T0134490

Law, Governance and Technology Series

Volume 54

Series Editors

Pompeu Casanovas, UAB, Institute of Law and Technology UAB, Barcelona, Spain

Giovanni Sartor, University of Bologna and European University Institute of Florence, Florence, Italy

The *Law, Governance and Technology Series* is intended to attract manuscripts arising from an interdisciplinary approach in law, artificial intelligence and information technologies. The idea is to bridge the gap between research in IT law and IT-applications for lawyers developing a unifying techno-legal perspective. The series will welcome proposals that have a fairly specific focus on problems or projects that will lead to innovative research charting the course for new interdisciplinary developments in law, legal theory, and law and society research as well as in computer technologies, artificial intelligence and cognitive sciences. In broad strokes, manuscripts for this series may be mainly located in the fields of the Internet law (data protection, intellectual property, Internet rights, etc.), Computational models of the legal contents and legal reasoning, Legal Information Retrieval, Electronic Data Discovery, Collaborative Tools (e.g. Online Dispute Resolution platforms), Metadata and XML Technologies (for Semantic Web Services), Technologies in Courtrooms and Judicial Offices (E-Court), Technologies for Governments and Administrations (E-Government), Legal Multimedia, and Legal Electronic Institutions (Multi-Agent Systems and Artificial Societies).

Vytautas Cyras • Friedrich Lachmayer

Essays on the Visualisation of Legal Informatics

 Springer

Vytautas Cyras
Faculty of Mathematics and Informatics,
Institute of Computer Science
Vilnius University
Vilnius, Lithuania

Friedrich Lachmayer
University of Innsbruck
Innsbruck, Austria

ISSN 2352-1902 ISSN 2352-1910 (electronic)
Law, Governance and Technology Series
ISBN 978-3-031-27959-1 ISBN 978-3-031-27957-7 (eBook)
https://doi.org/10.1007/978-3-031-27957-7

This Springer imprint is published by the registered company Springer Nature Switzerland AG
The registered company address is: Gewerbestrasse 11, 6330 Cham, Switzerland

To Ilmar Tammelo (1917–1982), a great Estonian legal philosopher

Preface

The discourse on legal theory of the 1960s was determined by Hans Kelsen's second edition of the *Pure Theory of Law* (PTL, for short) (see *Reine Rechtslehre*) and its 1967 English translation (Kelsen 1967). In PTL, Kelsen created methodical prerequisites for jurisprudence to be constituted as a methodically conscious discipline. Nevertheless, a new avant-garde position had already emerged. Based on Georg Henrik von Wright's seminal work *Deontic Logic* (1951) (the logic of obligation, permission and prohibition), the formal consideration of law increased. This view, especially since the 1970s, in the form of 'legal logic', has become the definitive legal-theoretical paradigm; compare also the 'paradigm shift' in Thomas Kuhn's *The Structure of Scientific Revolutions* (1970). Georges Kalinowski (1973), Leo Reisinger (1977), Ilmar Tammelo (1978), Jean-Louis Gardies (1983), Herbert Fiedler, Fritjof Haft and Roland Traunmüller (1988), Ota Weinberger (1989), Enrico Pattaro (2007), Giovanni Sartor, Pompeu Casanovas, etc. (2011) should be mentioned here. The scientific concern was to gain a completely new access to law by transforming the legal content into a formal language or a notation. From today's point of view, this was the beginning of a machine culture in law, because in this context, textual language is no longer sufficient. This approach was initially pursued through the development of legal expert systems (see, e.g., Fiedler et al. 1988) and, subsequently, Artificial Intelligence and Law (AI and Law) and has become fully established in the scientific community (see ICAIL,[1] JURISIN,[2] JURIX[3] and other conferences).

A proponent of the formal analysis of law was Ilmar Tammelo (1917–1982), most recently professor of legal philosophy at the University of Salzburg. He has

---

[1] International Conference on Artificial Intelligence and Law, see, e.g., http://www.iaail.org/.

[2] International Workshop on Juris-informatics, held annually in Japan, see JURISIN 2022, https://www.niit.ac.jp/jurisin2022/.

[3] The Dutch Foundation for Legal Knowledge-Based Systems and its annual conference, see http://jurix.nl/proceedings/.

creatively turned his attention to formal problems, such as his preoccupation with a proto-logical calculus. Tammelo also tried to take account of the non-traditional dimension of law through, for example, his work on justice and the philosophy of survival. Tammelo investigated the problem of notation. Although he did not experiment with visuals, he was interested in them and encouraged their development.

Currently, several types of visualisation have emerged. The spectrum ranges from automatic visualisations, in which legal terms are arranged by a computer like the stars of a galaxy, to situational drawings (Walser Kessel 2011) and metaphors for robots (Weng et al. 2019; Takeda et al. 2019). Klaus Röhl and Stefan Ulbrich (2007) and Colette Brunschwig (2021), for instance, have dealt in detail with questions of visualisation on the theoretical level.

The advantage of a non-strict visualisation lies in the fact that the subject and the context are not always distinguished and strictly structured. Notations for such visualisations are usually more open and thematically more elastic than logical notations. For the most part, the syntax is not set and can be changed to suit the topic. This is an advantage in case other notations are not sufficient to represent newly occurring structures. In such case, an experimental notation is needed, which can be quite intuitive in its origin. The visuals probably have two components: an intuitive view and a rational order in a regular syntax.

In the following contributions, we deliberately use different visual patterns as it does not seem possible at this stage to develop an overall visual model of law and its documentation. However, it is realistic to make different cuts and to try to deal with the complexity of the subject and its contexts in a methodical multi-level approach to law (Krawietz 2009).

The complexity of law is one of the major challenges of both legal theory and legal informatics. The aim is to build a bridge between the bank of legal content on the one side (with all its textual precision, but more or less diffuse) and on the other bank, a formal notation, which is required for the technical implementation in the context of legal informatics. To stay with the metaphor of the bridge between two banks: a visual is an island in the river, which facilitates the transition from the textual side to the formal side, as it were a tertium comparationis (cf. Kaufmann 1982). Anyhow, it was an island in the river, which was historically important for the emergence of a city, such as Rome, Paris, Budapest or Vienna.

In this respect, visualisations as a periphery of notations can also have a considerable place in the representation of legal knowledge. In a dialectic between the centre and the periphery, the latter can provide innovative impulses. We believe that intuitive–structural visuals are suitable for use in legal informatics. Often it is not clear how a legal text is to be interpreted. Therefore, a cognitively practical way is to use affirmative interpretation patterns first and then make cognitive decisions. In terms of law, it is a double subsumption. It concerns a cognitive subsumption, that is, which interpretation pattern to apply, and a normative subsumption, that is, which norm to invoke.

Consider the question 'Can the meaning of legal norms be comprehended by machines?' We approach it similarly to Alan Turing's (1950) question 'Can machines think?' Turing begins with the definitions of the meaning of the terms 'machine' and 'think', and each word is open-textured. Analogously we consider the term 'norm'. A norm has multiple meanings such as content meaning, institutional meaning, cultural meaning, etc. In computing, different approaches have been undertaken to model norms and to represent them in computers. Institutional thinking and the concept of a legal institution distinguish legal informatics from formal-theory reasoning, which typically is used in computer science.

Each chapter is a kind of exploratory research; an abstract theory is being developed. The limitations of our research lie in the fact that the issues are tackled on an abstract level. Thus, we follow a top-down approach. We stand in a position of a theorist and prefer a 'bird's-eye view'. There are two options for analysis in the law: either the content of norms is analysed or not analysed. In the first case, you encounter specific norms of a certain branch of law. In the second case, you stay in a position of legal theory. A practical implication is that concrete recommendations can be provided in the design of a concrete legal information system.

In summary, the subject matter of this book is rooted in legal informatics, a discipline that builds a bridge between law and computing. We explain their interconnectedness abstractly, as a whole. We insist on the holistic view and hold that neither law nor legal documentation can be successfully reduced to its component parts.

The authors acknowledge that the content of this book is partially experimental. The reason is that the language of pictures is not standardised. This is a difference from textual systems in which the language conforms to an exhaustive list of strict rules. In visualisation, the attribution to regulation and semantics is still widely open and can be freely shaped. The presented beginning should be treated according to a trial-and-error principle.

We are aware that the compressed presentation of different approaches to visualisation appears unconventional and does not meet the expectations of legal theory texts. However, it is precisely the peculiarity of the current situation of legal visualisation that the standards of presentation are currently approached experimentally and that different forms and design concepts of the view are possible. The discussion about the future development of legal visualisation is still open and the contributions presented here are, as it were, workshop discussions, which nevertheless serve as a guide in their diversity. The concept is exploratory, but conceived methodically at the meta-levels.

The present book is based on papers that were co-authored from 2006 onwards. Most of these have been first given at IRIS, the International Legal Informatics Symposium,[4] held annually at the University of Salzburg. Each chapter of the present book, as a rule, is based on a separate paper and was revised and compiled for this volume.

---

[4] https://iris-conferences.eu/. IRIS proceedings are available online in Jusletter IT, the serial edition by Weblaw, Bern, https://jusletter-it.weblaw.ch/.

The book is divided into eight parts. Part I concentrates on visualisation, Part II—Legal Theory, Part III—Legal Norms, Part IV—Text–Document Relation, Part V—Legal Subsumption, Part VI—Legal Machines and Compliance, Part VII—A Path from Digital Humanities Towards Human Digitalities and Part VIII—Legal Argumentation. Each part is divided into several chapters.

All URLs were last visited on 15 December 2022.

Vilnius, Lithuania   Vytautas Cyras
Wien, Austria   Friedrich Lachmayer

References

Brunschwig CR (2021) Visual law and legal design: questions and tentative answers. Jusletter IT, 27 May 2021. https://doi.org/10.38023/8b70bb88-de0c-4034-a54c-68409bb9549e

Fiedler H, Haft F, Traunmüller R (eds) (1988) Expert systems in law – impacts on legal theory and computer law. Neue Methoden im Recht, vol 4. Attempto, Tübingen

Gardies J (1983) Logique de l'action (ou du changement) et logique déontique. Logique et analyse 26(1):71–89. https://www.jstor.org/stable/44084062. Accessed 15 Dec 2022

Kalinowski G (1973) Norms and logic. Am J Jurisprud 18:165–197

Kaufmann A (1982) Analogie und "Natur der Sache": Zugleich ein Beitrag zur Lehre vom Typus, 2. Auflage. Decker & C.F. Müller, Heidelberg

Kelsen H (1967) Pure theory of law, 2nd edn (trans: Knight M) (Reine Rechtslehre, 2. Auflage. Deuticke, Wien 1960). University of California Press, Berkeley

Krawietz W (2009) Modern society and global legal system as normative order of primary and secondary social systems—an outline of a communication theory of law. ProtoSociology 26:121–149. https://doi.org/10.5840/protosociology2009266

Kuhn TS (1970) The structure of scientific revolutions, 2nd edn. The University of Chicago

Pattaro E (2007) The law and the right: a reappraisal of the reality that ought to be. Series A Treatise of legal philosophy and general jurisprudence, vol 1. Springer, Dordrecht

Reisinger L (1977) Rechtsinformatik. de Gruyter, Berlin

Röhl KF, Ulbrich S (2007) Recht anschaulich. Visualisierung in der Juristenausbildung. Halem, Köln

Sartor G, Casanovas P, Biasiotti MA, Fernández-Barrera M (eds) (2011) Approaches to legal ontologies. Law, governance and technology series, vol 1. Springer, Dordrecht

Takeda M, Hirata Y, Weng Y, Katayama T, Mizuta Y, Koujina A (2019) Accountable system design architecture for embodied AI: a focus on physical human support robots. Adv Robot 33(23):1248–1263. https://doi.org/10.1080/01691864.2019.1689168

Tammelo I (1978) Modern logic in the service of law. Springer, Vienna
Turing A (1950) Computing machinery and intelligence. Mind 59:433–460
von Wright GH (1951) Deontic logic. Mind 60(237):1–15. https://www.jstor.org/
    stable/2251395. Accessed 15 Dec 2022
Walser Kessel C (2011) Kennst du das Recht? Editions Weblaw, Bern
Weinberger O (1989) Rechtslogik. Duncker & Humblot, Berlin
Weng Y, Hirata Y, Sakura O et al (2019) The religious impacts of taoism on ethically
    aligned design in HRI. Int J Soc Robot 11(5)829–839. https://doi.org/10.1007/
    s12369-019-00594-z

Contents

Part I
Legal Visualisation

Chapter 1
Introduction

1.1 Textuality Will Decline and Programming Will Increase

This book deals, on the one hand, with the communication technology of visualisation and, on the other hand, with the peculiarities of law as an object of visualisation. At present, there is no standard and comprehensive model of legal visualisation. A distinctive feature of the law in connection with its visualisation consists in the abstractness of legal texts. Legal texts reside in an abstract frame that is not linguistically structured. It is the task of legal visualisation, in addition to considering the types of legal situation, to make visible these pre-textual interdependencies of the legal terms (Lachmayer and Hoffmann 2005).

Traditionally, law is textual. Jurists transform texts into texts. There are various kinds of texts: laws, contracts, claims, judgments, etc. Text transformations require abstracting, reasoning and other legal methods. Legal texts contain legal terms and legal sentences that we may call Kelsen's legal sentences. Judgments, guidelines and their head notes are formulated in abstract legal terms. Abstracting and extracting are therefore needed and are performed by jurists and secretaries.

Legal terms that were detached, for example, by Georg Puchta in the nineteenth century, were textual. Thus, the phenomenon was called Begriffsjurisprudenz—jurisprudence of concepts. Legal terms are also central in Roman law. Hence, the initial position is that traditionally legal texts are transformed with the aid of the richly formed area of legal terms.

The law appears, on the one hand, in legal texts and, on the other hand, in legal situations, which are mostly typed. The dominance of textuality began in modern times with the reception of Roman law. Previously, customary law had been situationally dominant. With the advance of the social and legal use of machines,

Based on Čyras et al. (2018).

© The Author(s), under exclusive license to Springer Nature Switzerland AG 2023
V. Cyras, F. Lachmayer, *Essays on the Visualisation of Legal Informatics*, Law, Governance and Technology Series 54, https://doi.org/10.1007/978-3-031-27957-7_1

the importance of textuality will decline and that of programming will increase (see e.g. Boehme-Neßler 2017). The visualisation of law fits into this trend.

Graphical notations are a strong support for a formalised view of the law. Key features are represented by images or graphics, even in cases in which the level of abstraction necessary for formalisation has not yet been reached. Legal visualisation deals with graphical representations and, in particular, with the visualisation of the abstraction of the law. Visualisation as a method tries to describe implicit relationships between various rules, concepts and documents. The complexity of legally relevant events, actions and documents is structured and put into a proper timeline that is sufficiently clear for laypeople in such situations. Text and picture accord a strong support for a formalised view of the law two levels, abstract and concrete. The situational function of pictures ("A picture is worth a thousand words") is not the only one (see e.g. Larkin and Simon 1987).

Related Work In recent decades, legal visualisation has been studied by many authors. Moreover, a separate section on legal visualisation runs yearly in IRIS. A 20-year IRIS multi-method literature analysis has described a large network of authors (Schoormann et al. 2017). In our study, however, we narrow the focus to situational legal visualisation. Commenting on a variety of visual legal communication practices would extend beyond the scope of this book.

Volker Boehme-Neßler (2011), p. ix writes about the "visualification" of law and its multiple facets, including the medium of television. He notes the complementarity of text and image, and their different functions (ibid., pp. 86–87). Techno-images such as "[s]tructures, relationships or dynamic processes are often understood more readily when presented as maps, diagrams, models, building plans or computer simulations" (p. 56). A reason for this is that they "are created by causal mechanisms" (p. 57). However, the latter are not prevalent in law.

1.2   A General Schema for Visualisation

A general schema for visualisation is shown in Fig. 1.1. This schema consists of seven layers. Layer 2 is the primary one and depicts a phenomenon such as law to be understood and described. This phenomenon is an object of cognition or, in other words, a thing. The phenomenon has different elements and can be viewed from different perspectives. Similarly, a metaphorical cube has eight vertices, twelve edges and six faces. Layer 2 corresponds to Aristotle's teaching that things are primary to universals (universalia in re).

Layer 1 depicts the realm of ideas. It corresponds to Plato's teaching that ideas are primary to things (universalia ante rem). Next are Layers 3 to 5, which serve as descriptive layers. Textual and visual descriptions are distinguished. Layer 3 refers directly to the thing on Layer 2 and, hence, describes it. The thing can be described with text or pictures or can be photographed, etc., but it is not reflected.

Layer 4 serves as a theory. It structures naive descriptions of Layer 3. This theory can be described textually or graphically. Layer 4 is on a meta-level in respect of Layer 3. Layer 5 serves as a meta-theory and is a meta-level in respect of Layer 4.

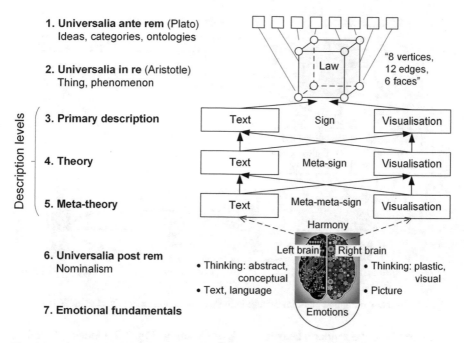

1. Universalia ante rem (Plato)
   Ideas, categories, ontologies

2. Universalia in re (Aristotle)
   Thing, phenomenon

3. Primary description

4. Theory

5. Meta-theory

6. Universalia post rem
   Nominalism

7. Emotional fundamentals

Fig. 1.1   A general schema for visualisation (Čyras et al. 2018)

Layer 6 concerns a model of a person. The left brain is linked to text/language, whereas the right brain is linked to visualisation. The goal is harmony. Layer 6 corresponds to the nominalists' teaching of universalia post rem. The nominalists hold that science is produced in the brain. However, Aristotle would disagree. We hold that both teachings are suitable as theories of facts. Plato taught that ideas for structuring come before things. Plato's teaching can be called a theory of products. Layer 7 concerns emotional fundamentals of cognitive science. This layer is additional to the other six layers.

1.3   Differences Between Verbal Writing and Pictorial Writing

This section compares verbal writing and pictorial writing in human communication. Verbal writing has its roots in the Latin language. Examples of pictorial writing are Chinese characters and the icons in public airports or in Olympic Games arenas.

Assume there is a human sender speaking to a human recipient (see Fig. 1.2). In addition to speech (Fig. 1.2, element 2a), verbal writing (2b) can be used. This verbal writing is parallel to speech and has certain advantages. However, one disadvantage of speech communication is that it cannot be distributed over time. Visualisation (2c) can also be added, but is mostly auxiliary.

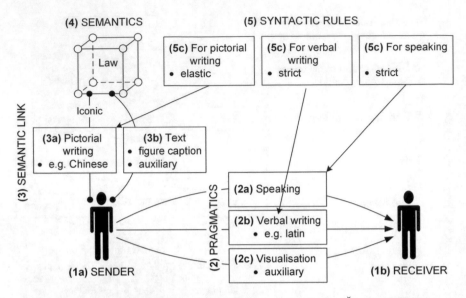

Fig. 1.2 Verbal writing and pictorial writing in human communication (Čyras et al. 2018)

Next comes the sender's semantic link to the thing (Fig. 1.2, element 3) and its semantics (element 4). The semantic link can also be autonomous and may have no association with the sender. Pictorial writing is a kind of magic. Examples of pictorial writing are also emoticons (pictorial representations of a facial expression). In the link to semantics, pictorial writing dominates, and textual descriptions such as picture captions are auxiliary (see Fig. 1.2, 3b). Pictorial characters refer to the type of the thing. In the semantic link, pictorial writing provides understanding. Textual captions provide efficiency and clearness—consider the phrase 'clare et distincte', 'clear and distinct', which is René Descartes' criterion of truth.

Communication is governed by rules (see Fig. 1.2, element 5). Both speaking (Fig. 1.2, element 2a) and verbal writing (2b) are strict, because there are strict speech and writing rules. Children's languages and a Babylonian confusion of languages are not desirable. Pictorial writing rules, however, are elastic. In the arts, for example, multiple interpretations are allowed.

Examples of Legal Visuals There is no general model for visualising the legal domain, but there are some promising approaches. However, certain aspects of law can be better explained with visuals. Further, several examples are presented (see Fig. 1.3). They stem from Friedrich Lachmayer's imagination of visualising insights, ideas and texts (see various examples on the web[1]). These visuals are logical pictures in the sense of Röhl and Ulbrich (2007), pp. 141 ff and their clues are further in this volume. Each visual in Fig. 1.3 is treated as a graphical representation of a concept in law. Thus, a graphical concept in law would supplement a verbal concept in law.

---

[1] https://jusletter-it.weblaw.ch/visualisierung.html, http://www.legalvisualization.com.

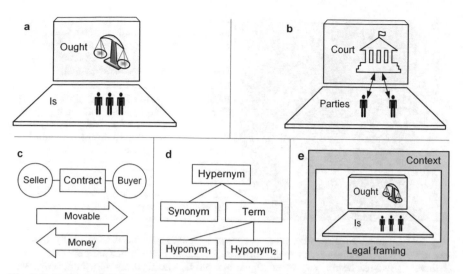

Fig. 1.3 Examples of visuals: **a** legal stage; **b** trial as a ping-pong process with a court; **c** legal institution such as a sales contract; **d** thesaurus/ontology; **e** legal framing (Čyras et al. 2018)

This supplement would be similar to supplementing a figure of speech such as a metaphor (like the metaphor of a bridge) with a visual in linguistics and semiotics.

1.4 Situational Visualisation

In a study of situational visualisation, the concept of situation is of primary importance. A situation with a complicated crossroad description is shown in Fig. 1.4. This scheme is familiar to candidates taking a driving theory test. The test has situation descriptions and questions. Road elements, cars, and road signs are involved. Drivers' intentions are described using text and symbols such as arrows. The description of the situation constitutes part of the situation's teleology. The alternatives are essential. The candidates answer multiple choice questions.

Term 'Situational Visualisation' in Computing Krum et al. (2001), for example, introduce a style of visualisation called Situational Visualisation in augmented and virtual reality systems. They note that "[m]any tasks require a detailed knowledge of the local environment as well as an awareness of rapidly changing and interacting events. This awareness is termed situational awareness or situation awareness." (Krum et al. 2001), p. 143. They quote Endsley (1988), p. 792 for a formal definition of situation awareness: "Situation Awareness is the perception of the elements in the environment within a volume of time and space, the comprehension of their meaning, and the projection of their status in the near future". Krum et al. (2001), p. 143 also note that "this type of spatio-temporal knowledge awareness is important in many tasks, including [. . .] law enforcement".

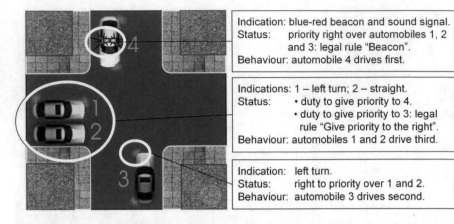

Fig. 1.4 A sample road situation presented to an examinee taking a driving theory test. The examinee has to answer a question. In this situation, the question is 'In which order does automobile 2 drive?' (Blue-red beacon and sound signal are on 4). The right answer: third, along with automobile 1 (see also Čyras and Lachmayer (2013) in Chap. 2 of this volume)

Conclusion   We have presented a schema for the visualisation of phenomena such as law and the differences between verbal writing and pictorial writing. Thus, the preliminaries of a theory on visualisation are introduced.

References

Boehme-Neßler V (2011) Pictorial law: modern law and the power of pictures. Springer, Berlin

Boehme-Neßler V (2017) Die Macht der Algorithmen und die Ohnmacht des Rechts. Neue Juristische Wochenschrift 42:3031–3037

Čyras V, Lachmayer F, Hoffmann H, Weng Y (2018) Introduction to legal visualization. Jusletter IT, 22 February 2018. https://jusletter-it.weblaw.ch/issues/2018/IRIS/introduction-to-lega_78b511cc94.html. Accessed 15 Dec 2022

Endsley MR (1988) Situation awareness global assessment technique (SAGAT). In: NAECON 1988, proceedings of the IEEE 1988 national aerospace and electronics conference, vol 3. IEEE, pp 789–795. https://doi.org/10.1109/NAECON.1988.195097

Krum DM, Ribarsky W, Shaw CD, Hodges LF, Faust N (2001) Situational visualization. In: VRST '01 proceedings of the ACM symposium on virtual reality software and technology. ACM, New York, pp 143–150. https://doi.org/10.1145/505008.505037

Lachmayer F, Hoffmann H (2005) From legal categories towards legal ontologies. In: Lehmann J, Biasiotti MA et al (eds) LOAIT – legal ontologies and artificial intelligence techniques. IAAIL workshop series, vol 4. Wolf Legal Publishers, Nijmegen, pp 63–69

Larkin JH, Simon HA (1987) Why a diagram is (sometimes) worth ten thousand words. Cogn Sci 11:65–100. https://doi.org/10.1111/j.1551-6708.1987.tb00863.x

Röhl KF, Ulbrich S (2007) Recht anschaulich. Visualisierung in der Juristenausbildung. Halem, Köln

Schoormann T, Hofer J, Behrens D, Knackstedt R (2017) Rechtsvisualisierung in 20 Jahren IRIS – eine multimethodische Literaturanalyse. Jusletter IT, 23 February 2017. https://jusletter-it.weblaw.ch/issues/2017/IRIS/rechtsvisualisierung_7e5897bef7.html. Accessed 15 Dec 2022

Chapter 2
Situation Versus Case

2.1 Examples of Situations

Situations and cases can be attributed with different methods of legal informatics. A 'situation' stands for a type of behaviour, and a case stands for an exemplar. Situations are governed primarily by the principle 'roles, not rules'. We aim to base the distinctions on legal theory and to develop a theoretical framework.

An example of a situation is a crossroad description (see, for example, Fig. 1.4 in previous Chap. 1). The roles comprise pedestrians and different types of drivers (car, bus, ambulance, etc.). Ex-ante interpretation of a situation is performed by citizens, whereas ex-post interpretation—by courts. Schematic representations of two situations in air traffic are shown in Fig. 2.1.

Legal Machine or an Expert System? Our thesis is that the situation dominates in a legal machine, whereas the case dominates in an expert system. A legal machine can be defined as a machine whose actions are legally significant and draw legal consequences (see part 6 in this volume). Legal machines are legal actors capable of triggering institutional facts and distributing permissions and obligations. An example is a traffic light, which distributes permission to cross the road. Traffic enforcement cameras are examples of successful legal machines.

The success of a legal machine is determined by the situation that is to be governed. In the implementation, open texture and non-determinism are minimised. A legal machine in a complicated situation risks taking a wrong action: for example, the action taken by a decision-making machine in a highly bureaucratic domain may be wrong. The simpler the situation, the simpler the legal machine: for instance, an automatic barrier to a car park can be simple.

Based on Čyras and Lachmayer (2013).

© The Author(s), under exclusive license to Springer Nature Switzerland AG 2023
V. Cyras, F. Lachmayer, *Essays on the Visualisation of Legal Informatics*, Law, Governance and Technology Series 54,
https://doi.org/10.1007/978-3-031-27957-7_2

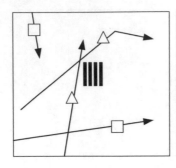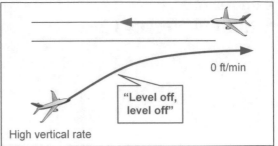

Fig. 2.1 Sample representations of two air traffic situations (Čyras and Lachmayer 2013)

2.2 Characterisation of Situations and Cases

Situations and cases are characterised differently:

1. **Type** A situation constitutes a generic behaviour pattern, whereas a case—a concrete one.
2. **Ex-ante/Ex-post** A situation is related with ex-ante analysis, whereas a case—with ex-post.
3. **Time** A situation concerns the future, whereas a case—the past.
4. **Alternatives** In a situation, alternatives are possible, and this is essential. In a case, however, there are no alternatives. Here, a concrete past behaviour is involved. However, alternatives can appear in hypothetical evaluations, such as 'Should the actors perform a different manoeuvre, the accident would not happen'.
5. **Language**

   Situations have no language at all. A situational language is non-professional.

   (a) A situation is mentally—visually, acoustically, sensibly—interpreted. Suppose a driver is in a crossroad. A mental language is non-textual and non-professional. Sensual (visual, aural, etc.) comprehension dominates, and textual descriptions appear on the periphery. A communication language does not need to be textual; for instance, gestures. Therefore, a situational language is loosened and differs from case languages.
   (b) Roles are inherent in situations, e.g. 'driver'. The actors' legal status may be implicit because rights and obligations are comprised by their roles.
   (c) Artificial agents can use formal languages. In multi-agent systems, the agents' beliefs, desires, and intentions are represented in computers.

   Cases have language: witnesses use a non-professional language, and jurists—a professional one.

   (a) Cases are explicitly formulated in documents. *Quod non est in actis, non est in mundo*—'What is not in the documents does not exist'. Cases are textually available. The major facts are described in an investigation report. However, statements about facts can be defeated during argument in the litigation. Visual descriptions (schemes) are supplementary and appear on the periphery.

(b) There are two kinds of languages: the non-professional language of witnesses and the professional juristic language. Legal subsumption serves as a bridge. The actors' roles comprise plaintiff, defendant, witness, etc.

6. **Placing on the 'Is' and 'Ought' Stages**
   Situation:

(a) Situations assigned to Is are always real and factual and of the moment. As an example, consider a crossroad with a red traffic light. You would like to cross, but do not want to set a bad example for your children, who learn the customary law from your behaviour.
(b) In contrast is the type of situation assigned to Ought. This situation type allows visual representations such as a schema in technical devices.

Case:

(a) Cases are also assigned to Is. Every case has passed. The reference range is not important. A case is fixed in the text.
(b) A case is on the Is stage, but can be viewed from two perspectives. First, the case is assigned to the subjective law. Second, the case is assigned to a legal proceeding, and hence, to the objective law. Here, argumentation arises. The players are assigned roles in the legal proceeding, such as plaintiff, defendant, witness, expert, etc.

7. **Web Applications** E-government application examples in Austria. For situations, see Austria's digital government agency;[1] for cases, see RIS.[2]
8. **Legal Instruments** Distinct legal instruments are concerned.
   Situation: the roles of actors, assumptions (hypothetical facts), rules which govern the situation, additional regulations which govern the situation, etc.
   Case: claim, evidence, attacks, etc. Adjudication can consist of several cases, e.g. criminal and civil.
9. **Representation Formalisms** Distinct legal instruments are concerned.
   Situation: deontic logic, abstract normative systems, etc.
   Case: case modelling approaches, factors, different narratives of the players, etc.
10. **Customary Law, Machine Law and Statutory Law**

---

[1] A government agency help site on the internet, which offers information necessary for those living and working in Austria (see https://www.oesterreich.gv.at/). It states the law that is applicable in various situations and supports ex ante analysis ("before the event").

[2] RIS (das Rechtsinformationssystem des Bundes), the Legal Information System of the Republic of Austria (see https://www.ris.bka.gv.at). It publishes cases and supports ex-post analysis ("after the event").

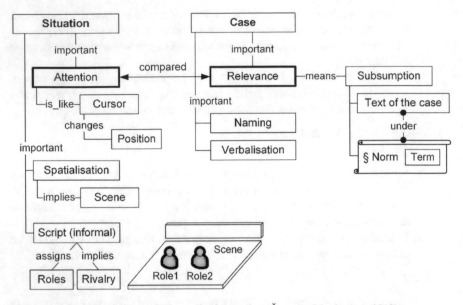

Fig. 2.2 Situation and case: attention and subsumption (Čyras and Lachmayer 2013)

> *Situation*: customary law and machine law are in the foreground. As an example, picture a pedestrian crosswalk. Pedestrians aim to cross it. Statutory law (the road rules) regulates this situation. However, ordinary people are governed primarily by customary law, which is superimposed. And finally, the situation is governed by traffic lights—machine law steps in.
>
> *Case*: the traditional hierarchies of legal sources prevail.

Subsumption (cognitive subsumption and normative subsumption, see Chap. 20 in this volume) are attributed to cases, not to situations, and are visualised "vertically". Legal rules also are visualised on the vertical Ought stage. This is distinct from both situations and cases that are visualised on the "horizontal" Is stage. Here, storytelling serves as a bridge between situations and cases. As an example, suppose a judge in a court announces the verdict of a case. The meaning of the judge's act of speaking is a legal act. The verdict contains a statement of grounds. It is presented as a kind of storytelling. It summarises the established facts and their interpretation and is the official version of the story.

Distinguished Elements in Situations and Cases Situations and cases are described by different concepts. Figure 2.2 shows the core elements that make the difference. A situation is viewed as a state in the world and is not finished. Different scenarios can evolve from a sole state. In terms of logic, the different worlds that can be accessed from a given situation are central. In terms of normative systems, the legal status of the players (normative positions) is key.

Cases are finished, and the outcome is known, e.g. 'Mr. Lammers is dead, shot with a gun'. Thus, the scenario is finished. However, the players may have different stories, and this is central. For example, the plaintiff and the defendant may render contrary arguments, e.g. 'Rijkbloem shot him' and 'Mrs. Lammers shot him'.

Which elements are important in the constellations of situations and cases?

- *Situation*. Here, attention is the most important element. Attention can be compared to a cursor that can move to different positions. The players behave as if they were on a stage. A script assigns roles to the players.
- *Case*. Here, legal subsumption, that is, bringing the text under norms, is in the forefront. It is important that the case elements are relevant to the norms. The elements of the issue have to be named in a professional legal language. Cases are marked by verbalisations. Here, the relationships—references—of the text to the relevant norms are addressed.

Representing Situations Graphically Representing a situation may involve a set of objects and relations, and the situation can also be represented as a graph. An example of a situation, which explains the right of succession in inheritance law, is provided in Zankl (2008), p. 269. Parent–child is a relation called 'ancestor'. This is an elementary, directed relation. Transitive closure of ancestor constitutes the descendent relationship.

Roles, not Rules A situation can be depicted with icons that represent the roles of the players. This is used in situational visualisation (see Butler 2010). For example, Florian Holzer (2010) is concerned with German penal law and distinguishes two kinds of visualisation: schematic (logical) legal visualisation and situational (scenery) legal visualisation. Schematic legal visualisation structures concepts, and situational legal visualisation represents situations, their elements, and their relationships. The pictures thus obtained are more suitable than texts, which are one-dimensional strings of words. Both methods are targeted at learning.

2.3 On a Notation for Situations

A situation is described by the following entities (see Fig. 2.3):

1. *Situational elements*. These elements are the constituents of the situation and exist in time and space. Let's denote them by small letters, e.g. a, b, *driver*, etc.
2. *Relations*. These are the relations between the situational elements. There are many kinds of relations: causal ($^{c}\rightarrow$), teleological ($^{te}\rightarrow$), instrumental ($^{instr}\rightarrow$), contextual ($^{contx}\rightarrow$), etc. These relations are comprised by both legal relations, such as debt, but also by empirical non-legal relations. The relations represent different perspectives.

A notation for a causality relation is $a\ ^{c}\rightarrow b$. In a situation, the alternatives of behaviour are of essential significance. Suppose you do not have money and, therefore, you cannot take a tram; but if you have money, you can take a transport.

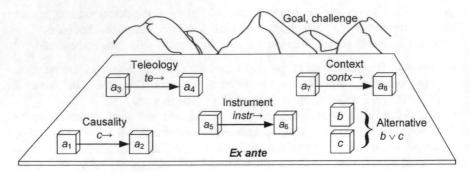

Fig. 2.3 A hint of the elements to be included in a notation for situations (Čyras and Lachmayer 2013)

A predicate language can serve to represent situations; compare block worlds in early artificial intelligence. Situational elements are represented by constants (0-arity predicates) and relations by predicates $P(a_1, \ldots, a_n)$.

Distinguishing Representations for Humans and Computers Humans and computers use different formats of representation and reasoning to act in a situation. Humans employ essentially more formats than computers. Humans comprehend a situation with their senses, and the brain makes a decision about which action to take. In a situation, a person reasons primarily in terms of roles, not legal rules. Predicate logic is not in the forefront in human decision making unless a computer decision support system is employed. However, computer knowledge representation formats can be employed to model and justify an action that was taken. Computers can be more effective than humans in specific tasks, for instance, emergency action based on instrumental sensors. In a situation like the crossroad in Chap. 1 Fig. 1.4, both drivers and unmanned vehicles could appear. Each actor would use a different representation of the situation and different decision making.

Conclusion Complete knowledge of a regulation in a non-trivial domain is unlikely to be achieved and represented in computers. However, a specific situation can be understood and dealt with by a legal machine. We hold that situational visualisation contributes to the development of the legal machines that govern a certain situation.

References

Butler DA (2010) Entry into Valhalla: contextualising the learning of legal ethics through the use of Second Life machinima. Leg Educ Rev 20(1–2):87–110. https://eprints.qut.edu.au/46275/1/Entry_to_Valhalla_LER_2010.pdf. Accessed 15 Dec 2022

Čyras V, Lachmayer F (2013) Situation versus case and two kinds of legal subsumption. Jusletter IT, 20 February 2013. https://jusletter-it.weblaw.ch/issues/2013/IRIS/2175.html. Accessed 15 Dec 2022

Holzer F (2010) Rechtsvisualisierung, Quo Vadis? Von der schematisch-logischen zur szenisch-situativen Rechtsvisualisierung. Jusletter IT, 1 September 2010. https://jusletter-it.weblaw.ch/issues/2010/IRIS/article_81.html. Accessed 15 Dec 2022

Zankl W (2008) Bürgerliches Recht. Facultas Verlag, Wien

Chapter 3
Visualisation as a Tertium Comparationis Within Multilingual Communities

3.1 A Link from the Visualisation of Meaning to Tertium Comparationis

A concern of this chapter are applications for visual navigation in legal document systems. We propose the visualisation of meaning as a tertium comparationis to act in the European Union as a commonality for all 24 linguistic versions.

Tertium comparationis (Latin—the third [part] of the comparison) is the quality that two things that are being compared have in common. "The third of comparison denotes a point of commonality without which no comparison seems possible" (Weber 2014), p. 155 (see Fig. 3.1).

In multilingual scientific communities we can see two discourse patterns. The use of English shows the top-down pattern. The use of other languages, for instance, German, shows the bottom-up pattern.

Another concept, *tertium communicationis*, denotes the communication intermediary between two agents who speak languages A and B, respectively. We can see the intermediary's conversion from tertium communicationis through *tertium translationis* to tertium comparationis.

We further tackle the structural legal visualisation approach (SLV) (see Chap. 4 in this volume). In SLV, diagrams are employed to represent legal meanings, in other words, to represent the semantics of law for the human user. The intended results concern visual navigation in information space, namely, information systems, which represent the law (henceforth: legal information systems). Such navigation can be compared with navigating a map (see e.g. Google Maps). The intended applications concern the already high, but not well recognised potential of visualisation in representing the deep structure of legal systems.

Based on Čyras et al. (2016).

© The Author(s), under exclusive license to Springer Nature Switzerland AG 2023
V. Cyras, F. Lachmayer, *Essays on the Visualisation of Legal Informatics*, Law, Governance and Technology Series 54,
https://doi.org/10.1007/978-3-031-27957-7_3

Fig. 3.1 An indirect
relation between A and B
through tertium
comparationis, the common
property (Čyras et al. 2016)

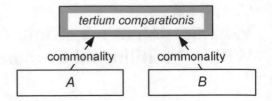

Visualising legal meaning differs from representing it as text, because its greater and easier expressiveness makes it capable of capturing structural relations between documents, legal concepts or events. Visualisations of timelines, events and concepts are commonly used, but only hint at the potential of visualisation. Results from legal theory research, in particular, tertium comparationis, are not well known, but are highly relevant. Relations between two entities can be manifold and are often insufficiently expressed in legal language. Visualisation as tertium comparationis represents these relations, but also constitutes an intermediate step towards a formal and machine-usable representation. There is a big variety of relationships in law such as weak/strong, direct/indirect, presumed/legally established, etc.

Related Work and Examples Examples of structural legal visualisation are slides by Lachmayer.[1] They provide diagrammatical visualisations of legal institutions. They also contain letterings that are translated from German to Chinese via English. Each lettering consists of one-three words and thus names the legal concept such as contract, unauthorised recording, abuse, etc. These examples demonstrate how text and visualisation are linked up to produce a comprehensible view (see Walser Kessel et al. 2016). We demonstrate that it is not enough to take into account German–English translation of words. The difference in legal terms in different legal systems (e.g. continental law and common law) is also important. Therefore the translation into Chinese has to take into account the legal system and the doctrine in China. In letterings, the rules of grammar do not prevail. Therefore, in translation, the syntactic structure of the letterings can be neglected. The cultural contexts of the languages are different and have an effect on visualisation.

3.2 Communication Patterns

Visualisation as Tertium Comparationis Tertium comparationis, a basis of comparison, describes the common quality. An example of tertium comparationis is the number. Suppose four apples are being brought into relation with four pears. This is about the number, in this case about the number four, which occurs as tertium comparationis. It does not compare apples with pears but compares four elements

---

[1] See https://jusletter-it.weblaw.ch/visualisierung/chinese.html.

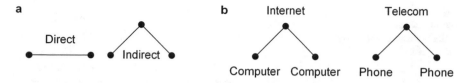

Fig. 3.2 **a** Direct relation and indirect relation. **b** Samples of indirect communication: via a third (Čyras et al. 2016)

with four other elements. A comparison can be performed through other common qualities such as 'fruitiness'.

In law, comparison can be interpreted broadly. In computer science, the interpretation is narrower and matching can be employed. For instance, the rule, 'All men are mortal', $\forall x\ man(x) \rightarrow mortal(x)$, and the fact 'Socrates is a man', $man(Socrates)$, in other words, *instance-of*($Socrates$, man), entail the conclusion 'Socrates is mortal', $mortal(Socrates)$. Here the constant *Socrates* matches *man*. The substitution is [*Socrates/x*]. The god Zeus, however, does not match *man* and there is no inference that 'Zeus is mortal'. Hence here we follow the *instance-of* relationship.[2]

There are also quite different approaches to visualisation—through semiotics, for instance. The classical philosophy of law, however, as approximately represented by Arthur Kaufmann (1963) (see Lachmayer 2005 and Chap. 22 in this volume), has provided a methodological introduction to visualisation with the thought pattern of tertium comparationis. In the European Union with its many official languages, in particular, visualisation, which appears as a tertium, can form a mental bridge between the different languages.

3.2.1   Tertium Communicationis—The Third in Communication

Tertium communicationis is not a word play: we are introducing a new term to denote the third part of communication. The subject matter of this abstract concept is, however, simple. A relation between two elements can be either direct or indirect (i.e. via a third, see Fig. 3.2a). A communication between two monads can be either direct or indirect. This theoretical basic concept comes from Leibniz: monads are uninteracting and each reflect the entire universe in a pre-established harmony.[3] In

---

[2] Weber writes: "the *tertium comparationis* may be related to *comparata* as a whole is to its parts, a substance to its accidents, an idea to its instances, or a generic concept to its subsumed concepts, and so on" (Weber 2014, p. 155).

[3] Leibniz's place in the history of the philosophy of mind is best secured by his pre-established harmony, that is, roughly, by the thesis that there is no mind-body interaction strictly speaking, but only a non-causal relationship of harmony, parallelism, or correspondence between mind and body (see Kulstad and Carlin at https://plato.stanford.edu/entries/leibniz-mind/).

Fig. 3.3 Tertium communicationis as an intermediate format (Čyras et al. 2016)

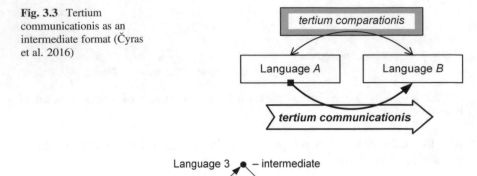

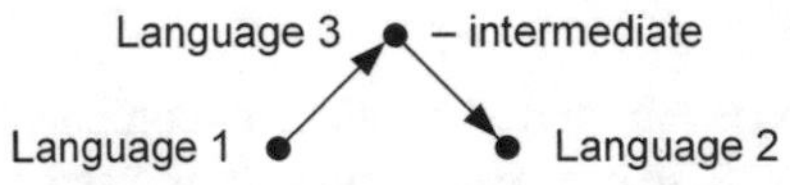

Fig. 3.4 Tertium translationis as an intermediate language (Čyras et al. 2016)

this way, for instance, the internet is a tertium communicationis for two-computer communication and the Telecom—for phone communication (see Fig. 3.2b).

We use tertium communicationis as a conceptual definition of something that improves communication between human beings or machines (see Fig. 3.3). This communication need not be visual. Text is not just verbal and in the end a textual document has a layout, its graphic structure. The question "Which formats contribute to better communication?" depends on various factors, such as the document type and the communication task, and is worth a separate study. Intermediate formats have their syntax and semantics.

An indirect relation can be made more dynamic and personal. In this way, tertium comparationis can be converted into tertium communicationis and lead further to *tertium identificationis* and *tertium socialisationis*. The latter can be foreseen in requirements engineering for an information system, which serves as a tertium.

Suppose a translation from language A to language B is being performed. Besides visualisation, other intermediate formats can be employed in translation. An intermediate language can serve as a *tertium translationis* (see Fig. 3.4). In natural language translation, for instance from Mandarin to German, the use of English as an intermediate can also make strong sense, especially in a scientific discourse.

3.2.2   Communication Top-down and Bottom-up and Translation

Our own model on multilingual legal systems takes into account that only English is now the reference language for translations, and the equal treatment of all languages is disregarded in practice. We can see two communication patterns in multilingual discourses: top-down communication and bottom-up communication. Different languages can be used in scientific discourse. Therefore, two situations arise

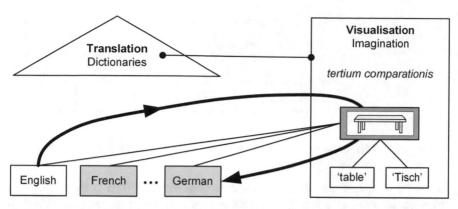

Fig. 3.5 Translation with visualisation (Čyras et al. 2016)

regarding the discourse language. On the one hand, English, a global language, can be used. (Other standards such as Latin could also be used, and thus the role of lingua franca emerges.) This is the top-down pattern. On the other hand, other (working) languages, such as German or French, can also be used. This is the bottom-up pattern. Native languages allow a scientist to unfold his ideas more naturally, and the discourse becomes more creative and productive. Hence, the bottom-up approach is also more meaningful than the top-down one.

Translation Problem The use of different languages brings translation problems. Therefore, dictionaries and translation machines, such as IATE (formerly Eurodicautom) emerge.[4] Currently, ontology-based approaches for document accessibility and semi-automatic extraction from legal texts are addressed in various projects (see e.g. Yoshida et al. 2013; Francesconi et al. 2015). A related work is also the Grammatical Framework[5] that provides abstract syntax trees as an intermediate format.

Visualisation Supplements Translation It is quite possible to go a long way around from one language into another language by going via a third language, the tertium translationis. Examples of this bridge language being visualisation can be found in books for visualised learning, where illustrations complement word translation; for instance, from the English 'table' to the German 'der Tisch' (see Fig. 3.5). In this way, visualisation supplements translation and brings an additional syntactic dimension to natural languages. Vividness is increased in the course of translation, so speakers obtain additional contemplation capabilities, and their discourse becomes more efficient. The more often use of visual dictionaries, in particular for

---

[4] Eurodicautom, created in 1975, was the pioneering terminology database of the European Commission. In 2007 Eurodicautom was replaced by Inter-Active Terminology for Europe (IATE), the inter-institutional terminology database of the European Union (https://iate.europa.eu).

[5] http://www.grammaticalframework.org/.

Fig. 3.6 Two kinds of tertium comparationis (Čyras et al. 2016)

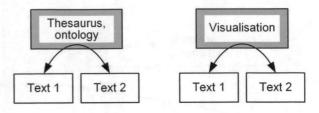

languages like Japanese or Mandarin, is evident. Thus, visualisation is shown to be important beyond legal informatics.

Lettering A special situation occurs with worded visuals. So far as the pictures are involved, no translation is required, since the pictures can be more or less "read" in all languages. If a visual is to be offered in another language, the wording must be replaced. Here, the tertium comparationis consists either in a text system or in the visual elements themselves, because they have a common reference to the different language versions.

Wording brings semantics to visualisation and may have various forms, such as figure captions, explanations, footnotes, labels, etc. A picture without a description is simply a graphic structure and can be viewed as mere visual chaos without semantics; it is therefore not acceptable in a discourse. The description could be in English and in other languages. Thus, the top-down and the bottom-up approaches can also be used in wording.

Transformation In summary, we are dealing with two kinds of tertium comparationis: thesauri/ontologies and visualisations (see Fig. 3.6). Visualisation in the role of tertium comparationis is the outcome of the following metamorphosis: from tertium communicationis through tertium translationis to tertium comparationis. In other words, the conversion of the roles of tertium is as follows: tertium communicationis changes into tertium translationis then into tertium comparationis. This transformation is aimed at applications in document space navigation.

3.2.3 Two Directions: From Natural Language to Professional Juristic Language and Vice Versa

In the projects that produce legal visuals, we single out two directions for the development of ideas: first, from the natural language to a professional language (legal language) and then to a formal technical language (see Fig. 3.7a), and, second, vice versa, from a professional legal language to the natural language (see Fig. 3.7b). Laypeople speak the natural language and jurists speak their professional language (s). Terms in a professional language may have specific metaphorical meanings, which are not intended in a natural language.

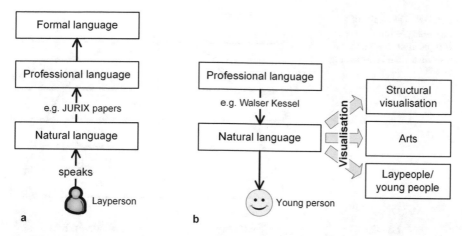

Fig. 3.7 Two directions: **a** from a natural language to a professional language, and **b** vice versa (Čyras et al. 2016)

A further step in the first direction (see Fig. 3.7a) up from the formal technical language is computer implementation. In this way the legal machines are produced. The first direction can be observed, for example, in Francesconi (2012). The second direction is demonstrated in Walser Kessel's (2011) informative book about law for young people. We point to three kinds of legal visualisation:

1. Structural visualisation (see e.g. Lachmayer's slide presentations).
2. Arts. Examples are novels and films about legal matters and also pictures and statues of Themis, etc.
3. Explaining law to laypeople or young people.

A topic to explore is the transformation of syntax when a diagram is produced from a text. For example, the text layout and font have to be changed to communicate legal content for young people.

3.3   From Text to Visualisation and to Model

There are two ways to move from a text in one language to a text in another language. One way is via visualisation, as we have discussed above. This path is shown in Fig. 3.3 and also Fig. 3.8 as the *tertium comparationis 1* arch. However, there is another way—via the model level (Fill 2014a, b). This way is shown in Fig. 3.8 as the *tertium comparationis 2* arch, and uses a model of the text, an ontology or a higher-level model.

Fig. 3.8 Two ways of producing tertium comparationis: via a visual and via a model (Čyras et al. 2016)

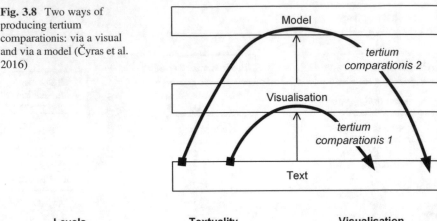

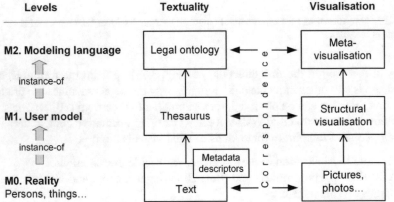

Fig. 3.9 Correspondence between textuality and visualisation at different levels of abstraction (Čyras et al. 2016)

3.3.1   Text–Visualisation Correspondence

We can see a correspondence between the textual world and the world of visualisation. This correspondence is shown in Fig. 3.9, where the traditional model-driven development infrastructure, which is addressed by Atkinson and Kühne (2003), is taken into account. We now explain the correspondence. Let us start from the world of textuality (see Fig. 3.9). Metadata descriptors are extracted from texts. Next, thesauri appear beyond texts and metadata. Then, beyond thesauri we place legal ontologies.

The visualisation world is shown on the right in Fig. 3.9. Pictures and other visually sensed raw materials correspond to texts. Above them we place structural visualisation, which denotes the graphical representation of the legal meanings of the texts. Above that we place meta-visualisation, which addresses the methods of visualisation and their components; cf. Moody (2009) and Fill and Karagiannis (2013).

3.3.2   Visual Products as Tertium Comparationis

We can see different examples of visuals that can serve as tertium comparationis products in law. A starting point is verbal metaphors. For instance, a pyramid represents the hierarchical structures of the branches of law or legal sources. Then comes a bridge (e.g., connecting the banks of law and technology), step working, etc. Here we can revert to the point of view that legal terms are also metaphors and have a specific meaning.

As ideal visual models we would mention the globe, the solar system, the atom model that is composed of a nucleus made of protons and neutrons surrounded by a cloud of electrons, and molecule models such as H_2O. We are talking of pictorial models and not formal graphic models. There are different types of models, depending on the legal task, the domain of law, and the scientific community. For instance, a norm can be modeled as 1) a graph consisting of the addressee, the deontic modus, the action, and the subject, or 2) a rule 'if C then A', $C{\rightarrow}A$ for short, or 3) a prescription to do A, $Norm(A)$, or 4) a sentence in deontic logic, for instance, an obligation **O**A, a permission **P**A, or a prohibition **F**A, etc. (see Fig. 3.10).

Conclusion In a multilingual scientific discourse we can see two communication patterns: top-down and bottom-up. We introduce the concept of tertium communicationis, which facilitates communication between human beings or machines. We aim to use tertium communicationis as a conceptual definition that improves communication. In the production of legal visuals, we single out two directions for the development of ideas: (1) from the natural language to a professional legal language and then to a formal technical language; and (2) vice versa.

We can see two ways of producing tertium comparationis: via visualisation and via a model. Therefore, we show the correspondence between textuality and

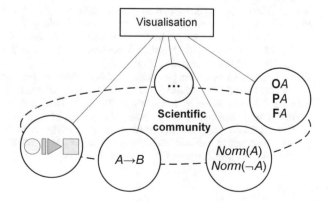

Fig. 3.10 A metaphor of different models for legal visualisation (Čyras et al. 2016)

visualisation at different levels of abstraction. We conclude with visual products that can serve as tertium comparationis.

References

Atkinson C, Kühne T (2003) Model-driven development: a metamodeling foundation. IEEE Software 20(5):36–41. https://doi.org/10.1109/MS.2003.1231149

Čyras V, Lachmayer F, Schweighofer E (2016) Visualization as a tertium comparationis within multilingual communities. Balt J Mod Comput 4(3):524–545. https://www.bjmc.lu.lv/fileadmin/user_upload/lu_portal/projekti/bjmc/Contents/4_3_12_Cyras.pdf.   Accessed 15 Dec 2022

Fill HG (2014a) Transitions between syntax and semantics through visualization. In: Schweighofer E et al (eds) Zeichen und Zauber des Rechts. Editions Weblaw, Bern, pp 935–944

Fill HG (2014b) Abstraction and transparency in meta modeling. Jusletter IT, 20 February 2014. https://jusletter-it.weblaw.ch/issues/2014/IRIS/2539.html. Accessed 15 Dec 2022

Fill HG, Karagiannis D (2013) On the conceptualisation of modelling methods using the ADOxx meta modelling platform. Enterp Model Inf Syst Archit 8(1):4–25. https://doi.org/10.18417/emisa.8.1.1

Francesconi E (2012) Supporting transnational judicial procedures between European member states: the e-Codex project. In: Schäfer B (ed) Legal knowledge and information systems. JURIX 2012: the twenty-fifth annual conference. Frontiers in artificial intelligence and applications, vol 250. IOS, Amsterdam, pp 41–50. https://doi.org/10.3233/978-1-61499-167-0-41

Francesconi E, Küster MW, Gratz P, Thelen S (2015) The ontology-based approach of the publications office of the EU for document accessibility and open data services. In: Kő A, Francesconi E (eds) Electronic government and the information systems perspective: proceedings of the 4th international conference EGOVIS 2015. Lecture notes in computer science, vol 9265. Springer, Cham, pp 29–39. https://doi.org/10.1007/978-3-319-22389-6_3

Kaufmann A (1963) The ontological structure of law. Nat Law Forum 8:79–96. https://scholarship.law.nd.edu/nd_naturallaw_forum/95/. Accessed 15 Dec 2022

Lachmayer F (2005) Das tertium comparationis im Recht. Variationen zu einem Thema von Arthur Kaufmann. In: Neumann U, Hassemer W, Schroth U (eds) Verantwortetes Recht: Die Rechtsphilosophie Arthur Kaufmanns. Archiv für Rechts- und Sozialphilosophie – Beihefte (ARSP-B), Band 100. Franz Steiner Verlag, Stuttgart, pp 67–77

Moody D (2009) The "physics" of notations: towards a scientific basis for constructing visual notations in software engineering. IEEE Trans Softw Eng 35(6):756–778. https://doi.org/10.1109/TSE.2009.67

Walser Kessel C (2011) Kennst du das Recht? Editions Weblaw, Bern

Walser Kessel C, Lachmayer F, Čyras V, Parycek P, Weng Y (2016) Rechtsvisualisierung als Vernetzung von Sprache und Bild – Anmerkungen zum Buch "Kennst du das Recht?". Jusletter IT, 25 February 2016. https://jusletter-it.weblaw.ch/issues/2016/IRIS/rechtsvisualisierung_c6b3190eb5.html. Accessed 15 Dec 2022

Weber R (2014) Comparative philosophy and the tertium: comparing what with what, and in what respect? Dao: J Comp Philos 13(2):151–171. https://doi.org/10.1007/s11712-014-9368-z

Yoshida Y, Honda K, Sei Y, Nakagawa H, Tahara Y, Ohsuga A (2013) Towards semi-automatic identification of functional requirements in legal texts for public administration. In: Ashley KD (ed) Legal knowledge and information systems. JURIX 2013: the twenty-sixth annual conference. Frontiers in artificial intelligence and applications, vol 259. IOS Press, Amsterdam, pp 175–184. https://doi.org/10.3233/978-1-61499-359-9-175

Chapter 4
Structural Legal Visualisation

4.1 Proposed Variants of Structural Legal Visualisation

This chapter investigates an approach which is called structural legal visualisation (SLV, also sequential legal visualisation). It is about diagrammatical views which facilitate comprehending the meaning of legal content. Complexity reduction is a motive. An issue is the complexity of the entire legal system and layman's limited abilities to understand legal institutions and the millions of documents. A sequence of views in SLV can be compared with a narrative. SLV has differences from information visualisation and knowledge visualisation. SLV relates to a scenario-centered graphical narrative rather than information display or user interfaces. Different pathways through the informational space are concerned. With respect to an object's change or non-change, two variations of SLV are identified: dynamic SLV and static SLV. The latter is divided into two: incremental SLV and alternate focuses SLV.

SLV is about the visualisation of statutory law rather than facts and leaves aside other important practices such as image-driven advocacy (Murray 2014; Porter 2014). SLV serves the user to comprehend the meaning of legal terms. Presentation of legal institutions is at stake. SLV is diagrammatical, relation-centered, model-based and is related to visualising legal ontologies.

SLV stems from Lachmayer's imagination, primarily in the domain of law. Visualising statutory law was already addressed at the beginning of legal informatics (Lachmayer 1976). SLV appears in the context of legal informatics that comprises the topics of legal document systems, navigation and information retrieval. SLV concerns visualising abstractions (see Lachmayer 2002). For decades, SLV was used in practice as slide presentations, where each slide can serve as a separate view. Among other things, we visualised Kelsen's Pure Theory of Law and Yoshino's

---

Based on two papers: Čyras et al. (2015) and Čyras and Lachmayer (2015).

© The Author(s), under exclusive license to Springer Nature Switzerland AG 2023
V. Cyras, F. Lachmayer, *Essays on the Visualisation of Legal Informatics*, Law, Governance and Technology Series 54,
https://doi.org/10.1007/978-3-031-27957-7_4

Logical Jurisprudence (see Chaps. 8 and 9 in this volume). Besides legal education, SLV is also aimed at e-government applications such as RIS or e-Codex.[1] Citizens' information systems use the internet to spread easily understandable public information. Figures in this volume are also examples of SLV visuals.

Suppose an object has two options: it changes or it does not change. Thus the object of visualisation (e.g. a diagram, scheme, mindmap, information space) can be either dynamic or static. Therefore, SLV can be divided into the following two major variations (that is, build-ups of the resulting views):

1. *Dynamic SLV*. A dynamic object is viewed; the object changes. The development in time is significant. The outcome is a series of images in time. This variation can also be compared with a film demonstration.
2. *Static SLV*. A static object is viewed; the object does not change in time. This variation can be divided into two sub-variations:

   - *Incremental SLV*. The process of adding items is significant. The object's presentation grows quantitatively. Graphical items are supposed to have links to the reference area and legal effect description.
   - *Alternating focuses SLV*. The process of changing the viewer's focus is significant. The user moves between broad overviews and detailed views.

Static SLV produces a series of views by highlighting individual items sequentially. The entire object is too complicated and visualising it at once would be too much. This variation can be compared with navigating a map. User-centric navigation in a state space is a characteristic. Static SLV is relevant to e-government Help applications, where hiding details is an essential feature.

In SLV, graphic elements commonly represent legal terms and relations. Slide tools such as PowerPoint have limited interaction capabilities and no camera, therefore slide functions can only be applied for animation. The camera concept is commonly employed in three-dimensional engines of three-dimensional virtual worlds or computer games. SLV has links to both *information visualisation* (Spence 2001; Card 2008; Cockburn et al. 2009) and *knowledge visualisation* (Eppler and Burkhard 2006), but stresses different issues.

4.2   Motivation

Interpreting (legal) requirements may require comprehending the law. Another trend is transferring legal texts and law enforcement to the web. There are terms such as 'service', 'contract', 'policy', etc., which are also used in computing, for instance,

---

[1]The e-Codex project "e-Justice Communication via Online Data Exchange" (https://www.e-codex.eu/) supports transnational procedures between EU member states. As an example, suppose Small Claims Procedure online form, into which data such as the plaintiff, the defendant, the claim, etc. are input (Francesconi 2012).

Fig. 4.1 A sample
incremental SLV. "Clare et
distincte", "clear and
distinct", is René
Descartes's criterion of
truth. **a** A text is
communicated from a
sender to a receiver. **b** The
text refers to the referential
area. **c** A visualisation refers
to clear and distinct
knowledge and hence
contributes to understanding
(Čyras et al. 2015)

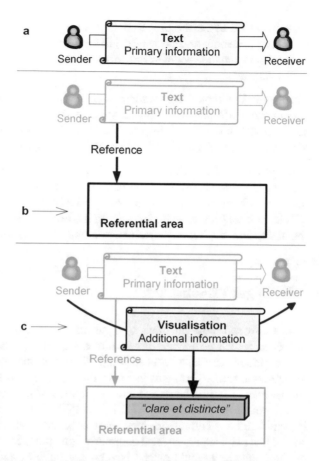

'web service', 'service-oriented architecture' (SOA), 'SOA contract' (see
e.g. Lupeikiene and Caplinskas 2014). Software engineers are typically laymen in
legal matters although they are required law awareness.

Complexity Reduction   Mastering the law as a whole and also in detail is difficult
even for a professional jurist. An issue is the complexity of the legal system;
cf. (Mazzega et al. 2011; Bibel 2004). SLV communicates a complex legal content
sequentially (see Fig. 4.1). Deep structures are comprehended step by step. An
overview can be shown first, then the details. Visuals can be more suitable than
reading a text, because various relationships (primarily implicit) can be shown.

Generation of Images   SLV is about the generation (synthesis) of diagrams. Images
can be represented by data and algorithms. The degree of automation—fully or semi-
automatic generation—is another issue. The sequence of images depends on the
user's goals. Pictures are merely reproduced in a simple slide preparation tool;
however, pictures are generated in advanced tools such as computer aided design
(CAD) systems or geographic information systems (GIS). There are interactive

systems which allow the user to navigate and to choose a visualisation sequence according to her needs. For instance, in Google Maps, the user can first overview a broad region and then zoom in and move to details, where images are generated from a GIS database.

Scenarios We think that scenario-centered visualised narratives can be used in the development not only of technical systems, but also of socio-technical ones.[2] A scenario is a narrative of foreseeable interactions of user roles (actors) and the technical system. A narrative is a time-threaded sequence of actions.

Evaluation of SLV The subject to be evaluated in the SLV approach is the recipient's comprehension of the communicated legal content. The recipient can miss implicit relations that are inherent in the legal domain. Explicit representation of relations contributes to understanding the domain. The better SLV visuals are in the navigation, the better the recipient comprehends the content.

4.3 Legal Visualisation

In (semi)formal representations of legal norms, on the one hand, there are formal notations, which go beyond the textual ones; on the other hand, there are visual representations that also occur in competition with the text. Two different types of visualisation can be distinguished: first, the visualisations formed according to strict formal rules; second, the more intuitive pictures which can detect situations better.

As noted in (Brunschwig 2014), p. 900, the concept of visual law (vox iurisprudentiae picturae) emerged in the seventeenth and eighteenth centuries. Visual law explores visual legal communication practices. Commenting on a variety of these practices would extend beyond our abilities and the scope of this book. Brunschwig also raises a question: What is legal visualisation and what is not?

We would also mention a study by Röhl and Ulbrich (2007) of visualisation in the legal area and the motivations behind using it. They are more separated from what they write about, whereas we are emotionally tied to the diagrams we create. The lack of pictures in jurisprudence becomes a learning obstacle (ibid.), pp. 15–17. A starting position is "Law is text" and therefore law is always textual for jurists. Hence there are reasons for jurists' reluctance to use visuals. Pictures bring a risk of drawbacks, such as redundancy, a low level of abstraction, trivialisation, and emotions (pp. 18–25, 100–102). However, the use of logical pictures[3] can bring advantages. Metaphors and symbols can be employed to represent norms and hence

---

[2] Alexander (2014), p. 3 writes that "[s]cenarios are a powerful antidote to the complexity of systems and analysis." He continues: "[S]cenarios are basically holistic... [T]he scenario is in essence, a single thing that conveys a human meaning" (Alexander 2014), pp. 4, 9.

[3] 'Logische Bilder' according to the sense of Klaus Röhl. The analysis of the term 'logische Bilder' in the sense of Ludwig Wittgenstein and his *Tractatus logico-philosophicus* would extend beyond the scope of this work.

Fig. 4.2 A sample dynamic sequential legal visualisation. Each of the three views shows the different roles of a person in the different stages of criminal proceedings (Čyras et al. 2015)

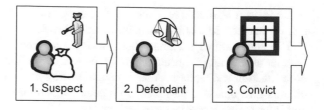

1. Suspect   2. Defendant   3. Convict

pictorial two-dimensional representations emerge (pp. 42–62). A historic example is the frontispiece of the book *Leviathan* by Thomas Hobbes,[4] where the state is represented by a giant crowned figure. To summarise, the combination of the words "law and visualisations" contains a kind of a paradoxical contradiction.

Visualisation is also possible through semiotics (see Fig. 4.1). A slide set is not a rich information space. SLV is intended for navigation in a state space, where visualising concepts lead first to scenarios and next to processes. The users may have different capabilities (laymen and professionals). A problem here is presenting explicitly a huge structure of legal terms and the variety of relationships.

Further, we observe two variations of SLV: first dynamic SLV, then static SLV. They differ in that the structure changes (in time) in dynamic SLV but does not change in static SLV. Although in static SLV the structure does not change, the visuals do change: elements can be added to or deleted from different views.

4.4 Dynamic SLV

Dynamic SLV considers that the structure of information space changes. In different phases of the process, the whole structure looks different. Here we talk about different pathways through the informational space. This is not about adding or deleting items to views as in the case of static SLV.

An example is as follows. Visualise the different roles of a person in the different phases of criminal proceedings (see Fig. 4.2): (1) Suspect in the pretrial stage; (2) Defendant (accused) in the judicial stage; and (3) Convict in the punishment stage.

Views in dynamic SLV can be compared with film frames. The above is an example whose object is a changing diagram. In addition to this, there is also dynamic SLV with moving pictures that are implemented in films (see Sect. 17.6).

The change of a structure (system) is a challenge for legal informatics. Consider the European law and decision making between the European Parliament, the European Commission and the Council of the European Union. The processes are complex and difficult to comprehend. However, they can be explained step by step.

---

[4] https://en.wikipedia.org/wiki/Leviathan_(Hobbes_book).

A novice can start with an overview.[5] Each phase is viewed differently and comprises branches. Modelling these procedures involves processes and their traces.

Different pathways through the informational space have to be considered in e-government Help applications, in which ordinary citizens seek advice depending on a situation and a phase. A user navigates the system according to her needs and obtains a sequence of information chunks. Modelling the user's degree of interest and information layers is a requirement.

In SLV, the trace of a navigation process is a series of displayed views. Here the event-recording symbols are graphical ones. The trace of a navigation process is a series of displayed views. A trace of the behaviour of a process is defined as a finite sequence of symbols recording the events in which the process has engaged up to some moment in time (Hoare 1985), p. 19. Hoare's *communicating sequential processes* is a mathematical abstraction of the interactions between a system and its environment. The basic building elements of a process are choice, sequential application and recursion (loop).

4.5   Static SLV

It is divided into two sub-variations: incremental SLV and alternate focuses SLV.

4.5.1   Incremental SLV

Diagram items are added sequentially and in the end the view becomes enriched quantitatively and complex. An example is shown in Fig. 4.1. Incremental SLV relates to focus+context views in information visualisation.[6] The following is a simple reference model for visualisation from Card (2008), p. 519, originally in Card et al. (1999):

$$Raw\ Data \rightarrow Data\ Tables \rightarrow Visual\ Structures \rightarrow Views$$

---

[5]See e.g. https://en.wikipedia.org/wiki/European_Union_legislative_procedure.

[6]Card (2008), p. 536 writes: "[C]onsider visualizations in which the machine is no longer passive, but its mappings from Visual Structure to View are altered by the computer according to the its model of the user's *degree of interest* [. . .] Focus+context views are based on several premises: First, the user needs both overview (context) and detail information (focus) during information access, and providing these in separate screens or separate displays is likely to cost more in user time. Second, information needed in the overview may be different from that needed in the detail [. . .] Third, these two types of information can be combined within a single dynamic display, much as human vision uses a two-level focus and context strategy."

Fig. 4.3 A complex context is illustrated with a static SLV with a numbered sequence of accumulated elements (Čyras et al. 2015)

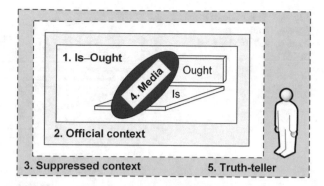

Another example demonstrates that each incremented view may be graphically simple, e.g., a rectangular box, but semantically difficult to understand, because it represents a complex (legal) concept. Figure 4.3 illustrates the idea of truth-teller (Tinnefeld and Lachmayer 2014). A conflict between an official context and a suppressed (taboo) context is displayed incrementally. The narrative sequentially introduces five notions: (1) everyday life; (2) the official context; (3) the suppressed (taboo) context; (4) the media's role; and (5) the truth-teller's role.

The picture format is not rich enough to show an incremental animation, because printed text provides fewer visual effects than a conference presentation, which is typically dominated by voice explanation. Examples of complicated artefacts in engineering are design drawings, such as the design of a machine. A CAD system visualises the machine. Its drawing set can be printed, but on many sheets.

4.5.2   Alternate Focuses SLV

In this sub-variation, single items are added and others are taken away, so the number of picture items per view remains manageable. Figure 4.4 shows a picture which can be analysed in depth using three different focuses.

The visual consists of a series of views each showing a perspective from a different focus. Here various methods of information visualisation can be applied. They emerge in the presentation problem, where different methods of scrolling, context map, and image magnification are used. This is exactly the problem that is explored in Spence (2001), p. 116: "the problem created by the need to have context information beneficially co-existing with detail of the focus of attention."

Other Variations of SLV Besides dynamic SLV and static SLV, other manners of visualisation are possible. Consider, for example, a big picture, which can be barely comprehended with a single view (e.g. a map). Experiments to view it can be made with the focus.

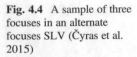

Fig. 4.4 A sample of three focuses in an alternate focuses SLV (Čyras et al. 2015)

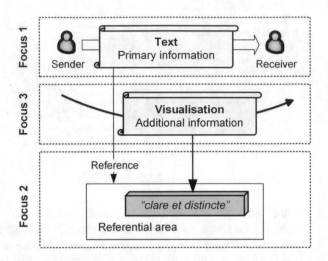

In three-dimensional virtual worlds, a virtual camera commonly moves with an avatar and machinima can depict the motion. Machinima is the use of real-time computer graphics engines to create a cinematic production. Desmond Butler (2010) examines legal education with the virtual world Second Life. He notes that machinima can contribute to a narrative-centered learning environment and "also offers a broad canvas for storytelling". Butler's machinima scenarios contain fact situations in legal ethics.

4.5.3 Legal Narratives

Visualisation brings narrative vividness (Anschauung, Anschaulichkeit, Latin imaginatio). The sequence of images within SLV goes hand in hand with a legal narrative. A point of SLV is that the legal narrative is about the law rather than the facts. We agree that the facts and cases are also significant, especially in legal practice and therefore scientific literature, particularly in the common law tradition, pays much attention to the legal narrative of facts (see Murray 2014). Visual narrativity and visual rhetoric are commonly used in advocacy. Porter (2014) provides a comprehensive scholarly treatment of images in written legal argument and offers suggestions for the fair regulation of multimedia persuasion.

Law and norms are normative whereas science is descriptive. Text is descriptive; however, legal text is normative. A narrative space is not descriptive, because the players may tell different stories (Bex et al. 2010). The narrative space of the text, e.g., the sales law, can also refer to normative elements, for example, a United Nations convention, such as CISG. General legal norms have the potential of a narrative space and its visualisation. This concerns, for instance, legal institutions that can be made more vivid.

Legal text can be processed with computers. However, text has no vividness. The text does not coincide with the narrative space; however, the text can constitute the narrative space. Visualisation forms the vividness space of the text's reference range. Hence visualisation does not compete with the text, but forms a narrative stage for it. For instance, Wolfgang Kahlig demonstrates that the German tenancy law is difficult to understand even for jurists. Different cost components are legal institutions. Kahlig develops software that explains the law and serves property management accounting (Kahlig and Stingl 2011). His diagrams are formally correct, but need even more vividness. Therefore we can see a future for legal visualisation in software.

The software system's front-office that is seen by the user is required to be simple and may comprise visuals such as icons. However, the back-office is complex, because it has to represent correctly formalised legal structures.

Metaphors The language of law is of a metaphorical nature. We maintain that metaphor is a matter of thought (see Lakoff 1993).[7] Metaphors serve to represent the meaning. Legal terms used by the language of law are not the same as those used in everyday discourse. Two kinds of interpretation in law are distinguished: the interpretation of norms and the interpretation of facts. The subsumption "the fact a is the legal concept A" also involves the metaphor of "is".

Metaphorical legal terms can be visualised accordingly. Cordula Kleinhietpaß (2005), p. 44 devotes a separate section to logical pictures in her dissertation on metaphors in the legal language and their visualisation. She lists 19 metaphorical means of style, such as allegory, analogy, comparison, hyperbole, parabola, symbol, etc. (Kleinhietpaß 2005), p. 82. Metaphorical styles employ entities and relationships between them. With SLV we aim to represent relationships explicitly. An example is a comparison which involves tertium comparationis.

No Formal Semantics for Diagrams We hold that diagrams may have formal syntax, but do not need to have uniform formal semantics. Diagrams can be composed of metaphorical graphical elements. UML, for instance, has formal syntax, but no uniform semantics. UML diagrams are declarative, their interpretation depends on the user, and software can be generated automatically up to a certain level. Programmers write source code for procedural knowledge.

---

[7]Lakoff treats metaphor as "a cross-domain mapping in the conceptual system": "[T]he metaphor can be understood as a mapping (in the mathematical sense) from a source domain [. . .] to a target domain" (Lakoff 1993), pp. 206–207.

4.6 Related Work

In visualisations in the legal domain, our attention is attracted by the following two specific features. First, legal visualisation is characterised by specific raw data. It cannot be limited to a specific norm or law and covers legal sources, legal doctrine, legal science, and other elements.

Second, the object of visualisation is a legal meaning. This differentiates legal visualisation from information visualisation. In the latter, computer-supported interactive visual representations are significant. However, this is not the case in legal visualisation. In the comprehension of law, communicating the meaning of law to the human user is of primary significance. In this sense legal visualisation is related to knowledge visualisation. The visual structure is a diagram that represents the meaning. Here diagrams serve well as legal norm visualisations (Rechtsnormbilder, Röhl and Ulbrich (2007), pp. 109–111).

Formalisation Versus Symbolisation Formalisation and symbolisation have to be distinguished (see e.g. Garnitschnig and Lachmayer 1979; Jordan and Lachmayer 1987). Symbolisation means to be a symbol of something (Hornby 2005). Formalisation, modelling, and representation can be defined more formally. In informatics this is done, for instance, by Sjaak Brinkkemper (1990), p. 21, who refers to Ogden and Richards (1923) and considers three types of systems (conceptual, concrete, and symbolic). A formalisation is defined as mapping onto a mathematical system of concepts with a corresponding representation. Here we remark that the immediate subject of a formalisation is a human. Further, the formalisation serves for a representation in a computer.

4.6.1 Specifics of SLV: Visualising Legal Meanings

The visualisation of legal meanings is distinct from information visualisations, such as the presentation of goods and services to potential customers who wish to search for a particular item. Three functions of instructive pictures can be distinguished (Röhl and Ulbrich 2007), p. 91:

1. Pointing function (e.g., an anatomy atlas).
2. Situational function ("A picture is worth a thousand words").
3. Construction (structure, design) function (the picture helps a viewer to build a mental model in her mind).

The semantics conveyed by a visual is addressed by Hans-Georg Fill (2009) in a chapter which is devoted to the analysis of visualisations.[8] Knowledge explication is

---

[8]Fill (2009), p. 163 writes: "Visualisation semantics are therefore related to questions such as *What may a user associate with the resulting graphical representation?* or *Is the intended meaning of the visualisation correctly transferred to the user or would another type of representation better fit?*"

a primary aim of legal visualisation in our approach. Here we refer to Fill (2009), p. 172, who holds that "the goal of *knowledge explication* [...] is to explicate knowledge that resides in the heads and minds of people and express it by a visualisation" and lists four basic aims of visualisation: knowledge explication, knowledge transfer, knowledge creation, and knowledge application. A subsequent aim, knowledge transfer, can be achieved by the following tasks: Diverge, Converge, Organise, Elaborate, Abstract, Evaluate, and Build Consensus (ibid.), pp. 173–174. In summary, the goal of comprehending the meaning of law is distinct from searching for items or information.

4.6.2 Relevance of Legal Visualisation to Computing

Computer usage changes legal tasks. A new task which is addressed by legal informatics is the development of legal machines. An example of non-compliant software design is provided in Oberle et al. (2012). Their example is about a user's consent, given by clicking 'yes' on his mobile phone, but not treated as an effective consent in the legal sense.

Causality and Imputation Kelsen (1991), § 7, pp. 24–25 explains in detail the distinction between causality and imputation. Imputation links a condition with a sanction brought about by a general moral or legal norm. However, software developers are accustomed to causality and mathematicians are accustomed to the axiomatic method. Therefore, they both may need to exert extra comprehension effort when they "encounter a principle which is different from the principle of causality expressed in the natural laws formulated by the natural sciences". These are two "different, but analogous" functional connections.[9] SLV aims at a qualitatively more complex phenomenon than problem domains in natural sciences and software engineering, where the complexity can be mastered by quantitative methods, for example, hierarchical decomposition, "divide and conquer".

Difficulties of Understanding the Meaning of Law by Software Developers Engineers who design legal machines might wish to make the following simplifications while modelling the law. First, representing legal norms as rules, and, second, automatic interpretation of a fact, *a*, and subsuming it under the legal term *A*, which is present in a norm. However, these simplifications and the plain interpretation are not always possible. The subsumption of *a* under *A* may be established through a complex relationship rather than a binary relation '*a instance-of A*'. Legal professionals are familiar with different methods of

---

[9]"The difference between the two is this: imputation (i.e. the relation between a certain behaviour as condition and a sanction as consequence, described by a moral or legal law) is produced by an act of will whose meaning is a norm, while causality (i.e. the relation between cause and effect described by a natural law) is independent of any such intervention" (Kelsen 1991), § 7, p. 24.

interpretation such as grammatical interpretation, systemic interpretation and teleo-logical interpretation. The interpretation of facts can lead to deep conclusions through multiple steps of different relationships. The plaintiff can argue that *a* is subsumed under *A*, but the defendant can argue for the opposite. Therefore a legal machine could make a balanced decision in routine cases and cannot in hard cases.

Standard Cases and Hard Cases Electronic procedures as in e-government appli-cations are likely to prevail in the middle areas of all kinds of proceedings. More and more situations are standardized and can be handled abstractly. However, things are different in the two peripheral areas. The hard cases will be handled as before with manual legal work.

For trivial matters of life, machines will continue to catch on. But these tasks, although legally performed, will still not be perceived by people as law. It is likely that a new type of situational personalisation will occur, such as intelligent traffic lights, a kind of animistic norm-setter.

4.6.3   Information Visualisation

In SLV, the user's primary concern in the approach is *what*, the content. We assume that the user chooses his path to navigate in the information space. *How* information is displayed is a secondary concern. In contrast, information visualisation addresses primarily *how* and secondarily *what*. The how can be maintained by different user interface mechanisms. These mechanisms have different features of separation. Overview+detail is characterised by spatial separation, lenses—Z-separation, zooming—temporal separation, focus+context—seamless focus in context, and cue-based techniques—selective highlighting or suppressing of items within the information space. Focus+context integrates focus and context into a single display (Cockburn et al. 2009).

SLV increases the ability to comprehend the information space, which is the law. The purpose of cognition in SLV outweighs perception. Cognitive skills are more important in SLV than perceptual ones as in the case of information visualisation. SLV focuses on cognitive tasks and not on search and target acquisition tasks as information visualisation.

While investigating SLV, the purpose of visualisation has to be agreed. Here we can refer to information visualisation that can be defined as "the use of computer-supported, interactive, visual representations of abstract data in order to amplify cognition" (Card et al. 1999). Hence, amplifying cognition is the purpose of infor-mation visualisation. Speaking about terminology, information visualisation is dis-tinguished from *scientific visualisation*, which is applied to scientific data and is typically physically based. Both belong to the broader field of *data graphics*, "which is the use of abstract, nonrepresentational visual representation to amplify cognition. Data graphics, in turn, is part of *information design*, which concerns itself with external representations for amplifying cognition" (Card 2008), p. 515.

Focus+context presentation techniques enable the user to discern information of interest. For example, multiple layers can be viewed from different focuses and with different transparencies of each layer. Suppression of data is used in situations where the display of too much information can be confusing. In this case, techniques for intelligently suppressing data are valuable. To summarise, the motivation is to provide balance between local detail and global context (Spence 2001, § 7). SLV has a commonality with the riffling technique Rapid Serial Visual Presentation and zooming and panning. "Panning is the smooth movement of a viewing frame over a two-dimensional image of a greater size" (ibid.), pp. 127, 130. They produce a series of images in time.

Incremental SLV has a commonality with the information visualisation notion of *semantic zoom* (Spence 2001), pp. 132–133. Both concern parts and the whole, but in opposite directions. Incremental SLV goes from a part to the whole diagram, whereas semantic zoom from the whole to a detail. Semantic zoom can be observed in air traffic control systems. In an overview an aircraft is shown on a display as a small circle. Semantic zoom-in allows the aircraft to be shown with flight information such as aircraft type, cruise level, destination, etc.

4.6.4 *Knowledge Visualisation*

Studies in visual cognition lead to the conclusion that visualisation dramatically increases our ability to think and communicate. Eppler and Burkhard (2006) link knowledge visualisation (KV) with knowledge management (KM) and list numerous benefits of visual representations. Hence, a longstanding objective is knowledge management. Knowledge visualisation is defined as a field that "examines the use of visual representations to improve the *creation* and *transfer* of knowledge between at least two people. Knowledge visualisation thus designates all graphic means that can be used to construct and convey complex insights" (Eppler and Burkhard 2006), p. 551. Hence the human is the subject of KV.

Knowledge visualisation is differentiated from other approaches, such as information visualisation or visual communication.[10] Information visualisation typically helps in human–computer interaction while knowledge visualisation is primarily used in communication among individuals. Knowledge visualisation aims at visual perception of the human. Graphic methods of representation are at the heart. A knowledge visualisation framework comprises three perspectives which answer three key questions with regard to visualising knowledge (ibid.), pp. 552–553:

---

[10]Eppler and Burkhard (2006), p. 551 write: "Information visualization aims to explore large amounts of abstract (often numeric) data to derive new insights or simply make the stored data more accessible. Knowledge visualization, in contrast, facilitates the transfer and creation of knowledge among people by giving them *richer means of expressing what they know.*"

1. Knowledge type (What? What type of knowledge is visualised (object)?).
2. Visualisation goal (Why? Why should that knowledge be visualised (purpose)?).
3. Visualisation format (How? How can the knowledge be represented (method)?).

The visualisation format perspective structures the visualisation formats into six main groups: (1) heuristic sketches, (2) conceptual diagrams, (3) visual metaphors, (4) knowledge animations, (5) knowledge maps, and (6) domain structures. The conceptual diagrams are important from the view of knowledge representation. Types of frequently used conceptual diagrams are: pie chart, Venn diagram, pyramid, circles, bars, lines, Gantt diagram, coordinates, sankey, radar/kiviat, tree, mind map, process, cycle, five forces, Ishikawa diagram, etc. (ibid.), p. 554.

Visualisation in Business Informatics We relate diagrammatical representations in the legal domain to Hans-Georg Fill's work (2009). He works in the area of fundamental research of business informatics, observes the fields which are related to the term 'visualisation', and surveys existing visualisation approaches. In the context of business informatics, Fill (2009), pp. 25–26 classifies the related fields into three categories:

1. Application level (knowledge visualisation, enterprise modelling).
2. Conceptual level (visual languages, graph theory and graph drawing, descriptive statistics, information visualisation.
3. Implementation level (computer graphics).

Visualisations in business informatics concern primarily business frameworks and business processes. The variety of their elements is very big (Fill 2009, § 3). A shared goal is to communicate business information. Fill's survey of visualisations in business informatics may serve as a template to perform a survey of visualisation methods in the legal domain.

Conclusion Structural legal visualisation is divided into dynamic SLV and static SLV. The latter is divided into incremental SLV and alternate focuses SLV. In SLV, the law (Ought, legal institutions) is in the forefront rather than facts (Is). SLV stresses a scenario rather than information display. Legal narratives with SLV are visual ones. Another point of SLV is the dynamic aspect, namely, user-centric navigation in the information space. For instance, laymen and professionals use different wordings and play different roles in informational processes. SLV can serve to show a bright-line distinction between legal terms, for instance, in e-government applications explaining the law to citizens.

SLV is a top-down approach rather than a bottom-up one, which is a feature of visualising facts in storytelling. SLV calls the user to become a "master of the law". The user is supposed to perform high-level cognitive tasks such as comprehending the information space rather than low-level mechanical tasks such as target acquisition. Each content creator would depict an object differently. Skills in art can also be important. Thus SLV calls for imagination.

References

Alexander I (2014) Introduction: scenarios in system development. In: Alexander IF, Maiden N (eds) Scenarios, stories, use cases: through the systems development life-cycle. John Wiley, Chichester, pp 3–24

Bex FJ, van Koppen PJ, Prakken H, Verheij B (2010) A hybrid formal theory of arguments, stories and criminal evidence. Artif Intell Law 18(2):123–152. https://doi.org/10.1007/s10506-010-9092-x

Bibel W (2004) AI and the conquest of complexity in law. Artif Intell Law 12:159–180. https://doi.org/10.1007/s10506-005-6742-5

Brinkkemper S (1990) Formalisation of information systems modelling. PhD thesis. University of Nijmegen, the Netherlands

Brunschwig CR (2014) On visual law: visual legal communication practices and their scholarly exploration. In: Schweighofer E et al (eds) Zeichen und Zauber des Rechts. Editions Weblaw, Bern, pp 899–933. Available at SSRN: https://ssrn.com/abstract=2405378. Accessed 15 Dec 2022

Butler DA (2010) Entry into Valhalla: contextualising the learning of legal ethics through the use of Second Life machinima. Leg Educ Rev 20(1–2):87–110. https://eprints.qut.edu.au/46275/1/Entry_to_Valhalla_LER_2010.pdf. Accessed 15 Dec 2022

Card S (2008) Information visualization. In: Sears A, Jacko JA (eds) The human-computer interaction handbook. Fundamentals, evolving technologies, and emerging applications, 2nd edn. Taylor & Francis Group, New York

Card SK, Mackinlay JD, Shneiderman B (1999) Information visualization: using vision to think. Morgan Kaufmann Publishers, San Francisco

Cockburn A, Karlson A, Bederson BB (2009) A review of overview+detail, zooming, and focus +context interfaces. ACM Comput Surv 41(1). https://doi.org/10.1145/1456650.1456652

Čyras V, Lachmayer F (2015) Logic oriented methods for structuring in the context of lawmaking. In: Araszkiewicz M, Płeszka K (eds) Logic in the theory and practice of lawmaking. Legisprudence library (Studies on the theory and practice of legislation), vol 2. Springer, Cham, pp 459–478. https://doi.org/10.1007/978-3-319-19575-9_17

Čyras V, Lachmayer F, Lapin K (2015) Structural legal visualization. Informatica 26(2):199–219. https://doi.org/10.15388/Informatica.2015.45

Eppler MJ, Burkhard RA (2006) Knowledge visualization. In: Schwartz DG (ed) Encyclopedia of knowledge management. Idea Group Reference, Hershey, pp 551–560

Fill HG (2009) Visualisation for semantic information systems. Springer Gabler, Wiesbaden

Garnitschnig K, Lachmayer F (1979) Computergraphik und Rechtsdidaktik. Manz, Vienna

Hoare CAR (1985) Communicating sequential processes. Prentice Hall. http://www.usingcsp.com/cspbook.pdf. Accessed 15 Dec 2022

Hornby AS (2005) Oxford advanced learner's dictionary of current English, 7th edn. Oxford University Press

Jordan P, Lachmayer F (1987) Symbolisierung von Metaphern. In: DOXA 13/1987, Semiotische Berichte, Heft 3,4/1987. Institute of Philosophy, Hungarian Academy of Sciences, Budapest, pp 137–141

Kahlig W, Stingl W (2011) Immobilien-Steuerrecht, 2. Aufl. Manz Verlag, Vienna

Kelsen H (1991) General theory of norms (trans: Hartney M) (Allgemeine Theorie der Normen, Manz Verlag, Wien, 1979). Clarendon Press, Oxford

Kleinhietpaß CM (2005) Metaphern der Rechtssprache und ihre Verwendung für Visualisierungen. Tenea, Berlin. https://docplayer.org/5921459-Juristische-reihe-tenea-bd-91.html. Accessed 15 Dec 2022

Lachmayer F (1976) Graphische Darstellung im Rechtsunterricht. Zeitschrift für Verkehrsrecht (ZVR) 8:230–234

Lachmayer F (2002) Visualisierung des Abstrakten. In: Schweighofer E, Menzel T, Kreuzbauer G (eds) IT in Recht und Staat, Schriftenreihe Rechtsinformatik, 6. Verlag Österreich, Vienna, pp 309–317

Lakoff G (1993) The contemporary theory of metaphor. In: Ortony A (ed) Metaphor and thought. Cambridge University Press, Cambridge, pp 202–251. https://doi.org/10.1017/CBO9781139173865.013

Lupeikiene A, Caplinskas A (2014) Requirements engineering for service-oriented enterprise systems: quality requirements negotiation. In: Haav H, Kalja A, Robal T (eds) Databases and information systems VIII. Frontiers in artificial intelligence and applications, vol 270. IOS Press, Amsterdam, pp 27–40. https://doi.org/10.3233/978-1-61499-458-9-27

Mazzega P, Bourcier D, Bourgine P, Nadah N, Boulet R (2011) A complex-system approach: legal knowledge, ontology, information and networks. In: Sartor G, Casanovas P, Biasiotti MA, Fernández-Barrera M (eds) Approaches to legal ontologies. Law, governance and technology series, vol 1. Springer, Dordrecht, pp 117–132. https://doi.org/10.1007/978-94-007-0120-5_7

Murray M (2014) Visual rhetoric and visual narrativity in five sections of a brief. Social Science Research Network, interactive, https://ssrn.com/abstract=2460357. Accessed 15 Dec 2022

Oberle D, Drefs F, Wacker R, Baumann C, Raabe O (2012) Engineering compliant software: advising developers by automating legal reasoning. SCRIPTed 9(3):280–313. https://doi.org/10.2966/scrip.090312

Ogden CK, Richards IA (1923) The meaning of meaning. Harcourt, Brace & World, New York

Porter EG (2014) Taking images seriously. Columbia Law Rev 114(7):1687–1782. https://live-columbia-law-review.pantheonsite.io/wp-content/uploads/2016/04/Porter.pdf. Accessed 15 Dec 2022

Röhl KF, Ulbrich S (2007) Recht anschaulich. Visualisierung in der Juristenausbildung. Halem, Köln

Spence R (2001) Information visualization. Addison-Wesley, Harlow

Tinnefeld MT, Lachmayer F (2014) Transparenz der Kontexte und die Rolle der Wahrheitssager. Jusletter IT, 20 February 2014. https://jusletter-it.weblaw.ch/issues/2014/IRIS/2531.html. Accessed 15 Dec 2022

Francesconi E (2012) Supporting transnational judicial procedures between European member states: the e-Codex project. In: Schäfer B (ed) Legal knowledge and information systems. JURIX 2012: the twenty-fifth annual conference. Frontiers in artificial intelligence and applications, vol 250. IOS, Amsterdam, pp 41–50. https://doi.org/10.3233/978-1-61499-167-0-41

Chapter 5
Distinguishing Between Knowledge Visualisation and Knowledge Representation in Legal Informatics

5.1 On Knowledge Visualisation

The notions of knowledge visualisation (KV) and knowledge representation (KR) are distinguished, though both are knowledge management (KM) processes. There are two theses of this chapter. First, the human is the subject of knowledge visualisation, whereas the computer is the subject of knowledge representation. Hence, KV is viewed from a social sciences perspective, whereas KR is viewed from the perspective of computing and artificial intelligence. Second, knowledge level representation of law is at the core of legal informatics.

Eppler and Burkhard (2006) link knowledge visualisation with knowledge management (see Sect. 4.6.4 in this volume). They refer to John Sparrow (1998) and indicate a longstanding objective in knowledge management: "making knowledge visible so that it can be better accessed, discussed, valued, or generally managed". We also view mind mapping (Buzan and Buzan 2006) as a kind of knowledge visualisation.

On the one hand, we hold that any conceptual diagram can be formalised as a graph $G = (V,E)$, consisting of a diagram-specific set of vertices V, a set of edges E, and marking mappings of the vertices and the edges. A problem is that vertices may correspond to lower level conceptual diagrams. In this way, a recursive definition is obtained. Besides this, a scalability problem arises.

On the other hand, the strength of a conceptual graph is viewed from a different standpoint than a semantically strict knowledge representation. The latter is computer oriented. In contrast, the human is the subject of semi-formal visual formats. The strength of all visualisation formats (including conceptual graphs) is informality (that is, open semantics and lack of strict formalisation). We hold that symbolisation is human oriented.

Based on Čyras (2009).

© The Author(s), under exclusive license to Springer Nature Switzerland AG 2023   41
V. Cyras, F. Lachmayer, *Essays on the Visualisation of Legal Informatics*, Law, Governance and Technology Series 54,
https://doi.org/10.1007/978-3-031-27957-7_5

Knowledge management concerns primarily an organisation. The objective of KM is to increase an organisation's value. Here, a conflict between organisation and individual can be observed. What contributes to the organisation does not necessarily contribute to an individual. Legal knowledge visualisation aims to increase the value of the individual. This is achieved when visualisation contributes to human cognition.

5.2 Knowledge Representation

Knowledge representation can be viewed from different perspectives—informatics and social sciences. The fact that the sociology of law is a well-established discipline supports the social perspective.

In informatics perspective, "knowledge representation developed as a branch of *artificial intelligence*—the science of designing computer systems to perform tasks that would normally require human intelligence" (Sowa 2000), p. XI. This view also accords with (Zarri 2006), where the roots of KR are examined. Zarri begins with a reference to Allen Newell (1982). The proposal is to distinguish between the knowledge level and symbol level representations, thus also conceiving relationships between knowledge management and computer science.[1] The knowledge level can be identified as a principle.[2]

Knowledge representation is a well-established discipline within AI in the ACM classification.[3] The branch 'Knowledge representation and reasoning' is included in 'Artificial intelligence', and the latter is included in 'Computing methodologies'. The inclusions $KR \subset AI \subset$ 'computing' express a rough view. Fine-grained views maintain that KR is also a management activity, because knowledge management is a management process. Hence, knowledge representation intersects, but is not a proper subset of, computing.

In computing, knowledge representation leverages the reasoning of software agents. Thus, KR becomes a branch of AI. The subject matter of KR comprises representation methods: (1) knowledge-level and symbol-level representations; (2) procedural and declarative representations; (3) logic-based, rule-based, frame-

---

[1] Newell (1982), p. 108 writes: "The knowledge level permits predicting and understanding behaviour without having an operational model of the processing that is actually being done by the agent."

[2] Zarri (2006), p. 467 writes: "According to this principle, the knowledge level represents the highest level in the description of any structured system [...] The knowledge level principle emphasises the *why* (i.e., the goals), and the *what* (i.e., the different tasks to be accomplished and the domain knowledge) more than *why* (i.e., the way of implementing these tasks and of putting this domain knowledge to use)."

[3] The 2012 ACM Computing Classification System, Association for Computing Machinery, https://www.acm.org/publications/class-2012.

or object-based representations (supporting inference by inheritance); and (4) semantic networks.

The computer, which is simply a tool in a person's life, is an immediate subject of AI and KR. The person using the computer is a longstanding subject of AI and KR. While reviewing the different solutions for representing knowledge, two main approaches are isolated: the symbolic approach and the soft programming approach (Zarri 2006), p. 468. Further, in the symbolic paradigm, two basic forms of KR are ranged:

- Rule-based representations (inference by resolution).
- Frame- or object-based representations (inference by inheritance).

Slight classification differences arise through emphasis on specific methods. Branches of AI and KR can be classified according to different criteria. Logic resides in the first place. Object-oriented representation and structured descriptions come second. Ontologies are emphasised by Sowa (2000) and form a symbolic approach.

Symbol-level representations of legal teleology are extensively used in AI and law (see e.g. Bench-Capon's work (2002) on legal teleologies). We find the knowledge-level representation a true challenge for legal informatics. The reason is that teleology of law—the 'why'—is mainly implicit, including its legal sources. In this way, a knowledge engineer meets a problem of understanding the meaning of fundamental legal concepts, such as the nature of law, a particular legal method, a legal interpretation, justice, value, and so on. Jurists, however, understand the meanings, as legal terms are studied at different levels of abstraction in specific branches of law, legal dogma, legal theory, jurisprudence, and legal philosophy.

5.3 Legal Informatics

We hold that knowledge-level representation is at the core of legal informatics, of which interdisciplinarity is a key feature. A separate effort on the subject of legal informatics is applied in Schweighofer (1999). Steinmüller and Garstka (1970)[4] must be quoted. Legal informatics is about building a bridge between law and informatics (see Fig. 5.1a). The bridge must be built in a balanced way. When informatics scholars lack legal knowledge when they build computational models of legal tasks, the bridge can collapse (see Fig. 5.1b). Similarly, when too much computing knowledge is expected from legal scholars, they can give up, and the bridge can collapse.

---

[4] Schweighofer (1999), p. 4 writes: "After Steinmüller and Garstka [...] legal informatics is the 'Theorie über die Beziehungen Zwischen EDV und Recht sowie deren Voraussetzungen und Folgen'. ('Theory about the relationship between EDP and law as well as the associated assumptions and consequences'.)."

Fig. 5.1 **a** Legal
informatics as a bridge.
b The bridge must be
balanced between law and
informatics; otherwise the
bridge can collapse

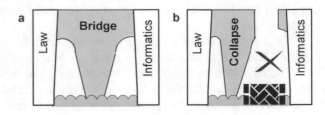

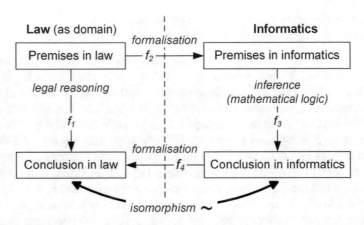

Fig. 5.2 Formalising legal reasoning. The diagram commutes: $f_1 = f_4 \circ f_3 \circ f_2$ (Čyras 2009). This is a requirement for legal reasoning to conform to formal inference. This is rarely a case in law

When identifying differences between law and informatics, distinctions between legal logic and mathematical logic emerge. A norm in the law can be compared with a rule in an artificial intelligence production system. This is in principle true, but both have key differences (cf. Hage 2005).

A formalism of informatics is involved when modelling legal activities such as legal reasoning, process flow, etc. Informatics is rich in formalisms, notations, and models, such as state transition diagrams, workflow diagrams, and UML[5] diagrams. Formal methods constitute a well-established branch of informatics.

Let f_1 denote legal reasoning. It is treated as a mapping from premises to a conclusion. Let f_2 denote the formalisation, which maps from law (or a legal domain) to informatics. The mapping f_2 maps from the legal domain to a formalism of informatics, for example, predicate logic. Let f_3 denote inference in informatics (for instance, with the modus ponens rule). Let f_4 denote the formalisation that returns from informatics to law. These mappings form a diagram shown in Fig. 5.2. If the legal reasoning and formal reasoning have 'good' properties, for example, 'correctness,' in a certain sense, the diagram commutes:

---

[5]The Unified Modeling Language. UML is a general-purpose modeling language in the field of software engineering, and is designed to provide a standard way to visualise the design of a system.

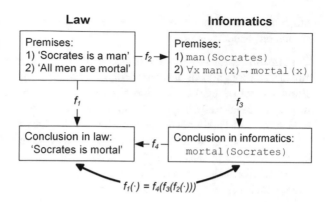

Fig. 5.3 Inference of 'Socrates is mortal' from 'Socrates is a man' and 'All men are mortal.' The diagram commutes (Čyras 2009)

$$f_1 = f_4 \circ f_3 \circ f_2, \text{that is, } f_1(\bullet) = f_4(f_3(f_2(\bullet))) \tag{5.1}$$

where the dot • denotes the premises. The explanation is as follows. The result of legal reasoning f_1 is congruent (isomorphic) with the sequential composition of three mappings: (1) the formalisation f_2; (2) the inference f_3; and (3) the formalisation f_4.

The equality (5.1) is a requirement for inference programs. This requirement can be rarely be implemented because "if not most, legal inference schemes are non-deductive" (Araszkiewicz and Płeszka 2015), p. 253.

Formalisation of the premises in the legal domain is not a trivial task. In our example, the premises are two statements. Figure 5.3 depicts the inference 'Socrates is mortal' from the premises consisting of two statements: 'Socrates is a man' and 'All men are mortal'. Figure 5.3 also shows that the diagram commutes.

5.4   Distinct Approaches in Legal Informatics

In legal informatics, we distinguish between two approaches called 'informatics in law' and 'information and communication technologies in law' (ICT in law). A human being is the final interpreter of legal knowledge in both approaches.

In the 'ICT in law' approach, legal knowledge is transferred from human to human. In the transfer, the knowledge must be recreated in the mind of the recipient (Zarri 2006), p. 552. The computer serves as an intermediary tool and does not interpret the knowledge. The subjects are linked as human–computer–human.

In the 'informatics in law' approach, the purpose of the final interpreter is to gain deep legal knowledge. Meaning is communicated to the interpreter. To this end, the legal knowledge is represented in the computer and a simple visual on paper may suffice. However, when legal knowledge is represented in an intelligent computer that 'understands' it, the knowledge engineer, the intermediary whose role is to assist the jurist in interpreting the knowledge, has satisfactorily served the jurist. The subjects are linked: human—a method of informatics in law—human, that is, human–informatics–human.

Conclusion Knowledge visualisation and knowledge representation are distinguishable, though both are knowledge management processes. The human is the direct subject of legal knowledge visualisation, whereas the computer is the direct subject of legal knowledge representation. However, thinking teleologically, the final subject of legal knowledge representation is also the human.

In the 'informatics in law' approach the subjects are linked human–*informatics*–human, whereas in 'ICT in law', the subjects are linked human–*computer*–human.

Legal informatics deals with the representation of legal knowledge. Deep knowledge, which is mainly tacit, is a problem.

References

Araszkiewicz M, Płeszka K (2015) The concept of normative consequence and legislative discourse. In: Araszkiewicz M, Płeszka K (eds) Logic in the theory and practice of lawmaking. Legisprudence library (Studies on the theory and practice of legislation), vol 2. Springer, Cham, pp 253–297. https://doi.org/10.1007/978-3-319-19575-9_10

Buzan T, Buzan B (2006) The mind map book. BBC

Čyras V (2009) Distinguishing between knowledge visualization and knowledge representation in legal informatics. Jusletter IT, 1 September 2009. https://jusletter-it.weblaw.ch/issues/2009/IRIS/article_157.html. Accessed 15 Dec 2022

Eppler MJ, Burkhard RA (2006) Knowledge visualization. In: Schwartz DG (ed) Encyclopedia of knowledge management. Idea Group Reference, Hershey, pp 551–560

Hage J (2005) Studies in legal logic. Springer, Dordrecht

Newell A (1982) The knowledge level. Artif Intell 18(1):87–127. https://doi.org/10.1016/0004-3702(82)90012-1

Schweighofer E (1999) Legal knowledge representation: automatic text analysis in public international and European law. Kluwer Law International, The Hague

Sowa JF (2000) Knowledge representation: logical, philosophical, and computational foundations. Brooks/Cole Thomson Learning, Pacific Grove

Sparrow J (1998) Knowledge in organizations: access to thinking at work. SAGE Publications, Thousand Oaks, CA

Steinmüller W, Garstka H (1970) EDV und Recht. Einführung in die Rechtsinformatik. JA-Sonderheft 1. J. Schweitzer Verlag, Berlin

Zarri GP (2006) Knowledge representation. In: Schwartz DG (ed) Encyclopedia of knowledge management. Idea Group Reference, Hershey, pp 467–477

Chapter 6
Criteria for Multidimensional Visualisation in Law

6.1 How Is Multidimensionality Exploited?

This chapter reviews visualisations in legal informatics by asking the question "How is multidimensionality exploited?". We focus on the transition from traditional rule-based linear textual representation such as 'if A then B' to two- and three-dimensional ones and films. A methodology of visualisation with the thought pattern of tertium comparationis can be attributed to Arthur Kaufmann. A tertium visualisation aims at a mental bridge between different languages. We explore how visuals are constructed and what types can be found here.

Review criteria comprise comprehension, relations, vertical-horizontal arrangement, time-space structure, the focus of attention, education, etc. There are multiple criteria to review and in turn different means to achieve multidimensionality in visuals: colours (including black-white-grey), mixed types of graphical elements, 1D-2D-2½D-3D, quantity-quality, statistics, etc.

Pictures for review are selected from JURIX 2012 proceedings. The mainstream of the visualisation in law, legal science and legal informatics can be determined with reference to JURIX. The annual JURIX conferences are among the most important in legal informatics regarding both the content and the form of scientific presentations. In many cases visuals make the text easier to understand, at least in terms of key points. On a meta-reflection level, however, the empirical question is how these visuals are constructed and what types can be found therein. Such an analysis may also affect the future design of visuals in legal informatics, especially as corresponding design principles are not yet in the canon. First we explain what we mean by multidimensionality in rule representations.

Based on Čyras and Lachmayer (2015).

V. Cyras, F. Lachmayer, *Essays on the Visualisation of Legal Informatics*, Law, Governance and Technology Series 54, https://doi.org/10.1007/978-3-031-27957-7_6

One-dimensional (1D) Visualisation Traditional norms (rules) are represented linearly: in text, both in natural languages and in artificial languages including mathematical notations, formal logic and programming languages such as Prolog. A traditional notation is 'if A then B'. There are other notations such as Polish prefix notation that comprises a deontic modality (see Tammelo 1978).

Two-dimensional (2D) Visualisation Metaphors and symbols can also be employed to represent norms and hence pictorial 2D representations emerge. An ancient example is the frontispiece of the book *Leviathan* by Thomas Hobbes. Besides pictorial visualisations, logical diagrammatical visualisations including info-graphics are widely used to represent legal content such as argumentation graphs, storytelling, legal workflow, etc. 2D diagrams can include pictures of three-dimensional real-world bodies such as cubes, cylinders, people, computers, houses, etc. and their icons, producing so-called 2½ representations. The icons of three-dimensional real bodies are used to contrast 2D diagramming elements and abstract concepts. Films serve well for situational visualisation (see Sect. 17.6).

6.2 Visualisations in JURIX 2012 Proceedings

Selected JURIX 2012 articles are reviewed below in the order of their appearance in the proceedings, where they are ordered alphabetically.

Araszkiewicz and Šavelka (2012) "Refined Coherence as Constraint Satisfaction Framework for Representing Judicial Reasoning" A constraint satisfaction framework as a potent tool for representing judicial reasoning is reported. Figure 1 on p. 8 shows a constraint network for conversion claim in the Popov v. Hayashi case. The picture is interesting, primarily from the point of view of relations, and open. A drawback of the picture is the absence of a legend for nontrivial abbreviations (FA—factual assertion, LA—legal assertion, FLR—FA to LA rules, LLR—LA to LA rules, LA_1—'Hayashi *is* liable. . .', LA_2—'Hayashi *is not* liable. . .', etc.) and three types of relationships (positive constraints, negative constraints, and the positively constrained chain). The reader has to guess whether the vertical arrangement means hierarchy and the horizontal one means flow.

Buchanan et al. (2012) "Computational Data Protection Law: Trusting each other Offline and Online" A collaborative project to develop a communication in infrastructure that allows information sharing while observing data protection law "by design" is reported. Figure 1 on p. 36 shows an overview of the architecture. This 2½D space-structured picture is composed of different subsystems. Two cloud-shaped "islands" that are connected with the "bridge" look better than white rectangles. Black and white textual elements interplay. Different icons of humans depict distinguished roles. The picture is comprised of different elements but is successful didactically. The same applies to figure 2 on p. 38.

Francesconi (2012) "Supporting Transnational Judicial Procedures between European Member States: the e-Codex Project" The e-Codex project is meant to implement building blocks for a system to support transnational procedures between EU member states so as to increase cross-border relations in a pan-European e-justice area. Figure 1 on p. 43 is composed of mixed elements that suggest clouds or islands and look like a territory map in 2½D. This is interesting; however, much of the text and graphics is too small and barely legible. Figure 2 on p. 47 is composed of mixed elements and a vertical static dichotomy between two models. It is interesting that dynamic flow is shown above with the interchange of grey and white ellipses. Figure 3 on p. 48 is composed of screenshots and arrow flows, but the dynamics is not elaborated.

Kubosawa et al. (2012) "Argument Analysis System with Factor Annotation Tool" An argumentation support tool which is based on a Toulmin diagram is reported. Figure 1 on p. 62 shows the architecture of the system. The flow is represented by arrows and rounded white and angled grey rectangles. The reader might be familiar with this type of flow diagram which dates from the 1970s. Figure 2 on p. 63 shows a screenshot that is composed of mixed elements (a table of textual factors and an argument graph) and contains two flows. Figure 3 on p. 65 does not define the meaning of the vertical placing: a hierarchy or a process in time? The meaning of computer symbols can only be guessed ("documents" or something else?). Do the dashed elements exist or not exist? Figure 4 on p. 66 is too abstract because contrasting white and grey circles is not intuitive, although the labels α, β, Λ, z, w, K, etc. are explained in the text of the paper. Figure 5 on p. 68 is also not intuitive. Figure 6 on p. 69 is a bad design pattern: the primary screenshots in the background are too small and illegible and the callout recalls comics.

Liang and Wei (2012) "An Argumentation Model of Evidential Reasoning with Variable Degrees of Justification" A gradual argumentation model of evidential reasoning is reported. The work is interesting and mature. At first glance, however, figure 1 on p. 74 seems too abstract. Time and space structure, different arrows and abbreviations are not clear. Likewise, figure 2 on p. 79 is elegant but also lacks a legend. This may be justifiable if the reader is familiar with argument graph formalisations, John Pollock's critical link semantics and the ASPIC$^+$ framework.

Lynch et al. (2012) "Comparing Argument Diagrams" Lynch et al. report the results of an empirical study into the diagnostic utility of argument diagrams in a legal writing context, namely, how law students employed the LASAD program. Figure 1 on p. 84 is a type diagram. It is drawn to read from right to left although you might expect time axis from left to right. Some texts are in an excessively small font, which may be the fault of a student.

Pace and Schapachnik (2012) "Types of Rights in Two-party Systems: a Formal Analysis" A formalisation of Kanger's types of rights in the context of interacting two-party systems, such as contracts, is reported. Figure 1 on p. 111 looks elegant although very formal and the reader has to judge if semantics complies with it. This picture recalls the logical square and cube which are known in modal logic (see

Philipps 2012, pp. 69–81). The table on p. 113 is not detailed although this may be reasonable for summarising just yes/no in each cell.

Poudyal and Quaresma (2012) "An Hybrid Approach for Legal Information Extraction" An approach and prototype software for legal information extraction is reported. They aimed to populate an ontology automatically. The approach combined a statistically-based method (machine learning) and a rule-based method. Figure 1 on p. 116 represents the ontology design. A reader could view it as a mind map and also ask whether the square of four concepts is a logical deontic square. All elements are in grey and therefore barely distinguishable. Figure 2 on p. 118 is not very creative.

Prakken (2012) "Formalising a Legal Opinion on a Legislative Proposal in the ASPIC$^+$ Framework" Prakken presents a case study in which the opinion of a legal scholar on a legislative proposal is formally reconstructed in the ASPIC$^+$ framework. Figure 1 on p. 127 demonstrates well-defined relations. This is achieved with texts in the boxes, dashed lines, labels and white vs. grey. Figures 2 and 3 on p. 128 look elegant thanks to the abbreviations, white/grey tones and arrows. Abbreviations make it hard to comprehend, however. A question arises about the patterns within the figures. The meaning of the horizontal-vertical arrangement—hierarchy or time—can be understood only after a thorough reading.

Ramakrishna et al. (2012) "The FSTP Test: a Novel Approach for an Invention's Non-obviousness Analysis" A mathematical approach called the FSTP Test for determining a non-obviousness indication in patent application during the examination stage is proposed. A table in figure 2 on p. 132 is a hybrid with process curves. This would benefit from elaboration, e.g. in a longer paper.

Robaldo et al. (2012) "Compiling Regular Expressions to Extract Legal Modifications" Prototype software for automatically identifying and classifying types of modifications in Italian legal texts is reported. The work employs the Italian standard NormeInRete (NIR), which was the outcome of a previous project. Figures 2 to 5 on pp. 137–139 attract attention with arced arrows (and a loop in figure 5) and two reading directions (from left to right and vice versa).

Szőke et al. (2012) "A Unified Change Management of Regulations and their Formal Representations Based on the FRBR Framework and the Direct Method" A unified change management of legislative documents and their representations is introduced. This is based on the Functional Requirements for Bibliographic Records (FRBR) framework and the direct method of legislative change management. Although figures 1 and 2 on p. 150 appear side by side, they have opposing reading directions. With regard to contents, figure 1 is very interesting because of the intermediate forms and four steps (Item–Manifestation–Expression–Work). Abbreviations (and formulas) make figures 2 to 6 on pp. 150–154 hard to comprehend for non-experts although bold face is used. Figure 6 has an opposing reading direction, ellipsis and rectangle-shaped elements with grey background and one with "dramatic" black. Relations are well-defined but formulas make the framework hard to comprehend.

Winkels and Hoekstra (2012) "Automatic Extraction of Legal Concepts and Definitions" The results of an experiment in automatic concept and definition extraction from the sources of law which are expressed in a simple natural language and standard semantic web technology are presented. The software was tested on six laws from the tax domain. Relations in figure 1 on p. 158 are well identified and good for learning purposes. Although composed of four layers, the figure seems too quantitative. White and grey elements are used and a dark grey in the focus, but the whole is confusing and not heuristic. Figures 2 and 3 on p. 160 are good for citations, but three schemes in two figures to save space is undesirable. The processes in figure 4 on p. 165 are bottom-up and right-left, and not usual. Therefore the picture is schematic and not intuitive. A line-approaching curve is shown in figure 6 on p. 166.

6.3   Visualisation Criteria

Our examination of selected pictures is done on the reflexive level of legal informatics. We discuss systematically different criteria:

- *Citation*. The names of laws and article numbers can be included in diagrams (Winkels and Hoekstra 2012), p. 160.
- *Colours*. In black and white press, dark and light grey tones aid comprehension (Winkels and Hoekstra 2012), pp. 158–166.
- *Dimensions*. Multiple dimensions on the paper can be achieved with 2½D. For instance, a wire-cube representation in Pace and Schapachnik (2012), p. 111 is supplemented with transitions and represents strength diagrams.
- *Domains*. Different problem domains can be referred to (Winkels and Hoekstra 2012), p. 158.
- *Elements with text*. Abbreviations may be difficult for non-experts (Szőke et al. 2012), p. 150. Similar may be with suspension points; see e.g. (Robaldo et al. 2012), p. 137 and (Szőke et al. 2012), pp. 150, 152.
- *Focus*. This is represented by bold face and a dark background. Important elements are coloured in dark grey and less important in light grey or white (Szőke et al. 2012), p. 154. There are also different shapes (angled, rounded).
- *Mindmapping*. Pictures in the form of mindmapping are creative. An ontology design (Poudyal and Quaresma 2012), p. 118 is shown with no cross-links.
- *Mixed types*. Different types of elements are combined (Szőkc ct al. 2012), p. 150. Good for education, but may be not very useful for formal semantics.
- *Quantity*. Too many elements confuse the issue. Therefore layers, levels and sub-elements are used (Winkels and Hoekstra 2012), p. 158.
- *Relationships*. Various relationships are depicted with different connectors. Different types of arrows are normally used: arced, curved, down, etc. Relationships

can have a predefined or a newly defined meaning and are represented with edges in graph-like diagrams. Examples of relationships can be found in argument diagrams and defeat graphs in argumentation-based inference (Prakken 2012), pp. 127–128, dependency relations (Robaldo et al. 2012), pp. 137–139, document generation and versioning (Szőke et al. 2012), pp. 150–154, relationships between concepts in the tax domain (Winkels and Hoekstra 2012), pp. 158–160.

- *Tables*. They contain much textual information but are not always creative (Pace and Schapachnik 2012), p. 113. Transitions can be added (Ramakrishna et al. 2012), p. 132.
- *Traditional formal diagrams*. Examples are argument diagrams (Lynch et al. 2012), p. 84 and statistical data visualisation (Poudyal and Quaresma 2012), p. 118; (Winkels and Hoekstra 2012), p. 166. They are clear, look good, but are nothing special.
- *Vertical and horizontal axes*. Placing elements top-down can mean different orders: hierarchy, time axis, etc. Horizontal arrangement from left to right can denote ordering in time. Other meanings can also be defined (Robaldo et al. 2012), pp. 137–139, where both the left arrows and right arrows show the rule-triggering sequence.

Conclusion Producing elaborated visuals as avant-garde as JURIX projects themselves is a tough task that requires the mastery of several problem domains: law, computing, visual media and semiotics.

References

Araszkiewicz M, Šavelka J (2012) Refined coherence as constraint satisfaction framework for representing judicial reasoning. In: Schäfer B (ed) Legal knowledge and information systems. JURIX 2012: the twenty-fifth annual conference. Frontiers in artificial intelligence and applications, vol 250. IOS, Amsterdam, pp 1–10. https://doi.org/10.3233/978-1-61499-167-0-1

Buchanan W, Fan L, Lawson A, Schafer B, Scott R, Thuemmler C, Uthmani O (2012) Computational data protection law: trusting each other offline and online. In: Schäfer B (ed) Legal knowledge and information systems. JURIX 2012: the twenty-fifth annual conference. Frontiers in artificial intelligence and applications, vol 250. IOS, Amsterdam, pp 31–40. https://doi.org/10.3233/978-1-61499-167-0-31

Čyras V, Lachmayer F (2015) Towards multidimensional rule visualizations. In: Araszkiewicz M, Banaś P, Gizbert-Studnicki T, Płeszka K (eds) Problems of normativity, rules and rule-following. Law and philosophy library, vol 111. Springer, Cham, pp 445–455. https://doi.org/10.1007/978-3-319-09375-8_33

Francesconi E (2012) Supporting transnational judicial procedures between European member states: the e-Codex project. In: Schäfer B (ed) Legal knowledge and information systems. JURIX 2012: the twenty-fifth annual conference. Frontiers in artificial intelligence and applications, vol 250. IOS, Amsterdam, pp 41–50. https://doi.org/10.3233/978-1-61499-167-0-41

Kubosawa S, Lu Y, Okada S, Nitta N (2012) Argument analysis with factor annotation tool. In: Schäfer B (ed) Legal knowledge and information systems. JURIX 2012: the twenty-fifth annual conference. Frontiers in artificial intelligence and applications, vol 250. IOS, Amsterdam, pp 61–70. https://doi.org/10.3233/978-1-61499-167-0-61

Liang Q, Wei B (2012) An argumentation model of evidential reasoning with variable degrees of justification. In: Schäfer B (ed) Legal knowledge and information systems. JURIX 2012: the twenty-fifth annual conference. Frontiers in artificial intelligence and applications, vol 250. IOS, Amsterdam, pp 71–80. https://doi.org/10.3233/978-1-61499-167-0-71

Lynch C, Ashley K, Falakmasir MH (2012) Comparing argument diagrams. In: Schäfer B (ed) Legal knowledge and information systems. JURIX 2012: the twenty-fifth annual conference. Frontiers in artificial intelligence and applications, vol 250. IOS, Amsterdam, pp 81–90. https://doi.org/10.3233/978-1-61499-167-0-81

Pace GJ, Schapachnik F (2012) Types of rights in two-party systems: a formal analysis. In: Schäfer B (ed) Legal knowledge and information systems. JURIX 2012: the twenty-fifth annual conference. Frontiers in artificial intelligence and applications, vol 250. IOS, Amsterdam, pp 105–114. https://doi.org/10.3233/978-1-61499-167-0-105

Philipps L (2012) Von deontischen Quadraten – Kuben – Hyperkuben. In: Philipps L (ed) Endliche Rechtsbegriffe mit unendlichen Grenzen: Rechtlogische Aufsätze. Editions Weblaw, Bern, pp 69–81

Poudyal P, Quaresma P (2012) An hybrid approach for legal information extraction. In: Schäfer B (ed) Legal knowledge and information systems. JURIX 2012: the twenty-fifth annual conference. Frontiers in artificial intelligence and applications, vol 250. IOS, Amsterdam, pp 115–118. https://doi.org/10.3233/978-1-61499-167-0-115

Prakken H (2012) Formalising a legal opinion on a legislative proposal in the ASPIC+ framework. In: Schäfer B (ed) Legal knowledge and information systems. JURIX 2012: the twenty-fifth annual conference. Frontiers in artificial intelligence and applications, vol 250. IOS, Amsterdam, pp 119–128. https://doi.org/10.3233/978-1-61499-167-0-119

Ramakrishna S, Karam N, Paschke A (2012) The FSTP test: a novel approach for an invention's non-obviousness analysis. In: Schäfer B (ed) Legal knowledge and information systems. JURIX 2012: the twenty-fifth annual conference. Frontiers in artificial intelligence and applications, vol 250. IOS, Amsterdam, pp 129–132. https://doi.org/10.3233/978-1-61499-167-0-129

Robaldo L, Lesmo L, Radicioni DP (2012) Compiling regular expressions to extract legal modifications. In: Schäfer B (ed) Legal knowledge and information systems. JURIX 2012: the twenty-fifth annual conference. Frontiers in artificial intelligence and applications, vol 250. IOS, Amsterdam, pp 133–141. https://doi.org/10.3233/978-1-61499-167-0-133

Szőke Á, Förhécz A, Strausz G (2012) A unified change management of regulations and their formal representations based on the FRBR framework and the direct method. In: Schäfer B (ed) Legal knowledge and information systems. JURIX 2012: the twenty-fifth annual conference. Frontiers in artificial intelligence and applications, vol 250. IOS, Amsterdam, pp 147–156. https://doi.org/10.3233/978-1-61499-167-0-147

Tammelo I (1978) Modern logic in the service of law. Springer, Vienna

Winkels R, Hoekstra R (2012) Automatic extraction of legal concepts and definitions. In: Schäfer B (ed) Legal knowledge and information systems. JURIX 2012: the twenty-fifth annual conference. Frontiers in artificial intelligence and applications, vol 250. IOS, Amsterdam, pp 157–166. https://doi.org/10.3233/978-1-61499-167-0-157

Part II
On Legal Theory

Chapter 7
Is and Ought

7.1 Distinguishing Ought from Is and Law from Legal Science

We will use a visualisation pattern that is composed of horizontal and vertical stages. The two stages depict Hans Kelsen's categorical distinction between the legal concepts of Is and Ought. The irreducible Is–Ought duality corresponds to a very old mythical and religious duality between Earth and Heaven; in other words, nature and spirit.

Kelsen (1967), § 4.b, p. 5 writes about Is and Ought in his *Pure Theory of Law*: "The norm, as the specific meaning of an act directed toward the behavior of someone else, is to be carefully differentiated from the act of will whose meaning the norm is: the norm is an *ought*, but the act of will in an *is*." Kelsen (1991), § 1.IV, p. 2 treats Ought as a basic category and points out that a norm can be created not only by the act of will but also by custom. The Is world is associated with causality and the Ought world with imputation (see Fig. 7.1). In the following figures, Is might appear in the light green colour and Ought is coloured blue. Law and legal science form two independent systems. Legal science is depicted on a separate vertical stage, which is parallel to the Ought stage (see Fig. 7.2).

7.2 Two Dualisms: Is–Meaning (Sein–Sinn) and Is–Ought (Sein–Sollen)

Is/Ought terminology was used already by Samuel Pufendorf (1672) (see his impositio). Pufendorf considered the dualism of Is (Sein) and Meaning (Sinn) and divided entities into physical entities (entia physica) and moral entities (entia

---

Based on Čyras and Lachmayer (2018).

© The Author(s), under exclusive license to Springer Nature Switzerland AG 2023
V. Cyras, F. Lachmayer, *Essays on the Visualisation of Legal Informatics*, Law,
Governance and Technology Series 54,
https://doi.org/10.1007/978-3-031-27957-7_7

Fig. 7.1 The horizontal and
vertical stages correspond to
the Is world and the Ought
world, respectively (see
Lachmayer and Čyras 2019
in Chap. 21)

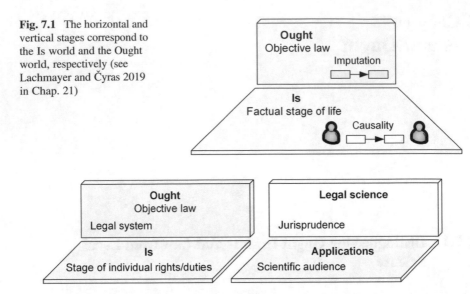

Fig. 7.2 Law and legal science form independent systems

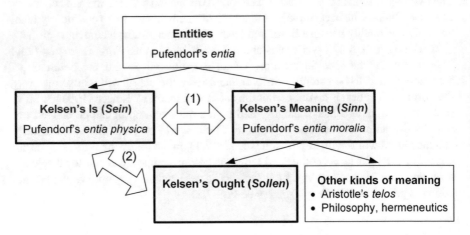

Fig. 7.3 Two types of dualisms: (1) Is–Meaning dualism considered by Pufendorf and Kelsen; and
(2) Is–Ought dualism considered generally in law (Čyras and Lachmayer 2018)

moralia)[1] (see Fig. 7.3). Later, Kelsen spoke about Meaning, and the Sein–Sinn
dualism was revealed. Kelsen's Meaning can be divided into distinct types: there is
the legal meaning (Sollen) on which Kelsen focused, and other kinds of meanings.
The latter exist because different sciences, such as philosophy, hermeneutics, etc.,
explain the world differently and have different ontologies. In sum, Kelsen concentrated on the dualism of Is and Ought.

---

[1] https://plato.stanford.edu/entries/pufendorf-moral/.

The Dualism of Is and Ought   Kelsen holds that Ought does not follow from Is.[2] In formal logic, no indicative statement logically follows from a modal ought-statement. In other words, *Obligatory p* does not imply *p*. However, this does not mean that there is no relationship between Is and Ought. The direction of the conformance relationship points from Is to Ought.[3]

Religion as the Roots of Is–Meaning (*Sein–Sinn*) Dualism   We hold that this dualism has roots in religion, where the Is world is related to Divine grace.

Enrico Pattaro (2007), pp. 57–82 links nature and God in the chapter devoted to the matrix of normativeness. Pattaro purviews "the problem of the foundation of the binding force of positive law – and hence of what is objectively right by virtue of norms posited through human will, that is, by enactment or convention" (ibid.), p. 57. He explains that a matrix is "what makes something be what it is"; consider, for example, the matrices used to print banknotes (p. 58). Pattaro writes about nature as the matrix of normativeness. First, he quotes William of Ockham who says that "nature is the will of God, and God has the power to turn evil into good" (p. 74). Second, after noting "Ockham's voluntaristic view", Pattaro writes about nature as biological instinct, namely, "the variant that identifies nature with animal and human instinct" (p. 75). Third, he provides a rationalistic version of nature as divine and human reason: "what is right by nature is the content of the norms inherent in human (and divine) reason understood as human (and divine) nature" (p. 77). Pattaro observes:

> The reality that ought to be is spiritual, ideal, and moral reality. With Hugo Grotius and Samuel Pufendorf the classical natural-law school uses the very terms "moral entities," "moral faculties," and "moral bonds" (*entitates morales, facultates morales,* and *vincula moralia*). Natural norms are conceived of as a class of norms that reason sets forth and that even stand above God, or at least will partake of God's nature, in that God cannot turn good into evil, or vice versa [. . .] In this conception, norms—understood as law that is binding per se—precede power. (Pattaro 2007), p. 77

Fourth, Pattaro writes about nature as the cosmic order and the origin of the term *jus positivum* and quotes Fassò's transliterations from Calcidium's Greek:

> Latin writers would use *positivus* in opposition to *naturalis* to express the Greek antithesis of *thései* and *phýsei*, which in the Hellenistic age had come to replace the older antithesis of *nomói* and *phýsei*, indicating the opposition between what is manmade, on the one hand, and what is natural, on the other (*thésis* is, in Latin, *positio*, and *positivus* thus rendered literally the concept expressed by the dative *thései*). (Pattaro 2007), p. 80

The latter quotations provide us terminological roots for the Is–Meaning (Sein–Sinn) dualism (see Fig. 7.4).

---

[2] "Nobody can assert that from the statement that something is, follows a statement that something ought to be, or vice versa" (Kelsen 1967), § 4.b, p. 6.

[3] "This dualism of is and ought does not mean, however, that there is no relationship between *is* and *ought*. One says: an *is* conforms to an ought, which means that something is as it ought to be; and one says: an *ought* is "directed" toward an is—in other words: something ought to be" (Kelsen 1967), § 4.b, p. 6.

7.3   Is Does Not Imply Ought

Although Ota Weinberger is not a proponent of natural law, but rather of positive law, he writes about arguments for natural law theories. We agree with Weinberger's grounds for adopting a natural law theory (criteria of fair law; law is more than power; and solving hard cases, for short). We also agree with his conclusions about positive law. Again, our thesis is that pure arguments for natural law conceptions do not imply Ought. Arguments can be of different kinds, for example, scientific, religious, etc. The good news about arguments is that they can be adduced to legitimate law through intermediate stages that have separate functions, bridge functions. For instance, religion justifies the natural law conception, which is not identical with law. The bad news is that, although pure scientific arguments aim at legitimating positive law, they do raise questions such as where do the values come from? (see Fig. 7.5).

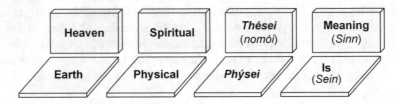

Fig. 7.4   The dualism of the physical reality and the spiritual reality in different discourses

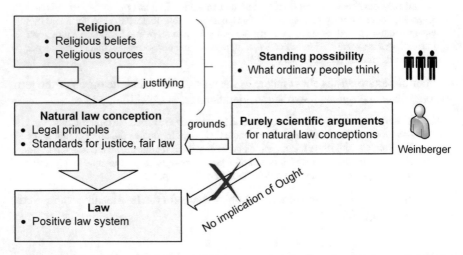

Fig. 7.5   On the way to positive law, arguments serve as intermediate stages and serve their bridge functions

7.4   Subsumption as a Bridge Between Is and Ought

Legal meaning is significant in subsumption. A fact, a, that appears in Is is subsumed under the legal term A, which is present in the legal norm N that appears in Ought. Further, we can follow the terminology by Pattaro (2007), ch. 1 and 2, especially pp. 13–17. He emphasises the distinction between token and type. Pattaro observes:

> [I]f a type is set forth and qualified in a norm [...] but is not expressed in any sentence, validity with regard to that type will be a token's congruence with the type, and invalidity its incongruence, whether this norm makes the type obligatory, permitted, or forbidden. (Pattaro 2007), p. 14

Pattaro notes that his "characterisation of validity therefore parts ways with the current legal-linguistic use of this term" (p. 14). Pattaro explains congruence:

> In geometry, "congruent" means "coinciding at all points when superimposed" – such is, for example, the meaning of "congruent triangles." Just as a triangle, a, can be incongruent with triangle b, but congruent with triangle c, so a token, t, can be incongruent with type U, and hence invalid with respect to it, but congruent with type V, and hence valid with respect to it. (Pattaro 2007), p. 20

Chapter 2 of Pattaro's book is devoted to the dualism and interaction between Ought and Is, and validity is metaphorically called a pineal gland. Pattaro refers, for instance, to Karl Engisch, Arthur Kaufmann, Karl Larenz and Riccardo Guastini and observes:

> There is a body of legal literature concerned with the so-called interpretation of facts (of actual states of affairs, events, or behaviours), namely, with the way in which to understand these things (as valid or invalid tokens, I would comment) with respect to the types set forth in and not forbidden by the law. The crucial point here is "not forbidden by the law." Thus, "paying your taxes" and "making a purchase" are types set forth in and not forbidden by the law, whereas "committing theft" is a type set forth in and forbidden by the law. (Pattaro 2007), pp. 24–25

On first impression, an idea can arise that Pattaro's validity explained as the congruence of a token, a, with a type U can be modelled in terms of an element, a, and a set U. Indeed, in mathematics, an element either belongs to the set or does not belong to the set (see Fig. 7.6). You might think that, in this way, the concept of legal validity can be reduced to truth: true (i.e. that which is congruent, valid) or false (that which is incongruent, invalid). But this is not correct.

Fig. 7.6 Token a is valid with type U, whereas token b is invalid with type U

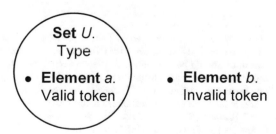

We think that Pattaro's argument has to be made more precise, distinguishing extensional definitions of U from intensional definitions of U.[4] We hold that Pattaro's argument is correct for an extensional set U. Suppose, however, an intensional definition of U. A computational problem arises here. To decide whether an element, a, is or is not an element of U for an intensional definition of U is an undecidable problem. In other words, there is no algorithm to determine whether the statement 'a is an element of U' is true or false. An example is the halting problem in computability theory—the problem of determining, from a description of an arbitrary computer program and an input, whether the program will finish running or continue to run forever (see Sipser 2006).

In law, legal terms are defined intensionally. Thus, an intensional definition of U is a proper model. Moreover, we point to two more complications. First, open texture applies to definitions. Second, an element, a, appears in Is in a situation that will occur in the future.

In summary, a legal definition of a legal term, T, differs from a definition of type U in computing. The institutional meaning of T appears in Ought, whereas U appears in a different realm, computer science.

References

Cook RT (2009) Intensional definition. In: A dictionary of philosophical logic. Edinburgh University Press, Edinburgh, p 155

Čyras V, Lachmayer F (2018) Meaning and meta-meaning as entities: content (is) and institutional meaning (ought). In: Jusletter IT, 24 May 2018. https://doi.org/10.38023/5c029a6a-619b-4558-bb74-69d57bf58b61

Kelsen H (1967) Pure theory of law, 2nd edn (trans: Knight M) (Reine Rechtslehre, 2. Auflage. Deuticke, Wien 1960). University of California Press, Berkeley

Kelsen H (1991) General theory of norms (trans: Hartney M) (Allgemeine Theorie der Normen, Manz Verlag, Wien, 1979). Clarendon Press, Oxford

Lachmayer F, Čyras V (2019) Formalising legal relations. In: Schweighofer E, Araszkiewicz M, Lachmayer F, Pavčnik M (eds) Formalising jurisprudence: festschrift for Hajime Yoshino. Editions Weblaw, Bern, pp 163–181

Pattaro E (2007) The law and the right: a reappraisal of the reality that ought to be. Series A Treatise of legal philosophy and general jurisprudence, vol 1. Springer, Dordrecht

Sipser M (2006) The halting problem. In: Sipser M (ed) Introduction to the theory of computation, 2nd edn. PWS Publishing, pp 173–182

---

[4]Cook writes: "An intensional definition provides the meaning of an expression by specifying *necessary* and *sufficient conditions* for correct application of the expression. An intensional definition should be distinguished from an *extensional definition*, which merely provides a list of those instances in which the expression being defined is applicable. For example, we might provide an intensional definition of "bachelor" by specifying that bachelors are unmarried men. An extensional definition of bachelor, on the other hand, would consist merely of a list of those men" (Cook 2009), p. 155. See also Wikipedia, https://en.wikipedia.org/wiki/Extensional_and_intensional_definitions, quoting Roy T. Cook.

Chapter 8
Visualisation of Hans Kelsen's Pure Theory of Law

8.1 Legal Theory as Middle-Ranged Abstraction

Hans Kelsen's Pure Theory of Law is among the most prominent and influential legal theories. Kelsen's book (1967) contains neither logical notation nor pictures, only text. In spite of this, our impression is that Kelsen himself had a very clear imagination. We make an attempt to visualise his theoretical models because it is important for legal informatics. Explicit visualisations of the structures of law and their theoretical representations are significant for the development of legal ontologies. Visuals also contribute to legal education and an understanding of the law that is expressed in a non-textual mode. In particular, the legal machinery has a non-textual effect in legal situations.

Kelsen created a paradigm of an up-to-date legal theory, so the visualisations of his ideas present an interesting way to understand PTL. This chapter concerns the core of PTL, and leaves out the marginal aspects. Our thesis is that PTL deals with middle-level abstraction (see Sect. 19.4 in this volume). We set forth a three-layer model (see Fig. 8.1). It can be shown that legal logic belongs to a higher layer of abstraction, PTL to the middle, and concrete decisions and laws are at the bottom. Ontologies are assigned to the highest layer.

The creation of formalisations is a substantial part of legal informatics. However, the application of formal notations may relate only to the details of law. This is because the textual systems of law contain details that can be exposed adequately and precisely. On the other hand, on a purely theoretical level, the need for contexts can arise, especially, in the context of legal theory. Here, PTL can be considered as a theory regarding the background. In this respect, a connection between PTL and legal informatics is provided.

Based on Čyras and Lachmayer (2021).

Fig. 8.1 *Machine =*
analogy of human on the
horizontal Is stage (Čyras
and Lachmayer 2021)

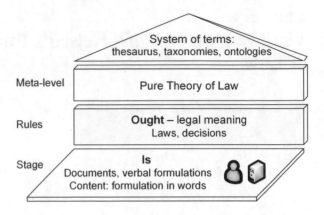

With regard to visualisations, there are inherently intuitive visualisations in addition to automatic ones. Automatic visualisations can show, for example, the structures of legislation and statistics. This chapter is devoted to intuitive visualisations, of which Fig. 8.1 serves as an example. Hence, strong visualisations exist alongside the weak ones. Both have their functions, and the problem that their syntax not uniform. This, however, provides the advantage of freedom to shape them. Visuals can make the context increasingly obvious. This is important for bringing legal informatics to action. Visuals can serve as maps that provide orientation in the textual landscapes of law, thus increasing the benefits of informatics.

Kelsen's texts are of great linguistic and intellectual intensity and are combined with a very clear pre-textual imagination. However, his imagination is not easy to grasp on first reading. A non-expert may wish to find a concise conceptual model of law as an accompaniment. Visuals can serve as a middle way to provide graphical models. Kelsen's works are not written as textbooks for freshmen.

8.2   Historical Position

Kelsen wrote two editions of the Pure Theory of Law: the first edition was published in 1934 and the second in 1960. A key feature of the Pure Theory of Law is a paradigm change of legal theory and the proposal of a new juridical methodology. Kelsen introduced new concepts and terms, such as norm, basic norm, the hierarchy of norms, legal act, etc.

Kelsen (1991), § 16.II, p. 70 stopped the scientific discussion and took over from the natural law doctrine. Here we recall René Marcic (1971; Marcic and Tammelo 1989) as one of the last important thinkers of natural law. Legal logic and legal informatics succeeded in the research. A scientific mainstream after Kelsen was the

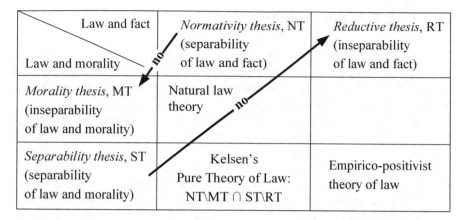

Fig. 8.2   Resolving the antinomy. Adapted from Paulson's introduction (see Kelsen 1992, pp. xxvi–xxix)

legal logic invented by von Wright (1951), with his article on deontic logic (the logic of obligation and permission).

To characterise Kelsen's position, we invoke Stanley Paulson's formulation on resolving the antinomy between the reductive thesis and the normativity thesis. In the introduction to the 1992 translation of the 1934 first edition of *Reine Rechtslehre*, Paulson expresses a view of "how Kelsen distinguishes his own position from those of the tradition" (Kelsen 1992), p. xxviii:

(i) Is the *normativity thesis* derivable from the *morality thesis*? The tradition: yes. Kelsen: yes.

(ii) Turning the question around, is the *morality thesis* derivable from the *normativity thesis*? The tradition: yes. Kelsen: no.

(iii) Is the *separability thesis* derivable from the *reductive thesis*? The tradition: yes. Kelsen: yes.

(iv) Turning the question around, is the *reductive thesis* derivable from the *separability thesis*? The tradition: yes. Kelsen: no.

Paulson finds that "Kelsen's answers to questions (ii) and (iv) suggest the hypotheses which he begins – the normativity thesis *without* the morality thesis, and the separability thesis *without* the reductive thesis". We can symbolise this: NT \MT ∩ ST\RT (see Fig. 8.2).

8.3   Is and Ought: Causality and Imputation

Kelsen (1967), § 3ff. uses a categorical distinction between Is and Ought. The Pure Theory of Law as a theory aims at cognition (ibid.), § 1. Therefore it appears on a meta-level (see Fig. 8.1). Other elements, such as the system of terms, form a modally indifferent substrate and appear on the meta-level, too.

Is represents the primary layer of the actors' actions and is visualised by the stage metaphor. Not only are persons among the actors, but also the requisites, for instance, things, as well as the actual substrates of speech acts and legal acts such as the paper of statutes and judgments. Verbal formulations are assigned to the Is even in a case in which the speech content is normative. The verbal formulations of 'ought', that is, the content, are distinguished from the legal Ought, which has a specific legal meaning (Sinn).

The next layer, that of rules, is in the realm of Ought. It is visualised by the vertical stage. According to Kelsen, it deals with legal meaning, namely, a specific legal significance. The Ought rises to the actual substrate, the Is. The legal acts of the law, such as judgments and private law (e.g. private contracts), constitute the Ought as the regulative background of the Is stage.

Material artefacts such as paper documents and verbal formulations appear in the Is and their legal meaning in the Ought. The Is world is factual—it comprises facts.

The Pure Theory of Law emerges as the next layer, namely, as a scientific descriptive meta-layer above the law, in the sense-sphere of Ought. The legal science must be descriptive in principle to remain "pure". But the PTL, though admittedly on the top layer, also contains prescriptive elements, such as, the command that legal science include only descriptive value-free sentences.

Kelsen spoke (1991, § 6.II) about a modally indifferent substrate that constitutes a system of terms that is built of terms contained in law. If you continue from this beginning, you can arrive at the modern system, which comprises thesauri, taxonomies and ontologies. In Kelsen's works, science reached a historical peak; however, it was not left standing and, in multiple phases, there has been distinctive further development. Ontologies can be viewed as the most modern developments in the system of legal terms (see e.g. Casellas 2011; Palmirani et al. 2011).

Further, the notion of imputation is analysed because it is central in distinguishing the Is and Ought layers that were introduced above.

8.3.1   Central and Peripheral Imputation

Kelsen distinguishes causality and imputation as two different kinds of functional connection (1991, § 7). Imputation links a condition with a sanction brought about by a general moral or legal norm.

The analysis of the fundamental notion of imputation reveals certain subtleties. Stanley Paulson (2011) writes about the "objectivity" motif in PTL and calls

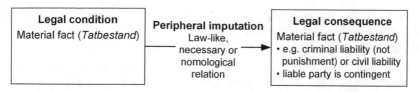

Fig. 8.3 Peripheral imputation relates two material facts, that is, the act and liability

Kelsen's thesis the "nomological normativity thesis". Kelsen distinguishes between central imputation and peripheral imputation:

> [Central imputation] is an entirely different operation from the peripheral imputation mentioned earlier, where a material fact is connected [...] to another material fact within the system, that is, where two material facts are linked together in the reconstructed legal norm. (Kelsen 1992), pp. 50–51

Paulson summarises that Kelsen's doctrine of central imputation manifests no personalised subject, and Kelsen's doctrine of peripheral imputation differs "in having, *strictu sensu*, no subject of attribution at all" (Paulson 2001), p. 51. We show the relationship within peripheral imputation in Fig. 8.3.

Paulson starts with the following formulation of peripheral imputation (with an 'and if . . .' clause inserted between parentheses as a shorthand reference to the other conditions associated with a legal proceeding):

> *Formulation I.* If an act of a certain type takes place (and if . . .) then that actor or a surrogate[1] is liable for that act. (Paulson 2011), p. 159

Paulson, however, rules out this formulation "by Kelsen's stipulation that peripheral imputation links material facts, where the latter material fact is understood to be the liability imputed to the legal act". He notes that "[t]o adopt formulation I as a representation of peripheral imputation would be to confuse peripheral imputation with central imputation" (p. 159).

Paulson proposes "[t]he alternative 'subjectless' counterpart [...] that does not include an ascription to a legal subject":

> *Formulation II.* If an act of a certain type takes place (and if . . .) then that act is treated as 'liability ascribing'. (Paulson 2011), p. 159

Paulson notes, that "formulation II seems counterintuitive in imputing liability to the act, not to the actor" and explains the reason that

> [w]e are accustomed to distinguishing between the imputation of liability individually on the one hand and collectively on the other [...] In the first case, the imputation of liability is either to the actor or [...] to a surrogate [...] say to the insurance company. (Paulson 2011), p. 161

---

[1] Here Paulson is using 'surrogate' to cover all variations on the theme of vicarious and collective liability, see also his notes 58–59.

Paulson analyses the imputation of liability to the act rather than to the actor and notes that "the character of the liable party – actor, surrogate, or collective body – is a contingent factor, a question of legal policy, not legal science":

> In any case it is precisely this necessary relation between act and liability that represents the core of what I am calling Kelsen's nomological normativity thesis. The relation is nomological in being necessary or law-like, and it is normative in being non-causal. (Paulson 2011), p. 161

Paulson concludes:

> Where the antecedent condition obtains, this marks the imputation of liability to the act, a necessary relation. Where the ascription of liability to a person is made, this marks a change in that person's legal position. The change, Kelsen insists, is a normative change, not a causal change. (Paulson 2011), pp. 164–165

8.3.2 No Long Series of Imputation

A difference in causality and imputation is that "by the very nature of causality – the chain of cause and effect is endless in both directions". On the contrary, "[t]he imputation series does not have an unlimited number of members as the causal series does: basically it has only two members" (Kelsen 1991), § 7, p. 24. Hence, a network of causes and effects can be depicted as a graph with two types of edges: one that denotes causality and the other that denotes imputation (see Fig. 8.4). A long series of causality may appear, but not a long series of imputation. We think that a challenge for AI and law is to explore different network patterns and to formalise distinguished theories of causality, fault, and legal responsibility, such as 'sine qua non', 'but-for', etc. (cf. Lehmann et al. 2004).

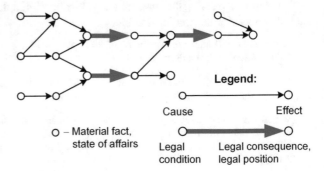

Fig. 8.4 A network of causalities (thin edges) and imputations (thick)

Legend:

O —● Cause — Effect

O – Material fact, state of affairs

O ═══► Legal condition — Legal consequence, legal position

Fig. 8.5 The interpretation
of the factual reality (Čyras
and Lachmayer 2021)

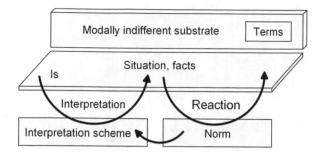

8.4 Interpretations

This section concerns two groups of concepts: (a) facts, norms and texts, and
(b) construction and deconstruction. Kelsen describes five (3+2) different interpretations regarding facts, norms and legal texts. We divide them into two groups (3+1):

1. The interpretation of factual reality (Is). Facts are the entities of the Is-world and
   are transformed into a legal meaning (Ought).
2. The interpretation of legal texts (content). Kelsen describes the interpretation of
   the content of legal texts and the transformation in a new version of textual
   understanding. This is associated with the procedure of subsumption.
3. The interpretation of legal acts. This addresses the interpretation of normative
   sources (normative texts) and their transformation into valid legal acts (e.g.,
   laws). The basic norm is regarded in this context. In this chapter, we express
   the main argument against Kelsen's basic norm concept: Such a (scientific) basic
   norm delegates a scientific qualification, but has no legal validity.
4. Construction.

8.4.1 The Interpretation of Factual Reality

A norm (from Ought) functions as an interpretation scheme of a fact (from Is).[2]
Hence, institutional facts are interpreted according to Ought (see Fig. 8.5). The
interpretation is erected on both Is and Ought. Here, Pufendorf's impositio should be
recalled (see also MacCormick and Weinberger 1986, pp. 49–92) for an institutional
theory of facts). It should be noted that a paper document of a draft law (bill) as such
has no legal meaning. The meaning is obtained when it is legitimated.

---

[2] Kelsen (1967), § 4, pp. 3–4 writes: "The external fact whose objective meaning is a legal or illegal
act is always an event that can be perceived by the senses [. . .] However, this event as such, as an
element of nature, is not an object of legal cognition. What turns this event into a legal or illegal act
is not its physical existence [. . .] but the objective meaning resulting from its interpretation. The
specifically legal meaning of this act is derived from a "norm" whose content refers to the act; this
norm confers legal meaning to the act [...]"

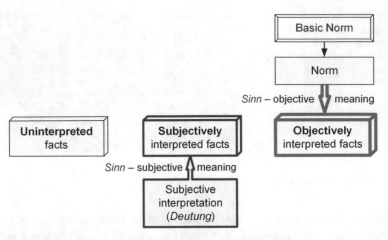

Fig. 8.6 Imposing the meaning to facts (Čyras and Lachmayer 2021)

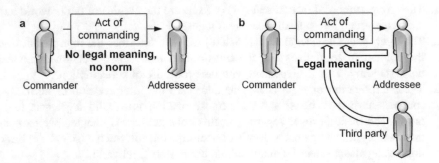

Fig. 8.7 **a** The subjective meaning and **b** objective meaning of the act of commanding

The interpretation above is supplemented by the imposition of meaning (see Fig. 8.6). First, facts—uninterpreted facts—appear on the Is-stage. Second, *subjectively interpreted facts* that are on the Is-stage are exposed to subjective meaning. Subjective interpretation appears on the layer of the mind. Third, *objectively interpreted facts* on the Is-stage have an objective legal meaning (Sinn) with respect to a legal norm in Ought:

> "Norm" is the meaning of an act by which a certain behaviour is commanded, permitted, or authorized [...] The command of a gangster [...] has the same subjective meaning as the command of an income-tax official [...] But only the command of the official, not that of the gangster, has the meaning of a valid norm, binding upon the addressed individual. (Kelsen 1967), § 4.b, pp. 5–8

Kelsen explains the subjective and objective meaning of the act of commanding (we illustrate this in Fig. 8.7):

> If the command is not empowered, then this is merely the *subjective meaning* of the act of commanding, that is, it is the meaning the act of commanding has from the point of view of the commander and not from the point of view of the addressee or any third party [...] Only an empowered command also has the *objective meaning* of Ought, that is, only an empowered command is a *norm* binding on the addressee, obligating him to act in the prescribed way [...] (Kelsen 1991), § 8.V, p. 27

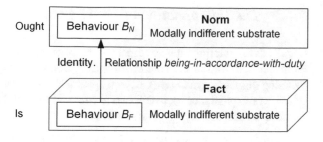

Fig. 8.8 Behaviour that agrees with a norm is formalised by the identity $B_F = B_N$ (in general, equivalence relation $\sim$ or *instance-of* relationship)

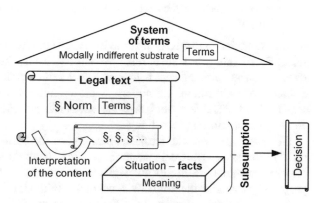

Fig. 8.9 The interpretation of legal texts (Čyras and Lachmayer 2021)

Legal norms conform to the basic norm. It appears at the meta-level, PTL.

Identity of Two Modally Indifferent Substrates Kelsen (1991), § 16.II devotes a whole section to the behaviour which agrees with a norm. The idea is expressed in the title: "Identity of the Modally Indifferent Substrate of the Behaviour Decreed to be Obligatory in the Norm with the Modally Indifferent Substrate of the Behaviour Existing in Reality" (p. 60). An example involves the fact '*A* pays his gambling debts' and the norm '*A* ought to pay his gambling debts'. The content of the Is and the content of the Ought constitute the modally indifferent substrate of 'paying-gambling-debts'. The fact sentence and the norm sentence are invested with the mode of Is and the mode of Ought, respectively. Here, we extract a formalisation that a behaviour that exists in reality, B_F, agrees with a behaviour, B_N that exists in the norm. Formally: there is an identity relationship between two modally indifferent substrates, $B_F = B_N$ (see Fig. 8.8).

8.4.2   The Interpretation of Legal Texts

The second interpretation is relative to the classical interpretation of the content of legal texts. The subsumption procedure is concerned. The terms that are found in the legal text appear on the meta-level and are a modally indifferent substrate (see Fig. 8.9). On adjudication by a court, see e.g. Kelsen (1967, § 35.g).

8.4.3   The Interpretation of Legal Acts

Legal acts are interpreted with respect to the basic norm (see Fig. 8.10). A thin arrow represents a transition from a normative text, a substrate (appearing in Is), to its legal meaning (appearing in Ought). Kelsen speaks about different degrees of the relation called 'correspondence' between two norms and the validity of a lower norm that is founded on the validity of a higher norm:

> A positive moral or legal order can never conflict with its Basic Norm [...] A conflict is always possible between Natural Law and a positive moral or legal order. (Kelsen 1991), § 59.II, p. 259

Again, we maintain that Kelsen views the basic norm as a scientific product that has scientific meaning, but no normative validity. Thus, the main argument against Kelsen's basic norm concept is that such (scientific) basic norms can only delegate a scientific qualification, but no legal validity. We think that this is a problem—a drawback of PTL. We hold that the scientific significance of the basic norm converges with normative validity.

However, here you can recall the function of the basic norm. Paulson maintains that "[w]heras fundamental norms in the juridico-philosophical tradition serve to impose constraints, Kelsen's fundamental norm – or basic norm (*Grundnorm*) – purports to establish the normativist character of the law" (Paulson 2000), p. 279.

Kelsen provides the example of the basic norm of Christian morality and holds that "only a norm can be the reason for the validity of another norm":

> It is a 'basic' norm, because nothing further can be asked about the reason for its validity, since it is not a posited norm but a presupposed norm. (Kelsen 1991) § 59.I.C, p. 255

He holds that the basic norm is not a positive norm, but a merely thought norm (i.e. a fictitious norm), the meaning of a merely fictitious, and not real, act of will:

> The cognitive goal of the Basic Norm is to ground the validity of the norms forming a positive moral or legal order, that is, to interpret the subjective meaning of the norm-positing acts as their objective meaning (i.e. as valid norms) and to interpret the relevant acts as norm-positing acts. This goal can be attained only by means of a fiction. (Kelsen 1991), § 59.I. D, p. 256

Fig. 8.10 The interpretation of legal acts (Čyras and Lachmayer 2021)

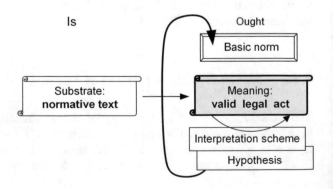

8.5   Construction

Structural interpretation involves scientific notions wherein Kelsen was very creative.

8.5.1   Double Norm

Kelsen (1967), pp. 100–101 makes a transition from the hypothetical norm concept to the categorical norm (see Fig. 8.11a). Other norm concepts exist (see e.g. Luhmann 2004). We depict this in Fig. 8.11b.

The difference is not easy to grasp and to formalise in terms of imputation and formal logic. However, Kelsen explains:

> Prosecutor *A* can demand that judge *B* punish *C*, who (in *A*'s opinion) committed theft; but the judge, who is willing to punish thieves, can reject the prosecutor's demand because the '*ought*-to-punish-*C*' is valid for the judge only if it his opinion that *C* has committed theft, and he is of the opinion that he has *not*. He can decide: '*C* is not to be punished.' What is lacking in this case is the condition for the *ought*-to-punish. (Kelsen 1991), § 5, p. 21

Kelsen (1991), p. 21 summarises: "All norms are valid merely conditionally". To explain the difference, Manfred Moritz's words can be used:

> If there is a conditional imperative 'If it rains, go home!', we can express the parallel judgment for instance in the following way: 'It is commanded to go home if it rains'. It should not be formulated so as to say 'If it rains, it is commanded to go home' […] The judgment which is parallel to a conditional imperative does not state under which conditions the action is *commanded*, but under which conditions the action ought to be *performed*. (Kelsen 1991), note 24, p. 290

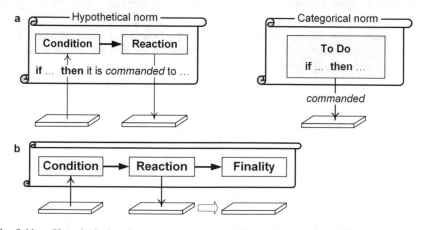

Fig. 8.11 **a** Hypothetical and categorical norms. **b** Niklas Luhmann's (2004) concept of norm (Čyras and Lachmayer 2013)

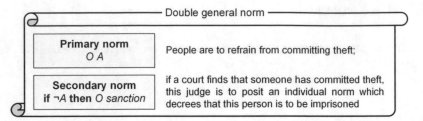

Fig. 8.12 A double norm is a unity of the primary and the secondary norm (Čyras and Lachmayer 2013)

Kelsen adds: "The imperative is 'conditional', not because it is subject to a condition [*bedingt*], but because it *sets a condition [bedingend]*" (Kelsen 1991), p. 290.

In the chapters devoted to primary and secondary norms, Kelsen views a general legal norm as a combination of them, that is, a double norm (see Fig. 8.12):

> It is assumed to be essential for law that a distinction be made between a norm commanding a certain behaviour and a norm prescribing a sanction for the violation of the first norm, then the former norm must be called the primary norm, and the latter the secondary norm [...] The primary norm can then exist quite independently of the secondary norm. But it is also possible for the primary norm—the one commanding a certain behaviour—not to be *expressly formulated*, and only the secondary norm—the one decreeing a sanction—to be expressly formulated. (Kelsen 1991), § 35, p. 142; see also § 15, p. 56

8.5.2   Hierarchy of Norms

This section presents a version of what Kelsen wrote that is bit more modern. Constitution, law, statute and decision form a hierarchy (see 1967, part V, especially § 35). This expresses governance by one nation-state (see Fig. 8.13). Kelsen speaks about the normative order and a hierarchical structure of norms.[3]

EU primary law and EU secondary law form another hierarchy, with the international law being above. A private treaty appears on the bottom. The basic norm is above all and is also in the mind.

---

[3] "A positive moral or legal order never constitutes a system of merely coordinate norms, but always one of superordinate and subordinate norms, i.e. a hierarchical structure of norms, whose highest level is the constitution whose validity is founded on the presupposed Basic Norm, and whose lowest level is made of the individual norms decreeing particular concrete behaviour to be obligatory" (Kelsen 1991), § 59.I.F, p. 258.

Fig. 8.13 A hierarchical structure of norms (Čyras and Lachmayer 2021)

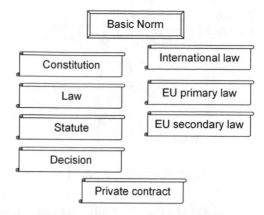

Fig. 8.14 A purification of the personality concept (Čyras and Lachmayer 2021)

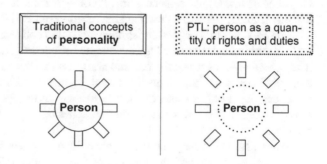

8.6   Purification: A Deconstruction

Kelsen's approach to purification rests on a critical interpretation of other theories. This is a deconstruction of the traditional legal theory.

Personality is a traditional key concept. In the Pure Theory of Law a person is only a quantity of rights and duties (see Fig. 8.14).

A traditional concept of institution comprises entities such as state. In PTL, institutions are only sets of norms (see Fig. 8.15). Therefore Kelsen devotes a separate chapter VI to law and state (1967), § 36 ff. esp. § 41.b.

An effect of the Pure Theory of Law is also that Kelsen provides new interpretation for traditional terms. State and person are examples where this arises. This is not new in the history of jurisprudence. Both happen: on the one hand adoption and, on the other, re-interpretation of previous terms and creating completely new terms. Guido Tsuno (2011) investigates these issues within the research on legal lexicon.

Fig. 8.15 A purification of
the institution concept

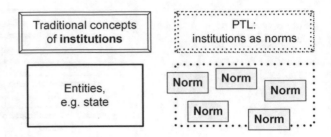

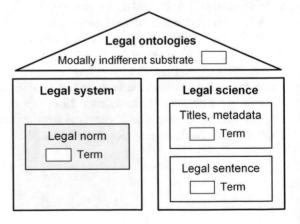

8.7 Legal Norms, Legal Sentences and Legal Terms

According to Kelsen, legal norms are part of a legal system, and therefore, are part of
Ought. In contrast, legal sentences are part of legal science, and therefore, are outside
of Ought. Legal sentences describe legal norms (see Fig. 8.16).

Hajime Yoshino's Logical Jurisprudence (2011) deliberately addresses Kelsen, as
well. Yoshino deals with the logical structure of legal science. Legal sentences form
a key element in his research. Yoshino aims to make the structure of legal sentences
explicit. Therefore, he brings in several layers: legal rule sentences, legal fact
sentences, legal object sentences and legal meta-sentences. Kelsen, with his terminology, stops at texts, whereas Yoshino reaches the logical layer and uses a formal
notation.

Tsuno (2011) investigates the legal lexicon and steps outside of the streams
above. Kelsen mentioned the concept of the modally indifferent substrate in the
General Theory of Norms, which appeared rather late. Thus, the terms do not form a
specific issue for Kelsen. In contrast, Tsuno investigates legal terms, namely, in their
historical dimension. He starts with medieval historical dissertations and law dictionaries. Legal terms allow the testing of these works. They also appear in titles and
headlines, and hence, in immanent metadata.

Fig. 8.16 Vertical Ought
stage and legal science
(Čyras and Lachmayer
2021)

Conclusion The Pure Theory of Law distinguishes between legal norms and legal statements (rules of law). Causality, which is attributed to Is, and imputation, which is attributed to Ought, form parallel systems. Imputation is treated as a quasi-causality. Kelsen makes a transition from hypothetical norms to double norms. In this model, the primary norm and the secondary norm come together. The imputation relationship connects the state of affairs of a norm (gesetzlicher Tatbestand, Normhypothese) with its legal consequence (Rechtsfolge). A legal norm determines a legal consequence given a state of affairs that falls within the scope of the norm.

The centrepiece of PTL is addressed in this chapter. Our thesis is that PTL deals with the middle layer of abstraction in the three-stage model. Legal logic and ontologies are assigned to the higher layer and individual decisions and laws to the bottom layer. A connection with legal informatics remains a separate issue.

References

Casellas N (2011) Legal ontology engineering. Law, governance and technology series, vol 3. Springer, Dordrecht. https://doi.org/10.1007/978-94-007-1497-7

Čyras V, Lachmayer F (2013) Extended legal thesaurus: legal terms as a modally indifferent substrate. Jusletter IT, 11 December 2013. https://doi.org/10.38023/4736480a-0978-43f1-b392-ad52256c17e9

Čyras V, Lachmayer F (2021) From Kelsen's Pure Theory of Law to Yoshino's Logical Jurisprudence. In: Yoshino H, Villa Rosas G (eds) Law and logic – making legal science a genuine science. Proceedings of the special workshop held at the 28th World Congress of the International Association for Philosophy of Law and Social Philosophy in Lisbon, Portugal, 2017. Archiv für Rechts- und Sozialphilosophie – Beihefte (ARSP-B), Band 166. Franz Steiner Verlag, Stuttgart, pp 29–63

Kelsen H (1967) Pure theory of law, 2nd edn (trans: Knight M) (Reine Rechtslehre, 2. Auflage. Deuticke, Wien 1960). University of California Press, Berkeley

Kelsen H (1991) General theory of norms (trans: Hartney M) (Allgemeine Theorie der Normen, Manz Verlag, Wien, 1979). Clarendon Press, Oxford

Kelsen H (1992) Introduction to the problems of legal theory. A translation of the first edition of the Reine Rechtslehre or Pure Theory of Law (trans: Litschewski Paulson B, Paulson SL). Clarendon Press, Oxford

Lehmann J, Breuker J, Brouwer B (2004) Causation in AI and law. Artif Intell Law 12(4):279–315. https://doi.org/10.1007/s10506-005-4157-y

Luhmann N (2004) Law as a social system (trans: Ziegert KA). Oxford University Press

MacCormick N, Weinberger O (1986) An institutional theory of law: new approaches to legal positivism. D. Reidel Publishing, Dordrecht

Marcic R (1971) The right to resist as an attribute of human dignity. University of Sydney, Sydney

Marcic R, Tammelo I (1989) Naturrecht und Gerechtigkeit: Eine Einführung in die Grundprobleme. Salzburger Schriften zur Rechts-, Staats- und Sozialphilosophie, Band 9. Peter Lang, Frankfurt am Main

Palmirani M, Cervone L, Vitali F (2011) A legal document ontology: the missing layer in legal document modelling. In: Sartor G, Casanovas P, Biasiotti MA, Fernández-Barrera M (eds) Approaches to legal ontologies. Law, governance and technology series, vol 1. Springer, Dordrecht, pp 167–178. https://doi.org/10.1007/978-94-007-0120-5_10

Paulson SL (2000) On the puzzle surrounding Hans Kelsen's basic norm. Ratio Juris 13(3): 279–293. https://doi.org/10.1111/1467-9337.00156

Paulson SL (2001) Hans Kelsen's doctrine of imputation. Ratio Juris 14(1):47–63. https://doi.org/
    10.1111/1467-9337.00171
Paulson SL (2011) The very idea of legal positivism. Revista Brasileira de Estudos Politicos 102:
    139–165.   https://pos.direito.ufmg.br/rbep/index.php/rbep/article/view/130.   Accessed
    15 Dec 2022
Tsuno G (2011) Repertorium Aureum: Rechtslexika im Geltungsbereich des Ius Commune und im
    19. Jahrhundert. Vico Verlag, Frankfurt am Main
von Wright GH (1951) Deontic logic. Mind 60(237):1–15. https://www.jstor.org/stable/2251395.
    Accessed 15 Dec 2022

Chapter 9
From Kelsen's PTL to Yoshino's Logical Jurisprudence

9.1 Introduction to Yoshino's Logical Jurisprudence

Hajime Yoshino's Logical Jurisprudence (LJ) aims for a logic-based systematisation in the legal domain. Legal reasoning and systematisation are its focus. Inevitably, embracing law as a whole brings us to Kelsen's Pure Theory of Law. We single out elements in PTL and LJ that function as parallels. The separation of law and legal science is also an issue. The notions of legal validity and scientific truth are differentiated. The thesis of the separation of law and legal science says that legal validity is determined by law and not by legal science. Analogically, the truth of scientific statements is determined by legal science and not by law. The question of whether or not a norm exists does not need legal science. Law and legal science are autonomous systems, although they are related. Both have their institutional meanings, which are called, respectively, legal institutional meaning and scientific institutional meaning.

Kelsen's PTL has numerous followers and an influence on other theories on law. It is only formulated in textual form. Logical Jurisprudence, as described by Yoshino (1997, 2011a, b) forms a transition to theories in the period after PTL and offers a self-contained architecture (see Fig. 9.1).

The Pure Theory of Law still appeals strongly to the past, although it strictly opposes the prevailing natural law. To this extent, PTL strives to separate itself from existing theories, but also to separate legal science from the politics that flow upstream from law. In contrast, LJ pursues an integrative concept, namely the explicit connection between the theory of law and the formal systems of logic in the forefront. The adoption of formal logic is a declared goal of LJ. The Pure Theory of Law, on the other hand, speaks of logic but a formal notation is completely absent.

Based on three papers: Čyras and Lachmayer (2017, 2019, 2021).

© The Author(s), under exclusive license to Springer Nature Switzerland AG 2023
V. Cyras, F. Lachmayer, *Essays on the Visualisation of Legal Informatics*, Law,
Governance and Technology Series 54,
https://doi.org/10.1007/978-3-031-27957-7_9

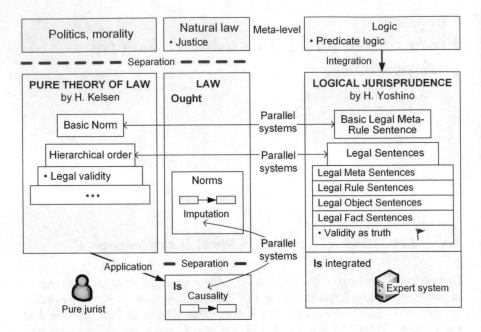

Fig. 9.1 Relationships between the Pure Theory of Law, law and Logical Jurisprudence

The Pure Theory of Law had a great influence on the self-understanding of legal practitioners, who just considered the term 'pure' when they took PTL into consideration. Logical Jurisprudence, on the other hand, is also adapted from a strict formal method to the machine culture of law in the future. This is expressed, for example, in the formal treatment of the subsumption problem.

The Pure Theory of Law distinguishes between legal norms and legal sentences that we may call Kelsen's legal sentences.[1] A legal sentence is not part of the law, but is part of legal science. Also a legal sentence is not part of a norm, but relates descriptively to it.[2] The Pure Theory of Law unfolds legal norms and develops a series of differentiations, which are then combined in a hierarchical model.

In contrast, LJ deals not with legal norms but with propositions that are called Legal Sentences. Formulae called Compound Predicate Formulae (Yoshino 1997)

---

[1] Kelsen uses the word 'Rechtssatz' in the German editions of his books. 'Rechtssatz' was translated as 'rule of law' in the translation of the second edition (see e.g. Kelsen 1967, pp. 57–58). However, the latter expression has a connotation of a legal principle 'rule of law' (*Herrschaft des Rechtes*) that differs from 'Rechtssatz'. This is unfortunate since the term 'rule' suggests a norm rather than a statement (see translator's note in Kelsen 1991, p. lvi). Therefore Yoshino suggests 'legal proposition' or 'proposition on law', thus following Stanley Paulson's translation of the first edition of Pure Theory of Law (see Kelsen 1992).

[2] Kelsen writes: "All legally relevant material contained in a legal order fits in this scheme of the rule of law formulated by legal science—the *rule of law* which is to be distinguished from the *legal norm* established by the legal authority" (Kelsen 1967), p. 58.

are used to represent Legal Sentences. In PTL the legal norms are linked to legal validity, whereas in LJ the Legal Sentences are linked to validity as truth.

Kelsen sees PTL as a science that is parallel to natural sciences: Is and Ought are parallel in the construction of these systems. In a similar way to how the cause and the effect are connected by causality, the behaviour's Ought and the sanction's Ought are connected through imputation. Regarding the hierarchical concept, parallels between PTL and LJ can also be found, since both have basic assumptions—the basic norm and the Basic Legal Meta-Rule Sentence, respectively.

Logical Jurisprudence occupies a prominent position in the scientific avant-garde after PTL. In the context of the works of Klug, Rödig, Weinberger and Tammelo, succeeding theorists of legal logic and AI built on Yoshino's LJ.

9.2   PTL and Logical Jurisprudence as Parallel Systems to Law

The relationships between the elements of PTL, LJ and law are shown in Fig. 9.1. Politics, morality and logic appear on a meta-level. They are separated from law. Natural law also appears separately on the meta-level, because PTL differentiates between justice (equity) and the law. The Is world is separate from the Ought world. In Logical Jurisprudence, however, the Is is integrated, because it is treated as a representation of reality in an expert computer system.

The Pure Theory of Law is separate from politics, morality and the natural law, and also from the legal system. Kelsen separates legal science from political and moral evaluations and also from the law. PTL helps jurists to apply the law. The basic norm is an essential element of PTL and determines the validity of norms. According to PTL, the legal order is built hierarchically. The basic norm is on the top, then come the constitution, laws, and individual contracts on the bottom.

Let us sum up the differences between Kelsen's PTL and Yoshino's LJ. Kelsen focuses on 'purification' from natural law theories. In PTL, law is separate from politics and morality, and Ought is also separate from Is. Yoshino, however, aims to integrate logic. As a consequence, a computer representation of the Is world is integrated in an expert system.

There are similarities between PTL and LJ, which makes them parallel modern systems. First, Yoshino's Basic Legal Meta-Rule Sentence and also Fundamental Legal Meta-Rule Sentence correspond to Kelsen's basic norm.

Second, Yoshino's hierarchy of legal sentences corresponds to Kelsen's hierarchy of norms. Yoshino's hierarchy also comprises Legal Meta Sentences, Legal Rule Sentences, Legal Fact Sentences and Legal Object Sentences. The interplay of legal sentences becomes clear from the Anzai–Bernard example (Yoshino 2011a).

Third, Yoshino's validity as truth corresponds to Kelsen's legal validity in Ought. Validity as truth can be modeled in computer language as a Boolean true or false flag. Fourth, Kelsen reasons in textual form and does not use formal notation.

Yoshino, however, uses predicate logic. This works on the syntactical level as a representation of the law. Fifth, Kelsen helps jurists, 'pure' ones, to apply the law. Yoshino's work is directed at future computer applications. Further LJ is explained in more details.

9.3 Visualisation of Yoshino's Legal Jurisprudence

Yoshino notes that there have been various theories of the systematisation of law. For instance, when speaking about natural law theory, Pufendorf (1672) tried to construct a deductive system of law (see Fig. 9.2).

Traditional legal concepts—on the vertical stage of law—are customary law, international law, legal hierarchy, etc. (see Fig. 9.3). Traditional juridical concepts—on the vertical stage of jurisprudence that concerns Yoshino—comprise legal

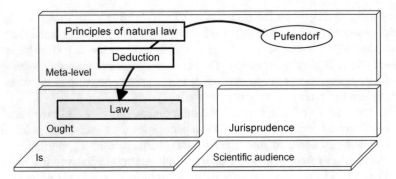

Fig. 9.2 Pufendorf takes the principles of natural law and constructs a deductive system of law (Čyras and Lachmayer 2017)

Fig. 9.3 Traditional concepts on the vertical stages of objective law and jurisprudence (Čyras and Lachmayer 2017)

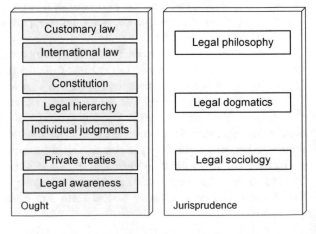

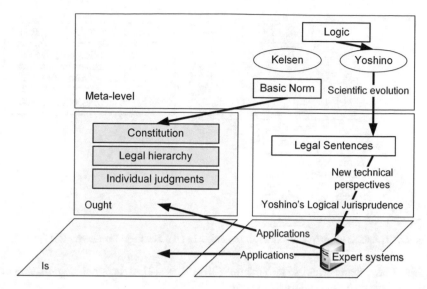

Fig. 9.4 Kelsen's basic norm and Yoshino's LJ (Čyras and Lachmayer 2017)

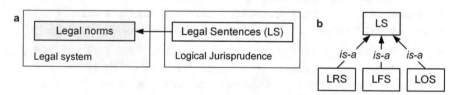

Fig. 9.5 From legal sentences to norms (Čyras and Lachmayer 2017)

philosophy, legal dogmatics[3] and legal sociology. Yoshino is concerned with the right vertical stage—jurisprudence—not the left one (which depicts objective law).

Kelsen's basic norm appears on the meta-level (see Fig. 9.4). Further the elements of LJ are explained.

9.3.1   Legal Sentences

Logical Jurisprudence starts from legal sentences, not from norms (see Fig. 9.5a). The traditional way to explain law and to make a bridge between the phenomenon of law and its formalisations works in the opposite direction: first try to understand the

---

[3] *Rechtsdogmatik*, no exact translation in the terminology of common law; legal science. Doctrine, 'black letter law', see MacCormick and Weinberger (1986), p. 1.

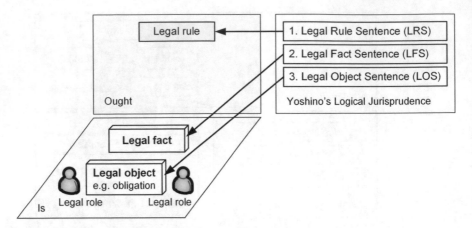

Fig. 9.6 The three primary kinds of legal sentences in LJ (Čyras and Lachmayer 2017)

spirit of law, then formalise it. Yoshino (2011a), p. 121 writes that "legal sentences are composed of three alternative types":

- Legal rule sentences (LRS) and legal fact sentences (LFS)
- Legal elementary sentences (LES) and legal complex sentences (LCS)
- Legal object sentences (LOS) and legal meta-sentences (LMS)

We start by observing the following kinds of entities: LRS, LFS and LOS (see Fig. 9.6). First, legal rule sentences (LRS) are in the world of Logical Jurisprudence, but describe legal rules that are in Ought. Second, legal fact sentences (LFS) describe legal facts that are in Is. Third, legal object sentences (LOS) also describe legal objects that are in Is. Here, obligations deserve special attention.

We can see that LS serves as a description and can be treated as a string. Validity, that is, a truth value, is concerned with legal meta-sentences. We treat LRS, LFS and LOS as being in *is-a* relation with LS (see Fig. 9.5b). In the same way, LMRS, LMFS and LMOS are in *is-a* relation with LMS (see below). Strict categorisations are demanded in computing. However, black-and-white formalisations may not be appropriate in the legal domain. However, theories should aim at conceptual purity.

LRS and LFS correspond to rule and fact in terms of logic programming. An example of an LRS structure is: *a(X) :- b(X), c(X,Y)*. Read: For all *X*, *X* becomes effective if *X* is an offer and *X* reaches the offeree *Y*. LRSs have the syntactic structure of rule as a hypothetical proposition (see e.g. Yoshino 2011a, p. 121):[4]

CISG Article 15(1) : An offer becomes effective when it reaches the offeree.

This is represented by *become_effective(offer(X,A), T) :- reach(offer(X,A), offeree(B, X), T)*.

---

[4]CISG—the United Nations Convention on Contracts for the International Sale of Goods.

Legal fact sentences have, for example, the following structure: *b(x1), c(x1,y1)*. Read, for example, *x1* is *A*'s offer and it reaches *B* on 5 April. Legal fact sentences have the syntactic structure of fact as a categorical proposition, for example, *A's offer reaches offeree B on 5 April*. This is represented by *reach(offer(o1,anzai), offeree (bernard,o1), April-05)*.

An LOS describes the obligations of a person, e.g., *It is obligatory for A to deliver the goods to B*. A *legal elementary sentence* is the smallest unit in legal sentences. An example is CISG Article 15(1) cited above. Another example is "One must drive a car at less than 100 km/hour on a highway". LES play the role of atoms.

9.3.2   Three Primitives: Legal Sentence, Validity and Inference Rule

Logical Jurisprudence works on the vertical stage of science (see the the right-hand section of Fig. 9.6). It aims, with a minimal number of elements, to explain the whole legal system, which is shown on the left-hand section of Fig. 9.6. LJ starts with three primitives:

1. *Legal sentence.* Logical Jurisprudence considers that norm as a meaning in Ought does not exist. Thus, LJ starts from sentences.
2. *Validity* of legal sentences.
3. *Inference rule.* The modus ponens rule is used: $P, P{\rightarrow}Q \vdash Q$. This is used for deduction from valid legal sentences (in the sense of LJ).

The validity concept in Logical Jurisprudence is treated as scientific validity, that is, a truth value in the world of science, *is_valid(sentence1, goal1, time1)*. This is shown further in Fig. 9.7. It is not the same as Kelsen's legal validity concept that refers to Ought. Yoshino speaks about the validity of legal sentences:

> The concept of validity is to be conceived of as a truth concept. That a legal sentence is valid means that it is true in the legal discourse of the world. If a legal sentence which describes a legal state of affairs is valid, it means that the legal state of affairs exists in the legal world. (Yoshino 2011a), p. 122

We should note that the legal domain can allow such a formalisation to a certain degree, namely, in formalising the deduction in law. The reason is that statements in the legal domain can be defeated. Arguments can also be assigned different weights. The reasons may be different. For example, an authority which provides an argument

Fig. 9.7 Validity of legal sentences—validity as truth (Čyras and Lachmayer 2017)

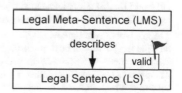

has a greater weight. Hence, both the concept of validity (Kelsen's Ought) and the concept of truth are inherent to law.

A legal meta-sentence describes the validity of a legal sentence, for example: *'It is obligatory for A to deliver the goods to B' is valid on 2010-05-01*.

Note again that this is scientific validity—in the world of science (i.e. LJ), and not validity in the world of Ought, which is Kelsen's validity concept (see Fig. 9.7).

Formalising the concept of validity is central in Yoshino's research.[5] Hence, legal sentences (comprised of LRS, LFS and LOS as above) are treated as syntactic entities—like strings. The validity of a legal sentence (i.e. whether it is true or false) is assigned through a legal meta-sentence. The representation of a model of a world in formal logic includes a set of assertions which are held to be true. Then formal inference rules step in to model legal reasoning.

Legal meta-rule sentence (LMRS) and legal meta-fact sentence (LMFS) describe the validity of an LMS or an LFS, respectively.[6]

9.3.2.1 Connections of Legal Sentences

There are are four kinds of connections of legal sentences:

1. 'and' (&)—conjunction
2. Connection into a legal complex sentence (LCS)
3. Connection between LOS and LMS
4. Connection between LMS and LMS

Each connection is described below.

Connector *and* (&) It connects two legal sentences, for example, *LS1* & *LS2*. A structure of legal sentences can be built in this way. The structure is treated as a group of legal sentences and can be assigned a unique name.

Connection into a Legal Complex Sentence (LCS) An LCS is composed of legal sentences, namely, a group of LS; but the way they are connected is not specified. Hence, an LCS is treated as an aggregate. An LCS has a unique name, such as, "*A–B* Contract", "The UN Convention", a part of statute, etc. (see Fig. 9.8a).

An important feature of LCSs is that if an LCS is valid, every LS is valid. This formalises the meaning of abstract concepts like contracts, judgments, administrative

---

[5] "[L]egal rules must be applicable to the case. In other words, legal rules must be valid to solve the problem of the case [...] That a legal sentence is valid means that it is true in the legal discourse of the world [...] If a legal sentence which describes a legal state of affairs is valid, it means that the legal state of affairs exists in the legal world" (Yoshino 2011a), p. 122.

[6] "A legal meta-rule sentence, which is applied to prove that a legal meta-sentence is valid, must also be valid [...] This can be done through the deduction from a legal meta-fact sentence declaring that the legal meta-rule sentence is valid or by the application of other legal meta-rule sentences. Therefore it is most important for the systematization of law to confirm legal meta-fact and rule sentences which make such deduction possible" (Yoshino 2011a), p. 122.

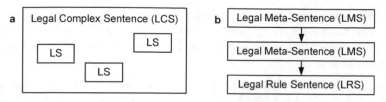

Fig. 9.8 **a** Legal complex sentence. **b** Connection between LMS and LMS (Čyras and Lachmayer 2017)

orders, statutes, etc. A legal complex sentence is treated as an aggregate (or a formula with the connector &, for example, *p1 & p2 & p3*).

Connection Between Legal Object Sentence (LOS) and Legal Meta-Sentence (LMS) An LOS describes an object. An example of an object type is an obligation. Examples of LOSs are, "*It is obligatory for A to deliver machinery to B*", or "*B must pay A the price of $58,000.*"

We have found that in Yoshino's examples an LOS describes an individual legal object, not a general one. Examples speak about the obligations of individuals, for example, *Anzai, A, Bernard, B.*

The modus of a legal object, e.g. obligation or right, is expressed by a distinct predicate: *s1: is_obligatory(A, deliver(A,B,machinery))*. The time for the obligation to become valid and to terminate is also represented with predicates, for example, *s2: become_valid(s1, 2010-04-09), s3: is_terminated(s1, 2010-05-01)*.

Both LOS and LMS can be represented with predicates. We also view predicates as expressions which can be represented as frames (or semantic nets)—for example, *deliver(sender, recipient, goods)*.

However, you can be surprised by the way Yoshino distinguishes rights from obligations. A right-duty duality may be expected. We would expect to treat an individual right and a duty in a similar way and to represent an individual right with an LOS, too. Yoshino probably focuses on objective (general) rights and subjective (individual) obligations (i.e. duties). He holds:

> A legal sentence which describes one's right is, however, not a legal object sentence but a kind of legal meta-sentence, because it is a legal sentence to afford him a legal power to settle a legal sentence. (Yoshino 2011a), p. 122

Yoshino treats the accrual of the validity of a legal object sentence by exercising the right as a fundamental meta-rule sentence (FLMRS; see the next sub-section) (see Yoshino 2011a, p. 123):

r3aa2 : If A has a right to require B to do Z at time T and

A requires B to do Z at T, then a legal sentence" It is obligatory for B to do Z" becomes valid
*   at T.*

The above rule asserts that a duty which is represented by a legal object sentence follows from a rule which represents the right. Yoshino (2012) analyses the concept of right in terms of legal meta-sentences. He aims to contribute to the "dynamic systematization of law".[7]

Connection Between LMS and LMS   A legal meta-sentence describes the validity of legal sentences. Some LMSs describe the validity of other LMSs. A connection is LMS–LMS (see Fig. 9.8b). The following are two examples of legal meta-rule sentences:

> *CISG Article 1(1) : This Convention applies to contracts of the sale of goods between parties whose places of business . . .*
>
> > *CISG Article 23 : contract is concluded when an acceptance of an offer becomes effective . . .*

Positive legal meta-rule sentences, LMRS, assist a fundamental meta-rule sentence (FLMRS) as its sub-rule sentences to decide on the fulfilment of each requirement of the FLMRS. Hence, a connection between LMRS and LMRS is produced. If the validity of a positive LMRS is regulated by other positive LMRS, the latter belong to a *higher meta-level* than the former (Yoshino 2011a), p. 123.

For terminological purity, an attempt could be made to give different names to the LMRS mentioned above, which are on the higher meta-level, and other LMRS, which are on the lower levels. Semantic differences can be probably be distinguished, too. However this may be difficult to formalise. The reason is that too many levels, or even a complicated hierarchical structure, can emerge.

9.3.2.2   Legal Inference

In Logical Jurisprudence, the modus ponens rule stands for the main inference rule. LRS are deduced from the existence of legal rules in Ought (see arrow (1) in Fig. 9.9). The LRS obtained, and legal fact sentences, LFS, are used to deduce legal object sentences, LOS (see arrow (2)). The LOS obtained point to legal objects on the Is stage (see arrow (3)).

Legal sentences are developed through the process of legal reasoning. Yoshino concentrates on two types of legal reasoning:

---

[7]"[T]he Hohfeldian logical formalization [. . .] fails to adequately systematize the dynamic changes of rights and duties in relation to changes in time. In contrast, we propose a system of analysis that recognizes the inherent hierarchy between a right on the meta-level and a duty on the object level language" (Yoshino 2012), p. 305.

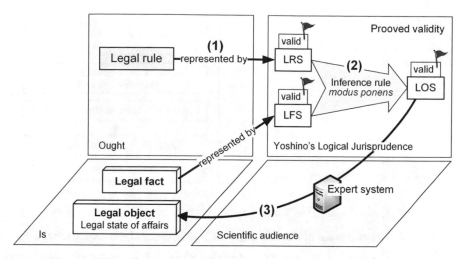

Fig. 9.9 Legal inference (Čyras and Lachmayer 2017)

1. *Reasoning of legal justification* based on deduction through modus ponens.
2. *Reasoning of legal creation* (or discovery). This is further divided into two parts: *abduction* (where the inference rule modus tollens is applied) and *induction*.

The legal sentence of a judgment may not be deduced from statutes and facts alone, but from the whole body of legal sentences, including legal principles, cases, theories and implicit legal common sense. Therefore, Yoshino emphasises two ways of legal reasoning:

1. *Concretisation*. Statutory terms are made tangible by creating LRSs which describe inclusion relations.
2. *Systematisation*. The sentences of legal principles are created and these enable us to bring mere collections of LS into a unified, coherent deductive system.

9.3.3 Fundamental Legal Meta-Rule Sentence (FLMRS)

A *fundamental legal meta-rule sentence* is implicitly taken for granted for all regulations. The following is an example from Yoshino (2011a), p. 122:

> *r0 : A legal sentence is valid at time T,*
> *if and only if a legal sentence becomes valid before T and*
> *it is not the case that the sentence is terminated before T.*

Yoshino notes that event calculus provides a hint for this rule, and the rule is treated as the most fundamental FLMRS. It is represented as follows:

Fig. 9.10 Basic Legal
Meta-Rule Sentence
(BLMRS) (Čyras and
Lachmayer 2017)

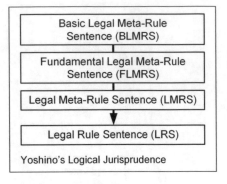

A legal sentence S is valid at the time T ⇔

(S becomes valid at time T1 before T) &   //First requirement

not (S is terminated after T1 and before T)   //Second requirement

Yoshino (2011a), p. 122 holds that all positive FLMRS regulate the fulfilment of the first requirement (*S becomes valid*) or the second requirement (*S is terminated*) of *r0* above.

9.3.4   Basic Legal Meta-Rule Sentence (BLMRS)

The validity of the final, highest legal sentence, whose validity cannot be deduced through the application of legal meta-rule sentences, is called the *basic legal meta-rule sentence* (Yoshino 2011a), p. 123 (see Fig. 9.10). (Again, validity is considered as truth—in the world of science). For example, in international law, LMRS that regulate the validity of conventions must be assigned to the highest level.

   The validity of the basic legal meta-rule sentence is to be *presupposed*, or asserted as a fact sentence. Yoshino holds that a BLMRS is sometimes found in constitutions or conventions, but sometimes in theories of constitutions or conventions which explain the basis of their validity.

9.4   Comparison of Yoshino's LJ with Kelsen's PTL

First, there is a similar solution at the top of the system: Yoshino's BLMRS and FLMRS correspond to Kelsen's basic norm (see Fig. 9.11).

   Second, Yoshino's hierarchy of legal sentences corresponds to Kelsen's hierarchy of norms. Third, Yoshino's validity as truth corresponds to Kelsen's legal validity in Ought. Fourth, Yoshino uses predicate logic while Kelsen reasons in textual form. Yoshino allows a differentiation between juridical sentences. Yoshino

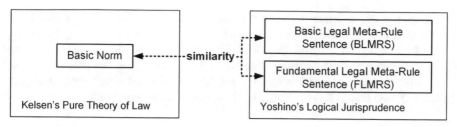

Fig. 9.11 A similar solution at the top of the system (Čyras and Lachmayer 2017)

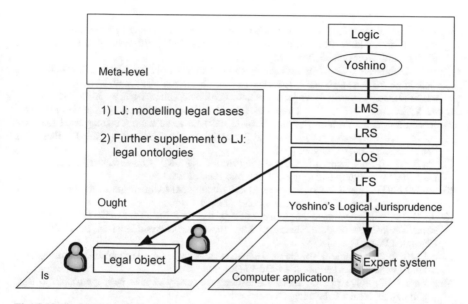

Fig. 9.12 Legal Object Sentences refer to legal objects in Is (see the left arrow). Yoshino goes through logic, Logical Jurisprudence and expert systems to legal objects in Is (see the right arrow) (Čyras and Lachmayer 2017)

departs from logic, and goes through Logical Jurisprudence—LMS, LRS, LOS, LFS—to expert systems which can contribute to legal objects in Is (see Fig. 9.12, the right arrow). Legal Object Sentences refer to legal objects on the Is stage of individual rights and duties (see the left arrow of Fig. 9.12). Fifth, Yoshino's work is directed at future computer applications while Kelsen's work is directed at jurists.

Conclusion Compound Legal Formula representation and Prolog remind us of the high expectations of knowledge engineers in the 1980s. Yoshino notes that a hint of the *r0* rule was obtained from (Sergot et al. 1986). However, nowadays the expectations of expert systems builders can be analysed from perspectives other than just logic programming (see e.g. Philip Leith 2010). Legal merit arguments have to be taken into account by knowledge engineers (see e.g. James Palmer 1997).

Logical Jurisprudence is within a traditional research of legal logic and is an achievement on the level of a model, however, it does not succeed in implementing the whole interconnectedness of norms. Nowadays, we would suggest expanding these concerns with, first, legal ontologies and, second, words (see Chaps. 12 and 19). We view the latter within the granularity of word–phrase–sentence–text. Different methods of legal informatics are applied to different units.

References

Čyras V, Lachmayer F (2017) Visualization of Hajime Yoshino's logical jurisprudence. Jusletter IT, 23 February 2017. https://jusletter-it.weblaw.ch/issues/2017/IRIS/visualization-of-haj_421 e705aff.html. Accessed 15 Dec 2022

Čyras V, Lachmayer F (2019) From legal symbolization via legal formalization towards human digitalities. In: Schweighofer E, Araszkiewicz M, Lachmayer F, Pavčnik M (eds) Formalising jurisprudence: festschrift for Hajime Yoshino. Editions Weblaw, Bern, pp 53–76

Čyras V, Lachmayer F (2021) From Kelsen's Pure Theory of Law to Yoshino's Logical Jurisprudence. In: Yoshino H, Villa Rosas G (eds) Law and logic – making legal science a genuine science. Archiv für Rechts- und Sozialphilosophie – Beihefte (ARSP-B), Band 166. Franz Steiner Verlag, Stuttgart, pp 29–63

Kelsen H (1967) Pure theory of law, 2nd edn (trans: Knight M) (Reine Rechtslehre, 2. Auflage. Deuticke, Wien 1960). University of California Press, Berkeley

Kelsen H (1991) General theory of norms (trans: Hartney M) (Allgemeine Theorie der Normen, Manz Verlag, Wien, 1979). Clarendon Press, Oxford

Kelsen H (1992) Introduction to the problems of legal theory. A translation of the first edition of the Reine Rechtslehre or Pure Theory of Law (trans: Litschewski Paulson B, Paulson SL). Clarendon Press, Oxford

Leith P (2010) The rise and fall of the legal expert system. Eur J Law Technol 1(1). https://ejlt.org/index.php/ejlt/article/view/14. Accessed 15 Dec 2022

MacCormick N, Weinberger O (1986) An institutional theory of law: new approaches to legal positivism. D. Reidel Publishing, Dordrecht

Palmer J (1997) Artificial intelligence and legal merit argument. PhD thesis. Balliol College, University of Oxford

Pufendorf S (1672) De Jure Naturae et Gentium. English edition (trans: Oldfather CH, Oldfather WA). Oceana, New York, 1964

Sergot MJ, Sadri F, Kowalski RA, Kriwaczek F, Hammond P, Cory HT (1986) The British Nationality Act as a logic program. Commun ACM 29(5):370–386

Yoshino H (1997) On the logical foundations of compound predicate formulae for legal knowledge representation. Artif Intell Law 5:77–96. https://doi.org/10.1023/A:1008289826410

Yoshino H (2011a) The systematization of law in terms of the validity. In: Proceedings of the thirteenth international conference on artificial intelligence and law, ICAIL '11. ACM, New York, pp 121–125. https://doi.org/10.1145/2018358.2018376

Yoshino H (2011b) The logical structure of a legal system proving the validity of law. In: Geist A, Brunschwig CR, Lachmayer F, Schefbeck G (eds) Strukturierung der Juristischen Semantik – structuring legal semantics. Editions Weblaw, Bern, pp 197–209

Yoshino H (2012) The logical analysis of the concept of a right in terms of legal meta-sentences. Jusletter IT, 29 February 2012. https://jusletter-it.weblaw.ch/issues/2012/IRIS/jusletterarticle_1063.html. Accessed 15 Dec 2022

Chapter 10
Semiotic Aspects of Law and Legal Science

10.1 Introduction

This chapter discusses the notion of legal meaning from the point of view of semiotics. Logic can be applied to the meta-level of law, and offers instruments for formal structuring in both law and legal science. From the perspective of a meta-level or a meta-meta-level, there are, however, other approaches that offer means for giving structure. These include semiotics, which is typically divided into syntax, semantics and pragmatics.

Pragmatics describes the signs associated with persons and their communication and, primarily, with the meaning of a corresponding speech act. The meaning of a speech act as a legal act can be called its *legal institutional meaning* (see Fig. 10.1). A hierarchical structure of the legal order contains sequences of elements of institutional meaning. The notion of the validity of law also belongs to the pragmatics of law because validity is concerned with the relational elements of legal institutional meaning. The pragmatic structure of law, including the institutional meaning of legal sources and the validity relationships of these sources, is created autonomously from the law. Law is a self-producing (autopoetic) system. Law does not therefore need legal science, either for content meaning or for institutional meaning.

The notion of a basic norm is a basic assumption. The basic norm as part of legal science was able to influence science regarding subject matter but not regarding legal validity. Whether the law exists or does not exist depends solely on the law itself or on the higher-level legal orders, in a similar way to how a state's law depends on international law.

The separation thesis applies not only to law and morality, but also to law and legal science. Previous chapter reveals these semiotic aspects through visuals.

Based on Čyras and Lachmayer (2021).

V. Cyras, F. Lachmayer, *Essays on the Visualisation of Legal Informatics*, Law, Governance and Technology Series 54, https://doi.org/10.1007/978-3-031-27957-7_10

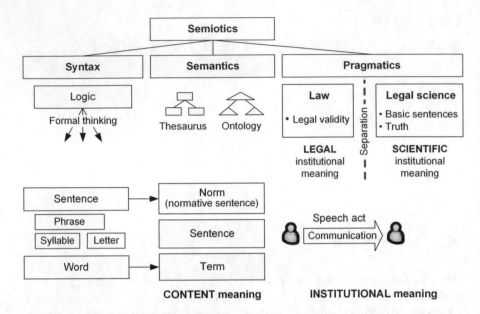

Fig. 10.1 Semiotics of law and the separation of law and legal science

10.2   Separation of Law and Legal Science from the Point of View of Semiotics

In semiotics, syntax, semantics and pragmatics are distinguished. Here one can follow Charles Peirce and Charles Morris and use the definitions of syntax, semantics and pragmatics that are widely accepted in semiotics:[1]

- Syntax: the relations among signs in formal structures (Seifert et al. 2013), p. 213. Syntax governs the structure of sentences, specifically word order and punctuation, in a given language.
- "Semantics: the relation between signs and the things to which they refer (i.e. their meaning)" (Seifert et al. 2013), p. 213. "Semantics deals with the relation of signs to their designata and so to the objects they may or do denote" (Morris 1938), p. 21.
- "Pragmatics: the relation between signs and the effects they have on the people who use them" (Seifert et al. 2013), p. 213; "the relation of signs to their users" (Morris 1938), p. 33.

The semiotic triangle by Ogden and Richards (1923), p. 11 explains the problem of meaning (see Fig. 11.8 in Chap. 11 and Fig. 18.4 in Chap. 18).

---

[1] See Wikipedia, https://en.wikipedia.org/wiki/Semiotics.

Syntax This deals with the rules governing the correct formation of symbol systems. There are levels of symbols: letters, syllables (which are important in voice communication), words, phrases, sentences and language structures beyond sentences. In law, words are important as they are the bearers of semantic concepts. In legal science, however, sentences are important as syntactically correct forms. In short, syntax is about building sentences.

Semantics This specifies the rules for how content is linked to syntactic units and how this content is further unfolded. There are different kinds of elements in semantics: terms, sentences, descriptive sentences, normative sentences, etc. For continental law, legal terms are decisive because the law is thought and argued about in legal terms. The terms have content that can be called *content meaning*. Semantics can be lifted to a meta-level that comprises thesauruses of legal terms and ontologies. Its meaning, however, refers to the content.

In short, semantics is about content. For thinking, however, it is mainly the terms that are important. More precisely, the meaning of terms, that is, their content meaning, is important here.

Pragmatics This is about the use of legal texts. Content is communicated between people. Here a different kind of meaning emerges, which is called *institutional meaning*. The latter is considered by Kelsen. Thus we obtain the institutional meaning of speech acts, norms, contracts, laws and constitutions.

Two Kinds of Systems: Law and Legal Science Validity is a key notion in law. Law itself brings validity into being and needs no impact from legal science or other systems. Statements and their truth values (true or false) are key notions in legal science. Law and legal science are autonomous, although related, systems. Both have their speech acts, namely, legal speech acts and scientific speech acts, respectively. They also both have their institutional meanings, which can correspondingly be called legal institutional meaning and scientific institutional meaning. The question of whether or not a norm exists in the law does not need legal science. There are other systems that are related to law and legal science, and ethics (morality) is an example of these. This is basically an issue for a thesis of the separation of law and legal science.

The thesis of the separation of law and legal science says that legal validity is determined by law and not by legal science. Analogically, the truth of scientific statements in legal science is not determined by law. Hence, scientific truth is distinct from legal validity.

Besides separation, we can also speak about linkages. First, natural law links legal science and law. Second, Kelsen writes about the basic norm that links his Pure Theory of Law and law. Third, Yoshino's Logical Jurisprudence also links legal science and law.

Conclusion Artificial intelligence approaches to law including Logical Jurisprudence were created decades after the appearance of PTL. Currently, the computational modelling of legal reasoning also needs a system of legal terms such as a thesaurus or an ontology.

Legal institutional meaning appears in the world of law. However, scientific institutional meaning appears in the world of legal science. Therefore to answer the question "What is the meaning of a legal act?", you have to specify "In which world?". Otherwise, the search for a meaning reminds us of the streetlight effect:[2] searching for a lost wallet not where you left it, but under the street lamp. Searching for the correct representation of a meaning is certainly not trivial. The reason is that there are many different meanings and they are viewed from different perspectives in different worlds.

The next chapter elaborates on content and institutional meaning further.

References

Čyras V, Lachmayer F (2021) From Kelsen's Pure Theory of Law to Yoshino's Logical Jurisprudence. In: Yoshino H, Villa Rosas G (eds) Law and logic – making legal science a genuine science. Proceedings of the special workshop held at the 28th World Congress of the International Association for Philosophy of Law and Social Philosophy in Lisbon, Portugal, 2017. Archiv für Rechts- und Sozialphilosophie – Beihefte (ARSP-B), Band 166. Franz Steiner Verlag, Stuttgart, pp 29–63

Morris CW (1938) Foundations of the theory of signs. In: Neurath O, Carnap R, Morris CW (eds) International encyclopedia of unified science, vol 1, no 2. The University of Chicago Press, pp 1–59. https://www.scribd.com/doc/51866596/Morris-1938-Foundations-of-Theory-of-Signs. Accessed 15 Dec 2022

Ogden CK, Richards IA (1923) The meaning of meaning. Harcourt, Brace & World, New York

Seifert U, Verschure PFMJ, Arbib MA, Cohen AJ, Fogassi L, Fritz T, Kuperberg G, Manzoli J, Rickard N (2013) Semantics of internal and external worlds. In: Arbib MA (ed) Language, music, and the brain: a mysterious relationship. MIT Press, Cambridge, MA, pp 203–232. https://scholarblogs.emory.edu/stoutlab/files/2013/07/Language-Music-and-the-Brain.pdf. Accessed 15 Dec 2022

---

[2] See, for example, Wikipedia, https://en.wikipedia.org/wiki/Streetlight_effect.

Chapter 11
Content Meaning and Institutional Meaning of a Legal Act

11.1 Content Meaning and Institutional Meaning

We distinguish two entities: an act and its legal meaning. We treat the legal meaning (henceforth institutional meaning) as an abstract objective entity. In this chapter, this entity is also viewed from an information systems perspective. Representing the institutional meaning in computers (legal machines) is a research question for future. We consider operations that strengthen or lessen the institutional meaning. Our idea is to link institutional meaning (which appears in Ought) with its representation (which appears inspiepr146 Is). Suppose a process is performed to modify the meaning of a legal act (including its content and its institutional meaning). Our idea is to link the process with events (institutional facts) which lead to this modification. Thus the modification in Ought is related with the modification of representation in Is. In this way we relate the modification in Ought with events in Is but do not reduce Ought to Is.

Kelsen holds that the norm is the meaning of an act of will.[1] An act is a "happening occurring at a certain time and in a certain place" and the legal meaning of this act is "the meaning conferred upon the act by the law" (Kelsen 1967), § 2, p. 2. Kelsen also writes about distinguishing between a norm and a statement about a norm.[2] Kelsen distinguishes between the content of an act and the legal meaning of an act. He uses the words 'content' and 'meaning':

Based on Čyras and Lachmayer (2018, 2021).

---

[1] "The Ought — the norm — is the meaning of a willing or act of will" (Kelsen 1991), § 1.III, p. 2.

[2] "[A] norm is not a statement and [. . .] must be clearly distinguished from a statement, especially a statement *about* a norm. For a statement is the meaning of an act of thought, while a norm [. . .] is the meaning of an act of will" (Kelsen 1991), § 8.II, p. 26.

© The Author(s), under exclusive license to Springer Nature Switzerland AG 2023
V. Cyras, F. Lachmayer, *Essays on the Visualisation of Legal Informatics*, Law, Governance and Technology Series 54,
https://doi.org/10.1007/978-3-031-27957-7_11

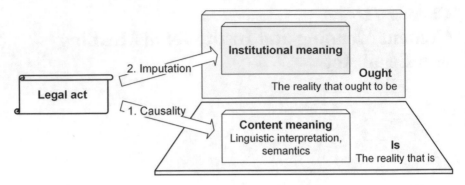

Fig. 11.1 The content meaning (Is) and the institutional meaning (Ought) of a legal act (Čyras and Lachmayer 2018)

> The commander expects the command-addressee to *understand* the command, i.e. to understand the *meaning* of the utterance *as a command*, i.e. to know:
>
> 1. *that* he is to behave in a certain way, and
> 2. *how* he is to behave, i.e. *what* he is to do or avoid doing.

The former is the *meaning*, the latter is the *content* of the act of will representing a command. (Kelsen 1991), § 9.II, p. 33

Hence, two kinds of "meanings" of a legal act can be distinguished (see Fig. 11.1):

1. *The content meaning.* It appears in Is, "the reality that is" (Pattaro 2007), pp. 3–5. It is determined by causality. It is established by the content, information, semantics, and linguistic interpretation of a legal act. It is an objective entity. It is an intangible, abstract entity but linked with a fact, a material object such as a document or event in Is. The content meaning can be represented and processed by computers as data, for instance, the text of a document.
2. *The institutional meaning.* It appears in Ought, "the reality that ought to be" (Pattaro 2007), pp. 3–5. It is determined by imputation (Kelsen 1967), p. 76. It is the objective legal meaning of the legal act. It exists as an intangible, ideal, nonfactual entity and not a material object. A computer cannot understand it and can process only representations (which appear in Is) of the institutional meaning.

The institutional meaning as an intangible objective entity can also be viewed from an information systems perspective. Legal validity is distinguished from documentary validity. Legal validity is treated according Kelsen's "ideell existence" of a norm in the Ought realm, that is, 'ought-to-be-observed'. This was first described in Kelsen's *Pure Theory of Law* (1967) then in his *General Theory of Norms*.[3]

---

[3] "As the meaning of an act of will, the norm has an *ideell* existence (as opposed to a real existence). But that does not mean that norms are ideas (i.e. thought-contents), as statements are" (Kelsen 1991), note 8, p. 278. "The 'validity' of a norm is its characteristic, *ideell, existence*. That a norm 'is

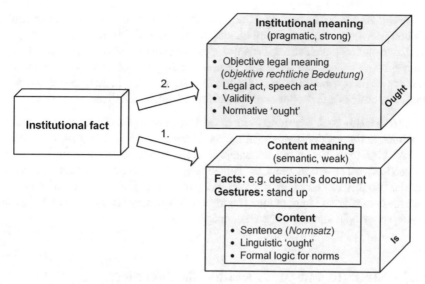

Fig. 11.2 The content meaning of an institutional fact and the institutional meaning (Čyras and Lachmayer 2018)

Analogically, a legal fact such as an act of will (institutional fact) also has two kinds of meanings: the institutional meaning and the content meaning (see Fig. 11.2). We follow Neil MacCormick and Ota Weinberger's terminology (1986) and their distinction of institutional facts and brute facts. Institutional facts like contracts, marriages, treaties, games, and so on are treated as objects that are not material.[4] The legal meaning (Ought) of institutional facts is in the focus.

Ought, the reality that ought to be, is characterised as a "spiritual, ideal, and moral reality" (Pattaro 2007), p. 77. Hence, institutional facts have two links: 1) to Ought, and 2) to Is, the reality that is. Following the first link, an institutional fact is an abstract, spiritual, and ideal entity and is an abstract object, analogically to the way in which norms and legal institutions are also abstract objects. They really exist and "sometimes specific physical objects may have non-physical characteristics ascribed to them" (MacCormick and Weinberger 1986), p. 10.

Content (further shorthand for content meaning) has to be legitimated through a process (which, for example, involves parliament) to become law.

---

valid' means that is exists. A norm which is not 'valid' is not a norm since it is not an existing norm" (Kelsen 1991), § 8.VI, p. 28.

[4] After introducing 'brute facts', MacCormick and Weinberger make the following observation about institutional facts: "However that may be, there are other entities which, albeit not material objects, we also commonly speak of as existing – things like contracts and marriages in the sphere of municipal law, treaties and international agencies (e.g. the Rome Treaties, the E.E.C. Commission) in the sphere of international law, games and competitions (e.g. the current World Cup Competition) in the sphere of social and sporting life" (MacCormick and Weinberger 1986), pp. 9–10.

Different Kinds of Meanings There are meanings such as scientific meaning, cultural meaning, religious meaning, and so on. A wedding ring is an example of cultural meaning which strengthens the legal meaning of marriage. A speech act in science obtains scientific meaning. Thus for example, Copernicus wrote in Latin, whereas Galileo wrote in Italian. A consequence was that laymen could not understand Copernicus's Latin but could understand Galileo's Italian.

Constructivism and Meaning We share the philosophical world view and the constructivist's position that social reality is constructed (Falkenberg et al. 1998), p. 29.[5] Our term 'institutional meaning' corresponds to what is called "shared conception".[6] The world view by Falkenberg et al. supposes actors and actands and the "quality of causation". We should remark that their "causation" comprises both the causality and imputation. The imputation concept is present tacitly because a group of people agrees on shared conceptions.

11.2   Strengthening or Lessening the Meaning

Jurists know the repertoire of legal means to strengthen or lessen the intensity of legal acts. The meaning can be lessened, for example, by deconstruction of legal acts. The research question is: How can the strengthen/lessen repertoire be modelled when modelling institutional meaning?

Content Meaning Institutional facts "are facts in virtue of being statable as-true statements" (MacCormick and Weinberger 1986), p. 10.[7] These as-true statements embody the content meaning. They can be expressed linguistically and strengthened with the help of formal logic. However, here the 'ought' words are linguistic ones and not normative ones. Therefore the content meaning can comprise even contradictory statements.

Although the content information can be divided into prescriptive, descriptive, and constitutive statements, they are purely factual and linguistic and have no normative significance; cf., for instance, a child's utterance. To add institutional

---

[5] Falkenberg et al. (1998), p. 26 write: "Constructivist: somebody who also believes that "reality" exists independently of any observer, but who is aware of the fact that we only have access to our own (mental) "conceptions"; for the constructivist, the relationship between reality and conception is principally subjective, and may be subject to negotiation between observers; any agreement – which we call "inter-subjective reality" – may have to be adapted from time to time."

[6] Falkenberg et al. (1998), p. 32 write: "When a group [of people] agrees on the meaning of a particular representation, we will call its interpretation a shared conception. It is then assumed that there is a unique domain it refers to, i.e. an inter-subjective reality."

[7] MacCormick and Weinberger (1986), p. 10 continue: "But what is stated is not true simply because of the condition of the material world and the causal relationships obtaining among its parts. On the contrary, it is true in virtue of an interpretation of what happens in the world, an interpretation of events in the light of human practices and normative rules."

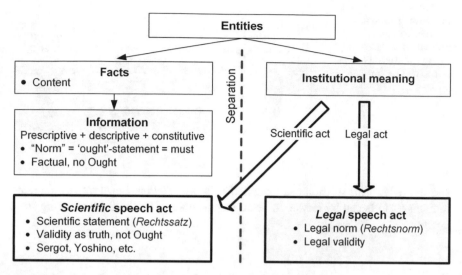

Fig. 11.3 A legal act (the right bold arrow) adds institutional meaning to statements. Scientific acts add no normative power but contribute to science and legal expert systems (the left arrow) (Čyras and Lachmayer 2018)

meaning, the statements have to be accompanied by a legal act, for example, a legal speech act (see Fig. 11.3, right bold arrow). Scientific acts add no normative power; however, they can contribute to science and legal expert systems.

Institutional Meaning Next to the content, we focus on the corresponding speech act, teleological statement, or legal act. Its intensity, that is, its quality, is important. It is, for instance, an officer's draft, a ruling, a law with the same content, or even a constitutional law. Hence, the meaning of a legal act resides in the existence of a draft, a ruling, a law, and so on. The institutional meaning of legal acts is concerned with their pragmatic effects. In summary, the intensities of the existence can be distinct, although with the same content.

Validity is the form of existence of a legal act in Ought whereas causal reality is the form of a fact's existence in Is. We hold that in Is the fact is either true or false (or unknown).

Semantics and Pragmatics The content meaning can also be called *semantic meaning*. The reason for this is that the linguistic interpretation is in the forefront here. Analogically, the institutional meaning can also be called *pragmatic meaning*. The content meaning has weak significance compared with the strong significance of the institutional meaning.

Weak and Strong Relations Legal acts can establish legal relations between persons. Consider a sales contract between individuals A, the buyer, and B, the seller (see Fig. 11.4). The content, the semantic meaning of the contract, is an attribute of the so-called *weak relation* between A and B. The institutional meaning of the contract implies a legal relation between A and B in the legal roles of the buyer

Fig. 11.4 The content meaning and the institutional meaning imply strong and weak relations (Čyras and Lachmayer 2018)

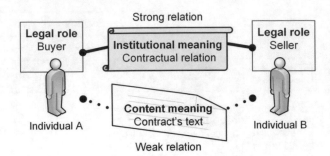

and the seller. This relation can be called a *strong relation*. Legal relations among individuals in Is can be viewed as strong projections of institutional meaning from Ought.

11.2.1 Strengthening or Lessening of the Content Meaning

The actors around a legal act have the means to strengthen or lessen its content meaning (see Fig. 11.5), for example:

1. *Logic*. Logical conclusions which follow from the premises can be stated clearly. Open texture can also be reduced. However, legal consequences (Ought) need not follow from a person's statement (Is).
2. *Adding objective legal terms*. Proper legal terms can be added, for instance, in contract use clauses such as performance, considerations, and so on.
3. *Material basis*. The medium of a legal act can be stressed, for instance, the substrate, an (electronic) document, or the whole legal machine.

The repertoire of means to modify the institutional meaning, however, differs from the repertoire to modify the content. Jurists know the essence of law, but laymen do not. Software engineers need to understand the essence in order to develop legal

Fig. 11.5 Strengthening the content meaning of a legal act (Čyras and Lachmayer 2018)

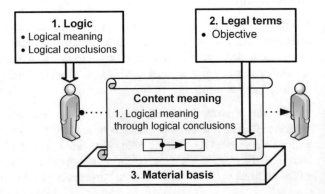

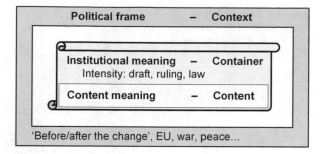

Fig. 11.6 The political frame corresponds to the context in semiotics (Čyras and Lachmayer 2018)

machines. The machines can raise institutional events (in Is) which modify—strengthen or lessen—the institutional meaning (in Ought).

11.2.2 Political Frame as Context in Semiotics

There are different types of frames such as the cultural frame, the legal frame, and so on. The term 'frame' corresponds to 'context' in semiotics. In cognitive linguistics and empirical semantics, a 'frame' means "any system of concepts related in such a way that to understand one of them you have to understand the whole structure in which it fits" (Fillmore 2006 [1982]), p. 373. We hold that 'content meaning' corresponds to 'content' and 'institutional meaning' corresponds to 'container'. There are different kinds of political frames such as "before the change", "after the change", "being a member state of the European Union", and so on (see Fig. 11.6). Another example is that legal acts are interpreted differently depending on whether the country is in a period of war or peace. A period of war severely affects, for instance, data protection law. In summary, the frame changes the interpretation of legal acts.

11.3   Relating Institutional Meaning with Representation

Our idea is to relate the institutional meaning of a legal act with its representation. We do not talk about the mental processes in our minds, because they cannot be observed. Knowing the meaning of words does not depend on understanding the nature of these processes.

Operations that modify the institutional meaning appear in legitimate workflow events (institutional facts conformant with the law). The events can be raised by authorities' decisions or computers. The process of modifying act_1 to produce a modified act act_2 involves representations in Is (see Fig. 11.7). Note that we do not reduce Ought to Is; we relate them.

Fig. 11.7 Modification in Ought is related with events in Is (Čyras and Lachmayer 2018)

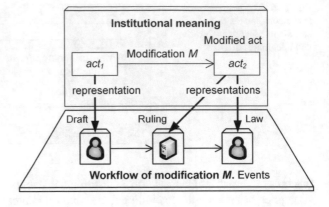

Fig. 11.8 The FRISCO semiotic tetrahedron, adapted from Falkenberg et al. (1998), p. 51

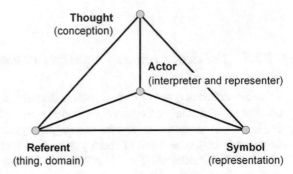

A legitimate modification of act_1 with the outcome act_2 appears due to a modification act M. The institutional meaning of M is the norm N that has an ideell existence. Hence the meaning of M is N. M prescribes to modify act_1 into act_2. M is enforced by a modification workflow in Is. Workflow events cause different representations in the transition from act_1 to act_2.

As an example, suppose that an act is strengthened, for example, from a minister's draft to a ruling and then to a law. Although the content may be similar, its meaning differs in the power.

In another example, suppose a car park with a traffic lights on the entry and the exit. You can violate the traffic-lights rule and drive on a red light. Suppose a barrier is added to prevent such violations. Thus the meaning is strengthened. First, the content meaning is strengthened—the barrier is added to the traffic lights. Second, the institutional meaning is also strengthened—the city authority's decision applies.

The idea to link the institutional meaning of a legal act with its representations is inspired by the FRISCO tetrahedron (see Fig. 11.8). The FRISCO semiotic tetrahedron extends the three classical categories (the semiotic triangle) by an additional actor, an interpreter. He is a representer, a human actor involved in a representing action (Falkenberg et al. 1998), p. 48. Meaning is defined as the relationship established by people in a language community between sign (symbol) standing for object (referent, thing) (ibid.), p. 195.

11.4   Representing Abstract Objects in Computers

Abstract objects and not only physical objects are assigned to the objective reality. Machines can physically manipulate with physical objects, for instance, a robot picks up a box. Abstract objects, however, cannot be manipulated physically. Machines operate with the representations of abstract objects, not the objects.

Consider the number π, a mathematical constant, whose meaning is "the ratio of a circle's circumference to its diameter." It is commonly approximated as 3.14159. Being an irrational number, π cannot be expressed exactly as a fraction. Hence, π cannot be represented in a format "real number" in computer with a fixed-length word. However, π is an entity (an abstract one) of the objective reality.

Universals can be represented in computers as symbols. Programmers who use software packages invoke π as a constant named "pi". A circle can be represented with its radius, r, and several symbolic equations, for example, the length of the circumference $C = 2*\pi*r$, and $Area = \pi*r*r$. In a computer-aided design system more properties are represented, for example, colour, texture, material, and so on. Modelling more complicated universal properties such as cupness or tableness can be attempted in a similar way.

Related Work on Representation   Representation is emphasised by Mihai Nadin (2011), p. 18, who writes about the semiotics of computation:

> The characteristic of semiotics, as Hausdorff understood and as Cassirer argued for is re-presentation. The fact that the means of representation can be called signs, or be defined as signs, is less relevant than the essential functions of semiotics. In close relation to representation is the function of interpretation through which meaning is conjured.

Richard Fallon's study (2015) of legal "meaning" can be related with our concept of content meaning. Fallon reveals many senses of the term 'meaning' in legal argumentation.[8] He advocates that "[g]iven the function of interpretive theories to guide or determine choices among otherwise plausible senses of legal meaning" such theories should do so on a case-by-case basis, not on a categorical basis (Fallon 2015), p. 1235.

Conclusion   Multiple representations of a legal act represent different aspects of the legal meaning. The separation of concerns principle,[9] which is common in software engineering, applies. Each stakeholder views a legal act differently.

---

[8] "Examination of familiar terms of legal argument reveals an astonishing number of possible senses of that term—and, correspondingly, an equally large number of possible referents for ultimate claims concerning what legal provisions mean. These referents include a statutory or constitutional provision's semantic or literal meaning, its contextual meaning as framed by shared presuppositions of speakers and listeners, its 'real' conceptual meaning, and its intended, reasonable, and previously interpreted meanings" (Fallon 2015, p. 1235).

[9] "The 'separation of concerns' principle is realized by the concept of views [. . .] The separation of concerns principle refers to the description of different characteristics of a software system that may or may not relate to the later execution of those systems. The principle will be applied in the division of complex description of even small portions of software into hopefully better understanding

The semiotic triangle by Ogden and Richards (1923), p. 11 has to be extended to model sender–receiver communication. The reason is that the semiotic triangle deals with one person, a human agent. A semiotic square is a proper model.[10] The FRISCO semiotic tetrahedron is a visual of a more elaborate framework.

References

Čyras V, Lachmayer F (2018) Meaning and meta-meaning as entities: content (is) and institution-al meaning (ought). In: Jusletter IT, 24 May 2018. https://doi.org/10.38023/5c029a6a-619b-4558-bb74-69d57bf58b61

Čyras V, Lachmayer F (2021) From Kelsen's Pure Theory of Law to Yoshino's Logical Jurisprudence. In: Yoshino H, Villa Rosas G (eds) Law and logic – making legal science a genuine science. Proceedings of the special workshop held at the 28th World Congress of the International Association for Philosophy of Law and Social Philosophy in Lisbon, Portugal, 2017. Archiv für Rechts- und Sozialphilosophie – Beihefte (ARSP-B), Band 166. Franz Steiner Verlag, Stuttgart, pp 29–63

Falkenberg ED, Hesse W, Lindgreen P, Nilsson BE, Oei JLH, Rolland C, Stamper RK, Van Assche FJM, Verrijn-Stuart AA, Voss K (1998) A framework of information system concepts. The FRISCO report (web edition). IFIP, the Netherlands. https://www.mathematik.uni-marburg.de/~hesse/papers/fri-full.pdf. Accessed 15 Dec 2022

Fallon RH (2015) The meaning of legal "meaning" and its implications for theories of legal interpretation. Univ Chic Law Rev 82(3):1235–1308. https://chicagounbound.uchicago.edu/uclrev/vol82/iss3/3/. Accessed 15 Dec 2022

Fillmore CJ (2006) Frame semantics. In: Geeraerts D (ed) Cognitive linguistics: basic readings. Mouton de Gruyter, Berlin, pp 373–400. Originally published in: Linguistic Society of Korea (ed) Linguistics in the morning calm. Hanshin Publishing Company, Seoul, 1982, pp 111–137

Goedicke M (1990) Paradigms of modular system development. In: Mitchell RJ (ed) Managing complexity in software engineering. IEE Computing series, vol 17. Peter Peregrinus, London, pp 1–20

Kelsen H (1967) Pure theory of law, 2nd edn (trans: Knight M) (Reine Rechtslehre, 2. Auflage. Deuticke, Wien 1960). University of California Press, Berkeley

Kelsen H (1991) General theory of norms (trans: Hartney M) (Allgemeine Theorie der Normen, Manz Verlag, Wien, 1979). Clarendon Press, Oxford

MacCormick N, Weinberger O (1986) An institutional theory of law: new approaches to legal positivism. D. Reidel Publishing, Dordrecht

Nadin M (2011) Information and semiotic process: the semiotics of computation. Cybern Hum Knowing 18(1–2):153–175

Ogden CK, Richards IA (1923) The meaning of meaning. Harcourt, Brace & World, New York

Pattaro E (2007) The law and the right: a reappraisal of the reality that ought to be. Series A Treatise of legal philosophy and general jurisprudence, vol 1. Springer, Dordrecht

---

partial descriptions – that we call views – that must later be superimposed to form a complete description" (Goedicke 1990), p. 5.

[10] https://en.wikipedia.org/wiki/Triangle_of_reference.

Part III
Legal Norm

Chapter 12
Extended Legal Thesaurus: Legal Terms as a Modally Indifferent Substrate

12.1 The Granularity Problem

We hold that the modes of obligation, in the same way as legal terms, constitute the subject matter of a legal thesaurus. Moreover, we propose to consider three more relations. These are three types of weak relations: dialectical relations, context relations and metaphorical relations. They augment the five types of strong logical relations of synonymy, semi-synonymy, antonymy, hypernymy/hyponymy and thematic relations. (A hyponym is a word or phrase whose semantic field is included within that of another word, its hypernym. For example, there is the hyponymic relationship between *red* and *colour* (see Wikipedia, https://en.wikipedia.org/wiki/Hyponymy_and_hypernymy).) We begin with combinations of ought modes, which result in obligation, permission, liberty and vetum. Then we explore the types of norms by combining structural parts such as condition, ought, which includes subject, modus, action, and object, and also purpose (telos).

Legal Terms as the Smallest Entities Consider the question "What is the smallest entity of a legal system?" This is similar to the question "What is the smallest particle of the world?" In ancient Greece, this question was asked by philosophers, and Democritus' answer was "the atom" ('indivisible'). Since then, physicists have discovered subatomic particles (chiefly electrons, protons and neutrons) and currently an answer to this question is "the meson". In legal theory, the smallest entity question above can have different answers. Kelsen answered "the norm", whereas Yoshino offered "the legal sentence". In legal documentation, different approaches exist. Some legal document systems take the entire document of a regulation as the smallest entity, whereas others take the articles or paragraphs of a legal act. However, others even distinguish between grammatical sentences.

Based on Čyras and Lachmayer (2013).

© The Author(s), under exclusive license to Springer Nature Switzerland AG 2023
V. Cyras, F. Lachmayer, *Essays on the Visualisation of Legal Informatics*, Law,
Governance and Technology Series 54,
https://doi.org/10.1007/978-3-031-27957-7_12

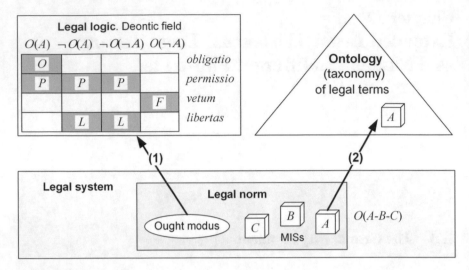

Fig. 12.1 Two themes to investigate: (1) different modes of obligation and (2) the elements of the modally indifferent substrate (Čyras and Lachmayer 2013)

This granularity and the different ideas could be viewed in connection with the modally indifferent substrate (MIS). Kelsen (1991, § 16) considers the legal norm to be the decisive entity: Ought is a mode that comprises MISs. In contrast, we think that, in addition to legal norms, legal terms can be viewed as a separate layer of self-dependent entities of law. A paradigm shift in the granularity is that, in addition to norms, the core legal elements comprise legal terms.

Suppose an act A is prescribed to the addressee of a norm. This can be expressed as *Obligatory*(A), $O(A)$, which connects the Ought O with the intended action A. According to Kelsen, A is an MIS that is imbedded in the mode O.

Different Modes of Ought In our view, it is interesting that O as well as A appears in a logical context. Therefore, we can treat O, the mode of obligation (prescription), abstractly. The reason for this is that the background of obligation involves the entire deontic field. The modes comprise concepts such as permission P, prohibition (vetum) F, liberty L and probably other modalities, and could therefore be defined alternatively (see arrow (1) in Fig. 12.1).

The formula $O(A)$ represents a simple form. In legal texts, multiple legal terms A, B and C, might occur in a single norm and, thus we have $O(A\text{-}B\text{-}C)$ (see Fig. 12.1). To summarise, both the modes of obligation and the elements of MISs could constitute the subject matter of logical analysis.

A legal term A could also be viewed in relationship to other legal terms (see arrow (2) in Fig. 12.1). Legal ontologies attempt to develop such relationships and make use of them, for example, in searching. In European Union law, such stereotypical relationships of legal terms occur as an MIS. In addition to this, there is the translation problem. The reason is that separate legal terms, e.g. A, B and C, in different national legal orders, could have different systemic significance. This produces different mappings of legal terms to the structural backgrounds of the terms in respective legal orders.

12.2 The Ought-Action Structure of Norm and Deontic Modalities

Relations between a norm $N(A)$ and the normative status of the duty can be discussed in more detail. Four cases can be created (Lachmayer 1977), pp. 75–76:

1. $N(A)$ – commandment (obligation; obligatory rule);
2. $\neg N(A)$ – absence of commandment;
3. $\neg N(\neg A)$ – absence of prohibition;
4. $N(\neg A)$ – prohibition (prohibitive rule).

Here the meaning of negation is based on intuition and is not formalised more strictly. Negation of an action, $\neg A$, means an omission of this action A. Negation of a norm, $\neg N(\ldots)$, means an absence of this norm in the regulation. From each of the four cases above, a respective normative status is derived:

5. $N(A) \rightarrow O(A)$	From a commandment, an *obligatory duty* arises.
6. $\neg N(A) \rightarrow \neg O(A)$	From the absence of a commandment, *no obligatory duty* arises.
7. $\neg N(\neg A) \rightarrow \neg O(\neg A)$	From the absence of a prohibition, *no prohibitive duty* arises.
8. $N(\neg A) \rightarrow O(\neg A)$	From a prohibition, a *prohibitive duty* arises.

The spirit of commandment and the spirit of prohibition are expressed by items 5 and 8 respectively. Sixteen subsets can be made from the set of four statuses $\{O(A),$ $\neg O(A), \neg O(\neg A), O(\neg A)\}$. In other words, its powerset consists of $2^4 = 16$ elements. Each element forms a row in the table which is depicted in Fig. 12.2.

One cannot agree to treat the negation of an action, $\neg A$, as an omission of A. Indeed, there is a difference between an omissive action and a negative action. The following example is presented in (Sartor 2007), p. 448:

- For the omissive action NON (Brings$_j$ [k is injured]) to take place, it is sufficient that j did not cause k's injury.
- For the negative action Brings$_j$ (NON [k is injured]) to take place, it is instead required that j prevents k from being injured (which presupposes that without j's intervention k would have been injured).

Sartor considers "this distinction to be sufficiently intuitive, though its analysis would require various philosophical considerations and distinctions".

To explain Fig. 12.2, Standard Deontic Logic (KD) can also be used. KD is formulated with the following axioms (see e.g. Valente 1995, p. 84):

KD0 All (or enough) tautologies of propositional calculus
KD1 $O(p \rightarrow q) \rightarrow (O(p) \rightarrow O(q))$ – the so called K-axiom

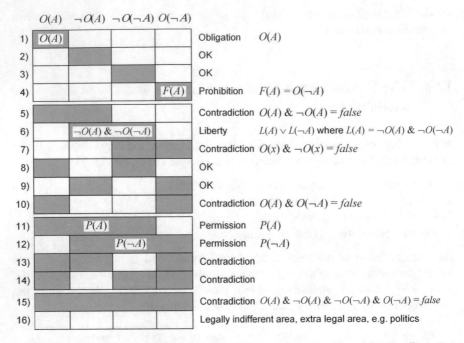

Fig. 12.2 Sixteen subsets of the set of four elements which head the columns (Čyras and Lachmayer 2013)

KD2 $O(p) \rightarrow P(p)$ – "obligatory implies permitted"
KD3 $P(p) \rightarrow \neg O(\neg p)$ – "obligation is the duality of permission"
KD4 $F(p) \rightarrow \neg P(p)$ – "forbidden is not permitted"
KD5 $p, p \rightarrow q \vdash q$ – *modus ponens*
KD6 $p \vdash O(p)$ – O-necessitation

12.3   Hypothetical (Conditional) and Categorical Norms

A subsequent theme to explore is the classification of norms according to their structure. Kelsen distinguishes categorical norms and hypothetical norms.[1] Categorical norms "command a certain behaviour unconditionally—under all circumstances". To begin exploring the structures of norms, we list some of them:

---

[1] "[E]very general norm establishes a relationship between two sets of facts, which may be described in the statement: Under certain conditions, certain consequences ought to take place. This is [. . .] the formulation of the principle of imputation, as distinguished from the principle of causality" (Kelsen 1967), § 25, p. 101.

Fig. 12.3 The structure of a norm (Čyras and Lachmayer 2013)

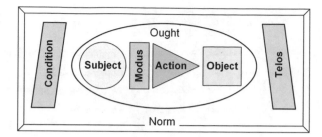

- *Hypothetical norm*, if condition then reaction (consequences), and *categorical norm* (see Kelsen 1967, § 25). They are depicted in chapter 8 figure 11, a.
- *Condition-reaction-finality* (see Luhmann 2004 and also Chap. 8 Fig. 8.11b in this volume). Luhmann distinguishes conditional programming ("if it is dark then switch the lights on") from finality programming ("switch the lights on in order to read").
- *Double norm:* state of affairs → commanded behaviour, otherwise sanction. Kelsen (1991, § 15 and 35) distinguishes primary norms that command a certain behaviour from secondary norms that decree sanctions for the non-observance of norms (sanction-decreeing norms) (see Chap. 8 Fig. 8.12 in this volume).
- *To-Do* norms and *To-Be* norms (see Sartor 2007, p. 446).

Consider the norm structure of three elements: (1) a condition, (2) an ought and (3) a finality (or, in other words, a purpose, goal or telos). An ought is composed of four elements: a subject, a modus, an action, and an object. Thus the structure of a norm is as follows (see Fig. 12.3): (1) condition; (2) ought (comprised of subject, modus, action, and object); and (3) finality.

Further, we aim to classify norms according to the presence of a subset of these elements as the structural parts of a norm. The types of norm are distinguished by taking into account three variables (*condition, ought, telos*) where each may or may not be present or, in other words, takes the value true, 1, or false, 0. Three elements allow us to build eight subsets:

1. (1, 1, 1): complete norm. "If it is dark switch the lights on to make it light".
2. (1, 1, 0): no telos. Conditional norm, a classical one. Example: "If it is dark switch the lights on".
3. (0, 1, 1): teleological norm, task norm (Aufgabennorm, Auftragsnorm) of Weinberger (2000), pp. 443–452. For example, in EU law purposes are usually set out in preambles.
4. (1, 0, 1): To-Be norm. Example: "If it is dark it should be light". The subject and other variables may be implicit. This makes an object-regulated structure.
5. (1, 0, 0): incomplete.
6. (0, 1, 0): categorical norm. A classical norm with "ought". Action is implicit.

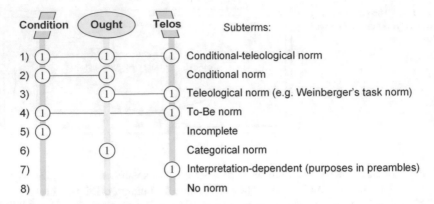

Fig. 12.4 A taxonomy of norms according to the three elements including telos (Čyras and Lachmayer 2013)

7. (0, 0, 1): too little, although this depends on interpretation, e.g., listing purposes in the preamble of a law. Legal principles can be modeled in this way. However, a principle is distinct from a norm.
8. (0, 0, 0): no norm.

The eight combinations above are shown in Fig. 12.4.

12.4   Taxonomy of Norms by Subject-Modus-Action-Object Structure

Further, we distinguish the types of norms taking into account the four elements: a subject, a modus, an action, and an object. Four elements allow us to build 16 subsets where each may or may not be present (see Fig. 12.5):

1. (1, 1, 1, 1): a complete norm. Results with transitive actions, that is, actions, which require a direct subject. Example: "You ought to open the door."
2. (0, 1, 1, 1): no subject. A To-Be norm. Example from construction laws: "Minimum ceiling height shall be 2.4 meters."
3. (1, 0, 1, 1): no modus. A description or an allegation. "You open the door."
4. (1, 1, 0, 1): no action. Action is not regulated or implicit. Examples: "You ought the car (keep in order)", "Police ought (keep) order."
5. (1, 1, 1, 0): no object. Results with intransitive verbs. "He ought to be punished."
6. (0, 0, 1, 1): no subject, no modus. Indicative descriptive interpretation, usually a passive sentence. Example: "A car is driven."
7. (0, 1, 0, 1): incomplete.
8. (0, 1, 1, 0): subject is interpretative, e.g., "everybody". Example: "No stopping."
9. (1, 0, 0, 1): incomplete.

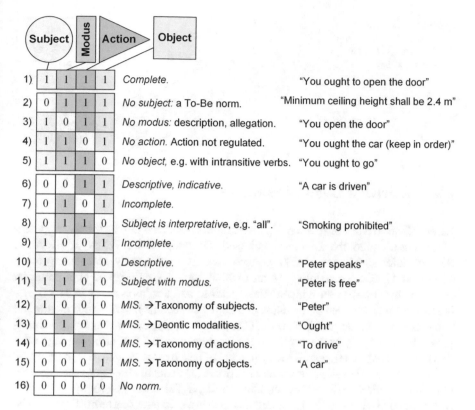

Fig. 12.5 A taxonomy of norms according to the combinations of four elements: subject, modus, action, and object (Čyras and Lachmayer 2013)

10. (1, 0, 0, 1): descriptive. Example: "Peter speaks."
11. (1, 1, 0, 0): subject with modus. Example: "Peter is free."
12. (1, 0, 0, 0): a modally indifferent substrate, MIS. Example: "Peter". Leads to a taxonomy of subjects.
13. (0, 1, 0, 0): MIS. Example: "Ought". Leads to a taxonomy of deontic modalities.
14. (0, 0, 1, 0): MIS. Example: "To drive". Leads to a taxonomy of actions.
15. (0, 0, 0, 1): MIS. Example: "A car". Leads to a taxonomy of objects.
16. (0, 0, 0, 0): no norm.

A subject and an action are essential in a To-Do norm, whereas an object and an action are essential in a To-Be norm. This is depicted in Fig. 12.6.

Fig. 12.6 Distinctions
between To-Do norms and
To-Be norms (Čyras and
Lachmayer 2013)

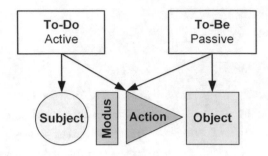

12.5   Extended Legal Thesaurus

Essentially five types of relationships have been considered during the development of an ontology in the LOIS project (see Tiscornia 2007; Peters et al. 2007; Schweighofer and Liebwald 2007). According to the generally accepted wording of Gruber (1995), an ontology is an explicit formal specification of a common conceptualisation with term hierarchies, relations and attributes that makes it possible to reuse this knowledge for automated applications. The five relations mentioned above are *logical*, monolingual, ones: (1) synonymy, (2) near synonymy, (3) antonymy, (4) hypernymy/hyponymy, and (5) implemented_as. See also language relations: eq_synonym, eq_near_synonym, and eq_has_hyperonym/eq_has_hyponym.

We propose to consider three more relations: (1) dialectical relation; this means a term of dialectical antithesis or, in other words, a dialectical antonym; (2) context relation, and (3) metaphorical relation; this means a metaphor of a term. These can be called weak relations—in contrast to strong logical ones. A legal thesaurus comes before a legal ontology. A thesaurus comprises terms and their relations whereas an ontology extends beyond this and comprises more advanced formalisations.

References

Čyras V, Lachmayer F (2013) Extended legal thesaurus: legal terms as a modally indifferent substrate. Jusletter IT. https://doi.org/10.38023/4736480a-0978-43f1-b392-ad52256c17e9

Gruber TR (1995) Toward principles for the design of ontologies used for knowledge sharing. Int J Human-Comput Stud 43(5–6):907–928. https://doi.org/10.1006/ijhc.1995.1081

Kelsen H (1967) Pure theory of law, 2nd edn (trans: Knight M) (Reine Rechtslehre, 2. Auflage. Deuticke, Wien 1960). University of California Press, Berkeley

Kelsen H (1991) General theory of norms (trans: Hartney M) (Allgemeine Theorie der Normen, Manz Verlag, Wien, 1979). Clarendon Press, Oxford

Lachmayer F (1977) Grundzüge einer Normentheorie: Zur Struktur der Normen dargestellt am Beispiel des Rechtes. Duncker & Humblot, Berlin

Luhmann N (2004) Law as a social system (trans: Ziegert KA). Oxford University Press

Peters W, Sagri M, Tiscornia D (2007) The structuring of legal knowledge in LOIS. Artif Intell Law 15(2):117–135. https://doi.org/10.1007/s10506-007-9034-4

Sartor G (2007) Legal reasoning: a cognitive approach to the law. A treatise of legal philosophy and general jurisprudence, vol 5. Springer, Heidelberg

Schweighofer E, Liebwald D (2007) Advanced lexical ontologies and hybrid knowledge based systems: first steps to a dynamic legal electronic commentary. Artif Intell Law 15(2):103–115. https://doi.org/10.1007/s10506-007-9029-1

Tiscornia D (2007) The Lois project: lexical ontologies for legal information sharing. In: Biagioli C, Francesconi E, Sartor G (eds) Proceedings of the V Legislative XML Workshop. European Press Academic Publishing, Florence, pp 189–204. https://docplayer.net/16605486-The-lois-project-lexical-ontologies-for-legal-information-sharing.html. Accessed 15 Dec 2022

Valente A (1995) Legal knowledge engineering. IOS Press, Amsterdam

Weinberger O (2000) Maastricht-Vertrag und die Theorie der Aufgabennormen. In: Weinberger O, Fischer MW (eds) Aus intellektuellem Gewissen: Aufsätze von Ota Weinberger. Duncker & Humblot, Berlin, pp 443–452

Chapter 13
Normative Resultants

13.1 The Structural Elements of Rule

This chapter is devoted to the concept of normative resultants of rules. Two concepts—unified status (einheitlicher Status) and summary status (zusammenfassender Status)—are explored. Here we follow the theory of norms and the concept of normative resultants (normative Resultanten) (see Lachmayer 1977, pp. 88–92). In summary, this chapter concerns structuring of legal semantics, in particular, duties and obligations.

Consider a set of rules $\{r_1, r_2,\ldots, r_n\}$, then different variants of normative status. For simplicity, a case of duties is analysed below and hence, the normative status of the addressee's duties is considered.

Denotations The structural elements of rule are the same in both the real and a virtual world. The essential elements of a rule, r, are denoted as follows:

1. Condition *CON*. Denoted by *condition(r)*.
2. Disposition:

   - subject *SUB*. It is denoted by *subject(r)*. This is the addressee;
   - action *A*. It is denoted by *action(r)*;
   - normative modus (*obligatio, permissio*, etc.). It is denoted by *modus(r)*;
   - object *OBJ*. It is denoted by *object(r)*.

3. Sanction. It is established by a secondary rule.

Hence the rule, r, is constructed of its elements:

Based on section 4 of Čyras and Lachmayer (2011).

V. Cyras, F. Lachmayer, *Essays on the Visualisation of Legal Informatics*, Law, Governance and Technology Series 54, https://doi.org/10.1007/978-3-031-27957-7_13

$r := \langle condition = CON, subject = SUB, action = A, modus = MOD, object = OBJ, \ldots \rangle$

The constructor of r is denoted in short by $r = \langle CON, SUB, A, MOD, OBJ \rangle$. The existence (validity) of the rule is denoted by a predicate, N:

$N(condition = CON, subject = SUB, action = A, modus = MOD, object = OBJ)$

This is also denoted by $N(A)_r$ or $N(A)$ – to stress the behaviour A.

Deontic Field   Relations between a norm $N(A)$ and the normative status of the duty $O(A)$ have to be commented. The four cases can be created (see Sect. 12.2 in this volume): (1) $N(A)$, commandment; (2) $\neg N(A)$, absence of commandment; (3) $\neg N(\neg A)$, absence of prohibition; (4) $N(\neg A)$, prohibition. From each of the four cases above, a respective normative status is derived: (5) $N(A) \rightarrow O(A)$, (6) $\neg N(A) \rightarrow \neg O(A)$, (7) $\neg N(\neg A) \rightarrow \neg O(\neg A)$, (8) $N(\neg A) \rightarrow O(\neg A)$. The spirit of commandment and prohibition is expressed by 5 and 8 respectively.

13.2   The Unified Status

The *unified status* (*eiheitlicher Status*) is obtained when two (or more) variants of normative status have the same contents. A simple example is of two rules, $r1$ and $r2$. The rules have the same addressee and the same action, A:

$$subject(r1) = subject(r2)$$

$$action(r1) = action(r2) = A$$

As mentioned previously, the contents are the same: $contents(r1) = contents(r2)$.

The existence (validity) of $r1$ and $r2$ is denoted respectively by $N(A)_{r1}$ and $N(A)_{r2}$; the notation in Lachmayer (1977), p. 88 is followed. The addressee is bound by two duties, $O(A)_{r1}$ and $O(A)_{r2}$, which have the same contents. A key question is "Can the two duties, $O(A)_{r1}$ and $O(A)_{r2}$, of the same addressee, be put together to form a normative resultant, which is called a *unified duty* and denoted by $O(A)_{e(r1-r2)}$?" The concept is depicted in Fig. 13.1.

The unified duty established by n rules $\{r1, r2, \ldots, rn\}$ is denoted by $O(A)_{e\ (r1-r2-\ldots-rn)}$ or simply $O(A)_{e(1-2-\ldots-n)}$. Each ri has the same condition, subject, action, etc. The construction of the unified duty brings a simplification. Separate duties and rules need not be broken up; instead, of many duties, the sole unified duty is regarded.

An example of two rules is as follows. The first, $r1$, is the road rule 'Crossing the road on a red light is prohibited'. The second rule, $r2$, is implemented with a technological devise—traffic lights.

Fig. 13.1 The unified duty denoted $O(A)_{e(r1-r2)}$ arises from two rules, $r1$ and $r2$ (*Čyras and Lachmayer* 2011)

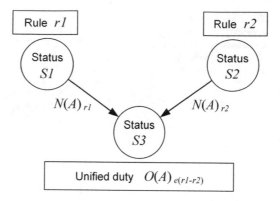

Rule $r1$

Rule $r2$

Status $S1$

Status $S2$

$N(A)_{r1}$

$N(A)_{r2}$

Status $S3$

Unified duty $O(A)_{e(r1-r2)}$

13.3   The Summary Status

Consider two rules, $r1$ and $r2$, with the same addressee, SUB, but different—though compatible—obligatory behaviours, A and B, respectively.

$$subject(r1) = subject(r2) = SUB$$

$$action(r1) = A$$

$$action(r2) = B$$

$$modus(r1) = modus(r2) = obligatio$$

Though actions A and B are different, the obligatory behaviour prescribed by the first rule, $r1$, is compatible with the obligatory behaviour of the second rule, $r2$. On the basis of $r1$, a duty $O(A)_{r1}$ arises. On the basis of $r2$, a duty $O(B)_{r2}$ arises. The second rule does not cover the obligatory behaviour of the first rule. Therefore, the duty to do A does not arise from $r2$. Absence of this duty is denoted by $\neg O(A)_{r2}$.

The same is valid for the first rule. Therefore the duty to do B does not arise from $r1$. Absence of this duty is denoted by $\neg O(B)_{r1}$.

If only one rule—not both—is considered, the situation is as follows. On the basis of one obligatory rule, a duty arises. Here a question can be raised "Can both cases of normative status (duty, nonexistence of duty) be summed up in a normative resultant?" Such a normative resultant, which totals different normative statuses, is called a *summary status* (*zusammenfassender Status*).

In the case of two rules, $r1$ and $r2$, one duty and the nonexistence of another duty lead to two variants. Thus, two summary duties arise, the first, $O(A)_{r1-r2}$, concerning the first obligatory behaviour, and the second, $O(B)_{r1-r2}$, concerning the second obligatory behaviour. The concept is depicted in Fig. 13.2.

In the case of n rules, $r1, r2, \ldots, rn$, consider a summary duty $O(X)_{r1-r2-\ldots-rn}$. The index shows that the obligatory behaviour, X, is commanded by at least one rule, ri. The index does not show how many of such ri exist. One thing is for sure—not all the rules prescribe the same X. Otherwise the unified duty is obtained. It is also true

Fig. 13.2 Two cases of summary duty resulting from two rules, *r1* and *r2* (Čyras and Lachmayer 2011)

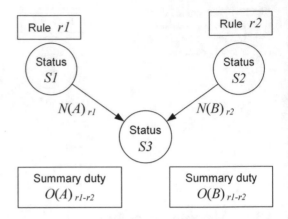

that no rule commands the opposite behaviour, $\neg X$, which is incompatible with X. The above example is built on two rules that lay down two different, though compatible, behaviours. How does the case of several rules *r1, r2,..., rn* look?

Let A_i denote the obligatory behaviour of *ri*. Consider rules $N(A_1)_{r1},..., N(A_n)_{rn}$. For each A_i of the compatible behaviours a summary duty can be established that is based on all the rules. A particular subset of rules induces a set of summary duties, which is equally large.

The construction of normative resultants is significant for the following reason. A behaviour prescribed by a separate rule is of little importance for the rule's addressee, respectively the rule's object. Instead, the behaviour that arises from the whole normative order is important.

Here the problem of rule contradictions can be tackled. Rules are produced by a certain subject (legislator). Therefore, rules can have contradictory contents. Science is not attributed the task of cleaning the contradictions. Science detects that the contradictions are available. The task of cleaning contradictions can be assigned to certain authorities.

13.4   An Example: A Girl with Her Father in a Café

Consider a situation—a girl with her father in a café. The girl's normative status is expressed as follows:

1. The father says 'Sit down'. Obligatio to sit $O(A)_{r1}$.
2. Implicit permission to speak. Permissio to speak $P(B)_{r2}$.
3. A general prohibition to smoke in the café. Vetum to smoke $V(C)_{r3} = O(\neg C)_{r3}$.
4. A specific prohibition to smoke for juvenile. Vetum to smoke $V(C)_{r4} = O(\neg C)_{r4}$.
5. The father asks 'What meals will you take?' Permissio for meals $P(D)_{r5}$.

The normative resultant can be expressed as a list of all five consequents: { $O(A)_{r1}$, $P(B)_{r2}$, $O(\neg C)_{r3}$, $O(\neg C)_{r4}$, $P(D)_{r5}$ }.

In further simplifications, indices can be omitted because rule numbers are of little importance for the addressee (the girl). Duplicated duties are abridged, hence $O(\neg C)$ will appear only once. The normative resultant is expressed with the list:

$$normative\_resultant_{r1-r2-r3-r4-r5} = \{O(A), P(B), O(\neg C), P(D)\} \qquad (13.1)$$

When interpreting the elements of the list, the common-sense understanding of the duties and strong permissions is taken into account. Duties are interpreted with intersection because of the O.M axiom of Standard Deontic Logic: $O(\varphi \& \psi) \Rightarrow (O(\varphi) \& O(\psi))$ (see Jones and Sergot 1993, p. 279). Therefore, the conjunction, &, is a connective in the formula: $duties_{r1-r2-r3-r4-r5} = O(A) \& O(\neg C)$.

Permissions are interpreted with union because of the O.∨ theorem of Standard Deontic Logic: $P(\varphi \vee \psi) \Leftrightarrow (P(\varphi) \vee P(\psi))$. Therefore, disjunction ∨ is a connective: $permissions_{r1-r2-r3-r4-r5} = P(B) \vee P(D)$.

In this example, duties and permissions A, B, C, and D are viewed as being independent and no partial ordering is introduced.

Connecting the duties with the conjunction and the permissions with the disjunction follows from deontic interpretation (see also Sartor 2007, pp. 453–497). In the case of duties with conflicting actions, such as $\{O(goNorth), O(goSouth)\}$, the smallest duty, their intersection $O(goNorth) \& O(goSouth)$, results. In the case of permissions with conflicting actions, such as $\{P(goNorth), P(goSouth)\}$, the largest permission, their union $P(goNorth) \vee P(goSouth)$, results.

Consider one other permission for the girl—to order a single soft drink:

6. The father asks 'What one soft drink will you have, cola $(E1)$, juice $(E2)$, or water $(E3)$?' Permission for one soft drink: $P(E1)_{r6}$ **xor** $P(E2)_{r6}$ **xor** $P(E3)_{r6}$.

The above permission is added to the normative resultant (Eq. 13.1):

$$normative\_resultant_{r1-r2-r3-r4-r5-r6}$$
$$= \{O(A), P(B), O(\neg C), P(D), (P(E1)\textbf{xor}P(E2)\textbf{xor}P(E3))\}$$

The normative resultant of the six rules, $r1, \ldots, r6$, comprises permissions expressed by the following formula:

$$permissions_{r1-r2-r3-r4-r5-r6} = P(B) \vee P(D) \vee (P(E1)\textbf{xor}P(E2)\textbf{xor}P(E3))$$

Related Work The interplay of obligations and strong permissions is studied by Boella and van der Torre (2008). They provide more elaborate examples in the context of hierarchies of authorities. They use Makinson's and van der Torre's framework of input/output logic (Makinson and van der Torre 2000); see also Evans et al. (2020). The 'Rex, Minister and Subject' game devised by Bulygin (1986) serves as an introduction. "If Rex permits hunting on Saturday and then Minister prohibits it for the whole week, its prohibition on Saturday remains with no effect" (Boella et al. 2009).

Incompatible Rules Result in 'Impossible' Summary Obligation In the case of incompatible obligatory actions, 'impossible' summary duty results. In logic, it is denoted by false, $\perp$ (bottom), or $\varnothing$ (empty). To illustrate, imagine a situation where only one of two subjects, mother or child, can be saved. This situation is governed by two valid but incompatible rules:

$$text(r1) = \text{'Save the mother'}, text(r2) = \text{'Save her child'}$$

Conflicting actions mean an empty intersection $A \cap B = \varnothing$. Formally, the set intersection of the operational implementations of the actions A and B is empty: $operationalisations(A) \cap operationalisations(B) = \varnothing$.

Another example of hardly compatible rules is when the father says 'go', $r1$, and the mother says 'stay', $r2$. The resultant is a contradiction, go & ¬go. Real-world pragmatic forces the addressee (child) to sum the arising duties to reach a middle behaviour, like staying in the yard. Hence, other criteria hold sway, which are not explicit in the rules, but implicit in the context.

13.5   Synthesizing Normative Status

The problem of semi-automatic synthesis of normative status is formulated below. A specification of a synthesizer for normative status can be formulated simply. Input is a list of rules, $r1, r2, \ldots, rn$. Output is the normative resultant, $O(X)_{r1\text{-}r2\text{-}\ldots\text{-}rn}$. This is depicted in Fig. 13.3.

Implementation of the machinery is not an easy task. Synthesis of both duties and permissions is in the scope. In reality, the task requires human intelligence. A reason is that legal rules would have to be formalised. Therefore, the concept of role may be an attempt to identify the resulting normative status.

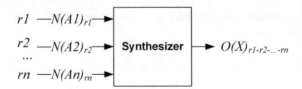

Fig. 13.3 The input and output of a synthesizer of the normative status. The rules $r1, r2, \ldots, rn$ serve as input. Output is the normative resultant of the rules (Čyras and Lachmayer 2011)

References

Boella G, van der Torre L (2008) Institutions with a hierarchy of authorities in distributed dynamic environments. Artif Intell Law 16(1):53–71. https://doi.org/10.1007/s10506-007-9059-8

Boella G, Pigozzi G, van der Torre L (2009) Five guidelines for normative multiagent systems. In: Governatori G (ed) Legal knowledge and information systems. JURIX 2009: the twenty-second annual conference. Frontiers in artificial intelligence and applications, vol 205. IOS Press, Amsterdam, pp 21–30. https://doi.org/10.3233/978-1-60750-082-7-21

Bulygin E (1986) Permisive norms and normative systems. In: Martino AA, Socci Natali F (eds) Automated analysis of legal texts. North-Holland, Amsterdam, pp 211–218

Čyras V, Lachmayer F (2011) From norms to obligations revisited: a case of three-dimensional virtual worlds. In: Geist A, Brunschwig CR, Lachmayer F, Schefbeck G (eds) Strukturierung der Juristischen Semantik – structuring legal semantics. Editions Weblaw, Bern, pp 213–234

Evans R, Sergot M, Stephenson A (2020) Formalizing Kant's rules: A logic of conditional imperatives and permissives. J Philos Logic 49:613–680. https://doi.org/10.1007/s10992-019-09531-x

Jones AJI, Sergot M (1993) On the characterisation of law and computer systems: the normative systems perspective. In: Meyer JJC, Wieringa RJ (eds) Deontic logic in computer science: normative system specification. John Wiley, Chichester, pp 275–307

Lachmayer F (1977) Grundzüge einer Normentheorie: Zur Struktur der Normen dargestellt am Beispiel des Rechtes. Duncker & Humblot, Berlin

Makinson D, van der Torre L (2000) Input/output logics. J Philos Logic 29:383–408. https://doi.org/10.1023/A:1004748624537

Sartor G (2007) Legal reasoning: a cognitive approach to the law. A treatise of legal philosophy and general jurisprudence, vol 5. Springer, Heidelberg

Chapter 14
Legal Frameworks of Three-Dimensional Virtual Worlds

14.1 Need for Legal Frameworks in Virtual Worlds

In this chapter, we reflect on constructing legal frameworks which affect computer applications which are called three-dimensional online virtual worlds. The normative regulation of avatars is concerned. Non-game virtual worlds such as Second Life, developed by Linden Lab (https://secondlife.com/), are in the primary focus. About 'serious' virtual worlds—opposed to leisure-based—see a scoping study by Sara de Freitas (de Freitas 2008).

To explore the above mentioned issues, normative multiagent systems are reviewed. The norms and obligations of software agents have been investigated traditionally in informatics: computer science researchers proposing formalisms and programming languages for operationalisation of norms in software.

Sketching the legal issues of virtual worlds is first dealt in this chapter. The metaphor of stage is employed here. It acts as a model, a symbolisation of the conceptual framework. It is generally called spatialisation.

Further the differences between the types of rules are addressed. Technical rules are impossible to violate, but legal rules (norms) can be violated.

All the rules are subject to implementation in virtual world software. In this context, law enforcement is a tough issue. The addressee concept of classical rules—persons—is supplemented with avatars. A sample "toy" rule 'Keep off the grass' can illustrate constraints on avatar behaviour. Various methodologies are investigated worldwide to program the rules. Programming languages include external tools and script languages (e.g. LSL, Python, Lua, etc.). As a programming exercise, consider a virtual world and the following scenario. Suppose you build a house with a door which is controlled by a rule which permits entering avatars from a certain group

Based on Čyras and Lachmayer (2010, 2011).

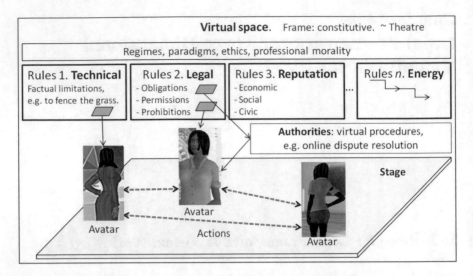

Fig. 14.1   The elements of a virtual world (Čyras and Lachmayer 2010, 2011)

only, e.g. your trusted friend avatars; other avatars are forbidden. In Second Life, this rule can be programmed by LSL (Linden Script Language).

The explored issues tackle the virtual world platform which was being developed within the VirtualLife[1] project (see below for a fuller outline). Here the legal framework being constructed comprises a Virtual Constitution (Bogdanov et al. 2009; Čyras and Lapin 2010; see also Čyras and Lachmayer 2010; 2011). The operational implementation of rules pays respect to Vázquez-Salceda et al. (2008).

14.2   The Frame of a Virtual World

This section describes informally different kinds of rules in three dimensional virtual worlds that are inspired by a metaphor of architecture. Such an immersive virtual environment is different from 2D menu paradigm.

The frame—the reality of a virtual world—is constitutive. The entities are comprised of avatars, and 3D objects such as buildings, rooms, information stands, avatar inventories, etc. An avatar is a computer user's representation (usually a 3D model). Every avatar is monitored by its user. The avatar can also be viewed as the cursor on the screen.

The frame of a virtual world is established from the outset. A conceptualisation of the "theatre" is depicted in Fig. 14.1. The entities of major importance are avatars,

---

[1] VirtualLife project "Secure, Trusted and Legally Ruled Collaboration Environment in Virtual Life", 2008–2010, co-funded by EU FP7 ICT under DG INFSO Networked Media Systems, https://cordis.europa.eu/project/id/216064.

their actions and rules, which regulate the behaviour. The avatars can also engage in joint actions. Avatar chat communication can be via voice or text chat.

Rules establish a regime (paradigm) of the virtual world. They can be divided into different classes such as technological rules (and furthermore, technical rules), legal rules, reputation rules, energy rules, professional rules, etc.:

Technical Rules They establish factual limitations. Real-world examples are to fence the grass, to close the door to forbid entering, to refuse money by a cash machine if you do not provide the PIN code, etc. Violations are impossible: there is no possibility of violating a technical rule unless you break the artefact completely. Hence technical rules are strictly enforceable.

Legal Rules Their nature is that they can be violated. For example, you can step the grass. But you risk being sanctioned. A procedure is enforced by an authority such as police, peacekeepers in a virtual world, etc. A sanction is imposed with a probability. Hence the legal rules are not strictly enforceable. Herein is the spirit of law. There is no strict boundary between technical and legal rules; a grey area exists. The structural elements of legal rules are the same as of real-world norms. The modus is a deontic notion: obligatory, permitted, prohibited, etc.

Legal rules are of two kinds. The primary rules come first. Sanctions are determined by secondary rules. They are associated with authorities which enforce the rules. Virtual procedures can be raised for violations. For instance, online dispute resolution is a kind of procedure.

The modes of effect can be different. A sanction can be raised randomly with a certain probability $p\%$. An example is a road rule which forbids crossing a street against traffic lights. You can go through a red light and if you are lucky a policeman will not punish you.

Legal rules are essential in virtual worlds—similarly as in the real world. It is impossible to implement normative regulation in a virtual world by means of technical rules only. Consider the norm that indecent content is forbidden in the virtual world. Such an abstract norm can scarcely be implemented by automatic checking.

In VirtuaLife a user agrees on a so called Virtual Constitution which consists of abstract legal rules. The Virtual Constitution is implemented as a click-wrap agreement. In this way it is part of End User License Agreement (EULA) and binds the users on the contractual level.

Energy Rules They sanction in the following way. If a prescribed behaviour is violated appropriate "energy" points are reduced. The addressee can be sanctioned effectively, that is, 100%.

This can be illustrated by security/trust rules, reputation rules and the avatar identity card in VirtuaLife. Each avatar has an ID card, which contains information about both his virtual and real life identities.

The ID card includes simple indicators of trust. A red (entrusted) bar means that the avatar is a guest and has not proved his identity; a yellow (weakly trusted) bar—

the avatar has an identity, but it has not been verified by any certification authority; and a green (trusted) bar—the avatar's identity has been verified by a certification authority. Each avatar also has an economic, social and civic reputation, whose indicators are handled by a sophisticated reputation system, depending on the avatar's behaviour. Thus the rules are implemented in software by hard constraints.

Professional Rules Other kinds of rules comprise moral rules, user community rules, etc. Examples are provided further from the VirtualLife project where the users can engage in a trusted community called Virtual Nation. Different communities are governed by different rules. For instance, Students and Teachers form distinguished Virtual Nations in a University Virtual Campus that is purposed at learning support (Čyras and Lapin 2010).

The users are not absolutely free to agree on the community rules. Spindler et al. (2010) emphasise that the users cannot escape from the real-world law.

Virtual Nation Scenarios A number of examples for allowing different scenarios can be proposed. Different values and rules are covered by NoCopy, CopyRight and CopyLeft nations. Permission language tables serve to implement distinguished rights. The permissions are represented explicitly in computer code.

In a NoCopy nation, no one is allowed to make copies. In a strict copyright nation, only the author of the object can make copies. The receiver of the copied object cannot make copies.

In a non-strict copyright nation, the original author of an object can decide if the new owner can copy the object or not. By default, an author or owner can copy.

In a CopyLeft nation, the creator's information is preserved. Each user can change and copy its own objects.

In a Second Life model nation, you can sell objects controlling whether they are editable, copyable or sellable. The creator cannot modify a sold object. Of course, you can always move your own objects. For example, the seller can decide to sell non-copyable objects. This object cannot be duplicated by the new owner. Therefore if she puts them in her inventory they disappear from the world.

14.3 Principles of Construction of a Virtual World Legal Framework

Rules can form different normative systems. Virtual world rules have different modes of effect or relevance, such as 'barrier', 'occasional', 'step-by-step', etc. (see Fig. 14.2).

Barrier Effect A door is an example of a barrier technical rule. The technical rules are implemented with hard constraints. For implementation see guideline 2 in Boella et al. (2009).

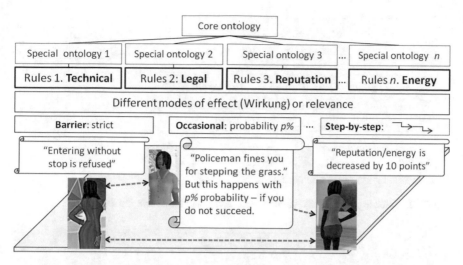

Fig. 14.2 Principles of construction of a virtual world legal framework (Čyras and Lachmayer 2010, 2011)

Occasional Effect The occasional type rule sanctions you with a certain probability. An example is a legal rule to buy the ticket when you take a train. However, you can succeed to travel without the ticket, but if a conductor does not sanction you.

A dream of computer scientists might be to implement the sanctions of each legal rule by means of technical rules. However this is against the spirit of law.

Step-by-Step Effect It is characteristic to reputation and energy rules. For example, each time you violate a rule, your points are decreased by 10%.

Ontologies A core ontology is immanent within the whole set of rules. A special (material) domain ontology is present within each kind of rules.

Technical Filters They can be set to enforce rules. For instance, in the context of e-law, legal texts can go through an Extended Markup Language (XML) filter. A document cannot be put on the "transport belt" of legislative workflow in case the document's XML structure is flawed. Such a filter is an example of a technical rule. The ruling is of the type "Entering without stop is refused".

14.3.1   Three Legal Stages

Three legal stages can be distinguished within a virtual world: (1) the legislative stage, (2) the negotiation stage—the stage of the game, and (3) the judicial stage (see Fig. 14.3). Their functions accord with the functions of law.

The legislative stage serves to produce rules. Here the whole in-world community can be involved. Next, the negotiation stage serves for everyday life. Social games

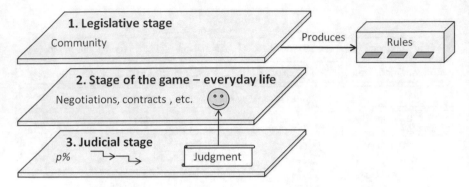

Fig. 14.3 Three legal stages of a virtual world (Čyras and Lachmayer 2010, 2011)

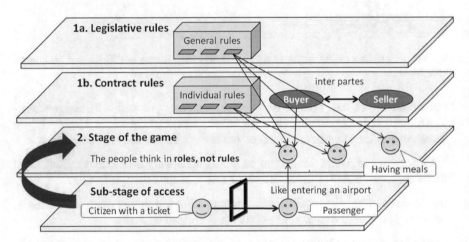

Fig. 14.4 Two legislative sub-stages serve to produce general rules and individual rules (Čyras and Lachmayer 2010, 2011)

including contracts are performed here. The judicial stage serves for judgments. This stage is not entered in each case. Distinguished modes of (virtual) legal proceedings are already identified above. Here activities such as storytelling, adjudication dialogs and legal disputes can be invoked.

The legislative stage consists of two sub-stages. On the first one, 1a in Fig. 14.4, legislative (general) rules are produced. It is compared with parliamentary activities, but performed by the community. On the second sub-stage, 1b, contract (individual) rules are produced.

A sub-stage of access can be distinguished within the stage of the game. It can be compared with an entering scenario. For example, in an airport a citizen with the valid ticket passes a procedure to become a passenger.

People Think in Roles, Not Rules In a virtual world, the concept of role is more significant than the rule concept. In the real world people think in terms of roles. The people do not even know rules and paragraphs of the law. An attempt to model the role is to put a label. Recall the roles of administrator, user, guest, etc. (in the case of computer users) and distinguishing their access rights.

14.3.2 Formalising Rules: Technical, Legal and Energy Rules

The concept of technical rule is formalised in terms of necessity (a causal relationship). A legal rule is formalised as a formula in mathematical logic. Energy rule prohibits certain behaviour; if violated, addressee's "energy points" are decreased.

Technical Rules They are based on natural necessity (causation). They are formalised 'If P, then Q'. In inference they can be employed with the modus ponens rule (P. If P, then Q. Therefore Q). Or in the sequent notation, $P, P{\rightarrow}Q \vdash Q$. An example of a technical rule is the cash machine's rule that is worded: '*if PIN code is provided then the cash machine gives money*'. Formally: *Rule(pin→money)*. The idea of the rule is the entailment that in the case the PIN code is not provided, the cash machine gives no money, formally: *Fact(¬pin), Rule(pin→money)* ⊢ *Fact (¬money)*.

Technical rules do not have the structural element modus. Therefore 'ought' (obligatory) or 'may' (permitted) is not included even in the grammatical formulation.

The technical rule concept can be viewed in the context of rule-based knowledge representation and compared with active rules in databases and business rules (cf. Vasilecas et al. 2009).

Legal Rules Deontic status (e.g. obligatory, permitted, prohibited, etc.) is a structural element of legal rules. The nature of the legal rules is that a prescribed behaviour, Q, can be violated. Following is an example of an observed situation:

$$Fact(P) \quad \text{–fact.}$$

$$Obligation(P \rightarrow Q) \quad \text{–rule.}$$

$$Fact(\neg Q) \quad \text{–observed violation fact.}$$

For example, the traffic lights rule permits you to cross only if the lights are green: 'Permitted to cross iff green'. However, you can cross against the lights:

$$Fact(\neg P) \quad \text{–red is on.}$$

$$Permission(P \leftrightarrow Q) \quad \text{–cross only on green.}$$

Fig. 14.5 Energy points are reduced upon the violations of a rule (Čyras and Lachmayer 2010, 2011)

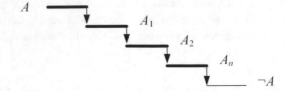

$$Fact(Q) \quad \text{--however you cross.}$$

The observed behaviour is interpreted that you are simply a bad guy and nobody can stop you crossing. Rule violations are sanctioned randomly.

Energy Rules Energy (reputation, etc.) rules prohibit certain behaviour. Consider you violate a rule. Therefore, your energy points are reduced. Hence, you are sanctioned 100%. An example is as follows:

$$Norm(\neg A) \quad \text{--}A \text{ is prohibited.}$$

$$Fact(A) \quad \text{--you violate the rule.}$$

Points of A are reduced--e.g., $A := 0.9^* A$.

The interpretation is that your energy points are reduced to A_1, then A_2 and so on until A_n. At last the state $\neg A$ is reached, which denotes no energy at all Fig. 14.5). The shark fish is an example in the nature. A shark drowns if swallows too much.

14.4   Related Work

Multiagent Systems Relevant formalisations are investigated by normative multiagent systems communities. Their formalisms are mathematically more precise than visuals in this volume. Boella et al. (2009) introduce five guidelines for the use of normative systems in computer science (see also a whole volume devoted to agents and AI & law). Boella et al. (2010) concern violations of legal rules and address goal-based interpretation and conflicting goals. Dignum et al. (2002) seek a long-term goal to extend the Belief–Desire–Intention (BDI) model, at a theoretical and practical level, with social concepts such as norms and obligations.

The Concept of Obligation With regard to the analysis of obligations, we have found useful the thesis of Adam Wyner (2008). He considers deontic logic as presented by Paul McNamara (2006) and provides linguistic considerations and natural language syntactic and semantic analysis. Wyner's analysis of the Contrary-to-Duty Paradox (the Gentle Murder Paradox and the Good Samaritan Paradox) contributes to better understanding of obligations.

Virtual Institutions Anton Bogdanovych' (2007) work on non-game virtual worlds is very relevant. He developed the concept of Virtual Institutions (VI) "being a new class of Normative Virtual Worlds, that combine the strengths of 3D Virtual Worlds and Normative Multiagent Systems, in particular, Electronic Institutions (Esteva et al. 2001; Esteva 2003)". Virtual Institutions are targeted at e-commerce. In Virtual Institutions an avatar can stop for a while interacting with its human master and continue independently as an agent that is governed by rules. Following is an example of a rule: "Only participants with certain roles are permitted to enter particular rooms". For instance, a Buyer is permitted to an Auction room but a Seller is prohibited. Esteva (2003) sees Electronic Institutions as structures and mechanisms of social order and cooperation governing the behaviour of two or more individuals.

The ancient city of Uruk project (Bogdanovych et al. 2009) is interesting for the following reasons. Its specification is rather simple and consists only of a dozen abstract norms. Virtual Institutions are defined as "3D virtual worlds with normative regulation of participant's interactions" (Bogdanovych et al. 2009), p. 141. A virtual institution is enabled by a three layered architecture. The Normative Control Layer employs AMELI to regulate the interactions between participants by enforcing the institutional rules. The Communication Layer causally connects the institution dimensions with the virtual world. The Visual Interaction Layer (supported by Second Life) visualises the virtual world.

Law-Governed Interaction The concept of 'law' in VirtualLife differs from that in Law-Governed Interaction (LGI) (see Naftaly Minsky 2005). LGI is a decentralised coordination and control mechanism for distributed systems—it can also be viewed as a "policy mechanism". The term 'policy' is used for an informal statement of a set of rules-of-engagement, reserving the term 'law' for a formalisation of this policy in a manner that can be enforced via LGI. LGI identifies two modes of law enforcement: (a) by preventing violations of the given law and (b) by reacting to violations.

LGI adopts the former stronger mode of law enforcement, (a). VirtualLife tackles both: the Virtual Constitution concept introduces the 'soft' interpretation of rules; thus (a) is tackled. VirtualLife adopts (b) by reacting to violations. Thus the 'strong' interpretation of rules is adopted. Mode (a) is difficult to implement as punishment cannot be implemented in full scale in VirtualLife; mode (b) is easier.

The role of a law L under LGI is to decide what should be done if a given event e occurs at an agent x operating under this law, when the control-state of x is s. This decision, the ruling of the law, can be represented by the sequence of primitive operations mandated by the law, to be carried out, automatically, at x. More formally, L is a function $L: E \times S \rightarrow O^*$, where E is a set of all possible regulated-events, S is a set of all possible states, and O is a set of all primitive operations. The event-condition-action rules have the form UPON event IF condition DO operation-list. The rules are implemented in Prolog or Java. Thus, LGI rules are implemented as technical rules.

Fig. 14.6 A spatialisation of norm and status. For the concept of unified duty $O(A)_{e(r1-r2)}$ see Chap. 13 Sect. 13.2 in this volume

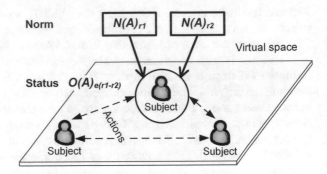

Computer Code Is Law The role of computer code in cyberspace can be compared with laws in real space.[2] In particular, MMOGs (massively multiplayer online games) are also "determined by the code—the software, or architecture, that makes the MMOG space what it is" (Lessig 2006), p. 14. Therefore software engineers have to have regard to the limits of programming in regulation by computer code, and jurists have to have regard to the limits of territorially-based sovereigns.

Conclusion We view avatars as subjects to normative positions of virtual world rules (see Fig. 14.6). Therefore the normative resultants of rules and their formalisations in the previous chapter apply.

In the approach worded "From rules in the law towards rules in artefact", we elaborate on an issue of regulation by computer code. The artefacts can be of different kinds. Additionally to embedded systems, the artefacts comprise software systems like virtual world platforms and virtual nations. Here software developers identify the rules and implement them in computer code. A part of rules can be explicitly represented—the 'strong' interpretation (Boella et al. 2009). A part of rules cannot be represented explicitly. They are formulated explicitly in the system specification, namely, in the EULA text—the 'weak' interpretation.

The rule of law is required for both human and artificial agent communities. Different persons can pursue conflicting interests. Therefore the need arises for governance by rules. Operating systems perform the role of "arbiters" in communities of computer programs that compete for common resources. Similarly, the behaviour of agents (avatars) in virtual worlds has to be regulated by rules that constitute the law of the virtual world. People think in terms of roles. The names of roles, such as an author, an owner, a NoCopy nation, serve to describe situations.

---

[2]"In real space, we recognize how laws regulate—through constitutions, statutes, and other legal codes. In cyberspace we must understand how a different "code" regulates—how the software and hardware (i.e., the "code" of cyberspace) that make cyberspace what it is also regulate cyberspace as it is" (Lessig 2006), p. 5.

References

Boella G, Pigozzi G, van der Torre L (2009) Five guidelines for normative multiagent systems. In: Governatori G (ed) Legal knowledge and information systems. JURIX 2009: the twenty-second annual conference. Frontiers in artificial intelligence and applications, vol 205. IOS Press, Amsterdam, pp 21–30. https://doi.org/10.3233/978-1-60750-082-7-21

Boella G, Governatori G, Rotolo A, van der Torre L (2010) A formal study on legal compliance and interpretation. In: Meyer T, Ternovska E (eds) Proceedings of the 13th international workshop on non-monotonic reasoning, NMR 2010, 14–16 May, Toronto

Bogdanov D, Crispino MV, Čyras V, Glass K, Lapin K, Panebarco M, Todesco GM, Zuliani F (2009) VirtualLife virtual world platform: peer-to-peer, security and rule of law. In: eBook proceedings of 2009 NEM summit towards future media internet, Saint-Malo, France, 28–30 September. Eurescom GmbH, pp 124–129

Bogdanovych A (2007) Virtual institutions. PhD thesis, University of Technology Sydney

Bogdanovych A, Rodriguez JA, Simoff S, Cohen A, Sierra C (2009) Developing virtual heritage applications as normative multiagent systems. In: Gleizes MP, Gomez-Sanz JJ (eds) Agent-oriented software engineering X. AOSE 2009. Lecture notes in computer science, vol 6038. Springer, Heidelberg, pp 140–154. https://doi.org/10.1007/978-3-642-19208-1_10

Čyras V, Lachmayer F (2010) Technical rules and legal rules in online virtual worlds. Eur J Law Technol (EJLT) 1(3) https://ejlt.org/index.php/ejlt/article/view/27. Accessed 15 Dec 2022

Čyras V, Lachmayer F (2011) From norms to obligations revisited: a case of three-dimensional virtual worlds. In: Geist A, Brunschwig CR, Lachmayer F, Schefbeck G (eds) Strukturierung der Juristischen Semantik – structuring legal semantics. Editions Weblaw, Bern, pp 213–234

Čyras V, Lapin K (2010) Learning support and legally ruled collaboration in the VirtualLife virtual world platform. In: Grundspenkis J, Kirikova M, Manolopoulos Y, Novickis L (eds) ADBIS 2009 workshops, proceedings of associated workshops and doctoral consortium of the 13th East-European Conference, Riga, Latvia. Lecture notes in computer science, vol 5968. Springer, Heidelberg, pp 47–54

de Freitas S (2008) Serious virtual worlds: a scoping study. The Serious Games Institute, Coventry University Enterprises, JISC. http://www.jisc.ac.uk/publications/reports/2008/seriousvirtualworldsreport.aspx. Accessed 15 Dec 2022

Dignum F, Kinny D, Sonenberg L (2002) From desires, obligations and norms to goals. Cogn Sci Quart 2(3-4):407–430

Esteva M (2003) Electronic institutions: from specification to development. PhD monography, vol. 19. Institut d'Investigació en Intel·ligència Artificial (IIIA), Spain

Esteva M, Rodríguez-Aguilar JA, Sierra C, Garcia P, Arcos JL (2001) On the formal specification of electronic institutions. In: Dignum F, Sierra C (eds) Agent mediated electronic commerce. Lecture Notes in Computer Science, vol 1991. Springer, Heidelberg, pp 126–147. https://doi.org/10.1007/3-540-44682-6_8

Lessig L (2006) Code version 2.0. Basic Books, New York

McNamara P (2006) Deontic logic. In: Gabbay D, Woods J (eds) Handbook of the history of logic, vol 7. Elsevier, pp 197–288

Minsky N (2005) Law governed interaction (LGI): a distributed coordination and control mechanism. An introduction, and a reference manual. Rutgers University. https://www.cs.rutgers.edu/~minsky/papers/manual.pdf. Accessed 15 Dec 2022

Spindler G, Anton K, Wehage J (2010) Overview of the legal issues in virtual worlds. In: Daras P, Mayora O (eds) User centric media: UCMedia 2009. Lecture notes of the institute for computer sciences, social informatics and telecommunications engineering (LNICST), vol 40. Springer, Heidelberg, pp 189–198

Vasilecas O, Kalibatiene D, Guizzardi G (2009) Towards a formal method for transforming ontology axioms to application domain rules. Inf Technol Control 38(4):271–282

Vázquez-Salceda J, Aldewereld H, Grossi D, Dignum F (2008) From human regulations to regulated software agents behavior: connecting the abstract declarative norms with the concrete operational implementation. Artif Intell Law 16(1):73–87

Wyner A (2008) Violations and fulfillments in the formal representation of contracts. PhD thesis. King's College London. http://www.wyner.info/research/Papers/WynerPhDThesis2008.pdf. Accessed 15 Dec 2022

Chapter 15
Legal Taboos

15.1 Definition of Taboo

We propose to formalise a taboo as a prohibition on speaking (in general, on informing). Three levels of norms are distinguished. First are basic prohibitions, *Forbidden X*. These are norms which prohibit basic actions, *Norm(¬X)*. Second-level norms comprise primary taboos which prohibit information about facts or fakes, *Norm(¬Inf(X))*, but permit them to happen. Third-level norms comprise meta-taboos, which prohibit information that a primary taboo exists, *Norm(¬Inf (Norm(¬Inf(X))))*. The message also is that a taboo on the essential causes *A* of an effect *E* can be officially camouflaged with a fake relationship between certain facts *B* and *E*.

The word 'taboo' means "a social or religious custom prohibiting or restricting a particular practice or forbidding association with a particular person, place, or thing."[1] A taboo is a vehement prohibition of an action based on the belief that such behaviour is either too sacred or too accursed for ordinary individuals to undertake.[2] In the fairy tale 'The Emperor's New Clothes', an example of a taboo is the prohibition on the mention that the Emperor is naked.[3]

Based on Čyras and Lachmayer (2018a, b).

---

[1] See https://www.oxfordreference.com/display/10.1093/acref/9780198609810.001.0001/acref-9780198609810-e-6931.

[2] See Encyclopædia Britannica Online, 'Taboo', and Wikipedia, https://en.wikipedia.org/wiki/Taboo. Common taboos involve restrictions on or ritual regulations for killing and hunting; sex and sexual relationships; reproduction; the dead and their graves; and food and dining (primarily cannibalism). See also the term 'nefas' in archaic Roman law.

[3] Danish author Hans Christian Andersen wrote about two weavers who promise an emperor a new suit of clothes, which they say is invisible to those who are unfit for their positions, stupid, or incompetent. When the Emperor parades before his subjects in his new clothes, no one dares to say

© The Author(s), under exclusive license to Springer Nature Switzerland AG 2023   139
V. Cyras, F. Lachmayer, *Essays on the Visualisation of Legal Informatics*, Law,
Governance and Technology Series 54,
https://doi.org/10.1007/978-3-031-27957-7_15

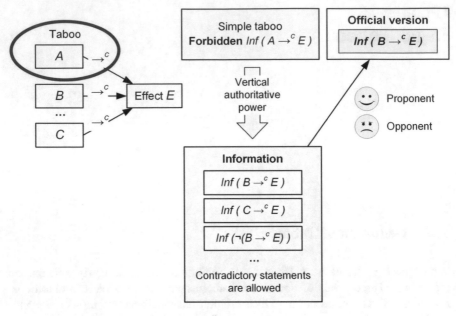

Fig. 15.1 The concept of taboo in context (Čyras and Lachmayer 2018a)

In this study, a taboo is treated as a prohibition on speaking (in general, informing). In this way, we narrow the broader meaning of a taboo, which is a prohibition on an action. We restrict ourselves to the prohibition of a specific action, namely informing.

Specifically, a taboo is imposed on giving information about the essential causes of an effect (which is typically evaluated negatively). We assume an effect E, and facts A, B, C that are in a causal relationship with this effect, as denoted by $A \rightarrow^c E$, $B \rightarrow^c E$, and $C \rightarrow^c E$. Suppose A is the main cause, and a taboo is imposed on it, that is, a prohibition on speaking caused by A. We also suppose that the official information is that B causes E, which is fake. This situation is depicted on the left-hand side of Fig. 15.1. Taboos can have various meanings and social reasons, such as top-down institutional repression, vertical authoritative power, odd morality, etc. Legal taboos may also be embraced by the system of norms.

The concept of a taboo is briefly overviewed by Duschinsky (2014).[4] He notes that according to Freud, "The meaning of 'taboo', as we see it, diverges in two

---

that they don't see any suit of clothes on him for fear that they will be seen as "unfit for their positions, stupid, or incompetent". Finally, a child cries out, "But he isn't wearing anything at all!" The story is about a situation where "no one believes, but everyone believes that everyone else believes. Or alternatively, everyone is ignorant as to whether or not the Emperor has clothes, but believes that everyone else is not ignorant" (Hansen 2011). See Wikipedia, https://en.wikipedia.org/wiki/The_Emperor's_New_Clothes.

[4] Duschinsky (2014) begins with the following definition: "'Taboo' is a Polynesian term, which has come to refer in Western academic and public discourses to topics, spaces, or practices that are consecrated as prohibited or to the process itself of marking them off."

contrary directions. To us it means, on the one hand, 'sacred' or 'consecrated', and on the other 'uncanny', 'dangerous', 'forbidden', 'unclean'" (Freud 2001), p. 18. In his book Taboo, Steiner (1956), p. 22 studies the subject from the perspective of sociology (or, more precisely, social anthropology). Taboos refer to danger.[5] Steiner notes that to make a comparative category the definition of taboo is narrowed (ibid.), p. 121. Next Steiner refers to Margaret Mead's article 'Tabu' in Encyclopaedia of Social Sciences, 1937: "Tabu may be defined as a negative sanction, a prohibition whose infringement results in an automatic penalty without human or superhuman mediation."

Taboos may be sensitive from several perspectives: morally, religiously, culturally, socially, politically, and also legally. Taboo norms can be evaluated negatively, although various positions can be explored. Broyde (2002) discusses three different problems: informing a bandit, informing an abusive government, and informing a (procedurally) just system of government. The view "No prohibition to inform when government is just" has a place in a discussion (Broyde 2002). We further focus on formalising statements about taboo; explorations of the function of taboos and social reasons are set aside.[6]

15.2 Formalising Taboo as a Prohibition to Speak

Let us denote by $Inf(X)$ that information about X exists (in reality or in a model such as a database). For example, information that A causes E is denoted by $Inf(A \rightarrow^c E)$. Let us follow the notation in deontic logic and denote that it is forbidden that X by $\mathbf{F} X$ or $\mathbf{F}(X)$. The obligatoriness of X is denoted by $\mathbf{O} X$ and the permissibility of X is denoted by $\mathbf{P} X$. The prohibition $\mathbf{F} X$ can be defined as $\mathbf{O} \neg X$ (obligatory to omit X, i.e. it is obligatory to not do X) or $\neg \mathbf{P} X$ (no permission to do X).

We start by defining taboo as a prohibition to speak. Thus, a restriction is imposed on a general prohibition $\mathbf{F} X$ of any action X. Taboo means that a phenomenon X may be permitted, but informing about X is prohibited. An example is a taboo on genitals: 'In our family, it is forbidden to speak about genitals'. However, it is not forbidden to have genitals. This is represented as $Taboo(genitals)$. Similarly, at a party, it is forbidden to speak about money. However, it is not forbidden to have money. This is represented as $Taboo(money)$.

A taboo can be expressed with a formula in modal logic $\mathbf{T} X =^{def} \mathbf{F} \, Inf(X)$, where $\mathbf{T}$ is treated as a modal operator that is syntactically analogical to the deontic

---

[5] Steiner (1956), pp. 20–21 defines: "[T]aboo is an element of all those situations in which attitudes to values are expressed in terms of danger behavior."

[6] Centola et al. write: "It is easy to explain why people comply with unpopular norms—they fear social sanctions. And it is easy to explain why people pressure others to behave the way they want them to behave. But why pressure others to do the opposite? Why would people publicly enforce a norm that they secretly wish would go away?" (Centola et al. 2005).

operators **O**, **P** and **F**. Formalisation of normativity implies a norm as an entity. A taboo on *X* means a norm that prohibits informing about *X*:

$$Taboo(X) = {}^{def} N(\neg Inf(X)) \tag{15.1}$$

In our formalisation, all the entities, including actions, facts and norms, exist as truth (true or false) in the realm of science, that is, in a model such as a database. Norms *N* (•) correspond to the Ought realm or its representation in the model, while *Inf* corresponds to the Is realm.

A norm *N(A)* must be assigned certain semantics. Consider *N(A)* as a commandment to do *A* and *N(¬A)* as a prohibition on doing *A*. The relation between a norm (rule) and the normative status of the duty can be explored (see Chap. 12):

$N(A) \rightarrow O(A)$–From a commandment, an obligatory duty arises.

$N(\neg A) \rightarrow O(\neg A)$–From a prohibition, a prohibitive duty arises.

Meta-Taboo Next we strengthen the above definition with a double prohibition called a meta-taboo. A *meta-taboo* is a prohibition on informing that there is norm that prohibits speaking about *X*:

$$Meta-taboo(X) = {}^{def} N(\neg Inf(N(\neg Inf(X)))) \tag{15.2}$$

In a literal sense, a meta-taboo can be linked with the expression "taboo on the mention of taboo", which is used in the literature (cf. Attridge 2014).[7]

15.3   Three Levels of Norms on Prohibition

A fact, its content and its institutional meaning are distinguished. A fact (in a broad sense) is treated as an act, and namely, as a "happening occurring at a certain time and in a certain place" (Kelsen 1967), p. 2. Fakes can be associated with false information (disinformation or hoaxes, also misinformation). Further facts in a narrow sense (or facts, for short) are defined as true information about the facts in a broad sense.

Consider a language *L* for expressing statements about facts, fakes and taboos. Its basic entities can be *Fact* (denoted by *FC*) or *Fake* (denoted by *FK*). The reference area of *L* sentences comprises more entities. Firstly there is *Meaning* (*ME*); then relations, such as *Causality* ($\rightarrow^c$), *Telos* ($\rightarrow^{te}$), *Equality* ($\rightarrow^=$), and *Transformation*

---

[7] John Attridge (2014) writes about the depiction of Englishness in novels. He notes that it was Archibald Lyall who "called the 'taboo on the mention of taboo', in his 1930 book 'It Isn't Done, or, the Future of Taboo Among the British Islanders'".

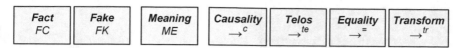

Fig. 15.2 Basic entities to which norms refer (Čyras and Lachmayer 2018a)

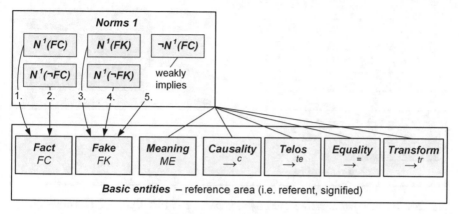

Fig. 15.3 Types of norms at the first level, *Norms 1*, and their references (Čyras and Lachmayer 2018a)

($\rightarrow^{tr}$) (see Fig. 15.2). The relations hold between the entities and express the semantics of *L*.

Norms 1 The next entity within *L* is a norm (denoted by *N*). There are several levels of norms. The first level (*Norms 1*) comprises norms about facts, $N^1(FC)$, and fakes, $N^1(FK)$ (see Fig. 15.3).

The following are examples of cases which can be created:

1. $N^1(FC)$ means a commandment to establish a fact *FC*. For instance, *N (door_closed)*, represents a commandment to close the door. Closing the door is a compliant action. This type of norm refers to *Fact* (see Fig. 15.3).
2. $N^1(\neg FC)$ means a prohibition of a fact *FC*. For instance, *N(¬door_closed)*, means a prohibition on closing the door. Opening the door is a compliant action. This type of norm also refers to *Fact*.
3. $N^1(FK)$ means a commandment to establish a fake *FK*. As an example, imagine a community of liars. This type of norm refers to *Fake*.
4. $N^1(\neg FK)$ means a prohibition of a fake. This is a normal case. In general, fake facts are prohibited. For instance, news with false content is prohibited; the use of counterfeit money is also prohibited. This type of norm refers to *Fake*.
5. $\neg N^1(FC)$ means an absence of commandment to establish a fact *FC*. We hold that an absence of a norm about a fact weakly implies a norm about a fake. As an example, we suppose a world with one door, and suppose that the door is closed. Hence, the proposition "*'The door is closed'* is a fact" is true. Suppose that

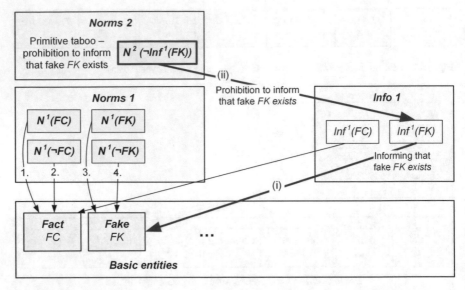

Fig. 15.4 Primitive taboos *Norms 2* and *Info 1* added to Fig. 15.3 (Čyras and Lachmayer 2018a)

$\neg N^1(door\_closed)$ holds in this world. The latter means the absence of any commandment to close the door. Next, suppose a fake news report of *'The door is opened'*. However, nobody is obliged to react to this fake, because of the absence of any commandment to close the door. In this sense, the fake is compliant in this world. Therefore we hold that the type $\neg N^1(FC)$ refers to *Fake*.

We do not explore case 5. It is important only to focus on cases 1 and 2, which refer to *Fact*, and cases 3 and 4, which refer to *Fake*.

Info 1 *and* Norms 2 Information is next entity in *L* to be explored. Information about *X* is denoted by *Inf(X)*. More precisely, the latter means the output of an act of informing about *X*. Information is primarily about facts, fakes and norms. The first-level information, *Info 1*, firstly comprises informing that *FC* exists as a fact, denoted by $Inf^1(FC)$, or, secondly, informing that *FK* exists as a fake, denoted by $Inf^1(FK)$ (see link (i) in Fig. 15.4). This can be treated as follows. Given a (news) statement *X*, the act of informing Inf^1 produces a flag (or a tag) which means that *X* is either of true content (thus assigning *X* to *Facts*) or false content (thus assigning *X* to *Fakes*).

Second-level norms, *Norms 2*, formalise primitive taboos (see Fig. 15.4). Here, norms are of the type

$$N^2\left(\neg Inf^1(FK)\right) \tag{15.3}$$

This means a prohibition N^2 to inform that *FK* is a fake (see link (ii) in Fig. 15.4). Hence, *Norms 2* secure fakes. Note that (Eq. 15.3) above coincides with the right-hand side of (Eq. 15.1) after substituting *X* with *FK*. Fakes flourish (on the basic

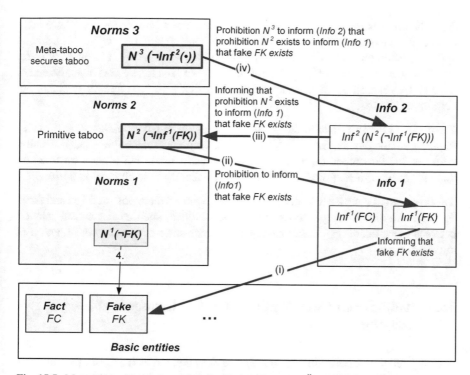

Fig. 15.5 Meta-taboos *Norms 3* and *Info 2* added to Fig. 15.4 (Čyras and Lachmayer 2018a)

level) because they are secured by *Norms 2*. Recall "All that is necessary for the triumph of evil is that good men do nothing".[8] Therefore *Norms 2* can be evaluated as evil.

Info 2 *and* Norms 3*: Meta-Taboo* The second level of information, *Info 2*, consists of information about primitive taboos (see link (iii) in Fig. 15.5). Indeed, $Inf^2(N^2(\neg Inf^1(FK))$ means an act of informing that a prohibition N^2 exists against informing Inf^1 that a fake FK exists.

The third-level norms, *Norms 3*, formalise meta-taboos. Here the norms are of type $N^3(\neg Inf^2(\bullet))$. This means a prohibition N^3 on informing Inf^2 about anything (see link (iv) in Fig. 15.5). Specifically, *Norms 3* comprise a prohibition N^3 to inform, *Info 2*, that a prohibition N^2 exists to inform, *Info 1*, that a fake FK exists. Thus a meta-taboo secures a primitive taboo (see the top-down path (iv)–(iii)–(ii)–(i) in Fig. 15.5).

Taboo on Fact Taboo on fact and taboo on fake form a duality. A taboo on a fact FC, denoted by *Taboo(FC)*, means a prohibition on informing that FC holds as a

---

[8]https://en.wikiquote.org/wiki/Edmund_Burke.

fact. The proof is based on the idea that FC being a fact implies that $\neg FC$ is a fake. Indeed, the content of FC being true implies that the content of $\neg FC$ is false. Let us apply the taboo on fakes, (Eq. 15.3), and substitute FK with $\neg FC$ to obtain $N^2(\neg Inf^1(\neg FC))$; this reads 'A prohibition to inform that $\neg FC$ is a fake'. This is equivalent to reading 'A prohibition to inform that FC is a fact'. This paragraph explains the definition (Eq. 15.1).

Example   In the fairy tale, a fact is that the emperor is naked. A taboo is formally imposed on this fact as a norm $N^2(\neg Inf^1(\text{'The emperor is naked' is a fact}))$. Dually, a fake is that the emperor is wearing new clothes. A taboo is formally imposed on this fake as a norm $N^2(\neg Inf^1(\text{'The emperor is wearing new clothes' is a fake}))$.

Taboo on Any Basic Entity   Above, we have explored the taboo on fakes and facts. A taboo can also be imposed on other basic entities, such as the causal relation between facts, teleology of actions, equality of meaning of facts, transformation of meaning, etc.

15.4   Taboo on a Combination of Three Elements of a Relation

A binary relation R between two sets S_1 and S_2 is defined as a subset of a Cartesian product $R \subset S_1 \times S_2$. For any $x \in S_1$ and $y \in S_2$ we write xRy to abbreviate $(x,y) \in R$. Elements of the set R are pairs (x,y).

Several meanings can be assigned to a taboo on the causal relation $A \rightarrow^c E$ between a fact A and an effect E. The original meaning is a prohibition to inform that A causes E. The second idea is a prohibition to inform about the fact A only, $Taboo(A)$. The third meaning is a prohibition to inform about the effect E, $Taboo(E)$, and fourthly, a prohibition to inform about the causality relationship $\rightarrow^c$ (its intentional description), $Taboo(\rightarrow^c)$. The last meaning appears, for example, in the case of a fake official version that the relation $A \rightarrow^c E$ is accidental or a correlation, in other words, the causality $\rightarrow^c$ is simply a mystery of faith (mysterium fidei).

The last taboo, $Taboo(\rightarrow^c)$, can appear, for example, in a network of facts, effects and other entities, such as actions, goals, teleological relations, etc. Suppose a taboo exists on the relation $A^- \rightarrow^c E^-$. To camouflage this taboo, a teleological relation $B^+ \rightarrow^{te} G^+$ can be introduced, where the goal G^+ is evaluated positively (see Fig. 15.6). Additionally, a fake official version can be introduced that the effect E^- is caused by a certain fact B^+. Thus the principle "the end justifies the means" is followed.

15.5   Related Work on Pluralistic Ignorance

We have modelled the meaning of Andersen's fable as a taboo on speaking that the emperor is naked. This tale illustrates the phenomenon of pluralistic ignorance, which defined as a situation where "no one believes, but everyone thinks that

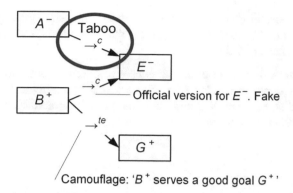

Fig. 15.6 A taboo on a causal relationship $A^- \rightarrow^c E^-$ is camouflaged in three steps, with a teleological relation $\rightarrow^{te}$ between B^+ and a certain goal G^+, which is evaluated positively: (1) in fact, both A^- and E^- are evaluated negatively; (2) therefore, the official version is announced that a certain cause B^+, which is evaluated positively, causes E^-; 3) a camouflage is that B^+ serves a good goal G^+, which outweighs E^- (Čyras and Lachmayer 2018a)

everyone else believes" and is mainly studied in social psychology. Hansen (2011) describes pluralistic ignorance as "the phenomenon where a group of people shares a false belief about the beliefs, norms, actions or thoughts of the other group members" and formalises it using epistemic/doxastic logic (based on plausibility models). Hansen focuses on the question of what it takes to dissolve the phenomenon, and talks about the dynamics of knowledge and beliefs of a group of agents. Public announcements are the simplest form of actions. In addition to Andersen's fable, Hansen provides classical examples including the "questions in a classroom".[9] Hansen formulates examples in terms of beliefs, but notes that pluralistic ignorance is often defined in terms of norms, for example, "a situation where a majority of group members privately reject a norm, but assume (incorrectly) that most others accept it" (see Centola et al. 2005). The latter also note that "It is not hard to find everyday examples of this fable in the academic kingdom. We can all think of prestigious scholars who are widely proclaimed as having the most brilliant new ideas, yet privately, people find the work entirely incomprehensible". Centola et al. study the "willingness to feign support for a public lie" and provide further examples.[10]

---

[9] "[T]he classroom example in which, after having presented the students with difficult material, the teacher asks them whether they have any questions. Even though most students do not understand the material they may not ask any questions. All the students interpret the lack of questions from the other students as a sign that they understood the material, and to avoid being publicly displayed as the stupid one, they dare not ask questions themselves. In this case the students are ignorant with respect to some facts, but believe that the rest of the students are not ignorant about the facts" (Hansen 2011).

[10] "It is not difficult to find other familiar examples of compliance with, and enforcement of, privately unpopular norms: 1. the exposure of the "politically incorrect" by the righteously indignant who thereby affirm their own moral integrity; 2. gossiping about a social *faux pas* by

We would model the classroom example with a primitive taboo on questions, that is, a norm that prohibits students from saying that they have questions. The fact is that students do have questions.

Conclusion Modelling taboo in this chapter gives rise to a terminological framework, which is depicted in Fig. 15.5. Three levels of norms and two levels of information are singled out. We introduce the terms 'primitive taboo' and 'meta-taboo', which secures the former.

References

Attridge J (2014) 'A taboo on the mention of taboo': taciturnity and Englishness in Parade's end and André Maurois' Les silences du colonel Bramble. Int Ford Madox Ford Stud 13:23–35

Broyde MJ (2002) Informing on others for violating American law: a Jewish law view. J Halacha Contemp Soc. http://www.jlaw.com/Articles/mesiralaw2.html. Accessed 15 Dec 2022

Centola D, Willer R, Macy M (2005) The emperor's dilemma: a computational model of self-enforcing norms. Am J Sociol 110(4):1009–1040. https://doi.org/10.1086/427321

Čyras V, Lachmayer F (2018a) Legal taboos. Jusletter IT, 22 February 2018. https://jusletter-it.weblaw.ch/issues/2018/IRIS/legal-taboos_483f370f96.html. Accessed 15 Dec 2022

Čyras V, Lachmayer F (2018b) Formalising taboo as a prohibition on informing. In: Lupeikiene A, Matulevičius R, Vasilecas O (eds) Baltic DB&IS 2018 joint proceedings of the conference forum and doctoral consortium, CEUR workshop proceedings, vol. 2158. https://ceur-ws.org/Vol-2158/paper6.pdf. Accessed 15 Dec 2022

Duschinsky R (2014) Taboo, overview. In: Teo T (ed) Encyclopedia of critical psychology. Springer, New York, pp 1921–1923. https://doi.org/10.1007/978-1-4614-5583-7_553

Freud S (2001) Totem and taboo, 2nd edn [1919]. Routledge. German original: Totem und Tabu, 1913

Hansen JU (2011) A logic-based approach to pluralistic ignorance. In: Academia.edu, https://www.academia.edu/1894486/A_Logic_Based_Approach_to_Pluralistic_Ignorance.   Accessed 15 Dec 2022

Kelsen H (1967) Pure theory of law, 2nd edn (trans: Knight M) (Reine Rechtslehre, 2. Auflage. Deuticke, Wien 1960). University of California Press, Berkeley

Steiner F (1956) Taboo. Cohen & West, London

---

snobs anxious to affirm their own cultural sophistication; 3. public adoration of a bully by fearful schoolboys who do not want to become the next victim; 4. "luxury fever" [...] among status seekers who purchase $50 cigars, $17,000 wristwatches, and $3 million bras, in an arms race of conspicuous consumption and one-upmanship that leaves the contestants no happier but perhaps a bit less affluent" (Centola et al. 2005).

Part IV
Text–Document

Chapter 16
Dual Textuality of Law

16.1 Textuality of Law

This chapter addresses the textual granularity of representation of law. Thus, both law and legal documentation are concerned. The word granularity questions what the smallest entity is. Furthermore, two standpoints are concerned—law and legal informatics—and building a bridge between these two realms is discussed.

This chapter is related to written language, and not speech. Textuality of law deals with different layers (see layers from 1 to 10 below and Fig. 16.1). In legal informatics, layers 4 to 9 are important, whereas layers 1 to 3 are not. Different applications can be built within each of the layers.

Layer 1 – Dot Dimension is zero. Dot properties such as colour may be important in a technical domain, but not in legal informatics.

Layer 2 – Letter No semantics are assigned to letters. However, in a technical domain different meanings can be assigned, for example, to letters in different fonts and sizes, such as bold or 10 pt/12 pt.

Layer 3 – Syllable Syllables are important in acoustics. They form a layer of analysis in speech processing.

Layer 4 – Word The word is a syntactical entity of the language. The word is the unit of thinking. A word is the smallest element that can be uttered in isolation with practical meaning. The word is the substrate whereas the term is a semantical entity; the term is related to its content. For example, numbers: there are Arabic numbers (1, 2, 3, etc.), Roman numbers (I, II, III, etc.), or numbers on a dice (•, ••, •••, etc.). However, in mathematics they denote the same abstractions. Ontologies are built on words, and the word is the minimal unit to translate.

Based on Čyras and Lachmayer(2019b).

V. Cyras, F. Lachmayer, *Essays on the Visualisation of Legal Informatics*, Law, Governance and Technology Series 54, https://doi.org/10.1007/978-3-031-27957-7_16

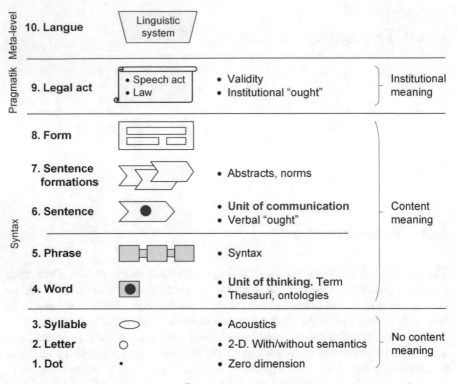

Fig. 16.1 Layers of textuality in law (Čyras and Lachmayer 2019)

Layer 5 – Phrase In linguistic analysis, a phrase is a group of words that functions as a constituent in the syntax of a sentence. Phrases are more important in professional languages and legitimation than in common language. A phrase, its synonyms, and translations can be distinguished.

Layer 6 – Sentence The sentence is the unit of communication. The sentence can serve as a unit of legal documentation (see e.g. Reimer (2008) about the Tasmanian legislation[1]). In mark-up languages such as XML, sentences are separated.

Layer 7 – Sentence Formation A sentence formation is a kind of formal sentence configurations, such as abstracts, head notes, and even norms. Sentence formations are not completely standardized in the legal domain. In arts, Haiku is an example. (Haiku is a very short Japanese poem with seventeen syllables and three verses.)

Layer 8 – Form (Formular) This is a more standardized formation of fields (see e.g. Gantner 2010). Forms can be represented in mark-up languages; an example is a paragraph.

---

[1] https://www.legislation.tas.gov.au/.

Layer 9 – Legal Act Here, speech acts are also comprised. Institutional meaning is assigned on this layer, and as such pragmatics is a characteristic. The meaning of the word 'ought' is raised from grammatical meaning to legal meaning. A legal act is a container that comprises its institutional meaning and content meaning.

Layer 10 – Langue This is a meta-level. Langue is viewed as a linguistic system; you speak in parole that is ruled by the rules of langue.

Layers 1 to 3 have no content meaning, whereas layers 4 to 8 are attributed to content meaning and therefore are most important for legal informatics. Different software systems can be built with each layer and various informational processes can be computerised. For example, ontologies traditionally concern words (layer 4), but they can also be built on phrases (layer 5).

16.2 Legal Informatics: A Bridge from Law to Its Representation in Computer

Legal documentation is not equal to legal informatics. Legal informatics is a science concerned with bridging law and legal documentation. Hence, a transformation 'law → legal documentation' is studied. Legal documentation speaks about different representations of law. Here, a duality of word and sentence has to be taken into account: the word is the unit of thinking, whereas the sentence is the unit of communication.

We distinguish the following representations of law:

- A – *Document representation.* The granularity question is a theme: what is the smallest unit—a sentence, a paragraph, or a document?
- B – *Syntactic representation.* Is it represented with a text again, a notation of formal logic, a mark-up language, or a graphical notation?
- C – *Semantic representation.* It deals, among other issues, with the relation between the factual and the normative.
- D – *Pragmatic representation.* It concerns a relation between an act of legal information and a legal act. Treating an authentic electronic document as a legal act is a theme, that is, layer 9 = representation D.

Building a bridge from law to legal informatics is about connecting layers 1 to 10 with representations A to D (see Fig. 16.2).

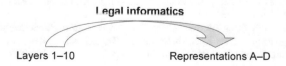

Fig. 16.2 Legal informatics is a science concerned with building a bridge from law to representation of law (Čyras and Lachmayer 2019)

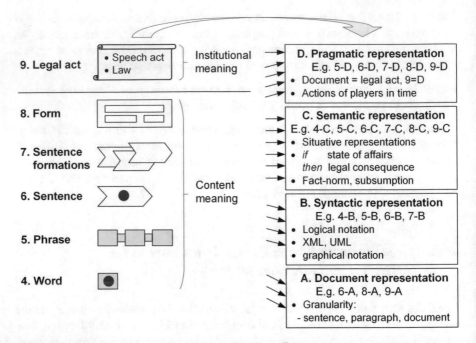

Fig. 16.3 Links between law and representations of law (Čyras and Lachmayer 2019)

Different links between layers 1–10 and representations A–D can be distinguished (see Fig. 16.3). For example, while speaking about document representation A, different granularity options can be studied: sentence (the link from layer 7 to representation A, 7-A for short), form (link 8-A), or document (link 9-A). While speaking about semantic representations, if-then rules, subsumption and situational representations are tackled. While speaking about pragmatic representation, the theme of authentic electronic documents is tackled (link 9-D, which can be marked with the identity 9=D).

References

Čyras F, Lachmayer F (2019) Dual textuality of law. Jusletter IT, 21 February 2019. https://jusletter-it.weblaw.ch/issues/2019/IRIS/dual-textuality-of-l_86b90aefea.html.   Accessed 15 Dec 2022

Gantner F (2010) Theorie der juristischen Formulare. Schriften zur Rechtstheorie, Heft 252. Duncker & Humblot, Berlin

Reimer S (2008) Rechtssetzung zwischen Österreich und Tasmanien. In: Schweighofer E et al (eds) Komplexitätsgrenzen der Rechtsinformatik. Tagungsband des 11. Internationalen Rechtsinformatik Symposions IRIS 2008. Boorberg, Stuttgart, pp 277–286

Chapter 17
Legal Norms and Legal Institutions as a Challenge for Legal Informatics

17.1 Impact of Legal Informatics from Periphery to the Centre of Law

Although legal informatics is on the periphery of jurisprudence, it can make a significant impact on the centre in respect of legal dogmatics. We believe that the impact from legal informatics can be reached through situational legal visualisation and situational terms, for example, by correcting the boundaries of legal terms. The latter is the subject matter of legal theory and hence contributes to the centre of jurisprudence.

This chapter makes analogy between Begriffsjurisprudenz (jurisprudence of concepts) in the nineteenth century and legal ontologies of the present, and stresses a situational treatment of law in addition to a normative one. Therefore both situational contents and institutional contents are important when representing legal semantics within legal informatics. However, the differences between legal norms, texts and documents have to be taken into account. Legal norms are interpretative products whereas legal documents are tangible products and are represented according to documentary rules. The themes of granularity and metadata remain aside from the norm–institution relationship but emerge in the law–legal informatics relationship. The granularity question, "What is the smallest entity?", can have different answers in legal documentation: the whole text of a law, an article, a paragraph, a sentence, a word (legal term) or even a symbol.

Legal dogmatics and legal theory lie at the centre of jurisprudence and both have their own expansion. Endogenous developments in judicature, for example, legal personality (e-persons, e-identity) etc. have a significant impact on jurisprudence. Legal theory also has its thematic mainstream. In contrast to the centre, there are

Based on Čyras and Lachmayer (2013).

© The Author(s), under exclusive license to Springer Nature Switzerland AG 2023
V. Cyras, F. Lachmayer, *Essays on the Visualisation of Legal Informatics*, Law, Governance and Technology Series 54,
https://doi.org/10.1007/978-3-031-27957-7_17

peripheral sciences such as legal philosophy, legal psychology, legal sociology, legal logic and legal informatics which form the surroundings.

There is a certain dialectic between the centre and the periphery. A specific feature is that innovations often and unexpectedly come from the periphery. An example is Colette Brunschwig's work (2011) on multisensory law[1], which brings legal psychology into service. Her research is more important to legal informatics than to legal theory. The reason is that legal machines need to imitate human beings in order to be effective in law enforcement. Humans perceive legally significant information with all of their senses and react accordingly. Therefore legal machines ought also to perceive and react multisensorily. Hence, Brunschwig's research in legal psychology has a direct impact on legal informatics.

Legal logic is another aspect of centre–periphery relations. Legal logic aims to reconstruct law, however, the way is not easy. The high expectations of the 1950s have not been achieved. Hence, a reconstruction of law in a shallow model is not fully successful. But there are partial models. One question is whether law is characterised by a special kind of formal logic or by applications of general logics.

We distinguish between applications of formal logic and specific legal notations. A notation is a writing system and not logic. Legal notations play the role of artificial languages. These are similar to chemical formula notations that are neither logic nor natural languages. However, there are connections between logic and notations, and this is a research field for legal informatics.

Although legal informatics appears peripheral, it is important for representing the law, namely, in the form of legal information. The law is represented by legal documents and this is part of legal culture. Nowadays legal information and informational processes are becoming more important than in past decades. For example, in Austria thousands of documents are added to the legal corpus database each month, and millions of legal documents are queried in RIS.[2] Legal informatics has moved from technical periphery to a power in practice, hence acquiring a new quality and becoming a player in the legal community. A subsequent step is that the challenges of legal informatics will affect law and legal dogmatics. This can happen through the judicature and shaping legal documents. Hence, the themes of the periphery can be displaced increasingly to the centre.

---

[1] "Multisensory" implies that, at all times, more than one stimulus is involved in affecting a human being (Brunschwig 2011), p. 581. Note the definition of the discipline is not trivial. Brunschwig writes: "Modifying the noun "law," the adjective "multisensory" refers to which kind of law or which law is at stake. The law in question is not, for instance, copyright law, family law, or penal law, but another legal discipline, that is, multisensory law. The term "multisensory law" not only has terminological implications, but also concerns its subject matter and cognitive interest" (Brunschwig 2011), p. 591.

[2] RIS, the Legal Information System of the Republic of Austria (see https://www.ris.bka.gv.at).

Fig. 17.1 Analogy of
methods in
Begriffsjurisprudenz and
legal ontologies (Čyras and
Lachmayer 2013)

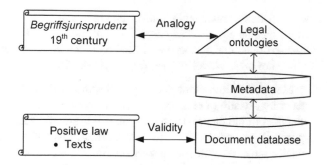

17.2   Legal Texts and Legal Documents

In legal informatics it is important to distinguish between legal text and legal
document (see Fig. 17.1). A legal text expresses the meaning of a legal act, such
as of a law or a court judgment, and is part of the legal realm, the Ought. On the other
hand, a legal document is part of the legal documentation realm that is determined by
legal technology. In modern legislation, legal documents include the medium of
electronic documents. However, this is only a change of substrate. From the view of
the model, there remains a difference between the legal text and the (electronic) legal
document. This can be seen in different treatments of corresponding structural parts.
Legal texts are structured according to legal rules, and namely, into sections, articles,
items, clauses, etc. On the other hand, (electronic) legal documents are structured
according to documentary rules, for example, the markup rules of XML.

Legal validity is distinguished from documentary validity. Legal validity, that is,
the validity of a legal text, such as a norm or a law, is treated according to "*ideell
existence*" (see Kelsen). On the other hand, documentary validity, that is, the validity
of a legal document in a legal database, is determined by the rules of electronic legal
documents. The dates of coming into effect and lapse are represented explicitly in a
legal document. In summary, documentary validity is determined by database time
events including the time of successfully obtaining an answer to a query.

The following is a side effect of distinguishing between legal validity and
documentary validity. Deciding whether a norm is valid or not valid can rest, on
the one hand, on a legal act and a legal text and, on the other hand, on a legal
document. Norms are mental constructs; however, documentary validity can also be
applied here. Legal reality thus demonstrates that a norm becomes valid when a
corresponding (electronic) legal document is uploaded to the database.

Metadata   The importance of metadata has emerged from the beginnings of legal
documentation in the European Union in the 1970s (currently see EUR-Lex[3]).
Metadata constitutes supplementary information that comes with documentary
structures and is primarily comprised of categories. In the beginning, categories

---

[3] Access to European Union law, https://eur-lex.europa.eu/.

were written as metadata within documents and could be handled separately. Nowadays metadata build a separate layer in documentation and are used more widely than in document management. Metadata can be represented in markup languages which are more powerful than former categories.

Metadata is important not only in the production of legal documents but also in searching, where queries are allowed to contain various combinations of tags. For example, in judicature databases you can search for full texts, abstracts, judgments, specific legal sentences, words, etc. A thesaurus allows queries in more abstract or specific terms than the relevant documents may contain. Hence, metadata contributes to a separate model of documents, which can be employed in searching.

Metadata contributes to making references. References can be made more explicit and rich using XML. Separate clauses of laws can be referenced, first, with cases and, second, with commentaries, in electronic commentaries of laws. Such XML structures form a separate layer and provide various opportunities for document management including search and actualisation. A reference is a kind of relationship. A variety of relationships comprises strong logical relations as well as weak relations.

Begriffsjurisprudenz and Ontologies   From the point of view of legal informatics, supplementing legal documents with metadata is insufficient. A tendency to build legal thesauruses has its roots in the 19th century Begriffsjurisprudenz.[4] Georg Puchta developed a legal system according to a pyramid of legal terms. A century later, since the 1990s, this research has come to be called legal ontologies. Here the term 'an ontology' is understood as in computing. It is distinguished from an uncountable noun 'Ontology' that refers to the branch of philosophy which deals with the nature and structure of reality. You can start with a definition that an ontology is a formal, explicit specification of a shared conceptualisation. Then you can arrive at a more formal definition that an ontology is a logical theory consisting of a set of formulas, designed so that the set of its models approximates the set of intended models (see Guarino et al. 2009). An ontology comprises term hierarchies, relations and attributes that makes it possible to reuse this knowledge for automated applications. Ontologies aim to collect legal terms into a semantic structure that comprises axioms about the terms. Nowadays see, for example, MetaLex[5] and research at the Leibniz Center for Law of the University of Amsterdam (see e.g. Breuker and Hoekstra 2011) and the CIRSFID Centre of the University of Bologna.[6]

---

[4] Jurisprudence of concepts. The term was coined by Rudolph von Jhering (see Wikipedia, http://de.wikipedia.org/wiki/Begriffsjurisprudenz).

[5] MetaLex stands for "Open XML Interchange Format for Legal and Legislative Resources". It concerns metadata standardization. The owner is CEN, European Committee for Standartization (see https://joinup.ec.europa.eu/solution/cen-metalex/about).

[6] https://site.unibo.it/cirsfid/it; especially see research by Giovanni Sartor and Monica Palmirani.

Begriffsjurisprudenz used metaphors such as vitality, pyramid (Begriffspyramide), etc., which differ from more formalised representations such as logic, informational techniques and relationships in modern ontologies. Of course, in the 19th century there was no emphasis on searching. However, the method was not so different. The aim was to organise modally indifferent substrate into a semantic structure.

17.3 Legal Norms and Legal Documents

The notion of legal norm is not as simple as it may appear from the first impression of the meaning in natural language. A legal institution comprises several norms. These norms are a modally indifferent substrate with respect to the legal institution. Legal texts are not made of norms but of structural arrangement units such as parts, sections, paragraphs, sentences, etc. Moreover, legal norm is not a primary elementary notion of law. Legal documents as a form of legal information do not know the notion of norm. Legal documents reproduce the structural arrangement units of legal texts and contain their own document units, for example, in XML.

According to Kelsen, legal norms belong to law whereas legal sentences belong to science, which describes the norms (see Fig. 17.2). Legal dogmatics holds that legal norm is a mental product. It extracts, reconstructs and formulates the content, that is, the legal meaning of a norm. A norm is obtained by interpreting legal text. A paragraph can contain several norms of behaviour or a norm can continue through several paragraphs, part here part there (see also Palmer 1997, pp. 27 ff). As a basic principle, legal norms are formulated in a natural language. A simple form is 'if A then B'. This is a methodological step which precedes formalisation.

The structural analysis consists in the rewriting of rules as logical statements or conceptual structures. In both cases, paper and electronic representations can be used. Without appropriate and fine-tuned conceptual structures and rule frames, such as decision trees, the application of rules remains cumbersome and time-consuming. For any well-defined process, this analysis is indispensable for automation. Further, (semi-)automated linguistic methods can be very helpful.

Fig. 17.2 Relationships between the notions of legal norm, legal text and legal document (Čyras and Lachmayer 2013)

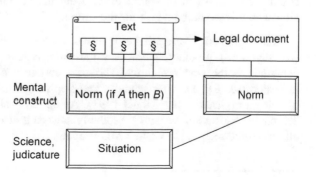

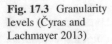

Fig. 17.3 Granularity levels (Čyras and Lachmayer 2013)

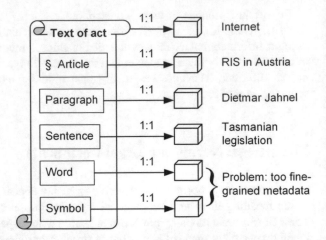

Institutional and Situational Contents of Law Besides legal norms as mental constructs, legal institutions and situations can be extracted interpretatively from legal texts. Institutional thinking is also a mental construct and is obtained through interpretation. This clearly shows in Roman law, where institutions make a systematic layer which is separated systematically from legal sources such as legal gestures.

The institutional and situational layers of the contents of law that are mental constructs are not dealt with explicitly in legal texts, but through interpretation within semantic spaces of law. Therefore there is no essential difference between a normative and a situational treatment of law. Both are interpretative, furthermore, they enter with the text, go through the text and aim to structure semantic spaces of law. When reconstructing law in legal informatics, it is important not only to capture legal texts in legal documents, but also to represent semantic spaces of law. This means that both normative contents and situational contents are important to represent legal semantic spaces within legal informatics.

Granularity There are structures in the background which are independent from the norm–institution relationship but which are important for the functioning of legal documentation, namely, for back-office software systems. Back-office contrasts with front-office which is concerned with the user-computer interaction. The granularity could produce structures which differ from the current documentary structures. However, this would be a task for the future.

The whole text of a regulation is nowadays a primary option in legal databases (see Fig. 17.3). Another option is a particular article of a regulation. In RIS, a paragraph is the smallest entity. The next option is a paragraph, a clause or a provision (see e.g. Dietmar Jahnel's text-step program of the federal constitution of Austria in Schäffer and Jahnel 1991). An option is also a sentence (see e.g. the Tasmanian legislation website[7]). Probably, a word is also an option. Automation of all this would require elaborate XML structures.

---

[7] https://www.legislation.tas.gov.au/.

Smaller entities provide flexibility in legal information systems. A big document can be synthesized from its parts. However, making entities too small significantly increases the amount of metadata. On the one hand, too fine-grained granularity may cause a metadata redundancy problem. On the other hand, too coarse-grained granularity may cause a problem while making amendments. Probably a middle level, such as the paragraph granularity, is the most reasonable happy medium.

17.4 Notations for Legal Norms

As noted previously, legal texts are not structured in the units of norms. In other words, a legal norm is neither a structural element of a legal text nor of a legal document. A norm is a product of interpretation. This is conducted by legal sciences, courts and the judicature. However, norms are linguistically formulated and jurists are linguistically-oriented. For example, this can be observed in a speech of a judge. A legal provision may be collected from several places.

A notation is the next question. A generally accepted one is 'if A then B', $A{\rightarrow}B$ or $N(A/B)$, which means "when A then ought to the case that B"; also read "if *condition* then *normative position*" (see Fig. 17.4). There are multiple attempts to represent legal norms as rules in a Prolog-like notation (see e.g. Sergot 1991).

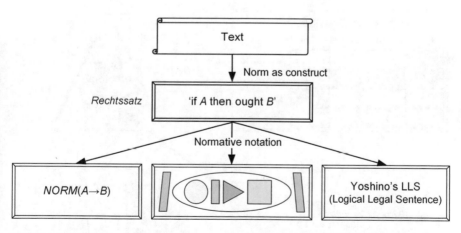

Fig. 17.4 Relationships between a legal text, a legal norm as an interpretative product which is linguistically formulated, and norm's representations in a certain notation (Čyras and Lachmayer 2013)

17.5   Modally Indifferent Substrate and Representing Normativity in Situations

Granularity could be viewed in connection with the modally indifferent substrate (MIS). According to Kelsen, Ought is a mode that comprises MISs. In contrast, we think that, in addition to legal norms, legal terms can be viewed as a separate layer of self-dependent entities of law. A paradigm shift in the granularity is that, in addition to norms, the central legal elements comprise legal terms.

Suppose an act A is prescribed to the addressee of a norm. This can be expressed as $O(A)$. In our view, O as well as A appears in a logical context. Therefore, we can treat the mode of obligation, O, abstractly (see arrow (1) in Fig. 17.5). A legal term, A, is viewed in relationship to other legal terms (see arrow (2) in Fig. 17.5).

Situational Elements   An idea we put forward in this chapter is also to consider situational terms besides normative terms. We hold that situational elements should build a separate layer that is supported by institutional elements, which are taken from ontologies, see arrow (3) in Fig. 17.5. Hence, a parallel virtual legal world shall be expanded with a normative notation for situations. A reason emerges from legal practice. Besides ex-post analysis and case law, which, for example, is supported by RIS, there is ex-ante analysis, which is supported by oesterreich.gv.at. The two forms—ex-post and ex-ante—correspond to two forms of legal thinking. Cases are at the core of jurists' professional legal thinking. A case is closed and a wrong behaviour cannot be reiterated in order to make a right choice. Lawyers (not

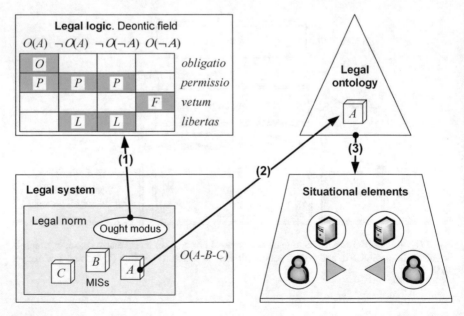

Fig. 17.5 Modally indifferent substrate, deontic field and situational terms (Čyras and Lachmayer 2013)

laypeople) deal with cases whereas laypeople think of situations. A situation is a type, it is open and a layperson may seek advice on the behaviour to adopt. A choice is possible. Therefore situational representations serve ordinary citizens. Hence, expanding legal ontologies from normative terms to situational terms is both an important theoretical problem for legal science and a practical one.

17.6 A Film Example: Situational Visualisation of a Court Judgment

Films serve well for situational visualisation (see, for example, the Tele-Jura[8] project). An example also is "Menzi-Muck Timber Case – the Film!".[9] This four-minute film takes a familiar case (BGE 129 III 181). In this 2002 decision, the Swiss Federal Court defined criteria to distinguish between favour (Gefälligkeit), gratuitous contract (unentgeltlicher Auftrag), negotiorum gestio (Geschäftsführung ohne Auftrag, GoA) and the claim to compensation by a person who gave voluntary help to another (Schadenersatzanspruch der unentgeltlich helfenden Person).

In the film, the type of situation is visualised with a Playmobil excavator–calf set (see Fig. 17.6, left). The film shows and explains the decision tree (see Fig. 17.6, right), which is employed by the visualised judge to make the judgment. The film is designed for educational purposes and can be used in electronic learning via the internet. To explain the law, clear graphic style descriptions are employed. Hence, situational visualisation is used in the film for multisensory learning.

The judgment in the "Menzi-Muck Timber" case demonstrates an influence from the periphery. The impact on the centre is that the boundaries of standards are made more precise. Standards often come from the periphery. Hence, the periphery–centre dialectic produces a progressive step.

The use of plastic characters and not real ones is important because a kind of relaxed mood is produced in this way, which is significant from a semiotic point of view. Cognition is easier in an abstract situation. The film represents a generalisation of the judgment in a concrete case.

We believe that in the future situational visualisations will influence normative representation of law in two directions: legal ontologies (see Chap. 19 Sect. 19.6)

---

[8]Tele-Jura is a project by R. Czupryniak, M. Frohn, P. Reineke, and S. Trebeß. Films run parallel to a course by Matthias Frohn at the Institute of International Private Law of the Free University of Berlin (http://www.telejura.de/).

[9]https://www.youtube.com/watch?v=KI7zeuayum4. The case concerned the claim for damages suffered by the person who gratuitously helps another. A farmer helped a neighbouring farmer to attach large logs to a Menzi Muck excavator for transport. The former fell from the ladder without any third party being at fault and was gravely injured. Is this a question of gratuitous contract, favour or negotiorum gestio? The distinction is relevant because only negotiorum gestio entitled him to compensation. The Federal Court limited the bases for claims.

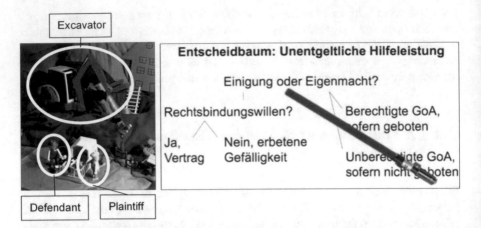

Fig. 17.6 A film visualisation of the "Menzi-Muck Timber" case of the Swiss Federal Court. On the right a decision tree shows criteria to distinguish between favour, gratuitous contract, negotiorum gestio (Geschäftsführung ohne Auftrag, GoA), and the claim to compensation by a person who gave voluntary help to another (Čyras and Lachmayer 2013)

and parallel virtual legal worlds. Figurative situational imaginary legal worlds can be implemented in three-dimensional online virtual worlds.

References

Brunschwig CR (2011) Multisensory law and legal informatics – a comparison of how these legal disciplines relate to visual law. In: Geist A, Brunschwig CR, Lachmayer F, Schefbeck G (eds) Strukturierung der Juristischen Semantik – structuring legal semantics. Editions Weblaw, Bern, pp 573–667

Breuker J, Hoekstra R (2011) A cognitive science perspective on legal ontologies. In: Sartor G, Casanovas P, Biasiotti MA, Fernández-Barrera M (eds) Approaches to legal ontologies. Law, governance and technology series, vol 1. Springer, Dordrecht, pp 69–81. https://doi.org/10. 1007/978-94-007-0120-5_4

Čyras V, Lachmayer F (2013) Legal norms and legal institutions as a challenge for legal informatics. In: Aarnio A, Hoeren T, Paulson SL, Schulte M, Wyduckel D (eds) Positivität, Normativität und Institutionalität des Rechts: Festschrift für Werner Krawietz zum 80. Geburtstag. Duncker & Humblot, Berlin, pp 581–592

Guarino N, Oberle D, Staab S (2009) What is an ontology? In: Staab S, Studer R (eds) Handbook on ontologies. Springer, Berlin, pp 1–17. https://doi.org/10.1007/978-3-540-92673-3_0

Palmer J (1997) Artificial intelligence and legal merit argument. PhD thesis. Balliol College, University of Oxford

Schäffer H, Jahnel D (1991) Ein Textstufenprogramm für Gesetzestexte. Darstellung am Beispiel des österreichischen Verfassungsgesetzes. Zeitschrift für Gesetzgebung 6(3):268–278

Sergot M (1991) The representation of law in computer programs. In: Bench-Capon TJM (ed) Knowledge-based systems and legal applications. Academic Press, pp 3–67. https://doi. org/10.1016/B978-0-12-086441-6.50006-4

Chapter 18
Different Views to Legal Information Systems: Separate Legal Meanings and Legal Sublevels

18.1 The Notion of Legal Sublevel

This chapter is concerned with the legal system and legal documentation systems, as well as their interconnectedness and introduces the idea of legal sublevels. Examples of legal sublevels are legal terms, annotations, commentaries, etc. A sublevel is treated as a representation level of the legal domain. In terms of software engineering, a sublevel can be defined as a level of infrastructural services for several domains. A key question is "What are the sublevels in law and legal informatics?". In this way, an exploratory research on the operational treatment of legal meaning is presented. The research question is based on how the legal meaning of a legal act should be represented. Different legal meanings are related to separate representations and various stakeholders view the act differently. We hold that views are related with representations. Thus different contents are revealed.

In this chapter we prefer the word 'sublevel' to 'meta-level'. The reason is that engineers understand the word 'sublevel' and do not accept 'meta-level'. In law, however, 'meta-level' would be preferred. In the word 'meta-level', we use the prefix meta with the meaning of with and across (German mit), and not higher or beyond. A legal sublevel can be defined as a representation level of the legal system.

From the standpoint of software engineering, a sublevel can be defined as a layer of infrastructural services for several domains (see Fig. 18.1). Sublevels are horizontal layers and, therefore, contrast from vertical slices. A sublevel corresponds to a subsystem and leads to a framework that comprises horizontal and vertical interfaces. Sublevels can be compared with horizontal layers of a more general matrix-shaped model, where vertical slices denote the branches of engineering and horizontal layers correspond to the features such as quality engineering, reliability engineering, safety engineering, etc.

Based on two papers: Čyras et al. (2016) and Čyras (2017).

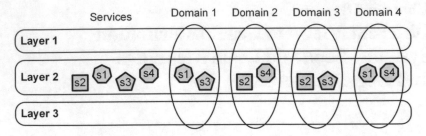

Fig. 18.1 A sublevel is defined as a layer of infrastructural services s_i (Čyras et al. 2016)

Fig. 18.2 Representing a
legal source in a legal
documentation system
(Čyras et al. 2016)

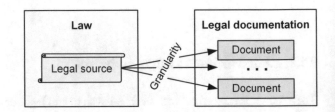

The subject matter of this study is the representation of legal meaning. The finding is that there is no unique meaning and no universal representation of a legal act. A layman's view to the legal system may comprise a sole information system, namely that of primary legal sources, such as laws. However, a legal professional's view comprises more representations. Both systems—the legal system and the legal documentation system—have their own sublevels and metadata.

We derive the idea of the legal sublevels from the granularity problem. Legal documentation does not reproduce a legal source one-to-one (see Fig. 18.2). The view is a means to master the complexity of the legal system and can be extended to the engineering of legal document systems.

This chapter can be split into two parts: sublevels in the law and sublevels in legal documentation. Section 18.2 describes a shift from a legal hierarchy to a network. Section 18.3 links the idea of legal sublevels with the notion of view. We think about the sublevels in light of views in Schweighofer's 8 views / 4 methods / 4 syntheses model (see Sect. 18.4) and project the core and peripheral areas around the legal system onto his model. Therefore Sect. 18.5 surveys the notion of view.

18.2   The Approach: Different Meanings in Distinct Representations

Software engineers may have difficulties understanding the differentiation between a fact and its legal meaning (Is and Ought). The reason is that nature and society are two distinct objects of scientific cognition, and we distinguish between natural and

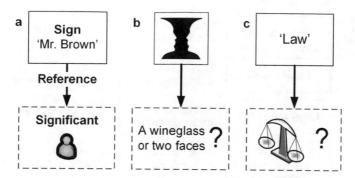

Fig. 18.3 A binary relationship of the reference between a sign and its significant (Čyras 2017)

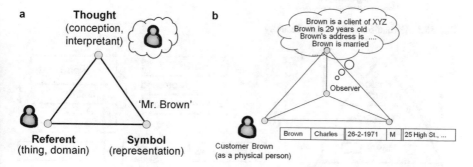

Fig. 18.4 **a** A tripartite relationship in the meaning triangle (see e.g. Sowa 2000, p. 192, and Ogden and Richards 1923, p. 11). **b** Example of the use of the FRISCO semiotic tetrahedron (adapted from Hesse and Verrijn-Stuart 2001)

social sciences. A layperson can scarcely know all the meanings of law. Therefore, most probably, she or he views the legal system as a collection of laws.

Suppose a person, a customer named Brown. The word (sign) 'Mr. Brown' refers to the real thing (significant) (see Fig. 18.3, a). However, the next graphical sign, shown in Fig. 18.3, b can be interpreted differently: a wine glass or two faces. Next, suppose that two persons—A and B—communicate about law. Law is a complex phenomenon and has multiple meanings. Therefore, most probably, A and B will have different conceptions in their minds (see Fig. 18.3, c). The problem is in making the conceptions of A and B consistent. Therefore, we arrive at the problem of representing a conception of law.

Figure 18.4 illustrates relationships between symbols, objects and meaning as a meaning triangle (a semiotic triangle by Ogden and Richards 1923). The idea is to relate the institutional meaning of a legal act with its representation. This idea follows the FRISCO semiotic tetrahedron (see Fig. 18.4, b). The tetrahedron extends the semiotic triangle by an additional actor, an interpreter who is a representer.

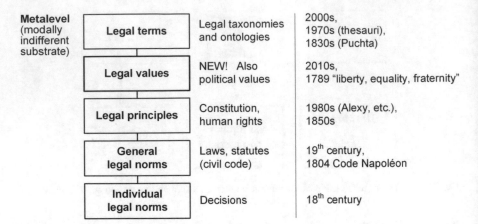

Fig. 18.5 Formation of the legal hierarchy

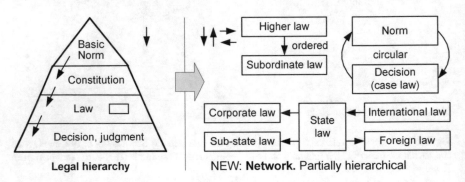

Fig. 18.6 A shift from a legal hierarchy (ordered) to a network (partially ordered) (Čyras et al. 2016)

18.3   A Shift from a Hierarchy to a Network

We do not propose to turn Kelsen's pyramid upside-down. Instead, our target is to explicate the network of legal sublevels. For example, political values are emphasised in Fig. 18.5, as they have been topical since the 2010s.

A hierarchical model of the legal system is presently too simple and strict. A network would be better suited (see Fig. 18.6). Such a network would be partially hierarchical and contain horizontal links. In addition to explicit links, implicit links are important. A network is a graph, and therefore, is a simple structure for reasoning in comparison with other formalisations such as formal logic. Paraphrasing Van Hoecke and Ost (1993), p. 1,[1] we can see a task for legal informatics to transform the

---

[1] "Econometrics, for example, attempts to transform economic science into a more 'rigorous' and hence more 'scientific' discipline by mathematical means" (Van Hoecke and Ost 1993).

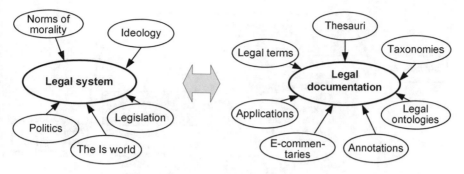

Fig. 18.7 Core–periphery subsystems around the legal system and the legal documentation system (Čyras et al. 2016).

network of sublevels into a more "scientific" discipline by mathematical means. An argument for a "network of networks" structure of the legal system can also be found in the theory of the autopoiesis of law of Karl-Heinz Ladeur (see e.g. Ladeur 1999, pp. 26, 32–35).[2]

The shift from a hierarchy also applies to legal document systems. Peripheral areas—sublevels—can be separated from the core, both in the legal system and in the document system (see Fig. 18.7). We relate the idea of a network to the interdisciplinary approach and a pluralist epistemological perspective to legal science which is advocated by Van Hoecke and Ost (1993) (see also Ost and van de Kerchove 1999).

The future "matrix of law" is discussed by Martin-Bariteau (2014), pp. 11–18. He comments about Ost, although it has been 15 years since Ost's original predictive work, and points out the distinctions of lawmaking in the information society.

18.4 Erich Schweighofer's 8 Views/4 Methods/4 Syntheses Approach

There are many stakeholders in a scenario to deal with a legal act. Each stakeholder may have a different view of the act. Each view produces a separate representation. Schweighofer's approach can be expressed using the formula *8 views + 4 methods = synthesis*. We visualise this approach in Fig. 18.8. This approach is a methodological framework to investigate legal sublevels. Schweighofer (2015) has developed new methods for the representation, analysis and synthesis of legal materials as legal data science. Legal data science, as part of legal informatics, serves as the integrative model of computer-supported representation and analysis techniques.

---

[2]Ladeur (1999) starts his study on understanding postmodern law with a pointed subtitle: "From the hierarchy of norms to the heterarchy of changing patterns of legal inter-relationships".

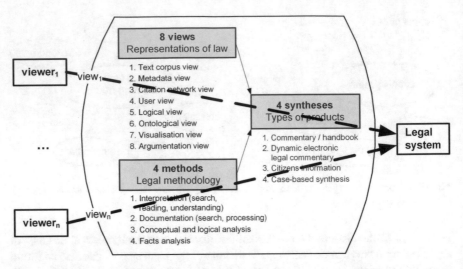

Fig. 18.8 Different perspectives of the legal system through a "lens", which comprises the 8 representations of law, the 4 methods and the 4 products (Čyras et al. 2016)

Schweighofer's model describes eight different representations of a legal system and four computer-supported methods of analysis, which lead to a synthesis, or a consolidated and structured analysis of a legal domain; this synthesis is (1) a commentary or electronic legal handbook; (2) a dynamic electronic legal commentary (DynELC); (3) a representation for citizens; or (4) a case-based synthesis. The eight views (or representations of law) are: (1) the text corpus view; (2) the metadata view; (3) the citation network view; (4) the user view; (5) the logical view; (6) the ontological view; (7) the visualisation view; and (8) the argumentation view. The four methods are: (1) interpretation (searching, reading, and understanding); (2) documentation (searching and processing); (3) structural analysis (both conceptual and logical); and (4) facts analysis.

The visualisation view is distinguished among the 8 views. Legal visualisation methods are human-oriented. The reason is that legal visualisation is primarily a means of information visualisation and serves humans. Therefore a challenge is computer-readable visualisations (i.e. computer-oriented) as well as computer-generated visualisations (human-oriented). Graphical notations should also support the formalisation of the law similarly as UML supports software development.

18.5 The Notion of a View

Lu and Conrad (2012, 2013) view the system of legal documents from the standpoint of legal search engines. However, the legal system (in a broad sense) can also be viewed from other standpoints, for instance, a software engineer's or a legal philosopher's. Thus, different perspectives (a synonym for the term 'view') emerge.

Both the legal system and the legal documentation system are systems. They can be described from the outside and the inside. A system can be described from the outside as a black box: inputs, outputs and their relation. A system is described from the inside perspective by its elements and the relationships between them. Figure 18.8 can serve as such a description.

We will compare the concept of view in Lu and Conrad's 4 views and Schweighofer's 8 views with a view in software engineering. The term 'view' denotes a representation of the law in the works by Lu and Conrad, as well as Schweighofer. Each viewer looks through a "lens", which comprises the 8 representations of law, the 4 methods, and the 4 products (see Fig. 18.8). Each viewer has his own perspective and projects the legal system onto the landscape of legal data science differently.

Lu and Conrad (2012, 2013) view the system of legal documents from the standpoint of legal search engines. However, search engines are not legal entities, and therefore, cannot be treated as stakeholders. Stakeholders are comprised of judges, document authors (e.g. West editors), search engine users (e.g. attorneys), etc.

Schweighofer considers Lu and Conrad's "4 views theory" and extends it with 4 more views: the logical view, the ontological view, the visualisation view, and the argumentation view. It should be noted that in the knowledge representation of law, it is not solely about the documentation; each view represents further insights on the law itself (Schweighofer 2015), p. 16.

Views of an Enterprise System Further, we consider an enterprise system in the role of a viewed object. Six views—the planner's, the owner's, the designer's, the builder's, the integrator's and the user's—are concerned in the Zachman framework (Sowa and Zachman 1992), which supposes that it is possible to manage an enterprise system using a multiperspective approach. Zachman's idea to decompose the system into a number of perspectives and focus areas serves as a theoretical basis for the vision-driven approach proposed by Čaplinskas (2009) (see also Sect. 24.6 in this volume). Zachman decomposes each perspective into six focus areas to be answered: what (data)? how (function)? where (network)? who (people)? when (time)? and why (motive)? Čaplinskas calls it the H3W decomposition. The concept of views is driven by the separation of concerns principle.

Five perspectives (views, levels) of the Čaplinskas' vision-driven methodological framework are: (1) business level requirements (the view of a business analyst), (2) user level requirements (the view of stakeholders), (3) IS (information system) requirements (the view of an IS analyst), (4) the requirements of IS subsystems (the view of an IS engineer), (5) software requirements (the view of a software analyst). More perspectives can also be concerned.

Conclusion The idea of core and periphery in law leads to the idea of legal sublevels. This idea contributes to the conceptualisation of the legal domain from the technological viewpoint. Such conceptualization will contrast from the jurisprudential outlines of law, where the branches of law or the functions of law (legislative, executive and judicative) play the key role. Soft law in the information society challenges "black-letter" law. To represent data and services in the legal domain, a proper conceptualisation is required. The views to a legal documentation system constitute a proper beginning.

Explicating legal sublevels contributes to the evaluative synthesis of legal decisions. Thus, explicit visual navigation through a legal information system would support the "wandering back and forth of the glance"[3] between the normative and the factual.

The sublevels of legal information should be taken into account in the engineering of legal information systems. The value lies in the explanations for engineers who analyse legal requirements and design legal machines. Various stakeholders observe different meanings that require representations in separate subsystems.

The research issues can be taken into account in a methodology for engineering. For instance, the layer of legal terminology is assigned to the ontological view and can be implemented in a separate subsystem of legal documentation. Thus, a separate layer of infrastructural services emerges. The periphery of the law can emerge in the core of legal document systems.

References

Čaplinskas A (2009) Requirements elicitation in the context of enterprise engineering: a vision driven approach. Informatica 20(3):343–368. https://doi.org/10.15388/Informatica.2009.255

Čyras V (2017) Different views on law determine the separate representations of legal meanings in information systems. Informacijos mokslai 79:58–70. https://doi.org/10.15388/Im.2017.79.11391

Čyras V, Lachmayer F, Schweighofer E (2016) Views to legal information systems and legal sublevels. In: Dregvaite G, Damasevicius R (eds) Information and software technologies. ICIST 2016. Communications in computer and information science, vol 639. Springer, Cham, pp 18–29. https://doi.org/10.1007/978-3-319-46254-7_2

Engisch K (1963) Logische Studien zur Gesetzesanwendung. Carl Winter, Heidelberg

---

[3] Karl Engisch's "Hin- und herwandern des Blickes" (Engisch 1963), p. 15 (see Pavčnik 2008).

Hesse W, Verrijn-Stuart A (2001) Towards a theory of information systems: the FRISCO approach. In: Jaakkola H et al (eds) Information modelling and knowledge bases XII. IOS Press, Amsterdam, pp 81–91

Ladeur K (1999) The theory of autopoiesis as an approach to a better understanding of postmodern law: From the hierarchy of norms to the heterarchy of changing patterns of legal inter-relationships. EUI working paper Law no. 99/3. https://cadmus.eui.eu/handle/1814/148. Accessed 15 Dec 2022

Lu Q, Conrad JG (2012) Bringing order to legal documents: an issue-based recommendation system via cluster association. In: Proceedings of the fourth international conference on knowledge engineering and ontology development (KEOD 2012). SciTePress, DL, pp 76–88

Lu Q, Conrad JG (2013) Next generation legal search – it's already here. VoxPopuLII blog, Cornell Legal Information Institute, 28 March 2013. https://blog.law.cornell.edu/voxpop/2013/03/28/next-generation-legal-search-its-already-here/. Accessed 15 Dec 2022

Martin-Bariteau F (2014) The matrix of law: from paper, to word processing, to wiki. Lex Electronica 19(1):1–23. https://www.lex-electronica.org/s/6. Accessed 15 Dec 2022

Ogden CK, Richards IA (1923) The meaning of meaning. Harcourt, Brace & World, New York

Ost F, van de Kerchove M (1999) Constructing the complexity of the law: towards a dialectic theory. In: Wintgens LJ (ed) The law in philosophical perspectives. Law and philosophy library, vol 41. Springer, Dordrecht, pp 147–171. https://doi.org/10.1007/978-94-015-9317-5_6

Pavčnik M (2008) Das "Hin- und Herwandern des Blickes". Zur Natur des Gesetzesanwendung. Rechtstheorie 39(5):557–572

Schweighofer E (2015) From information retrieval and artificial intelligence to legal data science. In: Schweighofer E, Galindo F, Cerbena C (eds) Proceedings MWAIL2015, ICAIL multilingual workshop on AI & law research, 15th international conference on artificial intelligence and law (ICAIL 2015). books@ocg.at, vol 313. OCG, Vienna, pp 13–23. http://fedora.phaidra.univie.ac.at/fedora/get/o:399570/bdef:Content/get. Accessed 15 Dec 2022

Sowa JF, Zachman JA (1992) Extending and formalizing the framework for information systems architecture. IBM Syst J 31(3):590–616

Sowa JF (2000) Knowledge representation: logical, philosophical, and computational foundations. Brooks/Cole Thomson Learning, Pacific Grove

Van Hoecke M, Ost F (1993) Epistemological perspectives in jurisprudence. Ratio Juris 6(1): 30–47. https://doi.org/10.1111/j.1467-9337.1993.tb00136.x

Chapter 19
Logic-Oriented Methods for Structuring in the Context of Lawmaking

19.1 Adding Logic-Oriented Information to Legislative Documents

With the transition from a text culture to a machine culture, the language changes, too. The language of the machine culture is the formal logic that is adequate for the machine, but not in the same way for people in their everyday language usage. In the mainstream of greater rationalisation, logic is increasingly used in legislation, especially allowing only correct interpretations. However, logic is not the only instrument which can be used to shape and improve legislative rationality. In the neighbourhood of logic there are further methods which can find application in structuring legislative texts. We propose to supplement legislative documents ex ante with explicit logic-oriented information which is relevant to ontologies and taxonomies. This information in a form of a mini-thesaurus can already be used in ex ante legislative procedure, and should not be added only in the ex post analysis of legal documentation.

A distinction between legislative texts and legal texts lies in open formulations. Legislative texts allow alternative formulations. In contrast, the wording of a valid legal text is fixed. The sole variation of a legal text is its interpretation. At a decision-making point in a legislative process the interpretation is basically open. However, it can be pushed in a certain direction with the help of additional materials, such as parliamentary reports. The subject matter of logic and lawmaking as investigated in this chapter concerns three themes:

Theme 1 – Three layers of a discourse
Theme 2 – Logic for the professional quality of the text
Theme 3 – Importance of the medium-level abstraction in law

Based on Čyras and Lachmayer (2015).

© The Author(s), under exclusive license to Springer Nature Switzerland AG 2023
V. Cyras, F. Lachmayer, *Essays on the Visualisation of Legal Informatics*, Law,
Governance and Technology Series 54,
https://doi.org/10.1007/978-3-031-27957-7_19

Each theme is discussed further in a separate section, after which we discuss selective application of logic. We think that in legal practice it is barely possible to translate an entire legal text in a logical notation, but it is possible to do so with a passage. Next, we discuss how logic expands legal interpretation.

19.2 Theme 1: Three Layers

The first theme comprises three layers (see Fig. 19.1):

1. *Political conflict*
2. *Argument.* The actors are political players from the political conflict above
3. *Meta-level: logic and rhetoric*

Political Conflict Political actors perform speech acts (usually in a parliamentary discourse) that are directed against each other. Here the goal is to universalise partial opinions, taking over in a draft and, finally, in legislation. The purpose is to achieve a compromise, to answer how to do the agreed, and to make capable of being used and understand by all.

Political discourse is a struggle of opinions. Its model comprises adversarial political actors. Each actor has adversarial goals. The actors compete to achieve a

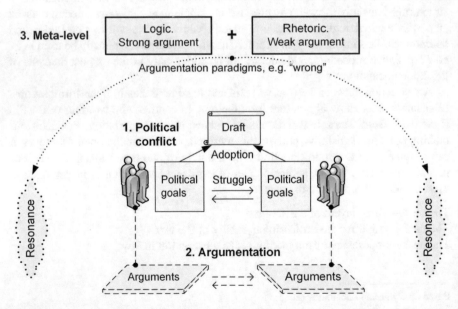

Fig. 19.1 Three layers of the subject matter. Dotted arrows show the use of logic and rhetoric on the meta-level and dashed arrows show argumentation (Čyras and Lachmayer 2015)

draft (see Fig. 19.1). The adversarial actors can also be called parties. They are not necessarily political parties and they number two in the simplest case.

Argumentation This is supplementary information which comes up with replies to the opinions. Argument's goal is acceptance, which is generally achieved by response. Argumentation strengthens political opinions and produces resonance, a bigger response from the public (is shown with dashed arrows in Fig. 19.1).

Logic and Rhetoric This forms a meta-level to the two paradigms above. Mostly it concerns rhetoric that determines the victory of political opinions. There is also logic as a meta-level of discourse, but it is an alternative and not dominant in the parliamentary debate. A decision in the parliament does not result due to the logical arguments. Yet they are not to be underestimated, at least not point-wise.

The importance of rhetoric is also emphasised by Fritjof Haft (2009), who is also a godfather of legal informatics; this can be illustrated with Fiedler et al. (1988). The notion of Normfall (in German) is introduced in Haft (2010); we would also use the phrase normal cases to stress that these cases are the opposite of extreme, boundary cases. Normfalls, which are assigned to politics, are taken into the law.

The question is about paradigms on the meta-level of logic and rhetoric. There are various paradigms. Some patterns are formed with all-round words such as 'always', 'from now on', 'henceforth', 'that is not true', 'wrong'. The use of the paradigms is shown with dotted arrows in Fig. 19.1. In summary, logical arguments can be used; however, logic is not central.

19.3 Theme 2: Logic for the Professional Quality of the Text

Logic in legislative texts is usually relevant for the professional quality of the texts. On the other hand, rhetoric is mostly important for the evolution of parliamentary discourse. Logic plays a small role here. Parliamentary discourse is determined by the will (in other words, free will, volition, intentions of the parties) and not rationality. The conflict of the wills is at the forefront. The parliamentary discourse is influenced by opinions and is brought to an end by the struggle of opinions.

Thus rhetoric determines parliamentary events in many parts. Speech acts during discourses in the parliament are political speech acts. A legislative draft is also a political act rather than a legal act. This is shown in Fig. 19.2.

Logic is important for professional legists (drafters of laws). Jurists in government departments are responsible for the professional quality of the texts. Professional drafters use logic to make texts correct and logically consistent. However, this is a serving, ministering function of logic. The drafters are also capable of intensifying the logic which was used in a parliamentary discourse.

Politicians are the dominant actors in a parliamentary discourse. The drafters, however, formulate their wills correctly and hence play a serving role. Thus the function of rhetoric dominates over the function of logic.

Fig. 19.2 Logic is important for the professional quality of legislative texts (Čyras and Lachmayer 2015)

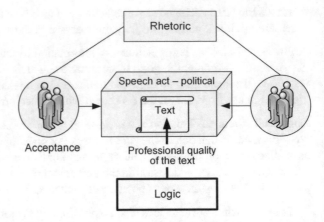

19.4   Theme 3: Middle-Level Abstraction

We first introduce three layers of abstraction in the legislative domain (see Fig. 19.3):

1. *formal abstraction* (in other words, high-level abstraction);
2. *middle-level abstraction* (interpretative abstraction). We focus on it as we hold that it contains more potential for legal informatics;
3. *substantive abstraction* (low-level abstraction).

Each abstraction layer is discussed further separately. We conclude that middle-level abstraction is more important in the context of logic and legislation.

19.4.1   Formal Abstraction

Formal abstraction is not as dynamic as middle-level and substantive abstraction. Once found, it stays that way. As examples, the following works can be mentioned: Tammelo's notation for the legal domain (1978), Jerzy Wróblewski's analytical

Fig. 19.3 Three levels of abstraction (Čyras and Lachmayer 2015)

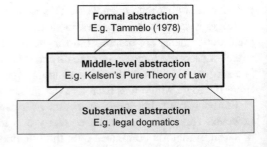

theory of law (1992), Weinberger's legal logic (1989), etc. Different sorts of formal logic, such as propositional logic, predicate logic, deontic logic, etc., are used here. These include, to mention just a few, studies in legal logic by Hage, modelling legal argument (Prakken and Sergot 1996), input/output logics by David Makinson and Leendert van der Torre, legal reasoning by Sartor (2007), pp. 3–85, and visualising normative systems by Silvano Colombo Tosatto et al. (2012).

The Logic of Political Will   Attempts to formalise the logic of willing (including political will) can be assigned to this level of abstraction. A formalisation of moral will was proposed by Ernst Mally in 1926.[1] Mally's deontic logic was an attempt to axiomatise strivings. This is connected with intentionality, that is, intending something. Mally's formalisation constitutes a preliminary phase of legal logic.

The logic of wishes (utinam), which is explored by Kazimierz Opałek (1986), is similar. His formalisation with the operator $Utinam(A)$ ("may it...") exceeds the logic of willing and leads to a whole theory of directives and norms (Opałek 1986), pp. 54–60. In this work, the analysis of a will $Will(A)$ leads to the analysis of a norm $Norm(A)$. This demonstrates a pathway from unconscious (political) willings to conscious norms. The logic of political will is a scientific concept and its formalisation, in preliminary phases, makes sense. We think that such formalisation could contribute further to the development of software that is capable of planning political wills in social domains.

19.4.2   Middle-Level Abstraction

Within the layer of medium abstraction, Kelsen's Pure Theory of Law is a relevant example. Here we find a mixture of formal structuring and material closeness. This is the area of scientific progress. This level is more elastic than other two. We find this level more creative, at least for legal informatics and our investigation. On the one hand, there is enough potential for abstraction in this layer; on the other, the substantive matters are not forgotten. It should be noted that the content of concrete norms is not examined in this layer.

An example of formalisation on this level of abstraction, though in chemistry, is a chemical formula notation such as H_2O. Practice shows that reasoning with such formulas and their graphical models is very effective. The following are examples of structural notation: relationships such as causation $A \rightarrow^{causal} B$ and teleology $A \rightarrow^{telos} B$, and a model of legal norms such as $Norm(A \rightarrow B)$.

Creativity with ontologies in the legal domain can also be assigned to this layer. For example, the formalisation of the norm graph concept is the starting phase in the approach of Oberle et al. (2012) on engineering compliant software. Here a norm graph consists of legal concepts (nodes) and links between them. Creativity is

---

[1] https://plato.stanford.edu/entries/mally-deontic/, https://plato.stanford.edu/entries/mally/.

required to build it. Norm graph formalisation is conducted by a legal expert and starts from extracting the required legal vocabulary. The vocabulary forms the basis of a legal lexicon which complements extracted terms by additional information. In turn, the lexicon serves as a basis for creating the computational model which consists of classes and relations.

Closed-World Assumption and Open-World Assumption In the development above we can see a transformation of a vocabulary (or ontology) into a computational model. We hold that there is a difference between a computational model (e.g. a database schema) and an ontology. A computational model follows the closed-world assumption. This means that what is not currently known to be true, is assumed false. In other words, what is not in the model is not in the world. An ontology follows the open-world assumption, which means that what is not currently known to be true is simply unknown.

The main components of ontologies as shared vocabularies are terms that are connected with links such as synonymy, hypernymy/hyponymy, etc. In contrast, the main components of computational models are entities (things) and the relationships that can exist among them.

19.4.3   Substantive Abstraction

Substantive disciplines, such as legal theory and legal dogmatics describe the object in principle with words. However, these disciplines are not really of interest here, because abstraction is too concrete and it is difficult to raise it to an upper layer. The content of concrete norms is examined in this layer and hence contrasts from the two upper layers.

It is difficult to invent on the top, that is, on the formal abstraction layer. For the same reason, we also do not focus on substantive abstraction. For instance, once an article in a law consists of a complete list of variations you can barely add more. However, we hold that creativity can be demonstrated on the middle abstraction layer. Formalising the interpretations of facts can be assigned to the middle abstraction. An example is ontologies. We aim at structuring the legal domain; namely, the big picture of the structure. In this layer, new formal notations could still be introduced, and they are not too far away from the substantive contents. This is in contrast to certain people who work on a low level and can interpret legal texts, but find it difficult to grasp the whole structure correctly.

19.5   Only Selective Application of Logic

A legal act comprises a legal text, which is Element 1 in our consideration (see Fig. 19.4). Legal texts are usually long and composed of structural parts such as sections, articles, paragraphs, etc., and are structured according to documentary rules.

In a legal text, there is a text passage which can be translated in a notation of formal logic. This text passage is Element 2. In legal practice, it is barely feasible to expect to reproduce (translate, transform) the entire lengthy text into a logical notation. A text passage can expand through several paragraphs and need not necessarily be a sentence. A legal norm is usually not formulated in one sentence and can expand through several places. For example, a norm's element, such as a condition, a subject, an obligatory action, or a provision, can be structured differently. The thesis that a universal model for reconstructing norms from legal text is possible can be rejected (see e.g. Wróblewski 1992).

Element 3 is logic, which is used to translate a passage into a logical notation. Element 4 is the result of the translation, that is, a product. Hence the product is a formal structuring of the text passage, whereas Element 3 is a system of logic.

Fig. 19.4 Selective application of logic. In legal practice, it is barely possible to translate the whole text in a logical notation, but possible to do so with a passage (Čyras and Lachmayer 2015)

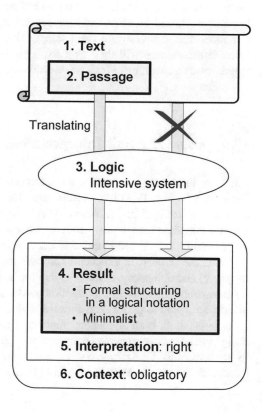

Translation has been attempted by many researchers. For example, Tammelo (1978) used Polish prefix notation that comprises a deontic modality. Jürgen Rödig (1980) employed predicate logic and inference rules. Less of formal notations have been used by Weinberger (1989). Up to now a success was translating only small passages such as a separate phrase, a provision, or a sentence.

The idea is that the translation is minimalist. Again, we hold that it is barely possible (at least at present) to reproduce the whole legal text in a logical notation. However, this is possible with smaller text passages. This thesis is backed by the cited research and numerous attempts to represent the meaning of a (legal) text using artificial intelligence. We would mention difficulties first in representing the inter-connectedness of norms and, second the open texture problem, which occurs while interpreting legal concepts.

The principle of selective application of logic is also true in legislation. Logic is not enough for an entire legal text such as a statute and allows only selective application. Only important passages can be represented in a logical notation. In legislation, hence, logic can be applied intensively but selectively. Here 'intensively' means providing less open texture, a higher degree shift from an open world to a closed world, or from loose to more strict interpretation.

One problem is the application of logic to reproduce the whole text and a corpus of texts. The selective application of logic can be compared with a scalpel. You cannot use a scalpel to chop as you would an axe. Logic is a precise tool and its limitations should be considered in legislation. It is meaningful to single out key sentences and to investigate them selectively: what interpretations do they allow? What consequences will they lead to? This is a targeted application of logic by legists. Such a checking of legislative drafts would be limited to selective analysis of key passages.

19.6   Logic Expands Interpretation

Logic is important in creating an interpretative space. This interpretation (see Element 5 in Fig. 19.4) is a correct one. Thus the system of logic contributes to eliminating wrong interpretations. Therefore the interpretation is interesting and various consequences follow from it. Of course, other factors such as different values can be considered in the creation of space for interpretation.

Next, the context is expanded through logic. Consequences are right (correct logically) and obligatory. In the case that the behaviour of a subject is expressed with deontic modalities such as obligation $O(A)$ and prohibition $F(B)$, the subject is clearly obligated to perform an action A and to refrain from B.

In legislation, both effects are important: the rightness of interpretation and the obligation of actions to pursue consequences. Hence, logic emerges as an instrument to achieve both. Obligatory consequences lead us to the roots of examining the deontic field (see e.g. Wesley Hohfeld (1913) and von Wright).

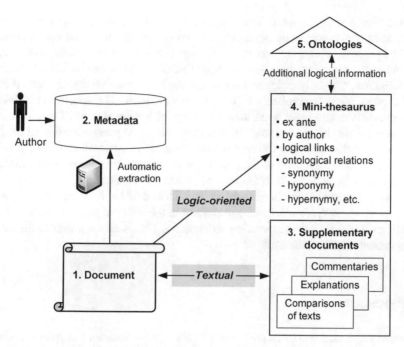

Fig. 19.5 Supplementary logical information to a document, a legislative draft (Čyras and Lachmayer 2015)

Proposal: Supplementary Logic-Oriented Information   Our proposal is to supplement a legislative document with additional logic-oriented information (see Fig. 19.5) such as a mini-thesaurus. This would be prepared ex ante (contrary to ex post documentalistic information which is added to legislative documents) by an author or an authority in a legislative process. A mini-thesaurus would contain links and ontological relations such as synonymy, hypernymy/hyponymy, etc. This is contrary to traditional metadata that is textual.

In a traditional legislative process, a legislative draft is supplemented with textual documents such as commentaries, explanations, comparisons of texts, etc. Our proposal is to activate logic-oriented ontology-relevant thinking and to add linking in the form of a mini-thesaurus with various links. A relevant research was conducted in the LOIS project where the five ontological relations have been identified.

Part of metadata is prepared by an author or authorities such as ministries and part is extracted from a document automatically. However, even more supplementary metadata could be extracted automatically or semi-automatically (see e.g. Le et al, and also Yoshida et al. in Chap. 3 of this volume).

In summary, the novelty of the proposal is to supplement legislative documents with explicit logic-oriented structural information which is relevant to ontologies, thesauruses and taxonomies. The purpose is neither supplementing the document with additional metadata automatically nor advancing general legal ontologies.

The proposed above appears in a pre-logical area, needs not strict semantics, and is intended for transforming into a logical notation. This can be called structural visualisation. Similarly as legislation is not yet law, so the proposed method is not yet a formal logic, but probably is in a perimeter to logic. The area of the legislation is more diffuse and more open than the range of applicable law. Therefore, other methods are also adequate. It may be that in the future 30 years more formal methods will be used than possible today. But now in a kind of transition phase, it is first necessary to leave the bank of the purely textual and go to an intermediate medium, and this may be well found in the area of structural visualisation.

Structural visualisation is relevant to legislative drafting as it can bring transparency to complex structures. This is important in formulating political wills and their public assessment in the sense of e-participation. This is also relevant to the idea of supplementary mini-thesaurus.

References

Colombo Tosatto S, Boella G, Torre L van der, Villata S (2012) Visualizing normative systems: an abstract approach. In: Ågotnes T, Broersen J, Elgesem D (eds) Deontic logic in computer science. DEON 2012. Lecture notes in computer science, vol 7393. Springer, Heidelberg, pp 16–30. doi: https://doi.org/10.1007/978-3-642-31570-1_2

Čyras V, Lachmayer F (2015) Logic oriented methods for structuring in the context of lawmaking. In: Araszkiewicz M, Płeszka K (eds) Logic in the theory and practice of lawmaking. Legis-prudence library (Studies on the theory and practice of legislation), vol 2. Springer, Cham, pp 459–478. https://doi.org/10.1007/978-3-319-19575-9_17

Fiedler H, Haft F, Traunmüller R (eds) (1988) Expert systems in law – impacts on legal theory and computer law. Neue Methoden im Recht, vol 4. Attempto, Tübingen

Haft F (2009) Juristische Rhetorik, 8th edn. Alber, Freiburg (Breisgau)/München

Haft F (2010) Das Normfall-Buch: IT-gestütztes Strukturdenken und Informationsmanagement, 4th edn. Normfall-GmbH, München

Hohfeld W (1913) Some fundamental legal conceptions as applied in judicial reasoning. Yale Law J 23:16–59. Reprinted with revisions as: (ed: Cook EE) Some fundamental legal conceptions as applied in judicial reasoning, and other legal essays, New Haven, Yale University Press, 1919, 1923, 1964, and (ed: Wheeler WC), Greenwood Press, 1978

Oberle D, Drefs F, Wacker R, Baumann C, Raabe O (2012) Engineering compliant software: advising developers by automating legal reasoning. SCRIPTed 9(3):280–313. https://doi.org/10.2966/scrip.090312

Opałek K (1986) Theorie der Direktiven und der Normen. Springer, Vienna

Prakken H, Sergot M (1996) Contrary-to-duty obligations. Studia Logica 57(1):91–115

Rödig J (1980) Schriften zur juristischen Logik. In: Bund E, Schmiedel B, Thieler-Mevissen G (eds) Springer, Heidelberg

Sartor G (2007) Legal reasoning: a cognitive approach to the law. A treatise of legal philosophy and general jurisprudence, vol 5. Springer, Heidelberg

Tammelo I (1978) Modern logic in the service of law. Springer, Vienna

Weinberger O (1989) Rechtslogik. Duncker & Humblot, Berlin

Wróblewski J (1992). The judicial application of law. In: Bańkowski Z, MacCormick N (eds) Kluwer Academic, Dordrecht

Part V
Subsumption. Legal Relations

Chapter 20
Legal Subsumption

20.1 Explaining Legal Subsumption

A novelty in this chapter is that legal subsumption is divided into two steps: cognitive (also known as factual or terminological) subsumption and normative subsumption. Subsumption refers to the application of the law, or more precisely, the application of a norm to a fact, thus concluding the legal qualification.

An English dictionary defines subsumption as: 1. that which is subsumed, as the minor clause or premise of a syllogism; or 2. the incorporation of something into a more general category. Subsumption is central in making a legal decision.[1] Legal subsumption concerns the relation between fact and normative condition (Lebenssachverhalt und gesetzlicher Tatbestand; Sachverhalt und Tatbestand der Norm) (see e.g. Larenz and Canaris 1995, pp. 91 ff.).

Raabe et al. (2012), pp. 53–58 differentiate between subsumption in the narrow sense and subsumption in the broad sense. The latter embraces all three steps:

1. Creating a major premise (Tatbestand→Rechtsfolge), e.g. $\forall x\, A(x){\to}B(x)$.
2. Producing a minor premise $A(a)$. The fact a is subsumed under A.
3. Conclusion $B(a)$.

Subsumption in the narrow sense concerns only the second step.

Legal qualification, which results in the subsumption procedure, is central to ontologies in law. For example, in relation to the question of whether a killing (world knowledge) is murder, legal sanction in the form of an execution or an allowed act within an international armed conflict is given only based on the legal qualification of the act (Schweighofer and Lachmayer 1997), p. 9 (see Fig. 20.1).

Based on Cyras and Lachmayer (2014, 2021).

---

[1] https://de.wikipedia.org/wiki/Subsumtion_(Recht).

© The Author(s), under exclusive license to Springer Nature Switzerland AG 2023   187
V. Cyras, F. Lachmayer, *Essays on the Visualisation of Legal Informatics*, Law,
Governance and Technology Series 54,
https://doi.org/10.1007/978-3-031-27957-7_20

Fig. 20.1 Different legal
qualifications of killing

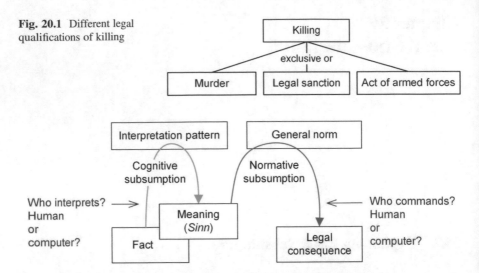

Fig. 20.2 The subsumption of a fact under a norm (Čyras and Lachmayer 2021)

Similarly, acts involving software within business processes can allow different legal qualifications. These acts can be matched with various legal concepts. Therefore subsumption can result in different decisions depending on a case.

Subsumption is of key importance when judging a violation. In order to judge whether there is a violation of the law, a factual situation has to be subsumed under a legal norm. Note that the factual situation can be subsumed under different norms. Therefore, conflicting norms and norm exceptions have to be taken into account. Here a balance is more important than an absolute rule.

Subsumption can be divided into two steps: cognitive (also known as factual or terminological) subsumption and normative subsumption (see Figs. 20.2 and 20.3).

The facts of a case are transformed into legal terms. A legal consequence arises in the form of a decision. Suppose that an action, a, is treated as a theft, A, rather than a burglary. This corresponds to the cognitive subsumption. We write $a \sim A$ (see Fig. 20.3). In computer science you can write *instance-of*(a,A). A pool of legal terms is used for the cognitive subsumption.

The second step is normative subsumption in which the general norm is applied and a legal consequence arises in the form of a decision. You can write $Norm(\forall x\, A(x) \rightarrow B(x))$ is applied to conclude B.

The first step, cognitive subsumption, corresponds to the unification. It is related to the minor premise. The second step, normative subsumption, corresponds to the major premise $\forall x\, A(x) \rightarrow B(x)$.

A key question is that of who interprets the facts in subsumption: a human or a machine (see Fig. 20.2). A typical example of a machine interpreter is a road radar system. In the case where a driver exceeds the speed limit (cognitive subsumption), the road radar system takes a photograph and sends it to a database to assign a penalty (normative subsumption). Thus, the radar system replaces the police officer

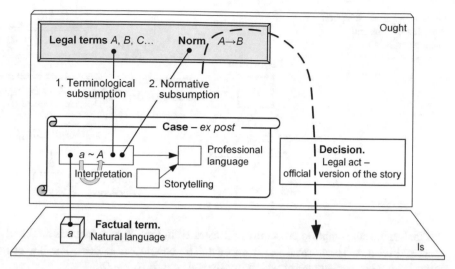

Fig. 20.3 Subsumption: the facts are assigned the legal qualification in accordance with a norm. A legal consequence arises in the form of a decision (Čyras and Lachmayer 2014)

or judge who would traditionally interpret the speed limit violation (cognitive subsumption) and assign a penalty (normative subsumption). In cybergovernance, competence in legal activities can be transferred from human to machine to carry out cognitive subsumption, normative subsumption or both. This transferring of competence can occur in both real-world activities and three-dimensional virtual world activities.

20.2   Modelling Cognitive Subsumption with the Instance-of Relationship

To model the subsumption procedure, conceptual modelling formalisms can be applied. Suppose we have the fact that *mydoor* is open and the norm N 'The doors ought to be closed'. The norm can be formalised with the following rule: if x is an instance of *Door*, then x ought to be closed. Formally, $\forall x \; x \in Door \Rightarrow O \; closed(x)$, where O is the deontic operator. A situation (a fact) with *mydoor* comes from Is. The fact is interpreted according to a norm from the Ought world which contains the term *Door*. Then *mydoor* is matched with *Door*. This can be simplified and expressed with a truth statement *instance-of(mydoor, Door)* or *mydoor∈Door*. This truth statement comes from Is. A duty which is conferred on me, to close *mydoor*, comes from Ought. However, in the Is world I can decide to leave *mydoor* open, thus violating the norm. Therefore a sanction can be conferred on me.

Fig. 20.4 The subsumption
procedure (Čyras and
Lachmayer 2014)

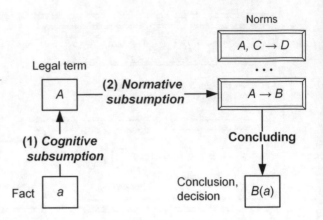

Finally, the subsumption procedure is illustrated in Fig. 20.4. A fact *a* is qualified
as a legal term *A*. The norm *A→B* is applied. The conclusion is *B*(*a*). The law can
comprise a more specific norm which involves *A*, e.g. *A*, *C* → *D*.

Next it is worth noting that the application of the law has to avoid formalism
(mechanistic approaches). This is stressed in legal theory. The idea of constructing a
subsumption machine (Subsumtionsautomat, or "mechanistic judge") is rejected
(see Ogorek 1986, pp. 212, 292 ff).

References

Čyras V, Lachmayer F (2014) Compliance and software transparency for the design of legal
    machines. In: Haav H, Kalja A, Robal T (eds) Databases and information systems VIII.
    Frontiers in artificial intelligence and applications, vol 270. IOS Press, Amsterdam, pp
    275–288. https://doi.org/10.3233/978-1-61499-458-9-275
Čyras V, Lachmayer F (2021) From Kelsen's pure theory of law to Yoshino's Logical
    Jurisprudence. In: Yoshino H, Villa Rosas G (eds) Law and logic – making legal science a
    genuine science. Proceedings of the special workshop held at the 28th World Congress of the
    International Association for Philosophy of Law and Social Philosophy in Lisbon, Portugal,
    2017. Archiv für Rechts- und Sozialphilosophie – Beihefte (ARSP-B), Band 166. Franz Steiner
    Verlag, Stuttgart, pp 29–63
Larenz K, Canaris C (1995) Methodenlehre der Rechtswissenschaft, 3. Auflage. Springer,
    Heidelberg
Ogorek R (1986) Richterkönig oder Subsumtionsautomat? Klostermann, Frankfurt am Main
Raabe O, Wacker R, Oberle D, Baumann C, Funk C (2012) Recht ex machina. Formalisierung des
    Rechts im Internet der Dienste. Springer Vieweg, Heidelberg
Schweighofer E, Lachmayer F (1997) Ideas, visualisations and ontologies. In: Visser PRS, Winkels
    RGF (eds) Proceedings of the first international workshop on legal ontologies, LEGONT '97.
    University of Melbourne, pp 7–13. http://www.di.unito.it/~guido/ontologie/articoli/ideas-
    visualisations-and-ontologies.pdf. Accessed 15 Dec 2022

Chapter 21
Formalising Legal Relations

21.1 A Variety of Relations in Law

This chapter concerns arbitrary relations in law and extends beyond concrete types of legal relations. There is no established ontology of relations in the legal domain, although ontologies of legal concepts are discussed in literature. Different legal terms, such as duty, contract, debt, husband, etc. can be viewed as relations. However, on the meta-level, there is no model of relation types in law.

To explore a notation for different types of legal relations, we would first mention Ulrich Klug (1982) who presented relation calculus in the context of legal logic. Hence, we articulate binary relations $R(A,B)$. They can also be written $A\ R\ B$. Binary relations can be represented in the form of pairs and also graphically (see Fig. 21.1).

A categorical distinction between Is and Ought implies two wide types of relations: causality relations A *causes* B and imputation relations A *imputation* B. A variety of causality relations appears in the nature and is studied in natural sciences. A central theme in law is legal relation between different entities. The following three cases can be distinguished:

1. A vinculum juris between persons ('bonds of law').
2. A relation between things.
3. The relation between the factual and the normative. The normative condition is expressed in legal terms, which constitute a modally indifferent substrate.

Creatively new is to name a relation R, for example, *counts_as*. Next, a pointing direction from the referent to the relatum is also significant because they are in different roles. This holds for asymmetric relations, such as '*inheritor*', '*self-defence*' and is of no importance for symmetric relations, such as '*be-in-contract-partnership*', '*sibling*', etc. Hence, different notations can be used: $A\ R\ B$, $A\ R{\to}\ B$

Based on Lachmayer and Čyras (2019).

V. Cyras, F. Lachmayer, *Essays on the Visualisation of Legal Informatics*, Law, Governance and Technology Series 54, https://doi.org/10.1007/978-3-031-27957-7_21

Fig. 21.1 A binary relation $R(A,B)$: without the name of a relation and with the name (Lachmayer and Čyras 2019)

and $A \leftarrow R\ B$, for example: A *legal_relationship* B, *parent care*$\rightarrow$ *child*, *parent* $\leftarrow$*obey child*, A *right*$\rightarrow$ B, A $\leftarrow$*duty* B. There may be inverse relations (see Klug 1982, p. 79). For example, the inverse of *employee*(A,B) is *employer*(B,A).

A relation, which is transitive, symmetric and reflexive, is called equality (or more generally, equivalence) relation (Gleichheitrelation) (see Klug 1982, p. 83). It is important from a mathematical point of view, because this allows it to divide tuples into a partition. In mathematics, a partition of a set X is a set of nonempty subsets of X such that every element x in X is in exactly one of these subsets (i.e. X is a disjoint union of the subsets) (see e.g. Halmos 1960, p. 28).

A huge variety of relations is immanent to law. A reason is that people are highly interrelated. The importance of this variety can be compared with knowledge-based systems in AI, where a huge variety of rules and facts outweighs an inference engine. The knowledge principle (Lenat and Feigenbaum 1987) sums up the importance of taking into account a huge variety of the world: "God is in the details."

Following are the themes to discuss in this chapter: different types of relations, distinguishing between relations and statements about the relations, and Peter Chen's entity–relationship model.

21.2 Definition of Relation in Mathematics

While attending the classes of law and while you can hear the term 'legal relations'. However, a formal definition of a relation is provided not always. Therefore a listener can raise a question what legal relation is. Deep studies can lead to philosophical problems, such as the problem of universals, meaning and reference. In ontologies (in the sense of computer science), this leads to defining the terms extensional relational structure and intensional relational structure (see Guarino et al. 2009).

A relation R over the sets $X_1, \ldots, X_n$ is defined as a subset of their Cartesian product, written $R \subseteq X_1 \times \ldots \times X_n$. A notation for an n-ary relation ($n \geq 1$) is $R(a_1, \ldots, a_n)$. We may also write $(a_1, \ldots, a_n) \in R$. A binary relation ($n = 2$) can be written in prefix notation Ra_1a_2, infix notation a_1Ra_2 and postfix notation a_1a_2R. A relation R corresponds to the n-ary predicate, which is usually given the same name:

$$P(a_1, \ldots, a_n) = true \text{ iff } (a_1, \ldots, a_n) \in R, false \text{ otherwise,} \quad \text{i.e.} (a_1, \ldots, a_n) \notin R$$

Unary relations ($n = 1$) are usually called predicates. Predicates for $n = 0$ denote atoms. In propositional logic, atomic formulas are called propositional variables. In a

Fig. 21.2 a A ternary relation $R(A, B, C)$. **b** A quaternary relation $R(A, B, C, D)$ (Lachmayer and Čyras 2019)

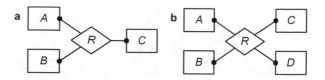

sense, these are 0-arity predicates. In mathematics, a predicate is commonly understood to be a Boolean-valued function $P: X \rightarrow \{true, false\}$, called the predicate on X. An extreme case $n = 0$ is obtained when the domain set X is empty.

Graphical representation of binary relations can be extended to n-ary relations that consist on n-tuples. Ternary relations consist of triples $R(A, B, C)$, quaternary relations consist of quadruplets $R(A, B, C, D)$, etc. They can be represented as bipartite graphs (see Fig. 21.2), where the node for the relation name differs from tuple element nodes.

Reification In computing, reification is defined as the process of turning a predicate or function into an object of the language.[1] As it is shown above, a relation implies a predicate and vice versa. Hence, a relation can be processed analogous to an object. This complies with Arthur Kaufmann's assertion that a relation can be processed analogous to a substance.

21.3 Relations in Law and the Layers of Law

We can decompose the Is realm into two layers: everyday life and subcultures (see Fig. 21.3). The Ought consists of other layers, such as a constitution, general norms and individual norms. Other elements form meta-layers, such as legal theory, meta-theories (e.g., Kelsen's Pure Theory of Law) and a system of legal terms.

We differentiate between the following types of relations:

1. *Horizontal relations.* A relation connects elements of one layer.
2. *Vertical next layer relations.* A relation connects elements of different layers.
3. *Vertical legal dogmatics relations.* A relation connects elements from the legal dogmatics meta-level layer with elements from Is and Ought layers.

---

[1] "The term "reification" comes from the Latin word *res*, or thing [...] There are two choices for representing categories in first-order logic: predicates and objects. That is, we can use the predicate *Basketball(b)*, or we can **reify** the category as an object, *Basketballs*. We could then say *Member(b, Basketballs)* (which we will abbreviate as *b∈Basketballs*) to say that *b* is a member of the category of basketballs. We say *Subset(Basketballs, Balls)* (abbreviated as *Basketballs ⊂ Balls*) to say that *Basketballs* is a subcategory, or subset, of *Balls*. So you can think of a category as being the set of its members, or you can think of it as more complex object that just happens to have the *Member* and *Subset* relations defined for it" (Russell and Norvig 2003), pp. 323, 341.

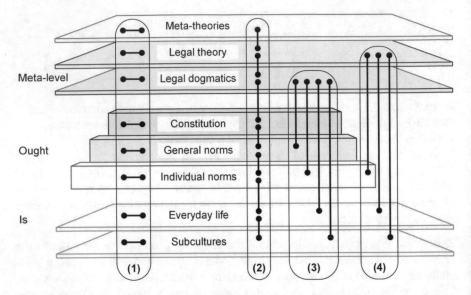

Fig. 21.3 The layers of law and relations: (1) horizontal relations, (2) vertical next layer relations, (3) vertical legal dogmatics relations, and (4) vertical legal theory relations (Lachmayer and Čyras 2019)

4. *Vertical legal theory relations.* A relation connects elements from the legal theory meta-level layer with elements of the individual norms layer and also with elements of the Is layers.

Vertically drawn relations include the subsumption relation. Ideology is also a meta-level layer. Therefore, the whole scheme, which is shown in Fig. 21.3, appears in ideological context. Hence, relations with ideological concepts are involved (see Fig. 21.4).

21.4   Statements About Relations

There is a difference between a relation *A R B* and a statement that *A* and *B* are in a relation *R*. There is a difference in who the teller is—for example, a judge or a layman. Therefore, we introduce a predicate STM(*A, R, B, statement, teller*) or STM [*A R B*]. This expresses that a teller says: '*A* and *B* are in a certain relation *R*'.

There is a distinction between two different categories: speech acts and statements. A speech act appears in Is, but its meaning appears in Ought. In contrast, statements appear as mathematical objects, such as propositions and predicates in the world of science. There is an essential difference if a speech act is pronounced by a

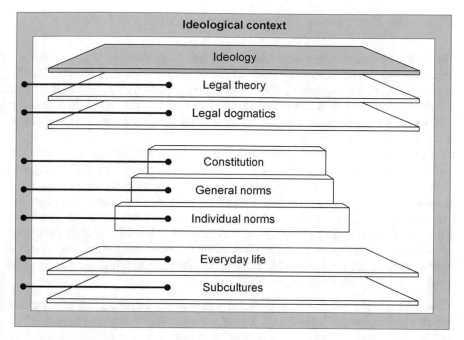

Fig. 21.4 The context of relations with ideological concepts (Lachmayer and Čyras 2019)

Fig. 21.5 A speech act, statement and a relation

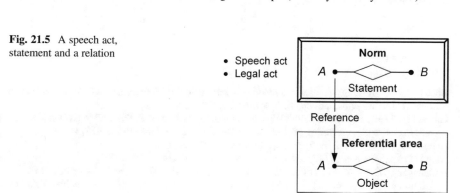

judge or a layman. In the first case, the speech act constitutes a legal act and, in the second case, does not. A speech act can be treated as an institutional fact and, hence, lead to a legal act whose meaning appears in Ought, for example, as a norm. This is shown in Fig. 21.5.

21.5 On Peter Chen's Entity–Relationship Model

We hold that a relation can be managed analogously as atomic entities. An entity–relationship model (ER model)[2] refers to the techniques proposed in Peter Chen's paper (1976). However, variants of the idea existed previously. Chen holds that "The entity–relationship model adopts the more natural view that the real world consists of entities and relationships. It incorporates some of the important semantic information about the real world."

Chen's notation for entity–relationship modelling uses rectangles to represent entity sets, and diamonds to represent relationships appropriate for first-class objects: they can have attributes and relationships of their own. If an entity set participates in a relationship set, they are connected with a line. There are related diagramming convention techniques, such as UML class diagrams. When speaking about the problem of visual dialects, Daniel Moody (2009) notes that ER modelling exists in a variety of dialects, such as the Chen notation (the most commonly used in academic context); the Information Engineering (IE) notation (the most commonly used in practice); the Bachman notation; etc.

Conclusion Relations in law is a theme that extends beyond concrete relations which are examined in legal theory. Investigations within this theme can extend to ontological theory of law. The goal of this chapter is to identify cornerstones of investigations.

References

Chen P (1976) The entity-relationship model—toward a unified view of data. ACM Transact Datab Syst 1(1):9–36. https://doi.org/10.1145/320434.320440

Guarino N, Oberle D, Staab S (2009) What is an ontology? In: Staab S, Studer R (eds) Handbook on ontologies. Springer, Berlin, pp 1–17. https://doi.org/10.1007/978-3-540-92673-3_0

Halmos PR (1960) Naive set theory. Springer Nature Switzerland

Klug U (1982) Juristische Logik, 4th edn. Springer, Heidelberg

Lachmayer F, Čyras V (2019) Formalising legal relations. In: Schweighofer E, Araszkiewicz M, Lachmayer F, Pavčnik M (eds) Formalising jurisprudence: festschrift for Hajime Yoshino. Edi-tions Weblaw, Bern, pp 163–181

Lenat D, Feigenbaum E (1987) On the thresholds of knowledge. In: Proceedings of international joint conference on artificial intelligence, IJCAI 1987, pp 1173–1182. https://www.ijcai.org/Proceedings/87-2/Papers/122.pdf. Accessed 15 Dec 2022

Moody D (2009) The "physics" of notations: towards a scientific basis for constructing visual no-tations in software engineering. IEEE Transact Softw Eng 35(6):756–778. https://doi.org/10.1109/TSE.2009.67

Russell S, Norvig P (2003) Artificial intelligence: a modern approach. Prentice Hall

---

[2] In software engineering, an entity–relationship model (ER model) is a data model for describing a database in an abstract way [...] Diagrams created to design these entities and relationships are called entity–relationship diagrams or ER diagrams (see Wikipedia, https://en.wikipedia.org/wiki/Entity%E2%80%93relationship_model).

Chapter 22
Tertium Comparationis in Law: Variations on Arthur Kaufmann's Theme

22.1 Legal Relations Replace Substances

This chapter tackles the following types of relations: (a) direct relation; (b) indirect relation through tertium comparationis (see Chap. 3 in this volume); (c) subsumption, that is, a relation between fact and the normative condition; and (d) amplitude relation. We follow Arthur Kaufmann's assertion that relations in law can be managed similarly to substances (see Lachmayer 2005). In the end, an ontology of legal relations is approached. Therefore legal relations are classified according to Is–Ought combinations.

Arthur Kaufmann (1982) replaces ontologies of substances by ontologies of relations (Relationenontologie). It is not straightforward to model a legal relation as a mathematical relation. There is a distinction between causality relations *A causal B* and finality relations *A telos B*, as they have different legal meanings. Similarly, the notions of correspondence (Entsprechung) and contradiction (Widerspruch) have also different meaning. Next, we differentiate between explicit and implicit relations and also between direct and indirect relations.

Software engineers need to model relations while implementing legal machines. However, engineers may meet difficulties understanding the meanings of legal relations. In legal theory and legal philosophy, the concept of relation has certain nuances. The meaning of legal relations differs from relations in an extensional relational structure and an ontology in computer science, and also in a (relational) structure in philosophy. Next, several complications on the way towards an ontology of relations are shown.

Based on section 5 "Legal relations" of Čyras et al. 2016.

22.2   Indirect Relations and Tertium Comparationis

Indirect Relation Tertium comparationis is the quality that two things that are being compared have in common (see Chap. 3 in this volume). A course through tertium comparationis modifies the relation. With tertium comparationis, you deal not with a direct relation between two elements, but, rather, with an indirect relation between them that is mediated over a third element. This indirect relation is a reflected relation and can also be characterised as a broken relation. A broken relation, a direct one, is replaced by two relations. For instance, a translation from Portugal into Lithuanian would be performed—not directly, but through English. Another example is making two information systems interoperable. Interoperability requires a bridge between the systems.

Overcoming Barriers with Tertium A reflected or broken tertium comparationis is able to make a connection through "walls" or other barriers. The situation is similar to a mirror, which allows you to survey areas that cannot be viewed directly. In this way, you can see not only the present, but also the past and the future. Tertium comparationis is a suitable technique to make connections in the unconscious, as they cannot be made directly.

Projecting a Relation Legal relations are generally not simple matters. In most cases, a relation is not like a bridge between two banks because it is not even observable in the outside world. Often, relations are projected and a relation becomes the result of projecting. Hence, projection is the content of a thought act, a speech act, or a legal act.

Comparison A comparison also concerns relations. Various elements can be compared, and hence, brought into a relation. If a relationship is projected, the elements that are connected in the relation are also projected. Hence, (a) Is can be compared with Ought (i.e. meaning), (b) Ought with Is, and (c) Ought with Ought.

Interpretation and Comparison A classical usage is a relation between the factual and the normative. It is meaningful to examine this relation because it usually appears in judgments, that is, legal acts. We hold that interpretation precedes comparison. The factual and the normative are compared not directly but through their meaning. This is then projected onto the factual and the normative, respectively (see Fig. 22.1). In legal language, it is not the case that a fact is compared directly with the content of a norm, but the interpreted fact is compared with the meaning of the norm. The interpretation is a prerequisite. The comparison compares the meaning-structure of the fact with the meaning-structure of the normative hypothesis. Legal terms serve as tertium comparationis.

Pretextual Universals A textual culture dominates in law and, therefore, there is little that is pretextual or non-verbal. However, there are also normative approaches that are centrally non-verbal. Examples are the simulated measurement units of the body, such as the radius or the cubit, the foot or the step. Hence, there are archetypes that are non-linguistic and have a social normative effect.

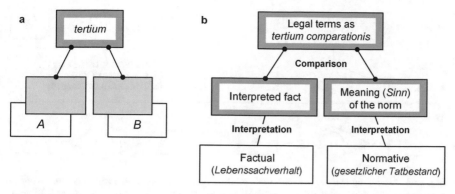

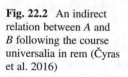

Fig. 22.1 An indirect relation between *A* and *B* through a common quality tertium comparationis: **a** pattern and **b** explanation (Čyras et al. 2016)

Fig. 22.2 An indirect relation between *A* and *B* following the course universalia in rem (Čyras et al. 2016)

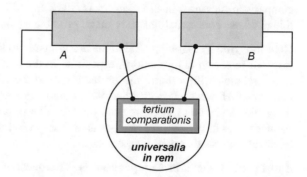

Subject-Internal Tertium Comparationis We spoke above about the abstract structural background that lies behind universal interpretation schemas, such as language, types, and terms, and that thus lies behind supposed objectivity. However, another course can be followed to facilitate tertium comparationis, specifically through the subject. Universals can also be derived from the subject. There are universalia in rem that are internally in the subject (see Fig. 22.2); they differ from universalia ante rem that are in the objective area before the subject and the thing. These universals can, but need not be formulated verbally. Such indirect relationships can be produced in the subject for a preliminary understanding. Since we hold that language is a distinct human competence, the pre-verbal ability may be associated with the development stages before humans. A comparison is also possible, to a certain extent, and thus a thought. The big advantage of language is less in the standardization in the projected meaning, but, rather, in the inter-subjectivity.

Two Poles of Tertium Comparationis There are, thus, two poles of tertium comparationis—namely, universalia ante rem that are assigned to the objective and universalia post rem that are attributed subjectively. Although you can find such

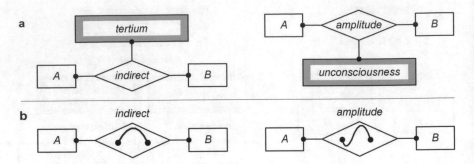

Fig. 22.3 Modelling *indirect* and *amplitude* relations in our dialect of the Chen notation. **a** Tertium comparationis and unconscious are modelled as separate entities in a ternary relation. **b** Relation names are written above relation icons (Čyras et al. 2016)

comparison measures in different areas, they are still functionally lifted from the things whose conceptual link they make possible.

Relations and Personality Relations are assigned to the meaning level. There are many different types of relations, especially in the area of law. If a case is brought into a relation with a norm, the projecting onto the relation of correspondence is performed. However, it is different with complementary roles. Here there is something like a vinculum juris between people. The personal relation of the complementary roles of two or more persons is probably what Kaufmann had in mind when he developed his theory of the person.

Substance of Tertium Comparationis The question "What is the substance of tertium comparationis?" is not trivial. A tertium comparationis, such as the meter or the kilogram (of the International Bureau of Weights and Measures), can be assigned a concrete substance. However, the substance of tertium comparationis can be weakened; think, for example, of merely projected units of measurement. Here, the substance is not as clear as in the case of concrete universalia in rem examples, like the meter or a cardboard/computer model of a house that is built by an architect.

Amplitude Relations We call an amplitude relation a relation which involves the unconscious and cognitive emotions. A goal of our investigations is to model indirect relations through tertium comparationis (*A indirect B*) and amplitude relations (*A amplitude B*). They both involve a third element (tertium and unconscious correspondingly) while relating two elements, *A* and *B*. This third element can be represented explicitly: *indirect*(*A*, *B*, *tertium*) and *amplitude*(*A*, *B*, *unconscious*). We would model this in our dialect of the Chen notation, as shown in Fig. 22.3 (we add line ends •).

Fig. 22.4 Towards an
ontology of relations in law
(Čyras et al. 2016)

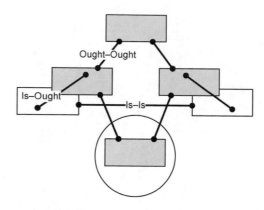

22.3 Towards an Ontology of Relations

Stressing the ontology of relations is a radical step that is interesting from a linguistic viewpoint. However, the practical consequence of this step has not been sufficiently considered. Is it, in fact, the case that only relations, and not the substances that are associated with them, are real? Through the elimination of the substances, you fall into a bottomless abyss, and the relations alone are not able to slow down this fall. An attempt to visualise the ontology of relations is shown in Fig. 22.4. This ontology can be treated as a classification of relations, which are grouped according to 'Is'–'Is', 'Is'–'Ought' and 'Ought'–'Ought' combinations. The proposed concept of the ontology of relations is at a very abstract level, and does not conform entirely to the treatment of ontologies in computer science.

Conclusion In this chapter, we focus on visuals that can serve as tertium comparationis. We continue from Chap. 3 and elaborate on the concept of tertium comparationis. Indirect and amplitude relations are introduced. We provide a classification of legal relations based on 'Is'–'Ought' combinations. We conclude that the substance of tertium comparationis may not be trivial, as in the case of units of measurement.

References

Čyras V, Lachmayer F, Schweighofer E (2016) Visualization as a tertium comparationis within multilingual communities. Baltic J Mod Comput 4(3):524–545. https://www.bjmc.lu.lv/fileadmin/user_upload/lu_portal/projekti/bjmc/Contents/4_3_12_Cyras.pdf.   Accessed 15 Dec 2022

Kaufmann A (1982) Analogie und „Natur der Sache": zugleich ein Beitrag zur Lehre vom Typus, 2. Auflage. Decker & C.F. Müller, Heidelberg

Lachmayer F (2005) Das tertium comparationis im Recht. Variationen zu einem Thema von Arthur Kaufmann. In: Neumann U, Hassemer W, Schroth U (eds) Verantwortetes Recht: Die Rechtsphilosophie Arthur Kaufmanns. Archiv für Rechts- und Sozialphilosophie – Beihefte (ARSP-B), Band 100. Franz Steiner Verlag, Stuttgart, pp 67–77

Part VI
Legal Machines and Compliance

Chapter 23
Multisensory Legal Machines and Production of Legal Acts

23.1 Machines and Humans Are Similar in Legal Context

A legal machine is defined as a machine in a system whose actions are legally significant and draw legal consequences. Simple examples are traffic lights and vending machines. Complicated examples are computer-based information systems in organisations, workflows for proceedings that use forms, and machines that replace officials in organisations. This chapter explores the creation of institutional facts by machines and multimodal communication of legal content to humans. Machines similarly as humans can be imposed status-functions of legal actors. Thus the concept of iustitia distributiva and societal distribution is enhanced. The thesis is that a machine can replace an organ, an office (Latin officium) or an executive agency in an organisation.

We focus on the analogy of machines with human beings. Legal content can be communicated by machines and can be perceived by all of our senses. The content can be expressed in multimodal languages: textual, visual, acoustic, gestures, aircraft manoeuvres, etc. Further the concept of encapsulation (Verschachtellung) of human into machine is proposed. Herein human-intended actions are communicated through the machine's output channel. Encapsulations can be compared with deities and mythical creatures that can send gods' messages to people through the human mouth. This chapter also aims to identify law production patterns by machines.

A first glance is as follows. An actor (a human being or a machine) executes an action (a legal transaction, Rechtsgeschäft). The action is addressed to another actor or actors (see Fig. 23.1). The term 'actor' is preferred to 'agent' which is reserved for meanings used by computer science community in the domain of multi-agent systems (MAS).

Based on Čyras and Lachmayer (2011, 2012, 2013).

Fig. 23.1 An actor (human or machine) executes an action which is legally significant (Čyras and Lachmayer 2012)

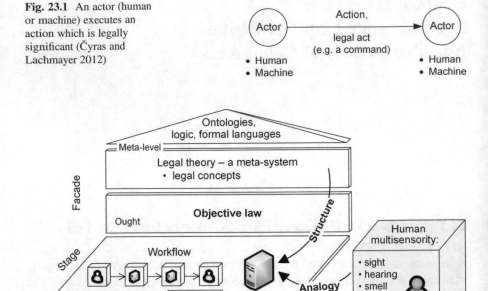

Fig. 23.2 Legal machines in context: *machine = analogy of human* on the horizontal Is stage (adapted from Čyras and Lachmayer 2013)

Context On the Is stage we view machines in the foreground and people in the background (see Fig. 23.2). Real-life workflows comprise both human beings and machines. Decisions are qualified as legal acts. Thus the workflows deal with conditions and effects. Legal theory appears as a meta-system. Objective law and legal theory impose a structure on machine behaviour.

Machines communicate acts to humans who perceive the legal contents by multiple senses (sight, hearing, smell, taste and touch). Thus a kind of multisensory legal communication is observed.

23.2   Legal Machines in Context

Paraphrasing Kelsen a purpose of this chapter is the cognition of legal machines, not their formation. Factual acts are from Is and do not have legal significance whereas legal acts have it and also an interpretation with respect to Ought.

Our departure point is that machines are tools. Technology is substrate and thus it is not part of law. However, institutional facts can also be triggered by machines. The context of legal machines is introduced by the following cases: (1) vending

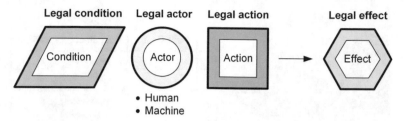

Fig. 23.3 From factual acts (raw facts) to legal acts (legal facts) (Čyras and Lachmayer 2013)

machines; (2) traffic lights; (3) form proceedings such as FinanzOnline;[1] and (4) machines that are auxiliary to officials in organisations. There are simple legal machines, such as the latter cases (1), (2) or automated barriers, and complex ones, such as e-government applications for the cases (3) or (4). The latter are examples of legal machines accessible in the internet according to the 'as-a-service' paradigm (see Raabe et al. 2012, pp. 33–51).

Thus the point of departure is that an actor makes an action with an effect and this is under a condition (see Fig. 23.3), e.g. 'Alice puts a coin in her piggybank'. Thus we start with the *condition-actor-action-effect* model. To illustrate the notation, following is an instance, *factualAct1*:

$$factualAct_1 = (condition = undefined,$$
$$actor = 'Alice',$$
$$action = 'drops\ a\ coin\ in\ her\ piggybank',$$
$$effect = 'making\ savings')$$

Besides a human being and a machine, the actor can also be a deity, a text, etc. Legal significance is observed in conclusive conduct (konkludentes Verhalten) such as Chris putting coins in a ticket machine. A fraud is committed when dropping fake coins in a vending machine whereas a child may put old coins in her piggybank.

Factual acts can be lifted to the legal acts category by the actor's role. For instance, you are obliged to stand up when the judge enters a courtroom, though you sit when ordinary people come in. Both factual and legal acts are raised by real-life events and can be represented by Boolean propositions, for instance:

$$factualAct2 = pedestrian\_Mike\_raising\_hand$$
$$legalAct2 = policeman\_Steve\_raising\_hand$$

No legal consequences are implied by *factualAct2*, whereas *legalAct2* implies: drivers are obliged to halt, $legalAct2 \Rightarrow \forall x \in drivers\ Obligatio(halt(x))$. Legal effects are significant whereas the types of legal acts—speech acts or implications—are not.

---

[1] FinanzOnline provides a one-click link to the Austrian tax administration (see https://finanzonline.bmf.gv.at).

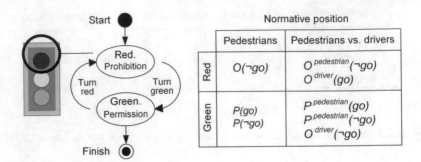

Fig. 23.4 The vertical effect of administrative law regulation by traffic lights. The algorithm is represented in the form of a finite-state automaton. On a pedestrian red light they are obliged not to go, $O(\neg go)$, and drivers are obliged to go. On a pedestrian green light they are permitted to go, $P(go)$, and they are also permitted to wait, $P(\neg go)$ (Čyras and Lachmayer 2013)

Persons putting coins into a vending machine engage in sales contracts. The condition can also have legal significance, for example, traffic enforcement cameras make photographs when the vehicle exceeds the speed limit. Hence, each element—the legal condition, the legal actor, the legal action and the legal effect—are qualified to have legal significance.

Traffic Lights: Vertical Effect In the contract example, the relationships *condition–actor–action–effect* have horizontal—individual—effect since they concern private law. Traffic lights have vertical—general—effect as regulated by administrative law. The traffic lights normativity can be expressed in different formalisms. The algorithm in terms of a finite-state automaton is shown in Fig. 23.4. A pedestrian is prohibited to go on a red light, $F(go)$, and permitted on green, $P(go)$, though he can wait on the pavement, $P(\neg go)$, too. The automaton's states are turned from red to green or vice versa. The algorithm changes permissions and obligations and distributes legal time and space between pedestrians and drivers. The regulation of pedestrian traffic lights can also be expressed with a formula:

$$O(\neg go) \vee T[O(\neg go) \rightarrow P(go)] \vee T[P(go) \rightarrow O(\neg go)] \vee P(go)$$

where $O = obligation$, $T = transition$, $P = permission$. Prohibition to do A, $F(A)$, is formalised as obligation not to do A, $O(\neg A)$. The yellow light is not taken into consideration above in order to simplify the model.

Workflow and Legal Machines In proceedings workflows, decision makers are comprised of humans and machines (see Fig. 23.5). Data input is a legally binding act. For instance, declaring income has legal qualification and you are obliged to input truthful data. You cannot excuse machines saying that you were joking with false data. Machines also check for your input correctness. Hence, all communication combinations are observed: human-to-human, human-to-machine, machine-to-human, and machine-to-machine. Each is of legal significance.

Fig. 23.5 In a workflow, decisions can also be made by machines (Čyras and Lachmayer 2013)

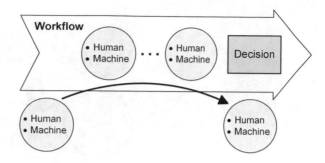

Fig. 23.6 Three layers within an organisation. A legal act establishes a relationship between two entities (Čyras and Lachmayer 2013)

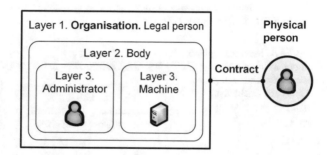

Computers that are comprised in information systems are substantially more complicated than simple legal machines. Here recall e-government applications. Suppose a machine is described in terms of finite state automaton. The number of its states can serve as a measure of complexity when comparing two machines. For instance, a simple traffic light consists of three states: 'red', 'yellow' and 'green'. On the contrary, information systems have substantially more states. Each keystroke can raise a different event and it brings the system to a distinct state.

Machines Replacing Administrators in Organisations There are no big differences between machines and humans in the production of legal acts by organisations. An organisation can be viewed on three levels (see Fig. 23.6). The first is the legal entity as a whole. The second level is a body (Organ) of the organisation, and the third one—an administrator (Organwalter) of the body, which can be a human being or a machine, too. Suppose an official selling train tickets. A traveller makes a contract with the organisation—not with the cashier. Therefore the cashier can be replaced with a ticket machine.

The Right of Representation Is an Issue
The question is, can machine represent an organisation's body? The answer depends on the legal position of machines. This is the subject matter of regulation by the law. The legal status results not from raw facts but from the legal order. Imposing regulations by machines is a prerequisite to change their status from tools to legal machines. A legitimisation is necessary.

The meaning of contract lies in the legal act—not the substrate. The institutional fact is of legal significance whereas the actual action of obtaining goods is not. The

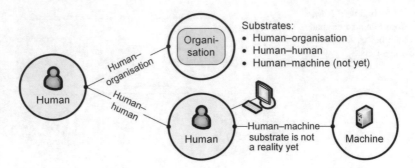

Fig. 23.7 Communication relationships. Machine is auxiliary to administrators: machine ≠ legal person (Čyras and Lachmayer 2013)

Fig. 23.8 Machine replaces an organisation and becomes a kind of e-person (Čyras and Lachmayer 2013)

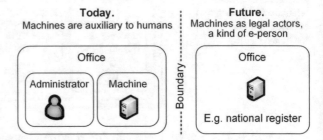

legal act is from the Ought whereas the substrate is from the Is. From this viewpoint, we draw an analogy between making contracts via administrators and machines. Then machine can count as administrator in organisation; see the formula "X counts as Y in context C" (Searle 1996, p. 114). A similar status can be imposed on different ontological categories of phenomena: people and objects (ibid., p. 97).

Hence, two alternative bridging relationships with a third person, the buyer, are: (1) organisation–*administrator*–person, and (2) organisation–*machine*–person. The first arch in (1) and (2) results respectively in two encapsulations, *organisation-in-administrator* and *organisation-in-machine*. In both cases the representation powers are scoped by the seller's function.

Machines replacing administrators result with the substrates human–organisation and human–human (see Fig. 23.7). The human–machine substrate is not a reality yet. Today machines per se still do not reach the level of legal persons. They lack legal capacity and contractual capacity.

Legal Personhood of Electronic Persons

The case of organisations draws a boundary of today. Imagine a future situation in which a machine replaces the whole organisation. Suppose national register organisations. Today they operate as legal persons. However, imagine a national register in future which is operated by a machine (see Fig. 23.8). It will become a kind of e-person. Schweighofer (2007, p. 18) states that "legal systems have to consider giving intelligent agents or robots some form of 'limited' legal personality in order to allow the application of the concepts of representation and responsibility." The question is to what level such a 'limited' legal personality can extend. A paradigm shift for future is to complement legal actors with machines.

Solaiman (2017, p. 172) maintains that "robots are presently recognised as a product or property at law". His review of a legal personhood is concerned mainly with industrial robots, and concludes that "robots are *ineligible* to be persons, based on the requirements of personhood" (ibid., p. 155), emphasis added. Solaiman (2017, p. 161) formulates three attributes of legal personhood, including "the ability to exercise rights and to perform duties". Bryson et al. (2017, p. 274) refer to Solaiman and stress two requirements for a legal person: first, "it is able to know and execute its right as a legal agent" and, second, "it is subject to legal sanctions ordinarily applied to humans". Bryson et al. (2017, p. 289) argue that "conferring legal personality on robots is morally unnecessary and legally troublesome." Bryson et al. (2017, p. 275) suggest that there is no moral obligation to recognise the legal personhood of artificial intelligence, and "recommend again the extension of legal personhood to robots, because the costs are too great and the moral gains are too few." Bryson et al. hold that legal personhood is all or nothing; conferring legal obligations on machines require procedures to enforce them.[2] It remains unclear how to operationalise dispute settlement procedures.[3]

Solaiman (2017, p. 170) presents an argument that "as the law presently regards, there is no 'in-between' position of personhood [. . .] because entities are categorised in a simple, binary, 'all-or-nothing' fashion". However, Bryson et al. (2017, p. 280) argues for legal personality to be divisible.[4] We agree that the legal position of a legal machine in the role of a governance body requires regulation by the law. Weng and Izumo (2019) suggest that with respect to rights and responsibilities a separate set of laws would be needed for robots.

Machine Is Analogy of Slave in Roman Law Administrator–organisation relationship is similar to that of a slave (servus) which makes a contract in favour of his master (dominus) (see Fig. 23.9). The slave is a thing (res). Therefore this is depicted with a box and a human inside. However it is significant that slaves could make contracts for their masters (in scope of their property, peculium). The contract is not for slave but via him. Thus two alternatives of negotium between Aulus Agerius and Numerius Negidius exist: via slave or directly. Machine's position in nowadays organisations can be compared with the legal position of a slave.

---

[2]Bryson et al. (2017, p. 282) write: "Just as legal rights mean nothing if the legal system elides the standing to protect them, legal obligations mean nothing in the absence of procedure to enforce them."

[3]Bryson et al. (2017, p. 288) continue: "Giving robots legal rights without counterbalancing legal obligations would only make matters worse   This would not necessarily be a problem, if 1. the other problems of legal personality—like standing and availability of dispute settlement procedures—were solved; and 2. the electronic legal person were solvent or otherwise answerable for rights violations. But it is unclear how to operationalize either of these steps."

[4]Bryson et al. (2017, p. 280) write: "Legal personhood is not an all-or-nothing proposition. Since it is made up of legal rights and obligations, entities can have more, fewer, overlapping, or even disjointed sets of these."

Fig. 23.9 Alternative
negotium between *AA* and
NN: via a slave and directly
(Čyras and Lachmayer
2013)

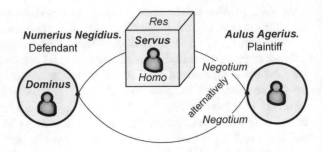

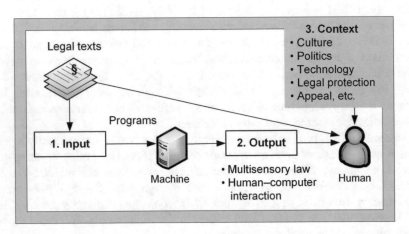

Fig. 23.10 Legal machines in the context (Čyras and Lachmayer 2013)

Context Law is transformed into machine's input, which has the form of programs
(see Fig. 23.10). The machine produces output to a human. The context is also
significant for human as it comprises various extra-legal contexts, such as cultural,
political, social, technical, and economic (Brunschwig 2011, p. 577) and issues,
e.g. legal protection, appeal, etc. The output raises an institutional fact and communicates it to the human. The interaction concerns multisensory law and human-
computer interaction. Hence, the issues of law and information technology (IT) are
tackled. The language to communicate the output from machine to human needs not
to be a natural language like English.[5]

Latency of Legal Forms New technological developments, especially ones involving the internet, can lack new legal forms. Recall the old forms, written and oral.
Suppose two natural persons intending to engage in a kind of a contract relationship

---

[5] Searle writes: "[s]ocial facts in general do not require language [. . .] My claim that language is
partly constitutive of institutional facts amounts to the claim that institutional facts essentially
contain some symbolic elements in this sense of "symbolic": there are words, symbols, or other
conventional devices that mean something or express something or represent or symbolize something beyond themselves, in a way that is publicly understandable" (Searle 1996, pp. 59–60).

and seeking a suitable form. Let us assume that no new legal form is available. Therefore the individuals start seeking for a workaround form. They decide on an old available form. However this old form which is drawn on the persons can have normative and institutional consequences, which are not suitable for the present situation. Examples are gratuitous service contracts which are seeking proxies to read university lectures. Recall also disastrous consequences of bank contracts when the whole loan was paid to individuals.

In summary, new technological situations may need to create new legal forms or to customise the old ones. Old form consequences can be undesirable.

23.3 An Analogy Between Machines and Humans

Four types of relationships to send legal content are possible: two types on the sender side—human and machine—and two on the receiver (see Fig. 23.11). These four interaction types are viewed differently in the context. The internal representations of information are different: texts for humans and programs for machines. Therefore, on the meta-level, different requirements arise for human–human and computer–computer interaction. The incoming texts can be read by people, but programs cannot be read by the users.

23.3.1 Actor, Norm and Role

We can associate an actor with a norm, N (a general and abstract norm from the reality that ought to be). Here we do not discuss whether this is one norm or a system of norms. The content of the norm is the subject matter of material law and is outside the scope of a jurisprudential survey.

A role can be assigned to an actor executing an action. A role is a set of rights, obligations, and expected behaviour patterns associated with a particular social status. A role identifies a whole type of behaviour—not an instance. Role's name is a label such as 'traffic light', 'vending machine', etc.

Fig. 23.11 Four types of communicating legal content (Čyras and Lachmayer 2013)

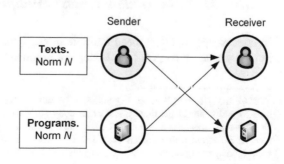

Fig. 23.12 Multisensority
in the *imago* doctrine:
machina = imago hominis
(Čyras and Lachmayer
2013)

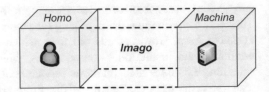

An actor complies with *N*. In the case of machine, software enforces *N*. Suppose a
norm model *condition-subject-modus-action*, where modus is 'obligatory', 'permitted', etc. The factual act model *condition-actor-action-effect* conforms to it. Every
concrete actual actor has to match the norm's condition and subject.

The sender who commits an action can be treated as an agent—"anything that can
be viewed as perceiving its environment through sensors and acting upon that
environment through actuators" (Russell and Norvig 2003, p. 32).[6] A vending
machine has a mechanism to cash money and a mechanism to give the item. A
traffic-light reacts to time and the light bulbs stand for actuators.

23.3.2   Situational Flexibility

Human–human interaction is more flexible than human–computer. People can adjust
their behaviour to a concrete situation. As an example suppose a train approaching a
station and a person under stress going to buy a ticket. It makes a difference to buy
from a cashier or a ticket machine.

Multisensority can ease layman's interaction. Multiple channels, such as voice,
face expression, eye contact, etc., can be used concurrently to explain situation
details to an administrator. Machines are less flexible in interpreting this
multichannel information.

Situational flexibility features can be foreseen in machine specifications. An
example is a rapid but expensive service instead of a slow but cheap. Communication in emergency situations, such as a need of ambulance, can be regulated by law.

23.3.3   Multiple Human Senses: Multiple Formats

Multisensory properties mean multiple input channels (see Fig. 23.12). Next question is how to manage outputs which are produced by output channels.

---

[6]Russell and Norvig (2003, p. 32) continue: "A human agent has eyes, ears, and other organs for
sensors and hands, legs, mouth, and other body parts for actuators. A robotic agent might have
cameras and infrared range finders for sensors and various motors for actuators. A software agent
receives keystrokes, files contents and network packets as sensory inputs and acts on the environment by displaying on the screen, writing files, and sending network packets."

command(*format* = *gesture*,   *content* = *'Policeman raising hand'*)

command(*format* = *acoustic*,   *content* = *'Policeman whistling'*)

command(*format* = *visual*,   *content* = *'Traffic light turns red'*)

command(*format* = *visual*,   *content* = ' 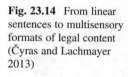 ')

command(*format* = *visual*,   *content* = ' Betreten verboten ')

command(*format* = {*visual, touch*}, *content* = *'Road barrier on the street'*)

Fig. 23.13 Examples of message representation *command*(*format, content*) (Čyras and Lachmayer 2012)

Fig. 23.14 From linear sentences to multisensory formats of legal content (Čyras and Lachmayer 2013)

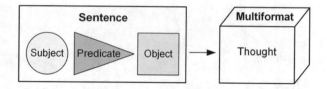

For instance, a legal act which forbids entering can be issued by different actors including machines and technical devices. In the case of a policeman raising hand and whistling, a human recipient perceives the message by sight and hearing. A traffic sign is sensed by sight only. A barrier can also be sensed by touch. The understanding of verbal signs such as 'Betreten verboten' can be limited on people understanding German.

The format of a recipient's input channel can be modeled with a parameter in the message representation *command*(*format, content*) (see Fig. 23.13). These messages mean the obligation to halt (with semantic nuances), *O halt* or *O no_action*. Hence, a need appears for a notation of normative multisensory messages.

This is similar to the multiple formats of text documents. A document can be produced in multiple output formats such as TXT, DOC, HTML, etc. Digital signature and other properties can also be foreseen. Similarly, a legal statement of the form *subject-predicate-object* can be outputted differently. Different levels and channels can be in the focus.

Multisensory Representation of Legal Content Suppose a linear structure *subject-predicate-object* to model sentences in a self-conscious language (see Fig. 23.14). What are sentence formats in the unconscious and could non-linear formats be more effective? The question can be formulated: Can the cognitive cube be diced in other formats for visual, acoustic, motor functions, textual, logical, etc. representations of legal contents (see Fig. 23.15)? Distinct formats result in different document types. For instance, the rules of computer actions are represented in programs, not in texts.

Fig. 23.15 The metaphor of unfolding multisensory cognitive cube to multiple formats (Čyras and Lachmayer 2013)

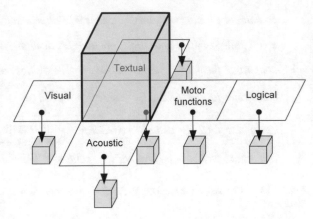

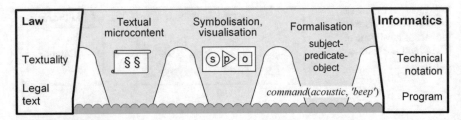

Fig. 23.16 The multibridge metaphor: transformations lead from norm to its machine implementation (Čyras and Lachmayer 2012)

23.3.4 Multisensory Law Is at the Periphery of Textual Law

Suppose designing a multisensory legal machine such as traffic lights for disabled people. It has to be equipped with sound devices and touch panels. Therefore, first, the (verbal) road rules concerning disabled have to be transformed into legal content (multisensory commandments), which would be perceived by disabled. Next transformation leads to technical statements which implement the legal content to be sensed by hearing and touch. The resulting acoustic implementation can be achieved with the following transformations:

$$Norm(subject-predicate-object) \rightarrow$$
$$command(acoustic, 'beep') \rightarrow$$
$$technical\ instructions$$

Consider multiple transformations from the law to informatics. The multibridge metaphor is shown in Fig. 23.16. In these transformations, multisensory law appears at the periphery whereas textual law is at the centre.

23.3.5 Multisensority in Procedural Law

Law concerns several tiers. The lowest tier is actors' behaviour on the Is stage where actors interact in different forms: written, oral, gestures, etc. The 'what' is regulated by material law whereas the 'how' by procedural law. Parliaments cannot regulate so flexibly comparing with technical standards which regulate multisensory communication. The reason is that legal systems have to satisfy the minimality principle. Therefore the weak rules of multisensory behaviour are placed in technical standards. Though, e.g. the written and oral forms of proceedings are regulated by the law. Examples of uni- and multisensory legal or legally relevant phenomena are given by Brunschwig (2011, pp. 592–599): voting in a parliament and video recording during the questioning of children.

The actors on the horizontal Is stage, humans and machines, communicate through various channels. Promulgation rules on the vertical tier of law could also be extended to multimodal channels such as Braille or voice. Reasonableness of this is next question.

Hence, normative multisensority is a matter for wide regulation by technical standards that are made by expert groups. Technical issues should not be overregulated by the laws. Outdating technologies would be illegitimate. Recall the data protection law which required the currently outdated RTF format.

23.4 Formalising Legal Machine as Encapsulation

Formal models of the issues which are raised above are a challenge. Actors can be classified into humans, animals, allegories, machines, etc. (see Fig. 23.17). Humans are legal actors whereas animals are not. Allegories such as the state and juristic person can denote legal actors. Legal machines are not juristic persons, however can be assigned a status-function. Next issue is the combinatorics of communication including the modes of communication such as text, acoustic, gestures, etc.

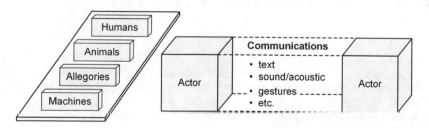

Fig. 23.17 The types of actors and communication (Čyras and Lachmayer 2013)

23.4.1   Human-in-Machine Is Similar to Human-in-Animal Encapsulation in the Ancient World

Examples of transformations of a human being into an animal and vice versa can be found in Greco-Roman myths. Mythical creatures such as minotaur,[7] centaur,[8] sphinx, etc. embody encapsulations. The Mechanical Turk (a fake chess-playing machine[9]) is an example of human-in-machine. In these ways human and animal combinations can be complimented with the encapsulations of machines: human-in-machine (e.g. The Turk) and machine-in-human.

The word 'person' is derived from Latin persona—actor's mask, character in a play, later human being. "The term 'person' refers to 'man as a player of roles'" (Pattaro 2007, p. 376). The word refers to an abstract thing and can be implemented by machine.

23.4.2   Transforming Humans into Animals and Machines

Human-to-animal transformations in the ancient world are about transforming a man into an animal such as a bird or an ass;[10] recall the myth about Midas[11] and Apollo. The combinatorics to explore concerns four kinds of entities: animal, human, mask—person (persona) including allegories such as state and juristic person, and machine. Each entity speaks a specific language. An example of acoustic output is a phone answering machine or GPS which give commands in voice. Formal logic is more a language of machines than people.

We define *encapsulation* of an actor *A1*, called *encapsulator*, into an actor *A2*, called *encapsulatee*, to be a new actor denoted *A1-in-A2* with the following capabilities (see Figs. 23.18 and 23.19):

(a) the encapsulator monitors (i.e. gives commands to) the encapsulatee in a language *L1* which is understood by both *A1* and *A2*;
(b) legal content is sent to third persons in a language *L2* of *A2*;
(c) encapsulator's goals (i.e. motives, objectives, values) are pursued;
(d) encapsulatee's, channels are used to transmit legal content.

---

[7] In Greek mythology, the Minotaur, as the Greeks imagined him, was a creature with the head of a bull on the body of a man or, "part man and part bull" (see Wikipedia, https://en.wikipedia.org/wiki/Minotaur).

[8] Composite race of creatures, part human and part horse (see Wikipedia, https://en.wikipedia.org/wiki/Centaur).

[9] See e.g. Wikipedia, https://en.wikipedia.org/wiki/The_Turk.

[10] See e.g. Wikipedia, https://en.wikipedia.org/wiki/The_Golden_Ass.

[11] See e.g. Wikipedia, https://en.wikipedia.org/wiki/Midas.

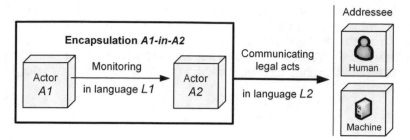

Fig. 23.18 Encapsulation *A1-in-A2* communicates legal act to addressee (Čyras and Lachmayer 2013)

Fig. 23.19 Encapsulation *A1-in-A2* (Čyras and Lachmayer 2013)

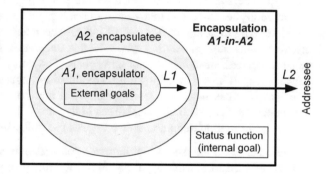

The idea is that a man *A1* is empowered with a tool *A2*. Not all human functions of *A1* are empowered, but a specific one that is regulated by a norm *N*. A purpose is to combine the capabilities of both *A1* and *A2*: *capabilities(A1-in-A2) = capabilities(-A1) ∪ capabilities(A2)*.

23.4.3 Encapsulation and Goals

Encapsulations are viewed as goal-governed systems. The encapsulator embodies the external goals concept. Here we follow Conte and Castelfranchi (1995) and their terminology; see their Chapter 8 "Towards a Unified Theory of Goals and Finalities", pp. 120–141. These external goals are intrinsic in a norm *N* for which the encapsulation *A1-in-A2* is designed. The legal texts which serve as input to the legal machine *A1-in-A2* can be viewed as a source of *N*.

The encapsulation *A1 in A2* can be assigned a status function. This status function can be viewed as goal of use value (to be apt to. . .) (Conte and Castelfranchi 1995, p. 124) on *A1-in-A2*. Goal definitions could be shared with the cognitive sciences: "a goal is a representation of a world state within a system" (p. 123).

Intentional goals (i.e. serving as external goals, values, intentional stance) cannot be assigned to every entity. Intentional stance is not intrinsic to machines. Deities and some allegories such as states and juristic persons can be assigned goals but machines cannot. "A stone *per se* does not have and cannot have any kind of goal" (pp. 123–124). Paraphrasing this, a machine (a tool, a gun) per se is neither good nor bad.

23.5   Examples of Encapsulation

Deities in Greco-Roman mythology have the form of human bodies. Recall gods, titans, etc. Personifications obtain both unnatural physical powers of gods and human bodily features. The human mouth sends legal content to people.

Which type to assign to this pair of human and machine: human-in-machine or machine-in-human? A starting point is that machines are tools monitored by humans. Second, machines do not have goals. The aim of coupling is to leverage human's capabilities. In a powerful combination, humans give intelligence to machines whereas machines leverage physical and computational capabilities of human beings. People obtain capabilities to fly, etc.

The encapsulation definition above implies the following consequences:

- *Human-in-machine* means that human's goals are pursued and machine's channels are used to transmit legal content. The human uses the machine as a tool, e.g. pilot-in-aircraft and driver-in-car.
- *Machine-in-human* encapsulation means that machine's goals are pursued and human's channels are used to transmit legal content.

Suppose a *policeman-in-machine* example. A policeman watches images on computer display that are transmitted from a distant camera which monitors a barrier. The policeman's command to stop the traffic is expressed in machine's gesture—the barrier is being dropped.

A meaningful example of *machine-in-human* encapsulation would scarcely be given. The reason is that machines do not have goals. Nevertheless, suppose a malfunctioning machine *A1* sending a false alarm to a human *A2* who commands alarm with bad consequences.

Human-in-machine examples below illustrate how human functions are assigned to machines and animals:

- *Pilot-in-aircraft*. Suppose two aircraft in the air. The first pilot orders the second one immediate landing. The signaling is in aircraft gestures, e.g. waving aircraft wings. The first pilot stands for *A1* and his aircraft for *A2*. The goal of *A1* is to force landing the second aircraft. Aircraft signal language stand for *L2*.
- *Policeman-in-car*. Suppose a policeman *A1* in a car *A2* commanding a violator driver to stop. Any communication channel can be used: car lights, manoeuvres, a

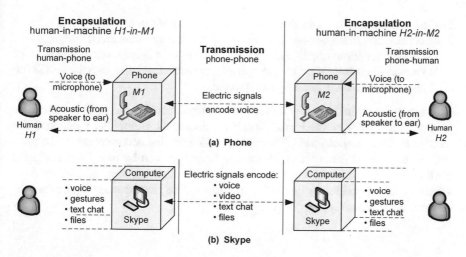

Fig. 23.20 Human-in-machine encapsulation in communication via (**a**) phone and (**b**) Skype (Čyras and Lachmayer 2013)

loudspeaker or even a gun. The goal is to stop the violator. Car signals stand for *L2*.

- *The Turk*. The type is *humanOperator-in-machine*. The operator stands for *A1* and the mechanical device that moves chess pieces for *A2*. *A1* aims to win against the opponent player thus cheating him that machine thinks. Chess moves stand for *L2*.
- *Human-in-animal*. The 'Golden ass' mythical story illustrates a transformation of a man into an animal. The man *A1* intends to spy with the goal to practice magic. Therefore he intends to transform into a bird *A2*. The *man-in-bird* would acquire the capabilities of both. However, while trying to perform a spell to transform into a bird, he is transformed into an ass.

23.5.1 *Representing Communication via Phone and Skype as Encapsulation*

Phone and Skype communication between humans *H1* and *H2* is described below to illustrate the *human-in-machine* notation. The communication chain between *H1* and *H2* is represented with two encapsulations and one transmission (see Fig. 23.20).

There are two channels between *H1* and his phone *M1*: (1) voice to the *M1*'s microphone, and (2) acoustic signal from the *M1*'s speaker to ear. The transmission between the two phones is through one channel: electric signal encodes voice. The whole chain is:

1. Encapsulation human-in-machine *H1-in-M1*: A message from *H1* to *M1* is transmitted by voice. *M1* encodes voice messages in electric signals.

2. Communication: The message is transmitted from *M1* to *M2*.
3. Encapsulation human-in-machine *H2-in-M2*: *M2* transforms electric signals into the phone's speaker vibration thus transmitting to *H2* via the acoustic channel. *H2* is encapsulated into *M2* with the purpose to receive electric signals, which are decoded to acoustic signals by the speaker.

A simple phone would scarcely be viewed as a legal machine but legal status can be imposed on intelligent machines. Skype communication employs video and file transfer as additional channels. Therefore people can also communicate in gestures and mimics via Skype. Other devices and languages can be used, especially for medium distance transmission. Examples are naval flag signalling and Morse code which can be transmitted by lights. Lighthouses can be viewed as legal machines for seamen, radio beacons—for pilots, etc.

23.5.2 Encapsulations into Human: X-in-Human

In contrast to encapsulations of human, *human-in-X*, following is an example of encapsulation into human, *X-in-human*, and into animal, respectively:

- *Allegory-in-human*: 'Leviathan' by Thomas Hobbes. This refers the frontispiece of the book.[12] The encapsulation type is *stateAllegory-in-humanFormSovereign*. The state allegory, *A1*, is encapsulated into the human-form sovereign Leviathan, *A2*. The *L2* language is that of rule by an absolute sovereign—to wield the sceptre, a gesture language.
- *Mask-in-animal*: Biblical Leviathan. This refers to a sea monster referred to in the Bible, one of the seven princes of Hell and its gatekeeper.[13] The encapsulation type is *gatekeeperMask-in-biblicalAnimal*. A gatekeeper mask, *A1*, is encapsulated into a biblical sea monster, *A2*. The allegory can be viewed as a *mask-in-animal*. The Hell gate keeping language stands for *L2*.

Actors such as animals, masks and allegories can be attributed intentions. The actors' demands can be viewed as goals. Therefore the encapsulations animal-in-machine, mask-in-machine and allegory-in-machine are meaningful. A question is: How to attribute responsibilities to the actors? Natural persons and juristic persons are held liable. The attribution of liability to animals and natural things is an issue of a historical survey.

---

[12] See Wikipedia, https://en.wikipedia.org/wiki/Leviathan_(Hobbes_book).
[13] See Wikipedia, https://en.wikipedia.org/wiki/Leviathan.

23.6   Related Work

Ordinary people think in terms of roles whereas jurists—in terms of rules. The mask and persona concepts can be modeled by roles. Actors send legal content to norm addressees, ordinary people. The addressee is attributed a role.

The Concept of Role In information systems engineering, a *User* is typically defined as a human or a software agent. Here we cite Matulevičius and Dumas (2011) who compare security models and adapt Role-based Access Control, RBAC (Ferraiolo et al. 2001) that restricts system access to authorised users. The main elements of the RBAC model are *Users*, *Roles*, *Objects*, and *Permissions*. A *Role* is a job function within the context of organisation. Role refers to authority and respon-sibility conferred on the user assigned to this role. *Permissions* are approvals to perform one or more *Operations* on one or more protected *Objects*. An Operation is an executable sequence of actions that can be initiated by the system entities. An *Object* is a protected system resource (or a set of resources). *User assignment* relationship describes how users are assigned to their roles. *Permission assignment* relationship characterises the set of privileges assigned to a *Role*.

Legal Machines in Multisensory Law Brunschwig proposed the term 'multisen-sory law' ('multisensory jurisprudence' as a synonym) and advocates that it is about multimodal (visual, audiovisual, etc.) representation and communication of valid legal content (geltendrechtliche Inhalt):

> The valid legal content denotes the content of valid law and also the content, which is significant for it. [Mit "geltendrechtlichen Inhalten" meine ich Inhalte des geltenden Rechts, aber auch Inhalte, die für das geltende Recht bedeutsam sind.] (Brunschwig 2003, p. 413)

Traditionally legal actors are comprised of lawyers, judges, administration officials, parliament members, etc. (p. 411). The subject matter of multisensory law consists of three phenomena (p. 592) (see Table 23.1). The subject matter of legal informatics is analogous (cf. p. 630). The words above are so interwoven that it is not easy to grasp the distinctions at once, but Brunschwig explains the meaning further in her analysis.

Table 23.1 The subject matter of two disciplines; adapted from figures in Brunschwig (2011, pp. 592 and 630)

	The subject matter of multisensory law	The subject matter of legal informatics
A	The uni- and multisensory phenomena in the law	The ICT-based phenomena in the law
B	The law as a uni- and multisensory phenomenon in the law	The law as an ICT-based phenomenon in the law
C	The law as a uni- and multisensory phenomenon (the law in uni- and multisensory phenomena)	The law as an ICT-based phenomenon (the law in ICT-based phenomena)

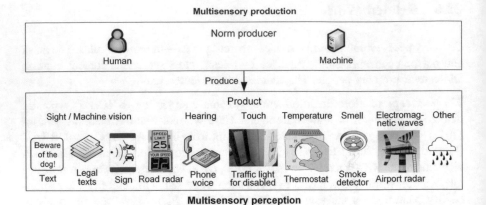

Fig. 23.21 A variety of modes in the production and perception of legal content (Čyras and Lachmayer 2011)

Her study raises deep questions and also serves as a reader on several fields.[14] Brunschwig's classifications enable us to relate the subject matter of the analysed disciplines to machines. For instance, legal visuals can be produced by computers. Thus machines would be related to the questions raised by her, for instance, "How do multisensory law and legal informatics relate to audiovisual law, auditory law, tactile-kinesthetic law, and olfactory-gustatory law?" (p. 648).

Some patterns of multimodal machine communication are illustrated in Fig. 23.21. Road and airport radar systems are examples of visual and radio communication where machine vision produces legal consequences. A voice example is hearing commands in your phone: 'In the case of... press 1, etc.' A thermostat perceives temperature changes and turns the heating system on. Prescriptive gestures can be performed by machines, too; see pilot-in-aircraft encapsulation in the previous section. Multisensory production and perception are distinguished.

Conclusion Briefly, a legal machine is defined as a machine in a system whose actions draw legal consequences. Legal machines shift raw facts into institutional facts. Moreover, a raw fact may have different legal interpretations. Thus, legal machines implement legal meaning. There are simple legal machines, such as traffic lights, barriers and vending machines, and complex ones, such as the electronic forms that are used in tax and finance. The software of legal machines implements legal rules and thus legal machines enforce the law.

We depart from the view that machines are tools. The target view is that legal machines are legal actors that are capable of triggering institutional facts. In

---

[14] "[F]irst systematic knowledge basis for multisensory law and particularly for its relationship to visual law [...] It has also added to what is known about legal informatics, notably about its branch artificial intelligence and law and its subarea visual legal representation" (Brunschwig 2011, p. 648).

organisations there is an analogy between the administrator's position and machine. Legal content can be expressed in multimodal languages (visual, audio, gestures, etc.), communicated by machines and perceived by all of our senses.

To express that a human *A1* is encapsulated into a machine *A2* we introduced the concept of encapsulation. Actions intended by *A1* are communicated to third persons via the output channel of *A2*. Encapsulations can be compared with mythical creatures, part human and part animal, which can send gods' messages through the human mouth.

Multimodal communication is regulated by technical standards that give flexibility to the 'how'. The promulgation law cannot regulate so flexibly.

References

Brunschwig CR (2003) Tabuzone juristischer Reflexion. Zum Mangel an Bildern, die geltendrechtliche Inhalte visualisieren. In: Schweighofer E, Lachmayer F (eds) Zwischen Rechtstheorie und e-Government: aktuelle Fragen der Rechtsinformatik. Schriftenreihe Rechtsinformatik, vol 7. Verlag Österreich, Vienna, pp 411–420

Brunschwig CR (2011) Multisensory law and legal informatics – a comparison of how these legal disciplines relate to visual law. In: Geist A, Brunschwig CR, Lachmayer F, Schefbeck G (eds) Strukturierung der Juristischen Semantik – structuring legal semantics. Editions Weblaw, Bern, pp 573–667

Bryson JJ, Diamantis ME, Grant TD (2017) Of, for, and by the people: the lacuna of synthetic persons. Artif Intell Law 25(3):273–291. https://doi.org/10.1007/s10506-017-9214-9

Conte R, Castelfranchi C (1995) Cognitive and social action. UCL Press, London

Čyras V, Lachmayer F (2011) Distributive multimedia and multisensory legal machines. Jusletter IT, 24 February 2011. https://jusletter-it.weblaw.ch/issues/2011/IRIS/article_362.html. Accessed 15 Dec 2022

Čyras V, Lachmayer F (2012) Multisensory legal machines and legal act production. In: 25th IVR world congress: law science and technology, 15–20 August 2011. Paper series A no. 026/2012. Goethe University Frankfurt am Main. https://publikationen.ub.uni-frankfurt.de/opus4/frontdoor/deliver/index/docId/24884/file/IVR_World_Congress_2011_No_026.pdf. Accessed 15 Dec 2022

Čyras V, Lachmayer F (2013) Legal machines and legal act production within multisensory operational implementations. In: Philipps L, Bengez RZ (eds) Von der Spezifikation zum Schluss. Nomos, Baden-Baden, pp 147–168

Ferraiolo DF, Sandhu R, Gavrila S, Kuhn DR, Chandramouli R (2001) Proposed NIST standard for role-based access control. ACM Trans Inf Syst Secur (TISSEC) 4(3):224–274. https://doi.org/10.1145/501978.501980

Matulevičius R, Dumas M (2011) Towards model transformation between SecureUML and UMLsec for role-based access control. In: Barzdins J, Kirikova M (eds) Databases and information systems VI. Frontiers in artificial intelligence and applications, vol 224. IOS Press, Amsterdam, pp 339–352. https://doi.org/10.3233/978-1-60750-688-1-339

Pattaro E (2007) The law and the right: a reappraisal of the reality that ought to be. Series A Treatise of legal philosophy and general jurisprudence, vol 1. Springer, Dordrecht

Raabe O, Wacker R, Oberle D, Baumann C, Funk C (2012) Recht ex machina. Formalisierung des Rechts im Internet der Dienste. Springer Vieweg, Heidelberg

Russell S, Norvig P (2003) Artificial intelligence: a modern approach. Prentice Hall

Schweighofer E (2007) E-governance in the information society. In: Schweighofer E (ed) Legal informatics and e-governance as tools for the knowledge society, LEFIS Series 2, pp 13–23
Searle JR (1996) The construction of social reality. Penguin Books, London
Solaiman SM (2017) Legal personality of robots, corporations, idols and chimpanzees: a quest for legitimacy. Artif Intell Law 25(2):155–179. https://doi.org/10.1007/s10506-016-9192-3
Weng Y, Izumo T (2019) Natural law and its implications for AI governance. Delphi – Interdiscip Rev Emerg Technol 2(3):122–128. https://doi.org/10.21552/delphi/2019/3/5

Chapter 24
Formulating the Compliance Problem

24.1 The Problem: Is Software Compliant with the Law?

We start with the Klaus Julisch's (2008) IT compliance problem definition and make an attempt to formulate the enterprise architecture (EA) compliance problem. The challenging issues comprise the complexity of the law phenomenon, compliance frameworks and methodologies to check EA for non-compliance with laws and regulations. We hold that a compliance methodology should take into account 'shared' relevant laws and a requirements engineering framework. We reflect mainly on the view of enterprise architects on legal informatics and a vision driven approach on requirements elicitation in the context of enterprise engineering, which was proposed by Albertas Čaplinskas (Informatica 20(3):343–368, 2009). Then we raise a question of placing the compliance problem into the Bonazzi–Hussami–Pigneur regulation and IT alignment framework (Information systems: people, organizations, institutions, and technologies. Physica-Verlag HD, pp 391–398, 2009).

This chapter attempts to overview some models which could contribute to formulate regulatory compliance problems. However, the field appears too broad to master with a sweep of the arm. A unified 'enterprise-wide' compliance process remains an ambition. Thus we present reflections on various issues. The message is that a compliance methodology should follow a requirements engineering framework because the latter combines business, IT and legal perspectives.

Consider the question 'Is software compliant with the law?' The answer need not be 'yes' or 'no' but can lie on an evaluation spectrum that ranges from optimistic to pessimistic. We find this question similar to the question, 'Can machines think?',

Based on Čyras and Riedl (2012a, b).

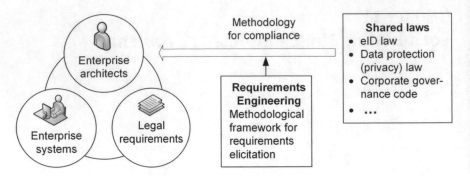

Fig. 24.1 The key concepts tackled in this chapter (Čyras and Riedl 2012a)

which was asked by Alan Turing. Analogously, we look at the terms 'software', 'compliant' and 'the law'.

The "naive" compliance problem formulation above is similar to bridging informatics and law (Fig. 23.16 in Chap. 23). We utilise the bridge metaphor because we can see a similarity, which is discussed further in Chap. 27. This bridge consists of multiple arches.

Transparency optimisation is a major purpose in EA. Legal requirements are one of a kind among all requirements tackled by enterprise architects. Different legal issues are concerned in every EA perspective. The enterprise architect's perspective has the task to integrate all the different views on EA, in particular, the business view, the ICT view, and the legal view. Figure 24.1 shows the key terms within the point of departure.

24.2   Motivating the Research

A practical motivation for academia can be illustrated by the STORK 2.0 project[1] that concerned the design and implementation of the foundations for a unified European identification and authentication space.

24.2.1   E-identity and E-banking Within the STORK 2.0 Project

STORK (Secure idenTity acrOss boRders linKed) [2008–2011] established a European electronic identity (eID) interoperability platform which allows holders

---

[1] Cofunded under EU ICT Policy Support Programme as part of the Competitiveness and innovation framework programme (CIP), https://cordis.europa.eu/project/rcn/191751/factsheet/en.

of national eIDs to access cross-border electronic services within six pilot applications. Its extension STORK 2.0 [2012–2015] extended the range of services within four new pilots. One of them is focused on e-banking, mainly retail banking, the scene for secure e-invoicing. Its key vision is to move identity and access management (IAM) out of the core banking IT system. Authentication should be possible with any eIDs issued by accredited eID providers guaranteeing the highest quality level of trustworthiness. Of course, a solution must include major national electronic identities in Europe, if they comply with highest quality standards. However, even for them legal issues are unclear.

The big picture for the whole project aims at a shift from interoperability for a few national eIDs to the creation of a single European identity space for borderless e-business. All trustworthy eIDs, both national and commercial, should be usable in this space upon the accreditation of the eID providers according to a 4-level quality standard for the trustworthiness of eIDs.

Non-repudiation is a critical requirement for electronic business. It is also a precondition for compliance as otherwise transactions could be repudiated. Both can be based on the authentication of interaction partners and a trustworthy recording of interaction activities.

Following is a use case to check for compliance. A company representative with an eID from country X (e.g. Germany), working in a company from country Y (e.g. Switzerland) logs into a banking platform in country Z (e.g. Austria, Lithuania or US). The number of potential customers comprises foreign nationals, for instance, those living in Switzerland and cross border commuters.

Do the requirements for e-banking comply with national eID laws? Can the proof of identity be transferred from the issuing of an eID to the opening of a bank account with this eID? In many countries this is an open question. For sure, some conflicts exist.[2] This indicates that compliance is a tricky and much broader issue than it appears to be at first glance. For instance, excluding some users may be legally compliant in one country and clearly non-compliant in another.

The STORK 2.0 project also tackled common infrastructure for federated e-government, in particular in Switzerland. Today's challenges are: (1) organisational and business models, (2) implementation of a government cloud, and (3) refinement of the existing enterprise architecture in order to get it "working". Tomorrow's challenge is enterprise architecture design for the implementation of the Lenk–Schaffroth–Schuppan vision of networked government, which links processes across different public administration organisations (Lenk et al. 2010). Apart from other challenges, there are highly complex compliance issues to be considered.

---

[2] Riedl et al. (2012, p. 440) write: "Seen from a European political perspective, eIDs are primarily in potential conflict with privacy protection rights and thus with data protection laws. However, seen from a broader political perspective, the design of a single identification and authentication space also touches the so far hardly discussed eventual right for being recognized by electronic services."

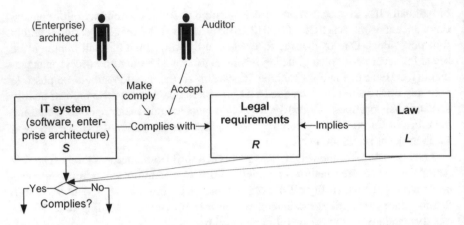

Fig. 24.2 The compliance problem (Čyras and Riedl 2012b)

As a final (much more simple) example, we may compare implementations for one-stop government, which depend on the integration of truly independent processes in different government agencies. For such implementations the choice of a tier for integration is critical. It makes a big difference whether it is done in the web-tier (front office integration) or in the application tier (back-office integration, e.g. with WS-BPEL, Web Services Business Process Execution Language). The latter is in many cases not legally compliant because it does not guarantee the immediate registration of incoming requests at every organisation.

24.2.2 Formulating the Regulatory Compliance Problem for Software

Julisch (2008) suggests academia a paradigm shift: from 'selling' security when organisations seek to 'buy' compliance to complementing current security research by additional research into security compliance:

> [A]s long as careers are terminated and people go to jail [. . .] for failures in compliance – rather than security – the commercial world will continue to pursue compliance rather than security as their primary goal. (Julisch 2008, p. 71)

Julisch (2008, p. 72) defines: "Security compliance, in IT systems, is the state of conformance with externally imposed functional security requirements and of providing evidence (assurance) thereof." He defines the security compliance problem as follows:

> *Definition*: Given an existing IT systems S and an externally imposed set R of security requirements. The *Security Compliance Problem* is to make system S comply with the security requirements R and to provide assurance that an independent auditor will accept as evidence of the compliance of system S with requirement R. (Julisch 2008, p. 72)

Following the definition above, we would formulate the *Compliance Problem*. It is (1) to make software S comply with requirements R that relate to a law L, and (2) to provide assurance that an auditor will accept this as evidence (see Fig. 24.2).

The enterprise architecture compliance problem formulation can be obtained as a specific case of the above—by 'software S' being replaced with 'enterprise architecture S'.

We have simply added a law L to Julisch's formulation. The semi-formal definitions above can only serve as a first iteration. In practice it will be difficult for solutions to the problem to result in a 'yes' or a 'no'. In practice, more elements are involved. Feedback loops would improve S, R and L. The conceptualisation of L may involve different elements, depending on the abstraction level. L may stand for a legal principle, a statute or a provision.

24.2.3 Limitations when Representing the Law in the Context of Enterprise Architecture

Attempts to represent the law in the context of the compliance problem will meet complexity issues. Failure to understand the law is one of the reasons why the program may be noncompliant (Silverman 2008, pp. 59–61). This failure can be examined from the software development perspective, and also from the legal perspective. First, the texts of laws constitute only a part of the whole legal system. The meaning of law—the Ought realm—would scarcely be understood from a single legal text. Therefore, a freshman can barely understand the meaning of the law when reading an isolated statute. Second, for this reason, only well-defined compliance problems can be implemented simply, for example, by ticking a box in an audit document. Hence, the law is not easily interpreted by the developers.

The variety of legal areas to consider is a challenge. There is a legal challenge even in a specific domain, such as the design of a federation of digital identities (an identity ecosystem) as an identity management system on the internet (Schweighofer and Hötzendorfer 2013, p. 238).

The limitations are raised by the following issues which are also related with the criticism of the use of formal logic in AI and law:

1. *Knowledge engineering problem.* Modelling the legal domain with rules would be scarcely possible.[3]
2. *Subsumption.* A factual situation can be interpreted differently. A fact can be subsumed under different norms.[4]
3. *Principle vs. rule.* The difference in regulatory philosophy between the US and other countries (Silverman 2008, p. 46).

---

[3] Palmer (1997, p. 30) writes: "Given that any rule can be cast in a large number of ways and that these potential formulations are simply not all able to be known in advance there exists a seemingly insurmountable knowledge engineering problem."

[4] Hart (1958, p. 63) writes: "Fact situations do not await us neatly labelled, creased, and folded; nor is their legal classification written on them to be simply read off by the judge."

4. *Abstractness of legal concepts.* Norms are formulated (on purpose) in abstract terms; they aim at types of behaviour and types of situations. For instance, predicates such as 'fair', 'just', 'reasonable' can be contested. Open texture can be illustrated by Hart's (1994, pp. 123 ff) example of the rule 'No vehicles in the park.'
5. *The myriad of regulatory requirements.* Compliance frameworks are multidimensional.
6. *Heuristics.* High level concepts are translated into invented low level ones.
7. *Teleology.* The purpose of a legal norm usually can be achieved by a variety of ways. They need not to be listed in a statute and specified in detail.
8. *Legal interpretation methods.* The meaning of a legal text cannot be extracted from the sole text. Creative interpretation is required. Apart from the grammatical interpretation, other methods can be invoked, such as systemic and teleological interpretation.
9. *Law as an autopoietic system.* A programmer expects an idealisation of the legal system as a closed system of rules, principles and procedures. However, the legal system is open and "[t]here is no absolute beginning of the system."[5]

The issues above can be treated as limitations in legal informatics. They can be compared with limitations in other sciences. There are limits in mathematics (see e.g. Chaitin 1998) and computing (Walker 1994).

24.3 A Variety of Factors to Comply with

Note that judges are allowed to have different opinions. Are auditors allowed too? The COSO framework[6] was issued prior to Sarbanes-Oxley Act of 2002 (SOX).[7] Deterring fraudulent financial reporting is an aim. The use of the COSO framework by company management shows the scale from 'no extent' to 'large extent' (Leech 2008). The Directive 2008/30/EC[8] on statutory audits can be compared with the impact of SOX in the US. Information technology internal controls are not an exclusive concern of COSO.

---

[5] Karl-Heinz Ladeur provides a critique of Niklas Luhmann, "The Unity of the Legal System", and continues: "There are no fixed rules of structures which command the process of self-preservation and self-reproductions of the system" (Ladeur 1999, p. 11).

[6] The Committee of Sponsoring Organizations (COSO) framework was originally issued in 1992 (entitled Internal Control—Integrated Framework) and updated in 2004 (Enterprise Risk Management), see https://www.coso.org.

[7] See Wikipedia, Sarbanes–Oxley Act, https://en.wikipedia.org/wiki/Sarbanes%E2%80%93Oxley_Act.

[8] Directive 2008/30/EC of the European Parliament and of the Council of 11 March 2008 amending Directive 2006/43/EC on statutory audits of annual accounts and consolidated accounts.

Tarantino (2008a) devotes the whole book to Governance, Risk and Compliance (GRC). He suggests taking a holistic approach. In particular, he addresses the risk concept (Tarantino 2008a, b, pp. 15–17, 236–237). Banking's categorisation accords[9] describe seven major areas of operational risk:

1. Internal fraud: unauthorised activities; theft and fraud
2. External fraud: external security; theft and fraud
3. Employment practices: employee relations; safe environment; diversity and discrimination
4. Clients, products, and business processes: suitability, disclosure, and fiduciary aspects; product flaws; improper business or market practices; advisory activities; selection, sponsorship and exposure
5. Damage to physical assets: disasters and other events
6. Business disruptions and system failures: systems
7. Execution, delivery, and process management: transaction capture, execution, and maintenance; monitoring and reporting; incomplete legal documentation; customer account management

This categorisation can serve as a framework. It illustrates a variety of risk factors, which have to be faced by auditors and other personnel.

Compliance is a multi-criteria problem. A single framework or standard would scarcely be a solution to all compliance and control needs.[10]

24.4 Elements of Enterprise System

According to the systems engineering view, an enterprise system consists of three subsystems listed below. However, there is no generally accepted agreement.

1. *Enterprise business system.* It is comprised of business actors, resources and business processes.
2. *Enterprise information system* (IS) "is a whole formed out of organisational memory and sets of information processing actors (IPA), information flows, and interrelated information processing processes implemented in accordance with the enterprise information processing policies and standards" (Čaplinskas 2009).
3. *Enterprise application system.* It is comprised of hardware agents, protocols, knowledge bases and software application programs.

---

[9] See Wikipedia, Basel II, https://en.wikipedia.org/wiki/Basel_II.

[10] Deluccia (2008, p. 62) writes: "Absolute adherence to a regulation by adopting a basic framework without considering the entire organization and threats that affect it make the organization compliant, but not secure or resilient to operational disruptions."

Other elements can also be distinguished. This depends on an author's view. Ross et al. (2006, p. 47) note that the term 'architecture' has acquired a negative connotation in some companies and quote saying "Architectures, like fondue sets [. . .] are rarely used." Ross et al. make emphasis on distinguishing between enterprise architecture and IT architecture. They also note that the IT unit typically addresses four levels of enterprise architecture (pp. 48–49):

1. *Business process architecture*. The activities or tasks composing major business processes identified by the business process owners.
2. *Data or information architecture*. Shared data definitions.
3. *Applications architecture*. Individual applications and their interfaces.
4. *Technology architecture*. Architecture services and the technology standards they are built on.

Subsystems and systems thinking are stressed in (Giachetti 2010, pp. 29–52). First a system is defined as "a set of discernible, interacting parts or subsystems that form an integrated whole that acts with a single goal or purpose" (p. 29). Then EA is characterised.[11]

One of the problems right now with enterprise architecture (cf. Giachetti 2010) is that for reasons of simplicity those practically usable in real life focus on very few aspects of a real-world IS, usually issues which are shared throughout the organisation. Depending on the operating model of the organisation, this is just technology, or in addition data and/or business processes. In the spirit of EA in the sense of Ross et al. (2006), it would make sense to define the "shared" relevant laws and integrate them.[12] Ross et al. (2006) suggest encapsulating enterprise architecture in a core diagram, which depicts a high-level view of the process, data, and technologies constituting the desired foundation for execution. Here we raise a question: how to formulate the EA compliance problem once such a one-page core diagram is provided? Writing a list of compliance requirements? An answer should concern a concluding remark that enterprise architecture is not a detailed blueprint of systems, data, and technology, but instead a business vision (Giachetti 2010, p. 206).

Enterprise architects check the architecture for potential conflicts with the law. The regulations which influence enterprise architectures, perhaps SOX, can be barely aware (Riedl 2011). The following relationships can be identified here:

- Architecture descriptions have to leverage checking compliance.
- Legal informatics experts can contribute to legislation, esp. in e-government.

---

[11] Giachetti (2010, p. 102) writes: "An Enterprise Architecture describes the structure of an enterprise, its decomposition into subsystems, the relationships between the subsystems, the relationships with the external environment, the terminology to use, and the guiding principles for the design and evolution of an enterprise."

[12] Giachetti (2010, pp. 12–13) writes: "Companies are buffeted by constant changes in regulations, such as Sarbanes-Oxley, Basel II, and HIPAA. As companies become global, they become accountable for increasingly complex reporting requirements [. . .] Companies may not be able to anticipate new regulations, but they can increase the likelihood that needed data is readily available or can easily be accumulated."

- Enterprise architects become important partners for legal informatics experts. This is possible in the revision of the law, e.g. in digital identity regulations.
- Contacts with authorities when anticipating ICT perspectives. Regulation of software exchange, for instance, modules in finance informatics.
- Ideas in legal informatics; patterns and anti-patterns.

24.5   Enterprise Compliance Process

Financial compliance process is an important but not the sole issue of conformance. Enterprise content management (ECM) systems are focused by Koo (2008) and a high-level compliance process is provided. Following is the list of standard requirements that any ECM vendor should provide: library services, repository search, document routing, central user administration, support for all popular text file formats, document imaging. More complex requirements: document-centric collaboration, compound documents support, digital assets management, records management, rule-driven work flow, process management, advanced security, etc. (Koo 2008, pp. 262–264).

24.6   The Legal Perspective in Enterprise Engineering

The only true purpose of the work of enterprise architects is transparency optimisation in an organisation. Three central perspectives to enterprise systems can be concerned: (1) Business perspective; (2) ICT (information and communication technologies) perspective; and (3) Legal perspective. Continuing the list above, other potential perspectives can be mentioned: (4) Internal communication perspective (a direction tool); (5) Public relations and marketing perspective; and (6) Political and economic perspective (probably in e-government).

In our research we focus on the legal perspective. More perspectives are concerned in architectural frameworks such as Zachman's one (Sowa and Zachman 1992):

1. Business level requirements (the view of business analyst)
2. User level requirements (the view of stakeholders)
3. IS (information system) requirements (the view of IS analyst)
4. The requirements of IS subsystems (the view of IS engineer)
5. Software requirements (the view of software analyst)

There are other perspectives, which are out of the Zachman framework (an architectural one).[13] Each perspective (level) presents a model of the system.

---

[13]"To be complete, it should additionally include the requirements of software components (the view of software architect), the implementation requirements (the view of software engineer), the

Each phase of system's life-cycle is subject to technical standards. The concepts of a to-be system and requirements are related to law. The requirements document (system specification) is part of the contract with a customer. Every requirement is based on a norm. This norm is present in a technical standard, business rule or other kind of legal source. The difference in the nature of requirements stems from the difference of norms.

24.7   Towards a Methodology of the Compliance with the Law

The end-to-end enterprise architecture compliance problem is too large and too complex for any one company to tackle. Similar is with compliance auditing, frameworks and good practices. Following are theme aggregates to shape the integration of different recourses compliant with the law (Riedl 2011):

1. Internal arrangement of transparency
2. Methods for the legal architecture view as part of enterprise architecture
3. Design methods for law-triggered changes in the enterprise architecture

We think that Čaplinskas' approach could provide a framework to shape the methods above. First, it is vision driven. Second, a legal perspective can be added. Further steps face the following problems. An analyst would scarcely be aware of legal norms in different branches of law. Therefore methodologies are needed. A trivial idea might be simply to check the requirements for compliance. This would be classified as an ex-ante solution "to design an artefact aimed at avoiding actions that are not compliant" (Bonazzi et al. 2010). However to lower the risk of violating strategic alignment, a holistic approach has to be undertaken. Ex-post solutions are "to design an artefact to assess the level of compliance".

Risk management for information technology is a growing challenge for GRC (Tarantino 2008a, p. 18). Recommendations involve three basic processes: risk assessment, risk mitigation, and evaluation and assessment. Absolute control measures are often cost prohibitive and require IT professionals to weigh the cost versus benefits. This process is complicated by the hundreds of software tool suppliers promising to fix their GRC problems (Tarantino 2008a, p. 19).

There is no silver bullet to solve the compliance problem. This is also explained for an IT compliance framework by Bonazzi, Hussami, and Pigneur, a work which is worthy of special attention (Bonazzi et al. 2010). Two dimensions, *Legal* and *IT*, and two kinds of sources for regulations with which a company must comply, *External*

---

process requirements (the view of process engineer), and the testing requirements (the view of tester) [...] The first five perspectives differ from corresponding ones provided by the Zachman's framework because they are designed for different purposes" (Čaplinskas 2009, p. 355).

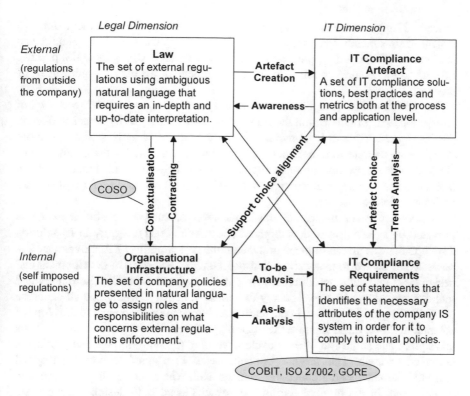

Fig. 24.3 The Bonazzi–Hussami–Pigneur regulation and IT alignment framework (adapted from Bonazzi et al. 2010)

and *Internal*, are depicted by rectangles (see Fig. 24.3). Different alignments are represented by arrows that point to the artifact that is defined.

Every concept in Fig. 24.3 denotes a broad field. Corporate noncompliance, corruption, etc., are just a few examples of violations. Noncompliance can be civil, criminal, or administrative, but also reputational or market-based. To analyse a company for compliance, legal norms in various branches of the law should be taken into account. This would make a task that is barely feasible for one analyst.

To-be Analysis can be treated in different ways, depending on controls or IT risks, e.g., COBIT,[14] ISO 27002,[15] GORE (Rifaut and Dubois 2008). COBIT

---

[14] COBIT (Control Objectives for Information and Related Technologies) is a framework for IT governance and control. See Wikipedia https://en.wikipedia.org/wiki/COBIT and https://www.isaca.org/resources/cobit.

[15] An information security standard, entitled Information technology—Security techniques—Code of practice for information security management (see Wikipedia, ISO/IEC 27002, https://en.wikipedia.org/wiki/ISO/IEC_27002). ISO 27001 is entitled Information technology—Security techniques—Information security management systems—Requirements. It is a specification. It uses words like 'shall'. ISO 27002 is a code of practice, not a specification (see Calder 2008).

concerns IT governance and best practices. COBIT view of the implementation of a system's infrastructure can be summarised as follows: plan and organise, acquire and implement, deliver and support, and monitor and evaluate (Rodgers 2008, p. 322). Like its COSO control counterpart, it is the framework for the management of IT processes.

The design of law-compliant information systems is an area on a lower level of abstraction, though falls within the framework above. As noted by Knackstedt et al. (2011), representation of legal requirements were lacking in early works. Therefore they propose a framework to model the area which is structured in three dimensions: (1) field of law (flow control, reporting, web applications, etc.); (2) modelling level (analysis level, model level, meta-model level); and (3) research goal (explanation- or design-oriented research).

A perspective for the actual implementation of such a holistic approach is provided by agile software development (Beck et al. 2001). Agility in IS solution development was first introduced in the extreme programming (XP) movement. It is nowadays extended to many IS related tasks and applied even in development and design tasks without much IS relationship but with a general multi-disciplinary and multi-stakeholder challenge. The key two ideas of agility is to involve all expertise needed for a good IS solution in the team working on the solution and to develop the solution in short cycles, where at the beginning of each cycle a requirements analysis takes place and at the end of each cycle a working (running) in-between-product is delivered to users. This original concept has been adapted to more conceptual contexts like enterprise architecture management, where no running products can be delivered. In the original setting the key challenge is to design a good basic overall structure, as the spirit of agility contradicts the planning. However, in principle agility proposes an interesting split for a holistic approach. The integration of multidisciplinary perspectives is split into a very rudimentary strategic core concept and a concrete teamwork, where requirements analysis and holistic solution development is done iteratively.

Conclusion This chapter presents reflections on different issues of compliance. The authors are influenced by both formal models which are used in computer science and descriptive methods of social sciences (including law). This is all for the best in the present research. However, there is no silver bullet to attack regulatory compliance requirements—no one-off, best-of-breed solution. Similar is with the theoretically formulated compliance problem. Positioning it in an IT alignment framework is a challenge. Though various compliance processes are positioned differently even within the two dimensions of IT and law.

In practice, an auditor can certify that software is compliant with a specific rule, a law, or an audit guide. A typical rule is 'A specific artefact X shall be present in an organisation'. However, the answer 'yes' can scarcely be given to a question about compliance with the whole body of law. The reason is that an expert can understand the legal meaning or, in other words, the Ought of this rule, this law or this audit guide respectively. However, a detailed understanding of every specific by-law in the whole body of law can scarcely be achieved. A big amount of work would exceed human abilities. Therefore a more experienced auditor can foresee a greater risk that the software does not comply with the law.

References

Beck K et al (2001) Manifesto for agile software development. Agile Alliance, 2001. http://agilemanifesto.org/. Accessed 15 Dec 2022

Bonazzi R, Hussami L, Pigneur Y (2010) Compliance management is becoming a major issue in IS design. In: D'atri A, Saccà D (eds) Information systems: people, organizations, institutions, and technologies. Physica-Verlag HD, pp 391–398. https://doi.org/10.1007/978-3-7908-2148-2_45

Calder A (2008) ISO 27001 and ISO 17999. In: Tarantino A (ed) Governance, risk, and compliance handbook. Wiley, pp 169–179

Čaplinskas A (2009) Requirements elicitation in the context of enterprise engineering: a vision driven approach. Informatica 20(3):343–368. https://doi.org/10.15388/Informatica.2009.255

Chaitin GJ (1998) The limits of mathematics: a course on information theory and the limits of formal reasoning. Springer, Singapore

Čyras V, Riedl R (2012a) Enterprise architects concern legal requirements for the compliance with the law. Jusletter IT, 29 February 2012. https://jusletter-it.weblaw.ch/issues/2012/IRIS/jusletterarticle_1057.html. Accessed 15 Dec 2022

Čyras V, Riedl R (2012b) Formulating the enterprise architecture compliance problem. In: Čaplinskas A, Dzemyda G, Lupeikienė A, Vasilecas O (eds) Databases and information systems. Tenth international Baltic conference on databases and information systems. Local proceedings, materials of doctoral consortium, DB&IS 2012. Žara, Vilnius, pp 142–153. CEUR workshop proceedings, vol 924. https://ceur-ws.org/Vol-924/paper14.pdf. Accessed 15 Dec 2022

Deluccia JJ (2008) IT compliance and controls: best practices for implementation. Wiley

Giachetti RE (2010) Design of enterprise systems: theory, architecture, and methods. CRC Press

Hart HLA (1958) Positivism and the separation of law and morals. In: Hart HLA, Essays in jurisprudence and philosophy. Clarendon Press, Oxford,. 1983, pp. 49–87

Hart HLA (1994) The concept of law, 2nd edn. Oxford University Press

Julisch K (2008) Security compliance: the next frontier in security research. In: Proceedings of the 2008 workshop on new security paradigms, NSPW'08. ACM, New York, pp 71–74

Knackstedt R, Heddier M, Becker J (2011) Fachkonzeption rechtskonformer Informationssysteme als Anwendungsgebiet der Rechtsvisualisierung. Jusletter IT, 24 February 2011. https://jusletter-it.weblaw.ch/issues/2011/IRIS/article_320.html. Accessed 15 Dec 2022

Koo J (2008) What to look for in enterprise content management for compliance. In: Tarantino A (ed) Governance, risk, and compliance handbook. Wiley, pp 259–266

Ladeur K (1999) The theory of autopoiesis as an approach to a better understanding of postmodern law: from the hierarchy of norms to the heterarchy of changing patterns of legal inter-relationships. EUI working paper Law no. 99/3. https://cadmus.eui.eu/handle/1814/148. Accessed 15 Dec 2022

Leech T (2008) COSO – is it fit for purpose? In: Tarantino A (ed) Governance, risk, and compliance handbook. Wiley, pp 65–75

Lenk K, Schuppan T, Schaffroth M (2010) Networked public administration. Organisational concept for a federal eGovernment Switzerland. eCH-0126 white paper. Federal Department of Finance FDF

Palmer J (1997) Artificial intelligence and legal merit argument. PhD thesis. Balliol College, University of Oxford

Riedl R (2011) Rechtsinformatik aus Sicht des Unternehmensarchitekten. In: Geist A, Brunschwig CR, Lachmayer F, Schefbeck G (eds) Strukturierung der Juristischen Semantik – structuring legal semantics. Editions Weblaw, Bern, pp 257–269

Riedl R, Bernold R, Brugger J, Selzam T, Smith E, Spichiger A (2012) A multiperspective view of unified identification and authentication spaces. Jusletter IT, 29 February 2012. https://jusletter-it.weblaw.ch/issues/2012/IRIS/jusletterarticle_1081.html. Accessed 15 Dec 2022

Rifaut A, Dubois E (2008) Using goal-oriented requirements engineering for improving the quality of ISO/IEC 15504 based compliance assessment frameworks. In: 16th IEEE international requirements engineering conference, RE 2008. IEEE Computer Society, pp 33–42

Rodgers I (2008) Internal controls best practices. In: Tarantino A (ed) Governance, risk, and compliance handbook. Wiley, pp 301–323

Ross JW, Weill P, Robertson DC (2006) Enterprise architecture as strategy: creating a foundation for business execution. Harvard Business School Press, Boston

Schweighofer E, Hötzendorfer W (2013) Electronic identities – public or private. Int Rev Law Comput Technol 27(1–2):230–239

Silverman M (2008) Compliance management for public, private, or nonprofit organizations. McGraw-Hill, New York

Sowa JF, Zachman JA (1992) Extending and formalizing the framework for information systems architecture. IBM Syst J 31(3):590–616

Tarantino A (2008a) Introduction. In: Tarantino A (ed) Governance, risk, and compliance handbook. Wiley, pp 1–37

Tarantino A (2008b) Operational risk management in financial services. In: Tarantino A (ed) Governance, risk, and compliance handbook. Wiley, pp 233–256

Walker HM (1994) The limits of computing. Jones and Bartlett Publishers, Boston

Chapter 25
Software Transparency for Design of Legal Machines

25.1 Compliance Implies Transparency

This chapter further investigates compliance. Software transparency is in the focus. The context is the changeover from a text culture to a machine culture in law. The target is the explainable legal machine. We remark that equal access to e-procedures does not guarantee justice. We formulate two requirements for legal machines: (1) the software architecture must be accessible, and (2) the software must provide legal protection. In the engineering phase for these requirements, the legal requirements must flow down to lower-level specifications.

Regulatory compliance is addressed as an ideal and is an element of the question 'Is software compliant with the law?', which was formulated in the preceding chapter. We start with a picture in Fig. 25.1. Legal norms appear in Ought, whereas the development of a machine appears in Is.

The software for a machine implements legal norms that are explicitly taken into account in the requirements' engineering phase. Here we call such norms *explicit norms*. The problem is that there are also norms that are not considered in the software life cycle. We call these norms *implicit norms*. These norms can be violated, and therefore they are important. There is no strict boundary between explicit and implicit norms, and a grey area exists due to the interconnectedness of norms in the whole legal system.

Compliance in the Design Phase It is important to detect the noncompliance of legal machines in the early stages of the software life cycle. It should be noted that legal knowledge need not lean heavily on the sources of law that are traditionally considered in compliance frameworks. Suppose we have a business process. Each link in the process can be considered to be compliant (at least at first glance) but the

---

Based on two Čyras and Lachmayer (2014a, b).

Fig. 25.1 A visual of the
compliance problem. The
legal machine appears on
the Is stage and has to be
compliant with the legal
norms that appear on the
Ought stage (Čyras and
Lachmayer 2014b)

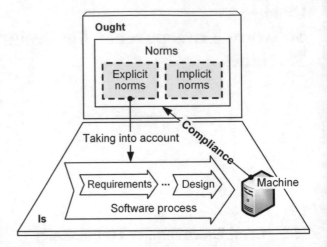

whole process can be noncompliant. Such noncompliant business processes are the
concern by Boer and van Engers (2011). Their new idea is the methodology that
stresses how noncompliance stories are elicited. Noncompliance in design is a
concern in their methodology.[1] For instance, a sales chain in which the initial seller
and the final buyer are identical gives rise to suspicions of tax evasion. Generic legal
tasks can be related to different kinds of legal knowledge, such as legal rules, design
patterns, social structures and evidence-based expectations.

A person who is not legally qualified (for instance, a software engineer) and a
jurist may have different views on the violation of a legal rule. The reason for this is
that a layperson can barely understand the whole interconnectedness of norms. Note
that an information system can cause harm, as can any misused artefact. For instance,
a computer generated message can cause a heart attack in the same way as a pencil
can serve as a murder tool.

25.2 Transparency of Legal Machines

This section formulates the problem that is termed 'legal machine transparency'.
Consider (a) a general norm that is formulated in a legal text such as a law or a
by-law; and (b) an individual norm that is formulated in a court judgment. The
following means of legal protection serve the different parties in the context of a text
culture:

---

[1] "We learned that specifications insufficiently leverage experience about the expected behavior of
agents in the domain. This weakness is most evident in the absence of explicit theory construction
about *noncompliance* in design, even though experience about critical incidents in the past, and the
ability to predict future incidents, is usually available in the organization and certainly plays a
leading, but largely implicit, role in design" (Boer and van Engers 2011, p. 171).

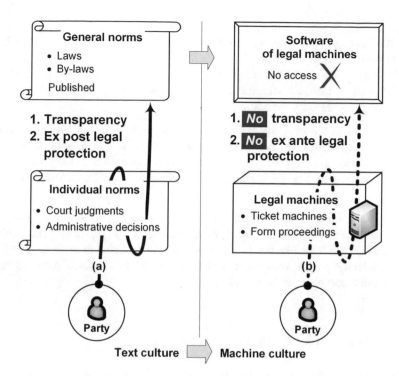

Fig. 25.2 Technical implementation of a changeover from a legal text to software. The problem is to ensure transparency and legal protection at the same level in both (a) and (b) (Čyras and Lachmayer 2014a)

1. *Transparency of law.* Legal texts are made accessible to citizens. An example is oesterreich.gv.at, which supports ex ante analysis; and
2. *Ex post legal protection.* An example of this is RIS in Austria.

These two types of information were not available years ago and have been improved over the course of time; they now come as standard. However, this standard was not set at the beginning of the machine culture. We can see the problem of a lack of transparency and of ex ante analysis support in the machine culture, as the machine culture is still young. A party cannot, for example, wait years to resolve a conflict with a machine (see Fig. 25.2).

Therefore two requirements for software can be proposed:

Requirement 1:   The architecture of the software for a legal machine must be made accessible to the user.
Requirement 2:   The software for a legal machine must provide trained, effective and rapid legal protection.

Concerning Requirement 1, it might be added that an explainable machine is a condition to trust it and to expect to solve conflicts with it. "We cannot trust a device unless we know how it works" (Parnas 2017, p. 31).

We aim to ensure that there is the same standard of transparency and legal protection in the machine culture as there is in the text culture. As examples, consider the following imaginary situation:

Example: The law provides for ten variations/possibilities but the program only contains nine. Let us suppose this applies to expenditure categories in tax law. Suppose you want to declare expenditure in the tenth category in your tax declaration, but the program does not allow this option. What do you do?

The latter situation can be observed in car parks equipped with unsophisticated ticket machines that give a very limited amount of money back. The different variations/possibilities like the ten in Example may be listed in different articles or laws. Ordinary people who are not legally trained or qualified would scarcely understand a complete list of variations.

25.3   Notes on Compliance

Suppose that a driver exceeds the speed limit in order to avoid greater harm, and a radar system records the violation. The speed limit rule is violated and a sanction applies. However, a more general question can be asked: 'Has the driver violated the law?' To answer this you have to understand what the law is. The answer is not a truth value, 'yes' or 'no', but a complex judgment that depends on the procedure and the parties. An expert in the law, and not a layperson, can understand competing formulations and exceptions in their entirety.

Again, we find that the question 'Is a program compliant with the law?' is similar to Turing's, 'Can machines think?' The term 'the law' denotes the whole system of rules that everyone in a country or society must obey. Understanding the system may lead to understanding law as a phenomenon. The complexity of our question could be reduced by substituting 'the law' with 'a rule': 'Is a legal machine compliant with a rule?' However the speed violation example shows that the reduction is not essential and does not reduce the problem to a mechanical decision 'yes – complies' or 'no – does not comply'.

Representing Legal Norms as Rules When formalising legal norms, we find it useful here to follow Oberle et al. (2012, pp. 291–294), where a list of references to related approaches is provided. We recall the early works on artificial intelligence and law in the 1980s and on modelling legal reasoning, and the good old days of Prolog (Bench-Capon et al. 2012).

Typically, a legal norm can be expressed as a logical rule 'if...then...'. Typically, legal norms determine a 'legal consequence' (*LC*), given one or 'more state of affairs' (*SF*) that fall within the scope of the norm. Schematically, this can be expressed as a logical rule $SF \rightarrow LC$. This is to be read as: "when state of affairs (*SF*) is given, then the legal consequence (*LC*) applies". In this respect the question is the extent to which business rules can implement norms. Therefore the research on implementing rules in information systems, business rules frameworks and ontologies is a talking point.

25.4   The Context of Justice in the Paradigm Change to E-Procedures

Kelsen pursued several objectives in his Pure Theory of Law:

- First, *a paradigm shift in legal theory.* PTL became a new jurisprudential standard and, in this respect, shaped the twentieth century.
- Second, *the overcoming of the natural law.* PTL has outlived the natural law.
- Third, *to stop arguments that use the concept of justice.* However, Kelsen did not succeed with this objective. The discussion today is more about injustice.

25.4.1   The Principle of Equality Before the Law

One of the principles of justice is equality. The application of justice is less of a normative problem, because it is preceded by a cognitive problem concerning matters such as interpretation. A preliminary issue is that what is found has to be interpreted. However, this is not a normative issue: subsumption is interpretative, that is, cognitive at its core. Depending on the legal concepts that are applied in the interpretation, the subsumption, which follows the interpretation, will be different.

The context of justice does not only affect politics (large and small), but also affects legal machines. The upcoming world of electronic administrative and judicial proceedings brings a new context for the application of justice. With e-proceedings, the context is all about everyday justice for those citizens who are affected, and about the procedurally mediated law that they enjoy. But even with IT-based everyday justice, the cognitive problem is upstream of the normative problem.

25.4.2   Subsumption Is Delegated to Parties in E-Procedures

The key to the application of the law and thus to access to justice is subsumption. The special feature of matters carried out with electronic forms (which we will refer to as e-proceedings or e-procedure) is that subsumption is accomplished by the parties and not by the court or the administrative authority. In traditional proceedings, the parties submit their allegations, these are confirmed or rejected in the course of the investigation, and finally the state of affairs is established by the authority. The state of affairs serves as the basis for the subsumption. Thus, there are a number of regulatory steps between the parties' assertions and the subsumption.

In e-procedures this is different. One party fills in the input fields. How the entries in these fields need to be made, however, is not commonly known but requires a knowledge of jargon. Thus, the performance of subsumption is delegated to the parties. To make entries, the parties have to use their knowledge of the legal terms that are defined by the sources of law in a complicated way.

Back-office programs for e-procedures are very quick and accurate at drawing legal conclusions from input data. However, the content of the conclusion depends to a large extent on the starting material that was completed in the parties' front offices. A party who is not skilful in law may be overwhelmed by this. This is an opportunity for intermediaries, allowing them to continue to position themselves professionally. The complexity of the law is not reduced by e-proceedings, but, as it did in the Middle Ages, continues to require intermediaries who now must be expert in information technology.

All parties are equal in e-procedures, and in this respect e-procedures seem to be fair. However, in the actual performance of an e-procedure there may be a big difference between communicating with a human operator and communicating with a machine. A human operator can offer flexibility, and this cannot be offered by a machine. As an example, suppose a traveller sees a train already approaching and tries desperately to buy an appropriate ticket from the ticket machine. A human being would assist better than the machine.

Equality ≠ Justice Equality is far from able to guarantee justice. An example is a transactional tax. This is the same for everybody, but has a greater impact on the income of the poor than on the income of the rich. Therefore, this is perceived as unjust. Knowledge of the law is similar. Today the law is conveyed electronically in the same way for all people. However, there are big differences in individuals' ability to deal with this knowledge, in addition to the differences in technical skills and aptitudes in dealing with the new media.

Ex Ante Legal Protection An open issue is certainly the lack of ex ante legal protection against incorrect electronic forms in e-procedures. Consider again Example, in which the law provides for ten cases but only nine of these cases are mentioned in the e-forms. The question arises of how someone should behave if he wishes to enter information in the tenth case, when he cannot do this electronically. Any ex post legal protection comes too late after the first instance of this and of the expiration of the deadline; and it is dysfunctional, since it only involves the input stage.

The paradigm shift to e-procedures provides small- and medium-range domains with a new standardized legal culture, which could not be achieved before. This paradigm shift provides equality and is 'fair', apart from the concern over different starting conditions. However, as in the past, injustice will be a massive problem in the areas in which it is so great that it cannot be consciously perceived. For nothing is as invisible as the things that may be overlooked. Here the paradigm shift to e-procedures will not change injustice.

25.5   Transparency in Software Engineering

Requirements 1 and 2 in the introduction are formulated at a very high level. The next question is how they can be implemented. In principle, the architecture of the legal machine can be made available to the user. Transparency of computer programs is a concern of software engineering.[2] Here transparency is combined with the principles of information hiding and separation of concerns. On different abstraction levels, a software element is treated as a black box that can be viewed in terms of its input, its output and its transfer characteristics without any knowledge of its internal workings.

There is no automatic way to achieve transparency. Different users may be interested in different architectural elements. Not every design solution can be made accessible to each user. This is for reasons of security and complexity, to mention just a few. Software requirements, including transparency requirements, are formulated in the early phases of the software development life cycle. Legal requirements are at a high level and are also a concern of requirements engineering. A flowdown of the requirements is needed to develop lower-level specifications, and these are formulated in the system specification. There is also a need to flow down the high-level Requirements 1 and 2. After this the software is designed and implemented. Thus, the resulting software can be made compliant with the initial legal requirements. However, in practice the story above is rarely so simple. There may be a wide gap between the legal requirements and the technical specifications (Riedl 2014).

On Implementing Requirement 2: Legal Protection Legal protection is even more difficult to implement than the architectural transparency in Requirement 1. The efforts of software engineers are not enough to make sure that Requirement 2 flows down. Organisational means and invention may be needed. The following paragraph sets out an imaginary situation.

Consider an automatic barrier to a pay car park. Suppose that the barrier does not lift up to let you out. Suppose that the cause is purely technical, such as a malfunction of the barrier's motor. What action can you take and what means of legal protection do you have? Some car parks provide a 24 hour/7 day voice connection to a human operator. You can therefore explain the matter to the operator and he can arrange for the barrier to be lifted manually.

---

[2]Transparency means that a distributed system hides its distributed nature from its users, appearing and functioning as a normal centralised system. In software engineering, it is also considered good practice to use different abstraction layers. There are many types of transparency (see Wikipedia, https://en.wikipedia.org/wiki/Transparency_(human%E2%80%93computer_interaction)).

As far as legal protection is concerned, the architect of the car park should, under Requirement 2, supply instructions for how the user should behave in an emergency. To summarise: although legal machines are typically treated as black boxes, transparency can be increased with a transparent flowdown of legal requirements.

Conclusion We have identified the transparency problem and formulated two requirements for legal machines. However, implementing these requirements is not an easy task, even if it is possible for it to be achieved at all. Moreover, there are different contexts of justice, and e-procedures do not guarantee justice. In the legal domain, mechanical judges are undesirable, and machine-assisted decision making outweighs machine-based decision making.

References

Bench-Capon T, Araszkiewicz M, Ashley K et al (2012) A history of AI and law in 50 papers: 25 years of the international conference on AI and law. Artif Intell Law 20(3):215–319. https://doi.org/10.1007/s10506-012-9131-x

Boer A, van Engers T (2011) An agent-based legal knowledge acquisition methodology for agile public administration. In: Proceedings of the thirteenth international conference on artificial intelligence and law, ICAIL '11. ACM, New York, pp 171–180. https://doi.org/10.1145/2018358.2018383

Čyras V, Lachmayer F (2014a) Program transparency for legal machines. Jusletter IT, 20 February 2014. https://jusletter-it.weblaw.ch/issues/2014/IRIS/2472.html. Accessed 15 Dec 2022

Čyras V, Lachmayer F (2014b) Compliance and software transparency for the design of legal machines. In: Haav H, Kalja A, Robal T (eds) Databases and information systems VIII. Frontiers in artificial intelligence and applications, vol 270. IOS Press, Amsterdam, pp 275–288. https://doi.org/10.3233/978-1-61499-458-9-275

Oberle D, Drefs F, Wacker R, Baumann C, Raabe O (2012) Engineering compliant software: advising developers by automating legal reasoning. SCRIPTed 9(3):280–313. https://doi.org/10.2966/scrip.090312

Parnas DL (2017) The real risks of artificial intelligence. Commun ACM 60(10):27–41

Riedl R (2014) Die Schwierigkeiten einer Transdisciplinären Rechtsinformatik. In: Schweighofer E et al (eds) Zeichen und Zauber des Rechts. Editions Weblaw, Bern, pp 175–183

Part VII
Human Digitalities

Chapter 26
Towards Human Digitalities

26.1 Evolution

A new term *human digitalities* is introduced intentionally to contrast with the well-established term *digital humanities*. The research subject of human digitalities is the machine, which is required to act in conformance with the law. Human digitalities are viewed in the context of the evolution from plants to animals to humans to machines. We can see an expansion and transfer of standards: digital standards for humanities and human standards for digitalities.

Digital Humanities and Human Digitalities The notion of multibridge is introduced in Chap. 23 and is shown there in Fig. 23.16. On the right bank of the multibridge between law and informatics there is the area called *digital humanities* (Burdick et al. 2012, p. 122) (see Fig. 26.1). The research subject of digital humanities is the human surrounded by digitally-based phenomena. We introduce another area—*human digitalities*—next to it on the right bank. Here the research subject—the machine—is different, and is structured according to human-centered rules.

Consider the line of evolution from plants to animals to human beings to machines, as shown in Fig. 26.2. In the proposed model, biological evolution leads to the development of human beings. The last step, the evolution from humans to machines, however, is a process of technological evolution in which humans produce machines. Moreover, humans strive to give human capabilities to their creatures, thus making machines artificially intelligent, a situation that is reminiscent of the ancient myth of Pygmalion and its modern variations.

Status Civilis or Status Naturalis? One question associated with the evolutionary step from humans to machines is whether machines reside in status civilis or status

Based on Čyras and Lachmayer (2019, 2020).

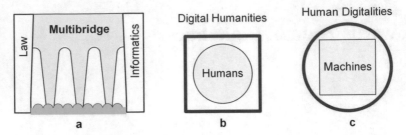

Fig. 26.1 (**a**) A multibridge from law to informatics. (**b**) Digital humanities. (**c**) Human digitalities (Čyras and Lachmayer 2020)

Fig. 26.2 The line of evolution from plants to animals to human beings to machines (Čyras and Lachmayer 2020)

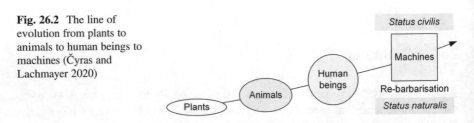

naturalis. A relapse to status naturalis is a permanent temptation of modern culture, although re-barbarisation is a kind of political atavism. Weapons are substitutes for the former raptors. The elements of re-barbarisation can, for example, be observed in EVE Online, a massive multiplayer online game (MMOG). In EVE Online, players take part in "harsh, unforgiving gameplay that lacks many amenities for players that other games of the genre possess".[1] We, however, maintain that machines have to be not monsters.[2]

The area of digital humanities belongs to the world of human beings, whereas the area of human digitalities belongs to the world of machines (see Fig. 26.3).

The theme of evolution leads further than legal formalisation to human digitalities. Wagner and Haag (1970) write about the step from symbolisation to formalisation (Symbolisierung → Formalisierung). They use the term symbolisation, but symbolisation is now interpreted in a broad sense, comprising

---

[1] Radosław Pałosz continues: "Game authors encourage a play style that would be treated as illegal or unethical in real life. EVE's world, because of its complexity, allows sophisticated frauds like financial pyramids identical in their essence to those known from real life to happen in-game" (see Pałosz's abstract "Virtual world as a state of nature: rule-creating activity of MMOG players" at the Special Workshop 3 Artificial Intelligence and Digital Ontology in conjunction with the IVR World Congress 2019 in Lucerne).

[2] Swend Erik Larsen traces a historical inquiry into the concept of monsters, and quotes the front page of the German magazine *Der Spiegel* from 15 February 2019 "which shows a whole-page photo of an airport by a caption in mega-sized letters: "Monster – Frankfurt Main – Der unmoegliche Flughafen" [Monster – Frankfurt Main – The impossible airport]" (Larsen 2019, p. 36).

Fig. 26.3 The area of digital humanities and the area of human digitalities (Čyras and Lachmayer 2020)

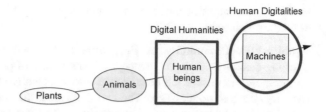

both symbolisation-in-the-narrow-sense and visualisation. Hence, we go further and investigate the evolutionary step that results in machines for digital processing.

26.2 From Digital Humanities Towards Human Digitalities

Digital Humanities In this section the right bank of the multibridge is studied (see Fig. 26.1a). This is where the area of digital humanities appears. This term "refers to new modes of scholarship and institutional units for collaborative, transdisciplinary, and computationally-engaged research, teaching and publication" (Burdick et al. 2012, p. 122). A field map of digital humanities can be proposed, and shows such methods as "enhanced critical curation", "augmented editions and fluid textuality", "visualization and data design", "the animated archive", etc. (ibid., pp. 30–31). Digital humanities "place a primacy on experiential navigation, epistemologies of representation, and the rhetorics of visualization" (p. 46). The human is the research subject of digital humanities, and this human is surrounded by digitally-based phenomena, including information and communication technologies.

Brunschwig starts out by noting that "both the digital humanities and what might (as a working hypothesis) be called digital law explore visualization, audiovisualization, and multisensorization" (Brunschwig 2018, p. 1). She brings the digital humanities and digital law closer together. We, however, go on to examine human digitalities.

Human Digitalities Next comes in the sphere that we call human digitalities. Its research subject is the machine, which is structured according to human-centered rules. We have coined the term to describe machines that are required to act in conformity with the law—in the same way as human beings ought to act. Human digitalities focuses on the concept of a legal machine whose purpose is regulation by computer code. After the text-to-program transformation, the program embodies legal rules, and the normative and digital expectations are amalgamated.

Karavas (2009, p. 464) argues that "the emergence of the computer as medium has triggered a transformation of the legal sphere that is culminated in the emergence of a techno-digital normativity that seems to undermine Luhmann's description of the legal system as an autonomous social system." The risks introduced by computers, and the dangers of AI, can be viewed both from the perspective of programming and from the perspective of law (see e.g. Graber 2020). Christoph Graber formulates recommendations to avoid the dangers of platforms using AI in relation to fundamental rights.[3]

Lyubimskii's Community of Programs Lyubimskii (2009) writes about the infosphere and introduces the concept of community of programs. Lyubimskii sees the problem "to ensure the coexistence and cooperative operation of programs". Lyubimskii's has two messages. The first message is that the interaction of programs should be ruled by human laws: "the structure of the community of programs and the means of their interaction are largely similar to the structure and means of interaction in human society". The second message warns us that "the human society becomes increasingly dependent on the community of programs, while the community of programs gradually becomes less dependent on the participation of people in its activity" (Lyubimskii 2009, p. 2). The infosphere will be a community of programs organised on the same principles as the human society. The worldwide computer network is the habitat of software.

A comparison of the interaction of programs in an information system with the interaction of humans in a social system is an oversimplification. In computer operation systems, for example, a core to rule computational processes is 'Do not jump the queue'. Human interaction, however, needs a qualitatively more complex system of rules.

Electronic Virtualities (E-Virtualities) In the evolutionary step from humans to machines, the evolution of spiritual spheres can also be observed. We can see the line of spiritual evolution from animism to magic to religion to e-virtuality. Technologies like television, which can be viewed as both macrocosm and microcosm, enable old animistic and magic dreams; for instance, an image projector can imitate the cave paintings of Altamira. The encapsulation concept and the examples of human-in-machine encapsulations (see Chap. 23, Sect. 23.4 in this volume) can also be linked with e-virtualities.

Eschatology by Technical Design The *Oxford English Dictionary* defines eschatology as "the part of theology concerned with death, judgment, and the final destiny of the soul and of humankind". There are various eschatological religions and ideologies.

We may formulate the question of whether machines can lead to the "end of the world", a final stage in eschatology, but this discussion is outside the scope of this book. A technological singularity is a hypothetical future point in time at which

---

[3] Graber begins with the observation that "[t]he expansionism of giant platform firms has become a major public concern, an object of political scrutiny and a topic for legal research. As the everyday lives of platform users become more and more "datafied", the "power" of a platform correlates broadly with the degree of the firm's access to big data and artificial intelligence (AI)" (Graber 2020). Graber writes about the affordances (the possibilities and constraints of a technology) and concludes with four recommendations concerning AI.

Fig. 26.4 Governing
body's computers
communicate with
computers in organisations

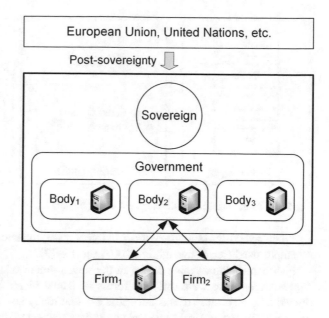

technological growth becomes uncontrollable and irreversible, resulting in unfath-
omable changes to human civilisation.[4] To disambiguate the different meanings and
assumptions, and for an overview of the models of technological singularity, see, for
example, the work of Anders Sandberg (2013).

26.3   Technocratic Governance in Instrumentalised National States

The thesis of this section is that, in the post-sovereign era, the national states are
more instrumentalised than they were centuries ago in the era of emerging sovereignty. A short historical review on the development of sovereignty is provided by,
for example, Grimm (2019) or Wilkinson (2019). The post-sovereign era began after
the Second World War and is characterised by a "new technocratic style" for the
governing function and "increasingly apolitical or technocratic governance" (Wilkinson 2019, pp. 14 and 16).

National states with different cultures may use the same computer programs. An
example is the software that was developed in the Akoma Ntoso project (see
Palmirani and Vitali 2011). Initially, this project was devoted to providing access
to African parliamentary proceedings. Later, a significant outcome was produced,
namely, Legal-RuleML, an XML-based language to represent rules and norms.
Another option is that information systems in different organisations communicate
with a centralised information system (see Fig. 26.4). Examples of this are EUR-Lex,
FinanzOnline and national or transnational registers.

---

[4] See Wikipedia, https://en.wikipedia.org/wiki/Technological_singularity.

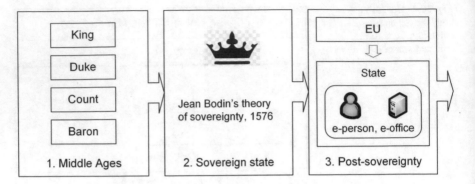

Fig. 26.5 Three stages in the development of sovereignty

When speaking about governance in cyberspace, the end of strict hierarchies may be emphasised (see Schweighofer 2007, pp. 16–17).[5]

Figure 26.5 shows three stages in the development of sovereignty. First, in the Middle Ages there were different forms of feudal hierarchical rule: a kingdom, a duchy, a county, etc. "It was thus possible that many sovereigns existed upon one and the same territory, and a person could be subjected to different sovereigns, yet to everyone only in one or another aspect and to no one totally" (Grimm 2019, p. 19). Second, in 1576 Jean Bodin developed a systematic theory of sovereignty. He concentrated dispersed prerogatives into a uniform public power that was attributed to a single person, the ruler, who became the only sovereign. "Where a ruler succeeded in becoming sovereign, the territory was transformed into a state" (Grimm 2019, p. 19). The words "I am the State" are attributed to the French King Louis XIV.[6] Third, the discussion about post-sovereignty concerns supranational organisations like the United Nations and the European Union.

Figure 26.6 shows two directions of attributing power: (1) from the top, the highest authority, God, and (2) from the people, who elect the parliament. Some of the governmental functions are performed by computers.

Conclusion In the evolutionary step from humans to machines, a theological problem of the second generation is that God creates the world, humans create machines imago Dei, imago hominis. Status civilis is the frame of modern life. Machines appear in the same context.

---

[5]Schweighofer (2007, pp. 16–17) writes: "The regulation is characterised by the end of strict hierarchies (governance by government), the competition of different regulation systems (governance with government), a strong transnational order [. . .], the exit option of citizens, companies and communities and a governance by recognition characterised by limited enforcement possibilities of the territorial state."

[6]See Wikipedia, Louis XIV, https://en.wikipedia.org/wiki/Louis_XIV.

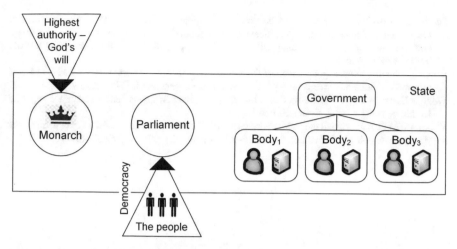

Fig. 26.6 Two directions of attributing power. Computers can act as governmental bodies

References

Brunschwig CR (2018) Perspektiven einer digitalen Rechtswissenschaft: Visualisierung, Audiovisualisierung und Multisensorisierung (Perspectives of digital law: visualization, audiovisualization, and multisensorization). Max Planck Institute for European Legal History Research Paper Series no. 2018-03. https://ssrn.com/abstract=3126043. Accessed 15 Dec 2022

Burdick A, Drucker J, Lunenfeld P, Presner T, Schnapp J (2012) Digital humanities. MIT Press, Cambridge

Čyras V, Lachmayer F (2019) From legal symbolization via legal formalization towards human digitalities. In: Schweighofer E, Araszkiewicz M, Lachmayer F, Pavčnik M (eds) Formalising jurisprudence: festschrift for Hajime Yoshino. Editions Weblaw, Bern, pp 53–76

Čyras V, Lachmayer F (2020) Legal visualisation in the digital age: from textual law towards human digitalities. In: Hötzendorfer W, Tschohl C, Kummer F (eds) International trends in legal informatics: festschrift for Erich Schweighofer. Editions Weblaw, Bern, pp 61–76

Graber CB (2020) Artificial intelligence, affordances and fundamental rights. In: Hildebrandt M, O'Hara K (eds) Life and the law in the era of data-driven agency. Edward Elgar, Cheltenham, pp 194–213. https://doi.org/10.4337/9781788972000.00018. https://ssrn.com/abstract=3299505. Accessed 15 Dec 2022

Grimm D (2019) Post-sovereignty? In: Leijssenaar B, Walker N (eds) Sovereignty in action. Cambridge University Press, pp 17–30. https://doi.org/10.1017/9781108692502.002

Karavas V (2009) The force of code: law's transformation under information-technological conditions. German Law J 10(4):463–482. https://doi.org/10.1017/S2071832200001164

Larsen SE (2019) Monsters and human solitude. In: Carpi D (ed) Monsters and monstrosity: from the canon to the anti-canon. Literary and juridical subversions. De Gruyter, Berlin, pp 35–44

Lyubimskii EZ (2009) On the path to building a community of programs. Program Comput Softw 35(1):2–5. [original Russian text published in Programmirovanie 35(1)]. https://doi.org/10.1134/S0361768809010022

Palmirani M, Vitali F (2011) Akoma-Ntoso for legal documents. In: Sartor G, Palmirani M, Francesconi E, Biasiotti MA (eds) Legislative XML for the semantic web, Law, governance and technology series, vol 4. Springer, Dordrecht, pp 75–100. https://doi.org/10.1007/978-94-007-1887-6_6

Sandberg A (2013) An overview of models of technological singularity. In: More M, Vita-More N
    (eds) The transhumanist reader: classical and contemporary essays on the science, technology,
    and philosophy of the human future. Wiley, pp 376–394. https://doi.org/10.1002/
    9781118555927.ch36
Schweighofer E (2007) E-governance in the information society. In: Schweighofer E (ed) Legal
    informatics and e-governance as tools for the knowledge society LEFIS Series 2:13–23
Wagner H, Haag K (1970) Die moderne Logik in der Rechtswissenschaft. Gehlen Verlag, Bad
    Homburg vor der Höhe, Berlin, Zürich
Wilkinson M (2019) Beyond the post-sovereign state? The past, present, and future of constitutional
    pluralism. Camb Yearb Eur Leg Stud 21:6–23. https://doi.org/10.1017/cel.2019.9

Chapter 27
Multiphase Transformation: From Legal Text to Program

27.1 Text to Program Transformation

This chapter explores the building of a multibridge between legal texts and their representations in computers. We hold that in the transformation from a legal text to the formalisation of that legal text, the path connecting the legal text to the computer implementation has intermediate steps. Formalising legal meanings reveals additional goals and makes them explicit. The thesis is that symbolisation and visualisation precede formalisation on the way to the representation of legal knowledge. Specifically, the open texture of the law can be decreased. Hence, visualisation serves as a syntactic bridge to technology.

The premise of this chapter is that it seems unrealistic to proceed directly in one step from legal texts to their formalisation (in the form of logic programming, e.g., Prolog). Intermediate steps are needed. In other words, we hold that a one-arch bridge is unrealistic and advocate a multi-arch bridge of some kind.

In the transformation *legal text* → *program* (see Fig. 27.1) we expect a formalisation in the form of a technical notation or a specification that further allows computer implementation. Hence, the target is a transformation where *program* means a technical language—computer code referring to software and hardware. A one-bridge approach metaphor can be used to specify the task. Next, a multibridge has to be built. Hence, an approach in legal informatics is proposed which is called Multiphase Transformation.

Based on Čyras and Lachmayer (2013).

Fig. 27.1 The task as a
one-bridge approach (Čyras
and Lachmayer 2013)

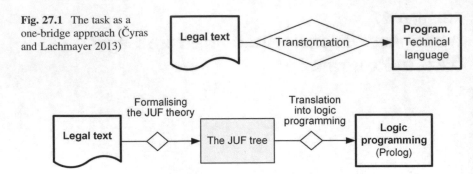

Fig. 27.2 Two steps in the research on JUF (Čyras and Lachmayer 2013)

27.2   One-Bridge Formalisations

There are many approaches to formalisations in the legal domain. Here, various
formalisms, notations, logics and modelling techniques are used. As a one-bridge
approach, Tammelo addressed logic-based representation. He was successful in
representing short legal texts in the prefix notation of binary operators. However,
such formal notation was not easy to read. Sergot et al. (1986) employed logic
programming while representing the British Nationality Act as a logic program.
Grabmair and Ashley (2005) examined two transformations: First, the statute text is
transformed into an Intermediate Norm Representation, and then to a rulebase.

Whilst the transformation is feasible in the case of a clear statement, difficulties
arise with complex texts and a scalability problem is faced. Hence, the quality of
transformation is acceptable for small texts only. However, the quantity (scalability)
is not acceptable. Similarly, a bridge from San Francisco to Hawaii is impossible.
However, nearly 8 km Öresund Bridge between Sweden and Denmark was built in
2000. Here the early attempts of artificial intelligence research on understanding
natural language can be recalled. You can succeed in a world of toy blocks, but it
would scarcely be possible to represent the meaning in the general case.

Ken Satoh's JUF Theory   Satoh's the Japanese Presupposed Ultimate Fact Theory
(the JUF theory, Satoh et al. 2009) is also a one-bridge approach. Satoh et al.
translated the JUF theory into logic programming. Satoh's one bridge can be divided
into two phases. The first is 'formalising the JUF theory' (see his section 2, pp.
165–167), where the JUF tree is an intermediate result. The second step is 'translation into logic programming' (see his section 3), the result of which is a Prolog
program (see Fig. 27.2).

Satoh's work concerns the non liquet (unknown truth value) problem in civil law.
Jurists are familiar with assumption rules and the burden of persuasion—who has to
prove what. The formalisation is an attempt to invoke computer science to solve the
non liquet truth value. We would also identify the next steps: 'developing the

PROLEG system' (see Satoh et al.'s section 4) and 'using the JUF theory', in particular by judges.

27.3   Multi-Arch Bridge Implies Multiphase Transformation

The building of a bridge is continued with the observation that legal knowledge representation is needed as an intermediate step. The input/output chain is *Legal text → Legal knowledge representation → Program* (see Fig. 27.3). Next, *Legal knowledge representation* is decomposed into three intermediate stages: *textual microcontent, symbolisation/visualisation,* and *formalisation* (see Fig. 27.4).

The four bridging steps in Fig. 27.4 are represented by 'input → output' pairs:

Step 1. *Microcontenting*: legal text → textual microcontent
Step 2. *Visualising*: textual microcontent → symbolisation/visualisation
Step 3. *Formalising*: symbolisation/visualisation → formalisation
Step 4. *Implementing*: formalisation → program

In Step 4, the program is implemented in a programming language. This program can be comprised in a complicated information system.

The four steps above can be worded in other ways or even divided into smaller steps. Intermediaries, such as draft and detailed design, can be taken into account. The boundaries of the intermediate steps depend on engineering methodologies.

The transformation above is introduced at the parole level. The transformation can also be viewed in the langue meta-level context (see Fig. 27.5). Therefore, the intermediaries can also be viewed in the parole and langue levels (see Fig. 27.6).

Next, two more levels are added: an ontology level and language reference level. The ontology level is comprised of the core ontology—how to build domain

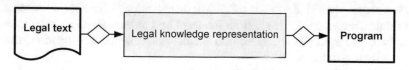

Fig. 27.3 Legal knowledge representation is an intermediary stage in a multibridge (Čyras and Lachmayer 2013)

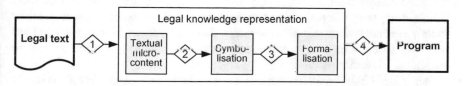

Fig. 27.4 The Multiphase Transformation approach—a multibridge (Čyras and Lachmayer 2013)

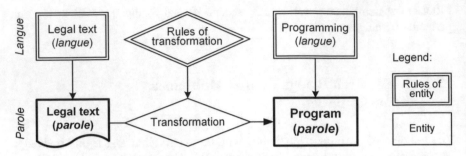

Fig. 27.5 Two levels—parole and langue—are comprised of entities and their rules (Čyras and Lachmayer 2013)

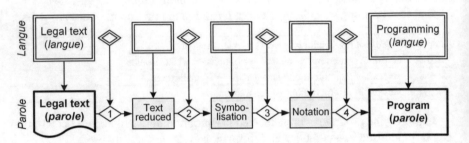

Fig. 27.6 The Multiphase Transformation in the parole and langue context (Čyras and Lachmayer 2013)

ontologies—and legal ontologies (see Breuker et al. 2004). Therefore, the trans-formations are both multiphase and multi-level (see Fig. 27.7).

Intermediate Phases Intermediate structures serve as semantic bridges and are necessary. A one-arch bridge is impossible to build when the gap is too wide. Another case is when the "banks" are blurred.

Four steps (phases) above are called Microcontenting, Visualising, Formalising, and Implementing. Step 1 leads from the legal text to textual microcontent. In this step, the linear legal text is divided into smaller portions that are organised, but not necessarily sequentially.

Step 2 takes the textual microcontent to symbolisation/visualisation. For the sake of formality, the text can be made more structured. Symbolisation is a good intermediary. The subject index, the lists (of references, tables, figures, etc.), abstractions, hypernyms/hyponyms, abbreviations, and other means can be used. Next, getting free of sentences and their grammar allows operating with symbols directly, and not with words as in the Greco–Roman tradition. Hence, a symbol and not a sentence becomes a communication unit. A grammar of symbols can be introduced, cf. traffic signs and Olympic pictograms.

Step 3 leads from symbolisation/visualisation to formalisation. This phase can be decomposed additionally. Step 4 leads from formalisation to knowledge

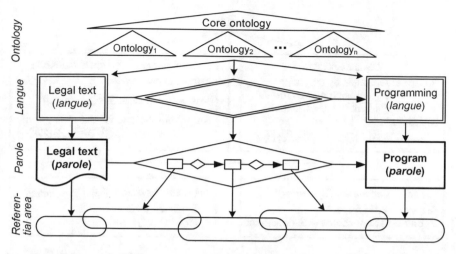

Fig. 27.7 Elements of multiphase multilevel transformations (Čyras and Lachmayer 2013)

representation/implementation in a computer. From engineer's view this step is a complex task that can also be divided into sub-phases. Various software engineering methodologies can be employed.

Intermediate steps can follow the life-cycle stages of knowledge-based systems. For example, the model of Stefik (1995, p. 350) identifies five stages: identification, conceptualisation, formalisation, implementation, and testing.

27.4   Approaches to the Transformation 'Legal Text To Program'

We distinguish between the different kinds of program, for example (see Fig. 27.8):

1. *Information retrieval systems* (IRS), also called IR systems
2. *Knowledge-based systems* (KBS). In the present context they are also called legal knowledge-based systems or legal expert systems
3. *Legal machines* such as traffic lights, cash machines, gates, etc.
4. *Information systems* (IS) such as enterprise resource planning (ERP) systems, management information systems (MIS), etc.
5. *Other* kinds of systems

Grey areas exist. The semantics of legal knowledge, which is represented in a system, is a criterion for distinguishing KBS from IRS. The spectrum of semantic features is wide, and therefore this criterion is not sharp. Search engines in KBS tend to become more intelligent; see a variety of search applications. In KBS, after the legal-to-program transformation, the program does not necessarily become the law.

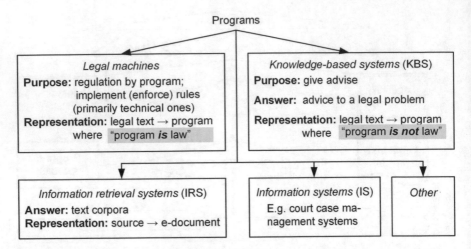

Fig. 27.8 A classification that distinguishes between legal machines, KBS, IRS and IS (Čyras and Lachmayer 2013)

Business rules in information systems represent different concepts, such as integrity constraints, epistemological, consolidation or derivation axioms, etc. (Vasilecas et al. 2009). They constrain database state transitions and can serve as enterprise policies. However, business rules implementations do not necessarily become legal machines.

The spectrum of legal machines as defined in Fig. 27.8 is wide, therefore the boundary between legal machines and KBS is not sharp either. As an example, assume a taxpayer who violates tax law. The tax office information system that fines the taxpayer can be classified as both a legal machine and a KBS.

Building information retrieval addresses the transformation *legal source → e-document*. For example, nowadays legal gazettes are being replaced by authentic electronic publications in databases and online systems such as EUR-Lex in the European Union. In IRS the answer to a query is legal text corpora. While in building IRS, the text-to-program transformation is not of primary importance.

In contrast, KBS face the *legal text → program* problem as the query answer is a guidance to the legal problem. In a KBS, legal knowledge is represented in the program (a knowledge base + inference engine, for short). Wisdom differentiates knowledge in law. Ill-structured knowledge and vague norms are immanent to law. Therefore we take into account Leith's (2010) scepticism about the value of expert systems in law. Underlying objections to expert systems are the "clear rule" idea and "the notion of being able to formalise symbol-level knowledge representation through some logical or semi-logical formalism".

A computational model of law is a temporary stop, while building the bridge from the legal domain to computer science. Thus, a vague legal rule is mapped to a strict rule in the model.

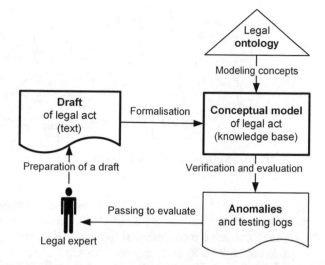

Fig. 27.9 Computer supported legislative drafting and traceability. The conceptual model of the legal act is tested for compliance with other acts (based on Paliulionienė 2008)

Legalese Within Information Systems Each IS, independent of its intelligence, is relevant to law to a certain extent. In the identification and specification stages, the purposes of the IS are identified. These purposes have to comply with the legal order. Part of IS requirements can be classified as legal requirements. Hence, a bridge from law to informatics is starting to be built.

The importance of formalisation can also be observed in legislative drafting and traceability (see Paliulionienė 2008; Fig. 27.9).

27.5   Emergence of Intermediate Phases

Intermediary structures as semantic bridges emerge in the following themes: communication, tertium comparationis and abstraction. The latter concepts form a kind of ontology for intermediaries. In communication the transformation leads from one language to another. Thus the purpose is to build a bridge from the legal text bank to the technical language bank. Tertium comparationis appears in the case of a relation which is not directly drawn from one element to another but through a third (see Fig. 27.10a, and also Chap. 3 in this volume).

In abstraction intermediate steps are also observed: first, by discerning parallel elements and comparing them, second, by seeing concrete examples such as celebrities, politicians, etc. Third, by producing schemes, fourth, through formal symbolisations, and fifth by developing ideas (see Fig. 27.10b).

Intermediate Steps in Context Legal knowledge representation is not an ultimate goal—either in law or in legal informatics. Logic programming is just one task within the context. Logic programming can occur, for example, as an argument task in judiciary, as a law enforcement task in execution, or as a technical filter in

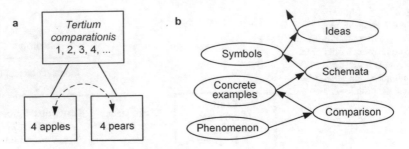

Fig. 27.10 Intermediaries in (**a**) tertium comparationis and (**b**) abstraction (Čyras and Lachmayer 2013)

legislation. Logical analysis of presumptions and burdens of proof in legal argument have been addressed, for example, by Prakken and Sartor (2008).

Legal knowledge representation appears in the context of other tasks. The four steps in Multiphase Transformation (see Fig. 27.4) can be identified and called differently. Therefore multi-arch bridges have neither a uniform arch number nor a unique construction.

Both knowledge representation and knowledge visualisation frameworks have to answer key questions such as 'what', 'why' and 'how'. The landscape of legal tasks can be subject to standardization similarly to software life-cycles. The questions including 'who', 'where' and 'when' have to be answered in software engineering in the requirements analysis phase. Therefore software life-cycle phases including specification, design and implementation can also be applied to legal tasks.

Reasons for Intermediate Steps One-bridge leading from law to legal expert systems was just a programmers' dream some decades ago. However realisations face difficulties. There are obstacles for one-bridge. The following difficulties can be mentioned:

1. When talking about cyberspace, at the very least, a software engineer cannot easily fully understand the question "What is the law applicable to a given situation?" (see Reed and Murray 2018, p. vii).[1]
2. Balancing in law is more important than rules.
3. A vast amount of legal knowledge is out of the text. Legal theory, doctrine, textbooks, etc. are the sources of legal knowledge, hence, explicit and implicit knowledge coexist. Technical domains are characterised by a smaller proportion of implicit and explicit knowledge.

The following lessons for intermediate phases can be learned from software engineering. One-arch technology such as writing a program from scratch is only feasible

---

[1] Reed and Murray (2018, p. vii) continue: "The answer has never successfully identified 'the law' but, at best, 'some of these laws'. At first we thought this was a defect in our own understandings, but over time we have come to the view that it is in fact the defect in law itself."

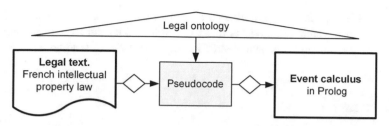

Fig. 27.11 A multibridge that can be extracted from Contissa and Laukyte (2008) who studied legal knowledge representation of French intellectual property law

for small programs. For complicated programs usually technology is used which considers the whole life-cycle.

Way Back and the V Model   A bridge implies two paths: first from one side to the other and then back again. A one way only—as in a catapult—is enough in cases where you do not need to return; in this case you may burn the bridge. The to-and-return metaphor can be compared with the V model (read as Vee model). The V-model is a graphical representation of a systems development life-cycle (see Forsberg et al. 2005).[2] The descending phases serve to implement the system, and the rising ones to verify and validate the requirements.

Importance of Islands   Text-to-program transformation phases can be compared with building bridges through a marsh. A constructor builds a series of bridges to smaller or larger islands. An island is often an improvement to a city's appearance: Seine Island → Paris, Tiber Island → Rome, Danube Island → Vienna, etc. In the legal domain, document transformation needs team cooperation, therefore the islands serve as stops to produce intermediate deliverables.

An Example of Observing Intermediate Steps   Contissa and Laukyte (2008) examine the legal knowledge representation of French intellectual property law; we depict their experience in Fig. 27.11. Legal texts serve as a bank from which to depart. The first island is a pseudo-code of the texts. The other bank is event calculus representation in Prolog. The ontology of the intellectual property law which is represented in LKIF language backs the development. The Legal Knowledge Interchange Format (LKIF) is a Semantic Web based language designed for legal applications (see Boer et al. 2008). It is built upon emerging XML-standards.

Conclusion   This chapter presents reflections about the phases on the way to legal knowledge representation. Each phase may have ill-defined inputs and outputs. Therefore a one-bridge approach seems actually unrealistic and Multiphase Transformation is proposed.

The intermediate steps are important, as additional goals can be revealed. It is complicated to focus concurrently on multiple, probably conflicting, goals.

---

[2] See Wikipedia, the V-Model, https://en.wikipedia.org/wiki/V-Model.

Intermediaries appear within multistep and multilevel transformations: ontology—langue—parole—referential areas and can be explained by the roles of communication, tertium comparationis, and abstraction in the process of cognition.

References

Boer A, Winkels R, Vitali F (2008) MetaLex XML and the legal knowledge interchange format. In: Casanovas P, Sartor G, Casellas N, Rubino R (eds) Computable models of the law, Lecture notes in computer science (Lecture notes in artificial intelligence), vol 4884. Springer, Heidelberg, pp 21–41. https://doi.org/10.1007/978-3-540-85569-9_2

Breuker J, Valente A, Winkels R (2004) Legal ontologies in knowledge engineering and information management. Artif Intell Law 12(4):241–277. https://doi.org/10.1007/s10506-006-0002-1

Contissa G, Laukyte M (2008) Legal knowledge representation: a twofold experience in the domain of intellectual property law. In: Francesconi E, Sartor G (eds) Legal knowledge and information systems. JURIX 2008: the twenty-first annual conference. Frontiers in artificial intelligence and applications, vol 189. IOS Press, Amsterdam, pp 98–107. https://doi.org/10.3233/978-1-58603-952-3-98

Čyras V, Lachmayer F (2013) Multiphase transformation in the legal text-to-program approach. In: Sturm F, Thomas P, Otto J, Mori H (eds) Liber amicorum Guido Tsuno. Vico Verlag, Frankfurt am Main, pp 57–70. https://ssrn.com/abstract=2632045. Accessed 15 Dec 2022

Forsberg K, Mooz H, Cotterman H (2005) Visualizing project management: models and frameworks for mastering complex systems. Wiley, New York

Grabmair M, Ashley K (2005) Towards modeling systematic interpretation of codified law. In: Moens M, Spyns P (eds) Legal knowledge and information systems. JURIX 2005: the eighteenth annual conference. Frontiers in artificial intelligence and applications, vol 134. IOS Press, Amsterdam, pp 107–108

Leith P (2010) The rise and fall of the legal expert system. Eur J Law Technol 1(1) https://ejlt.org/index.php/ejlt/article/view/14. Accessed 15 Dec 2022

Paliulionienė L (2008) Teisės aktams rengti skirtų sistemų vartotojo interfeiso ypatumai [in Lithuanian] (Peculiarities of the user interface of a legal document drafting system). Proc Lithuanian Math Soc 48(49):360–364

Prakken H, Sartor G (2008) More on presumptions and burdens of proof. In: Francesconi E, Sartor G (eds) Legal knowledge and information systems. JURIX 2008: the twenty-first annual conference. Frontiers in artificial intelligence and applications, vol 189. IOS Press, Amsterdam, pp 176–185. https://doi.org/10.3233/978-1-58603-952-3-176

Reed C, Murray A (2018) Rethinking the jurisprudence of cyberspace. Edward Elgar, Cheltenham. https://doi.org/10.4337/9781785364297

Satoh K, Kubota M, Nishigai Y, Takano C (2009) Translating the Japanese presupposed ultimate fact theory into logic programming. In: Governatori G (ed) Legal knowledge and information systems. JURIX 2009: the twenty-second annual conference. Frontiers in artificial intelligence and applications, vol 205. IOS Press, Amsterdam, pp 162–171. https://doi.org/10.3233/978-1-60750-082-7-162

Sergot MJ, Sadri F, Kowalski RA, Kriwaczek F, Hammond P, Cory HT (1986) The British Nationality Act as a logic program. Commun ACM 29(5):370–386

Stefik M (1995) Introduction to knowledge systems. Morgan Kaufmann, San Francisco

Vasilecas O, Kalibatiene D, Guizzardi G (2009) Towards a formal method for transforming ontology axioms to application domain rules. Inf Technol Control 38(4):271–282

Part VIII
Argumentation

Chapter 28
Three Layers of Legal Argumentation: Content, Speech Act, and Role

28.1 Content-Based Argumentation

This chapter distinguishes the three layers in legal argumentation. First, the content layer has the following elements: two points of view (A and not A), the parties, pro- and counter-arguments, and the goal (to establish the winner). This layer attracts the attention of artificial intelligence and law researchers who model legal reasoning within general theories of argumentation. The second layer—speech acts—concerns the quality of legal acts. Its elements are the players, a discourse authority, discourse rules, and the goal (to decide upon the validity of speech acts). The third layer—roles—concerns the roles of participants. Its elements are the parties and the rivalry between them. A participant can appear in the role, and would be classified as a non-player, which forbids him to act as a player. Hence, we distinguish between three kinds of issues which are connected with argumentation in law. They are based on the content, speech act validity, and player roles, respectively. Legal argument can be concerned with different concepts, for example, values, teleological structures, and theories. Another dimension distinguishes between Is and Ought, where Is refers to facts and Ought refers to norms.

Two conflicting points of view, A and $\neg A$ constitute a starting point. Next come the parties: the proponent and the respondent. Each of them therefore pursues an opposite factum probandum (what has to be proven): the proponent A and the respondent $\neg A$. Then come attitudes (pro or contra) that are expressed as opposite statements. Subsequently come pro- and counter-arguments that provide the ground and thus back the standpoints are presented. Counter-arguments express evaluative opinions. The goal of content-based argumentation is to establish the winner, thus bringing the argument to universal prevalence (see Fig. 28.1).

Content-based argumentation allows for different ways of modelling. Formal notations and logic can be applied to models of legal reasoning. This has been explored by a long list of researchers from the artificial intelligence and law

© The Author(s), under exclusive license to Springer Nature Switzerland AG 2023
V. Cyras, F. Lachmayer, *Essays on the Visualisation of Legal Informatics*, Law,
Governance and Technology Series 54,
https://doi.org/10.1007/978-3-031-27957-7_28

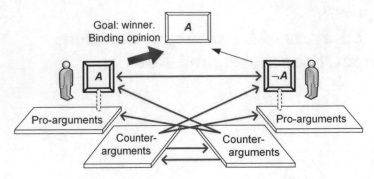

Fig. 28.1 Content-based argumentation

communities (see e.g. Gordon 2007). Argumentation schemes, material implication, universal generalisation, and deductively valid inference with the modus ponens rule are used herein. Rebuttal and undercutting are two forms of defeasible reasoning that are modelled.

Logical tools for modelling legal arguments (Prakken 1997) stand for general methods. They can help to represent statements about any entity, including the content, speech act validity, and player roles. For example, the predicates in the formula $\forall x\, A(x) \Rightarrow B(x)$ can denote any entity.

Specific content can be implicit. For example, argument diagramming in Bex et al. (2003) is devoted to modelling legal reasoning related to evidence. Hence, the nodes of argument schemes that represent propositions and conclusions are primarily related to the content, though the propositions can examine speech act quality and player roles, for example, 'The witness is biased'. To address speech act validity and player roles, a specific substantial law is essential. Here, legal proceedings law can step into the foreground.

28.2   Speech Act Based Argumentation

Here we deal not with sentences but with speech acts; they can also be classified as legal acts or performance acts. Next come the players; then a discourse authority appears. A discourse is comprised of two acts (see Fig. 28.2a), which can be valid or non-valid. They stand for the legal meaning of players' speech acts. The discourse authority's rules decide the validity of the discourse acts. Following is a classical example of a non-valid speech act. A lawyer who makes an appeal after the deadline has passed is a classic example of a non-valid speech act.

One can attempt to model this in an argument diagram (see Fig. 28.2b). Speech acts or roles are not addressed specifically with Wigmore's diagram elements (e.g. "testimonial assertion" T, "circumstance" C; see Walton 2005, p. 9). However, the statements that are denoted by the diagram elements can address both speech acts and roles similarly with argumentation schemes. The 26 typical defeasible

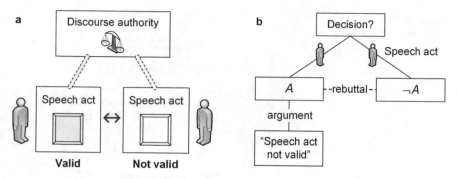

Fig. 28.2 (**a**) Speech act validity in discourse. (**b**) A sketch of an argument diagram

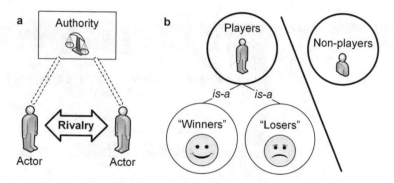

Fig. 28.3 The roles of actors. (**a**) A rivalry relation. (**b**) The classification of actors

argumentation schemes that are listed in Walton (2005, pp. 10–11) are relevant to speech act and the role to different degrees. Some schemes do not show direct relevance. However, some schemes are relevant, for example, schemes 19 and 20:

Scheme 19   "The Situationally Disqualifying Ad Hominem Argument: arguing that an opponent has no right to speak on an issue because he is not in a situation to credibly do so."

Scheme 20   "Argument from Bias: arguing that one should not pay too much serious attention to a person's argument, or should discount it, because he is biased."

28.3 Role-Based Argumentation

Here the actors (participants)—primarily the rivals—come first. The discourse authority establishes how the actors in the rivalry perform (see Fig. 28.3a); these actors can be divided into players and non-players (see Fig. 28.3b). A person may be not a player. For example, suppose a stranger from the audience in a trial tries to make a claim or object a prosecutor; such a person is not in charge of performing this

Fig. 28.4 "Rational discourse" (cf. e.g. Alexy 1978)

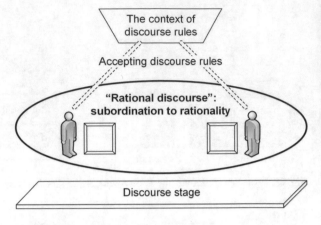

Fig. 28.5 Different cultural contexts

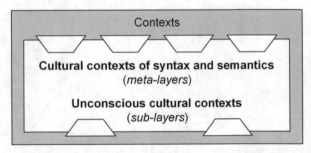

legal act. Players in argumentations have certain roles such as the proponent, respondent, witness, etc. Next the players can be divided into 'winners' and 'losers'.

The roles of actors are regulated by the rules of the proceedings. For example, a proceedings statute can make classify roles such as the plaintiff, the defendant, the expert, etc., giving them different rights and duties. Thus the burdens and standards of proof are included in the statutes.

28.4   Subordination to Rationality

Alexy (1978) writes about "rational discourse". Argumentation is subordinated to rationality and the acceptability of the discourse rules (see Fig. 28.4). First come the audience and the stage of rational discourse. Second comes an authority which decides the rules; the authority also establishes meta-levels of rationality.

28.5   Contexts

Different contexts are important. First, different contexts of syntax and semantics may appear (see Fig. 28.5). They form meta-layers; for example, different statutes can emerge. Suppose a district court deciding one way, a constitutional court another way, and a European court yet another. Second, unknowingly cultural contexts—sub-layers—appear. For instance, witnesses are more or less likely to be accepted in different cultures. There are different forms of mental unconscious acceptance. Here the unconscious, and not the rationality, emerges in the foreground.

Conclusion In argumentation in law, we stress three layers—content, speech act, and role. Legal reasoning can be based on factual or legal matters or on both.

References

Alexy R (1978) Theorie der juristishen Argumentation: Die Theorie des rationale Diskurses als Theorie der juristishen Begründung, 4. Auflage [2001]. Suhrkamp, Frankfurt am Main

Bex F, Prakken H, Reed C, Walton D (2003) Towards a formal account of reasoning about evidence: argumentation schemes and generalisations. Artif Intell Law 11(2-3):125–165. https://doi.org/10.1023/B:ARTI.0000046007.11806.9a

Gordon TF (2007) Visualizing Carneades argument graphs. Law Probab Risk 6(1-4):109–117. https://doi.org/10.1093/lpr/mgm026

Prakken H (1997) Logical tools for modelling legal argument: a study of defeasible reasoning in law. Kluwer Academic, Dordrecht

Walton D (2005) Argumentation methods for artificial intelligence in law. Springer, Heidelberg

Chapter 29
Transparent Complexity by Goals

29.1 Why Goals? A Variety of Conceptions

Making explicit the teleological structure of e-government can contribute to its understanding and reduce its complexity. E-government can be viewed from distinct perspectives—those of authorities and citizens, and also from conception and construction. This view of administrative and legal informatics requires paradigmatic changes in the development of e-government. We think that currently dominant normative thinking is not enough to solve specific problems of e-government. Here, a new concept of legal teleology is required. We propose to supplement norms, and even structural parts of a whole legal system, with teleological relations. This will form a separate structural layer of legal-knowledge representation and metadata of legal documents. Proposed notation $A \xrightarrow{te} B$ contains three elements: a basic element A, a target element B, and a teleological relation $\xrightarrow{te}$.

Legal order as a societal instrument is characterised by mostly implicit and rarely explicit teleological structures. Teleology concerns not just a single norm, but a whole legal system. An early attempt to analyse legal teleological structures was 'Interessenjurisprudenz' performed by Jhering (1877). Nowadays, the recent challenges of e-government require a new concept of legal teleology (see e.g. Wimmer 2006). Governance entails teleology, too. This concept resides in Westerman's (2007) idea that 'governance is governing by goals'. In e-government, theoretical concepts have also to be concerned and a formalisation on a large scale is required. Automatic indexing of purposes which appear in a statute, for example, EC Treaty, can scarcely be expected as a breakthrough approach (see e.g. *AI in law practice? So far, not much* by Oskamp and Lauritsen 2002).

Therefore, the term 'goal' deserves to be placed in a top legal ontology. This is especially trues in the branches of law where legal materials are in the process of

---

Based on Čyras (2007, 2009) and Čyras and Lachmayer (2008).

© The Author(s), under exclusive license to Springer Nature Switzerland AG 2023
V. Cyras, F. Lachmayer, *Essays on the Visualisation of Legal Informatics*, Law,
Governance and Technology Series 54,
https://doi.org/10.1007/978-3-031-27957-7_29

development. On the one hand, 'goal' can be treated as generalisations of 'objective', 'purpose', 'aim', 'result', 'value', 'end', 'finality', etc. For instance, the purpose of the law is considered in Hart's 'No vehicles in the park'. On the other hand, the goal generalises low-level measurable results such as targets, benchmarks, best practices, etc. The second argument is the teleological method. It is one of the major legal methods (Larenz and Canaris 1995, pp. 209 ff), and is widely used in European Union law.

We can see several reasons to consider goals. First, teleology is innate in normative legal systems. Therefore, representation of teleological structures should be an inherent task of legal-knowledge management. Second, legal reasoning, especially by non-experts in law, is driven primarily by goals rather than by norms. Third, teleological structures are mostly implicit and rarely explicit. Therefore, their representation is a true challenge in knowledge management. Fourth, teleological statements are extensively used in legal drafting. We maintain that listing the purposes of a statute in its preamble is not enough. Kelsen in his *Pure Theory of Law* focuses on the model of an action within a norm. We think that action-oriented models have to be supplemented with teleological relations.

Sartor (2006) treats the goal as a fundamental legal concept[1] and proposes a notation $A \Uparrow^G$ "to mean that the adoption of a proposition A advances the goal (or the set of goals) G". Purposes are also addressed by Jhering (1924), who distinguished the purpose of a duty as the interest it is intended to serve. Artosi et al. (2007), while proposing elements for a formalisation of the theory of norms, treat a propositional assertion and an action as constituent elements of a norm. We think that goals are also elements of the legal system. There are more theoretical beginnings in this direction. Teleological relations enter a broad field of relations. There exist many subterms of different relations (see e.g. Kaufmann et al. 2004).

Normative teleological structures can be compared with institutional teleological structures. The viewpoint 'roles, not rules' leads to analysis of, first, Jhering's interessenjurisprudence, then MacCormick and Weinberger's institutional theory of law, etc.

Summers (2006, pp. 42–47), while speaking about form and function, says that "the overall form of a functional legal unit as a whole must be designed to serve purposes". He distinguishes the following types of purposes of a functional legal unit: (1) founding purposes; (2) internal operational purposes; (3) public policies; and (4) political values—general values of the rule of law.

These works show possible methods to approach teleological structures in law on a methodological basis. We note that the following three levels are not well distinguished: (1) the nature of law; (2) the functions of law, as well as of an authority; and (3) the purposes of an authority. For example, an official speaks about

---

[1] Sartor (2006, p. 108) writes: "More articulate normative notions and, in particular, the idea of a right, cannot be built on the basis of obligations and permissions alone. Such notions embed a *teleological* perspective, namely, a focus on purposes or interests (final or intermediate values, ends, objectives) which a normative proposition is meant to serve."

computerisation as an aim of e-government. However, here the computerisation is a means—not the goal. As being the means it can contribute (positively or negatively) to certain values.

Although two Hohfeldian squares (see e.g. Sergot 2001) do not contain the term 'goal', one understands that it is among the fundamental legal concepts. The function of an artifact is considered as a teleological concept in philosophy (see Dennett 1989). When speaking about intentionality, Dennett refers to scholastics in the middle ages. The intentional nature of law is considered in artificial intelligence.

We consider the teleological method of interpretation because text-retrieval systems and experts in domains outside law rely primarily on the grammatical method of interpretation. However, "the historical and teleological dimensions of the law entail that the liberty of interpretation enjoyed by the reader of a statute from a linguistic point of view becomes even wider within a legal context" (Van Hoecke 2002, p. 150). Legal drafting is also a theme. A statement of the purposes of a legal act is required in a legislative procedure. This is usually presented in the preamble of the act, where the social relations to be regulated form an element of the purpose.

29.2 Motivation

This chapter is motivated to gain from explicit representation of teleological structures in law. This motivation is viewed from the following perspectives:

- *Using the teleological method* in legal reasoning. This is a *legal perspective*. It is reasonable to make purposes explicit, because purposive interpretation of law is broadly used by courts.
- *Tracing purposes*, a *computing perspective*. Purposes in the law should be validated and verified, especially while creating law. Thus ex ante and ex post analysis and XML-based tools are in the focus. We expect similarity to goal tracing in information systems (IS) development.

Teleology in Legal Argument Modelling teleology in legal argument is elaborated, in particular, in a special 2002 issue of the journal, 'Artificial Intelligence and Law'. A series of papers (Bench-Capon 2002; Hafner and Berman 2002, etc.) recapitulate the ideas of Berman and Hafner (1993) regarding the role of teleology in legal argument and elaborate theories based on (teleological) values. A distinction between factors and values is made. An exercise of three cases results in a list of values: legal certainty; social utility; and sanctity of property. A list of elicited factors includes 'the plaintiff/defendant was pursuing his livelihood', 'the plaintiff was on his own land', 'the plaintiff was not in possession of the animal', etc.

We think that modelling teleology in legal argument is important, but only one of several levels of teleological structures. The latter should rest, primarily, on legal theory, then on observations. Therefore, what is needed is a 'theory of goals'.

Legal Engineering and Systems Engineering This chapter is also motivated by the following intent regarding legal drafting. From a systems engineering (SE) standpoint, the law can be viewed as a formal system. This view is backed by the legal theory that the law is a system of norms. Such a system can be compared to a production system in AI. However, the complexity of the system is an issue.

Considering the view above, a legal engineering task should include the following stages (similarly to analysis–design–implementation stages in a software life-cycle—as requirements engineering methods recommend):

- First, formulate the goals of the system under consideration.
- Second, derive requirements from the goals.
- Third, design the system from the requirements.

However, the intention above is an ideal. It is based on the idea of treating a statute as a system (Čaplinskas and Mockevičius 2002). The following example was given by Albertas Čaplinskas while discussing the powers of a judge to determine the limits of custodial sentence duration. Two distinct principles are inherent in criminal law: punishing a person, or punishing for a crime. These principles can be treated as distinct goals. They can differentiate two distinct legal systems, for instance, continental law and common law. Top-down development and goal tracing techniques, which are known in systems engineering, might result in two distinct criminal codes. Luckily, the world is not that black and white. In each country, the two principles are intertwined distinctively and result in different criminal codes.

What Is Law and What Is Goal? Here we try to discover the essence of law through the category of goal. Can the related categories in legal theory be built on its basis? The Aristotelian concepts of finis and telos have to be distinguished. Finis is treated as a state (status) of the world, the final end; telos—a way, a direction, or a process.

Dworkin (1986, p. 15) shows what problems are faced while answering 'what is law?' In his analysis of Elmer's case, we find that the teleological concept of 'intentions' is formalised as coherence with legal principles. In the endangered species case, we find a classical comparison of alternatives: one value (endangered species) vs. another value (a hydro station). Which is heavier?

Teleological Structure Depends on a Legal Task We share the view of Valente (1995, p. viii) that "another path to develop models of problem solving, complementary to the one based on the ontology, is the development of models of typical legal tasks". He proposes typology of legal problems comprising some main views on the use and design of legislation (emphasis added): "the perspective of elaborating legislation, the perspective of an agent *using the legislation*, and the perspective of elementary *internal problems* implied or indicated by the ontology". Hence, legal-knowledge engineering should rest on legal theory.

29.3 Requirements and Goals of E-Government

Teleological statements are especially found in the legislative workflow: governmental drafting, parliamentarian decisions, etc. In high-level political and legal acts, e-government is expressed in terms of goals (see, e.g. European Information Society programmes such as i2010 or EU eGovernment Action Plan 2016–2020). In particular, "[i]t is widely accepted that the goal [of e-government] consists in increasing the performance of the governance" (Costake 2007). Thus e-government is related to governance (see e.g. Grönlund 2007). Grönlund identifies three goals as typically explicitly mentioned: more efficient government, better services to citizens, and improved democratic processes.

Goal orientation in e-government is inherited from European Union law which is very goal-centered. The objectives of the EU are set in Article B (now Article 2) of the Maastricht Treaty on European Union. Article I-2 of a constitution for Europe lists the values of the Union.

Political goals, legal goals, and information system goals shall be distinguished. They appear in the acts of different levels and in different terminology. For example, a high-level political aim, 'common market', can be decomposed to the AND-tree of four sub-goals of a type 'right': 'free movement of goods'; 'free movement of persons'; 'free movement of services'; and 'free movement of capital'.

A detailed analysis of e-government goals is done on lower-level issues. Requirements can be extracted from e-government issues (see Traunmüller and Wimmer 2004). Costake (2007) examines general requirements for e-government. Requirements that engineer for methodologies distinguish between functional requirements, non-functional requirements, and goals. Following are examples of business requirements for digital government (DG) as they are categorised by Costake in the form of a goal tree:

- General: transparency and accountability of the governance; easy access to public information; easy access to DG services; etc.
- Citizens-oriented: user-friendly access to public information and services; international recognition of personal e-documents; etc.
- Business-oriented: provision of complete online public e-services; e-procurement for public acquisitions; etc.
- Oriented on users in state institutions: possibility to simulate and assess the effects of drafts decisions or regulations; decision support services; etc.

29.4 Formalisation of Goals Should Be Taken Seriously

In Kelsen's *General theory of norms*, the norms are not associated with values. Kelsen devotes chapter 2 to norms and the means-goal-relationship. This comprises the teleological necessity between a norm and a goal. However in the contemporary context of e-government and governance, the goal emerges as a primary concept.

Who shall care about goals?—politicians, lawyers, governmental agencies or software engineers? There is a reason why lawyers are not interested in goals.[2] The practicing lawyer is "continuously engaged in demarcating valid from invalid law". This position is scarcely sustainable: "If we want to understand the products – the rules and principles [...] we should also understand the process that has helped to form those products" (Westerman 2007, p. 53). Westerman further characterises governance as a new style and introduces "*result-prescribing norms*" (RP-norms). In the EU law, this can be observed in framework-directives. Directives formulate aims and goal-prescriptions.[3] Examples of such aims are 'reliable care', 'good labour conditions', etc.

Westerman's statement, "The conventional rule as a device that indicates a concrete manner to achieve ends is replaced by direct prescriptions of those ends. Rule-making is supplanted by end-setting" (ibid., p. 55), suggests to us the following formalisation. A classically formed action-centered rule:

$$do\ action\ A\ to\ achieve\ the\ goal\ G$$

is replaced with the rule which has an open action X:

$$do\ whatever\ X\ to\ achieve\ the\ goal\ G$$

Norm-addressees are paradigmatically changed from individual ones to networks of numerous institutions. The next issue is the benchmarking of low-level goals. Suppose a high-level goal, 'reliable care', can be decomposed to contain a sub-goal, 'short waiting list'. Then "the question immediately arises what should be counted as sufficiently 'short'" (Westerman 2007, p. 55). Thus, specifications of goals lead to "*performance-indicators* that enable the various supervisory bodies to monitor the degree in which the desired aims and policies are realised" (ibid.). The requirement that "at every more specific and concrete level, there is less scope for alternatives routes by means of which the results can be obtained" (ibid., p. 56) accords with general top-down decomposition principles of systems design. There are reasons to prefer goals to rules when the disadvantages of rules emerge. The difficulties are discerned (ibid., p. 58) as the choice of rules, the enforcement of rules, the reception of rules, and the effectiveness of rules.

The above-listed difficulties also accord with the preference for declarative knowledge when disadvantages of procedural representation are observed. The nature of requirements engineering (RE) is to tell *what* to attain, not *how* to attain.

---

[2] Westerman writes: "The prevailing attitude of most legal scholars or students of legal theory is to regard policy-making – with or without politics – and governing – with or without government – as activities that should be kept separate from law. Lawyers deal with the product, not with the process that precedes it. They usually deal with rules and regulations, but not with the art of rule-making" (Westerman (2007, p. 53), referring to Wintgens (2006)).

[3] Article 249 (ex 189) of the EC Treaty sets: "A directive shall be binding, as to the result to be achieved [...] but shall leave to the national authorities the choice of form and methods."

Rules are useful when goals (interests, values) are conflicting. Consensus on shared goals (what is vital in governance) leads to explicit representation of the goals. The tenet that people should reach consensus leads to the emphasis on learning (ibid., p. 60). A shared goal (general interest) should be learned. Here e-government can serve as a collective process of guided learning.

"Tyrannical goals" are identified in demarcating a "facilitative rule (allowing people to pursue their own goals) and a manipulative rule (serving the interest of the legislator only)" (ibid., p. 68). Such tyrannical goals are avoid-goals that are distinguished in RE. Explicit representation of goals might serve when "within governance, there is no systematic place for such a forum in which conflicting interests can be brought together" (ibid.). Identification of the means as heavier or lighter in order to achieve certain goals can contribute to the principle of proportionality. Here the following formalisation can be extracted:

1. A mean $M1$ serves to achieve the goal G.
2. A mean $M2$ serves to achieve the goal G.
3. $M1$ is heavier than $M2$.

29.5   Structure of Teleological Notation

The teleological structure we propose contains three elements: the basic element A; the target-element B; and the teleological relation $^{te}\!\rightarrow$. The proposed notation is

$$A \;^{te}\!\rightarrow B$$

To illustrate the notation, consider three statements:

A goal g is achieved by a legal act a_1.
A goal g is achieved by a legal act a_2.
A legal act a_1 implies less quantitative restrictions (QR) than a_2.

A very simplified meaning of these statements can be represented:

$$a_1 \;^{te}\!\rightarrow g, \quad a_2 \;^{te}\!\rightarrow g, \quad a_1 \;^{QR}\!< a_2$$

Within the legal taxonomy there are different kinds of semantics of legal teleology, depending on different teleological order like time horizon, for example, $A \;^{te\_short\_term}\!\rightarrow B$, or $A \;^{te\_long\_term}\!\rightarrow B$.

Pragmatically, the teleological structure is embedded within a speech act, which must be represented by a separate notation, e.g. $te\_statement(\ldots)$. Also, the speech act can be qualified in different ways, e.g. legal, political, scientific: $te\_statement\_legal(A \;^{te}\!\rightarrow B)$; $te\_statement\_political(A \;^{te}\!\rightarrow B)$; or $te\_statement\_scientific(A \;^{te}\!\rightarrow B)$. Consequently, the notation leads to a theory of relations in law.

The Aristotelian philosophical concepts of entelechie, telos, and finis (Aristotle 1954) can be treated as the roots of the teleology of current normative systems. Aristotelian entelechie denotes the immanent telos goal of a thing. We represent the telos B of a thing A as $A \xrightarrow{te} B$. The natural law has been developed around the concept of entelechie. A norm allows behaviour that aims at a telos that is evaluated positively, and forbids behaviour that aims at a telos that is evaluated negatively. Hence, we advocate the relational nature of goals. In such a context, three subjects can be identified:

- The first subject establishes a goal relation $A \xrightarrow{te} B$.
- The second subject evaluates the goal B. For example, B is positive or negative.
- The third subject establishes a norm $N(A)$ concerning the goal relation.

According to Kelsen, a statement about the norm must contain no evaluation of the goal. This is the essence of his Pure Theory of Law. We further distinguish between the following kinds of goals:

- *Instrumental* goals. A goal is treated as a product.
- *Situational* goals. A goal is treated as a social landscape.

Here we consider different kinds of telos B in $A \xrightarrow{te} B$. In *instrumental teleology*, A is an instrument—a (technological) means—to reach the goal B, which is treated as a product. In *situational teleology*, the goal B is treated as a certain situation and the action A leads from one situation to another. Here goal B is not a product, but a landscape. The following metaphors apply. Instrumental teleology is compared to the teleology of hands. Situational teleology is compared to the teleology of feet. The hands produce products; the feet take us to another landscape. An instrumental goal sets a certain step. A situational goal sets, not a step, but a campsite, a migration goal, or a social scene that may not be declared. Next we distinguish between two projections of goals, which would be visualised differently:

- *Officially binding* goals—to be represented explicitly in a legal act.
- *Subjective* goals. These may be expressed by an external evaluator.

Two notions—a goal and a means—have to be distinguished. Usually a means to achieve a certain high-level goal can be treated as a goal, albeit a lower-level one. Such coercion can happen recurrently. This can be observed in governance and public administration law. For example, the means 'computerisation of a country', which is set by a high-level governmental agency, is treated by lower-level agencies as a goal. The lower-level agencies decompose the goal to sub-goals, set lower-level means, and pass them on to the next lower-level agencies.

Goal Set as a Vector of Values Goals play a central role in Hage's (2005, pp. 101 ff.) research on qualitative comparative reasoning. He gives an example of choosing between a Mercedes, a Volvo, and a Porsche.

A natural way to formalise goals is to represent them as coordinates of n-dimensional space. Here, two preferences are compared as two vectors. The bad news is that there is no total ordering relation $\leq$ in n-dimensional space. In the event that the weights are assigned to goals, then a natural ordering on real numbers is obtained (by summing up the weighted goals). However, the concept of legal goals is not so simple (see Dworkin's (1986) analysis of hard cases).

Teleological Phrases in Legislation   Legislation is a kind of societal practice and, therefore, can be approached from a teleological point of view. However, two forms of teleology have to be distinguished: explicit and implicit. Explicit teleological formulations can be provided in the texts of legislative materials, both in the texts of laws and in accompanying texts. Implicit teleological formulations are next. However, implicit teleology forms a contextual dimension that frames the legislation. Within this analytical framework, one can try to isolate teleological phrases and then formalise them as newly-discovered structures.

Legislative practice often uses teleological phrases. Teleological statements extracted from such phrases can be represented by the proposed notation $Act \xrightarrow{te}$ *Goal*. Multiple teleology is feasible, too. The goal may be formed of a set of sub-goals, for example, $Act \xrightarrow{te} \{g_1, g_2, \ldots, g_m\}$. Here, the column can be interpreted as a certain operation, such as *and, or, xor*. Decomposition of goals leads to graph-like structures that are already used in goal-oriented requirement engineering, where goals are associated with actions and agents. Actions in legal norms, too, are expected to have such a similarity.

29.6   Goals in Law and in Requirements Engineering

We advocate the following approach: a teleological network in the legal domain shall take into account goal modelling in requirements engineering. Why RE? It provides us with goal-oriented RE methodologies. We hypothesise on the assumption that a legal act is a system. Consequently, system design methods might be used in legislative drafting (Čaplinskas and Mockevičius 2002). However, the universe of discourse in law is on a higher level than that of IS design.

We make a comparison of two systems: a legal act and a software system. A norm corresponds to a requirement. Structural elements of the norm and of the requirement are compared correspondingly. The subject of the norm corresponds to the agent of the requirement. The telos of the norm corresponds to the goal of the requirement. A whole teleological network in the legal domain corresponds to the goal model in RE.

Van Lamsweerde (2009) lists the reasons why goals are so important in the RE process and formulates the problem of verification/validation. One of the benefits of goal analysis in information systems RE is to identify conflicting goals. Conflicts must be identified as early as possible in order to improve the design of an information system (of a socio-economic system, too). In the legal domain, conflicting goals are also a reality. They are identified in legislation, observed in law enforcement, claimed in judicial procedures, etc. An example is procedures of a bureaucratic agency versus efficiency of management. The nature of a conflict in the legal domain is expressed in different terminology than in goal-oriented requirements engineering. Here, different sorts of models (goals, agents, actions) are used. "A goal is a desirable state or effect or property of the system or of any part of it" (van Lamsweerde 2009, p. xviii). The identification of conflicting goals is one of the purposes of a graphical notation. An AND/OR tree can serve this purpose.

Different types of goals are distinguished in software engineering. For example, KAOS goal-oriented requirements-engineering methodology (van Lamsweerde 2009) distinguishes:

- *Achieve goals*—requires that some property eventually holds; $\lozenge$G.
- *Maintain goals*—some property always holds; $\square$G in deontic logic.
- *Cease goals*—some property eventually stops holding (opposed to achieve).
- *Avoid goals*—requires that some property never holds (opposed to maintain).

Additionally, *optimise, test, query, perform* and *preserve* goals are distinguished in multi-agent systems (see e.g. Braubach et al. (2005) about belief-desire-intention agent systems). In KAOS, the bottom-level goals in a goal tree are assigned to agents who are responsible for them. Time logic is used to represent the semantics of goals. The variety of goal-related concepts in requirements engineering demonstrates the expected variety of notions in the legal domain.

29.7   Functions of Law as High-Level Teleological Structure

The functions of law can be treated as a high-level teleological structure. The context is of the nature of law. Values are considered as a teleological concept: "the (main) aim of the law" is reduced to values; more precisely, to "realise values such as 'justice', 'equality', 'individual freedom' and the like" (Van Hoecke 2002, p. 61). Legal theory classifies the functions of law into three categories: the judicial function; the legislative function; and the executive function. From a societal perspective (ibid., p. 62), Hoecke distinguishes two main functions: structuring political power, and creating and keeping social cohesion. Achieving social cohesion implies the function of consolidation of the social system and the legal system. The latter statement can be represented as state transition. We would attach a teleological attribute 'social cohesion' to the final state. This transition is achieved by the function 'consolidation', which is represented as an edge in a kind of a semantic network.

Remarks on overestimating the aims of law can also be found (see e.g. Van Hoecke 2002, p. 61): "[I]n traditional jurisprudence attention often has been paid too exclusively to the aims of law. This is narrowing the analysis to deliberate lawmaking". Continuing this quotation, again, we discover the dimension, which has been already identified earlier—aims are formalised as values.[4]

---

[4] Van Hoecke writes: "When taking such a position, moreover, jurists tend to mingle a descriptive analysis with normative points of view. This is especially the case when it is posited that the (main)

A teleological notion of function is considered by Dennett (1996, p. 68): "[W]hat makes something a spark plug is that it can be plugged into a particular situation and *deliver a spark when called upon*" (emphasis in the original). Here we find a challenge to apply the functionalism and intentionality in the legal domain. However, law is qualitatively on a higher level of complexity than such artifacts as mechanical machines.

Different Meanings of the Term 'Law'   You can find the following different meanings of the term 'law': (1) a social phenomenon; (2) a legal or judicial system, i.e. structure and contents, e.g. continental law and common law; (3) a (logical) system of rules (a statute is treated as a (logical) system of norms); (4) a body of rules made by legislature (statutory law) (5) science or knowledge of law (jurisprudence); (6) the principles originating and formerly applied only in courts of common law (equity).

Goals may be assigned to a structural part of the law, too. You may speak about goals of a norm, goals of a contract, aims of the norm-sender—the will of the legislator, etc. (Van Hoecke 2002). Therefore, ontological structures are subject to different formalisations depending on their level.

The Teleological Method in Law   This is our next focus because "teleological or purposive method takes the objective of the statute as interpretation context. In certain cases the interpretation of a statute in the light of the purpose of the statute, or that of the entire legal system, is necessity" (Van Hoecke 2002, p. 140). His statement, "purposive interpretation is by far the most used method by the European Court of Justice" is also backed by other authors. One of the most striking characteristics of the legal order established by the Treaty is the competence vested in the Community institutions to enact legislation for the purpose of carrying out the objectives of the Treaty (Arnull et al. 2000, p. 83). A ground for looking at the aim of the statute is the clearly absurd or unjust result of applying the statute in its plain prima facie meaning. Another ground concerns historical developments that have arisen since the enactment of the statute. At times the immediate cause for a teleological construction is the absurd result of a literal interpretation (Van Hoecke 2002, p. 147).

Motivation to Formalise Purposes of an EU Directive   A challenging example for goals elicitation is found in European Union law, namely, interpreting the supremacy of Community law and direct applicability of EC Treaty provisions.

Purposes of an EU directive have to be transposed into the national legal systems. Thus, the legislation adopted to implement a directive need not use the same words as the directive itself. Here, natural questions can be raised: are the purposes explicit enough in the text of the directive? How one can verify that the purposes are implemented correctly in the national legislation?

---

aim of the law is to realise *values* such as "justice", "equality", "individual freedom" and the like, thus offering an idealistic picture of law" (Van Hoecke 2002, p. 61), emphasis added.

Aim ≠ Obligation!? Barnard (2004) presents analyses and examples of ECJ decisions that are based on teleological interpretation. For example, the list of benefits of free trade (ibid., p. 2) can be represented as a causal sequence of goals: 'free trade' → 'specialisation' → 'comparative advantage' → 'economics of scale' → 'consumer welfare' & 'efficient use of world-wide resources'.

After analysis of numerous Court decisions and quotations, which include the terms 'purpose', 'function', etc., we find the following conclusion important. After examining external economic relations of the EU, Barnard (2004, p. 227) concludes that "trade liberalization has always been an aim rather than an obligation". The above quotation illustrates a difference between the notions of aim and obligation. This also draws a border between AI and law. A task of AI is to model aims, whereas a legal task concerns the content of obligations.

Conclusion The different nature of goals is inherent to human agents and artificial agents. This differentiates human intelligence from artificial intelligence.

We agree with Van Hoecke (2002, p. 119) that "when analysing the structure of legal systems we have to take into account this intertwinement of form and substance". We back his conclusion that "the structure of legal systems cannot be studied in isolation from its content". To discover ontological structures, studies of the structure of law are not enough; studies of the content are required.

References

Aristotle (1954) Nicomachean ethics (trans and ed: Ross WD). Oxford University Press

Arnull A, Dashwood A, Ross M, Wyatt D (2000) European Union law, 4th edn. Sweet & Maxwell, London

Artosi A, Rotolo A, Sartor G, Vida S (2007) Elements for a formalisation of the theory of norms developed in this volume. Appendix to Pattaro E (2007) The law and the right. A treatise of legal philosophy and general jurisprudence, vol 1. Springer, Dordrecht, pp 413–423

Barnard C (2004) The substantive law of the EU. The four freedoms. Oxford University Press, Oxford

Bench-Capon TJM (2002) The missing link revisited: the role of teleology in representing legal argument. Artif Intell Law 10(1–3):79–94. https://doi.org/10.1023/A:1019501830692

Berman DH, Hafner CD (1993) Representing teleological structure in case-based reasoning: the missing link. In: Proceedings of the fourth international conference on artificial intelligence and law, ICAIL '93. ACM, New York, pp 50–59. https://doi.org/10.1145/158976.158982

Braubach L, Pokahr A, Moldt D, Lamersdorf W (2005) Goal representation for BDI agent systems. In: Bordini RH et al (eds) Programming multi-agent systems. ProMAS 2004, Lecture notes in computer science (Lecture notes in artificial intelligence), vol 3346. Springer, Heidelberg, pp 44–65. https://doi.org/10.1007/978-3-540-32260-3_3

Čaplinskas A, Mockevičius R (2002) Sistemų inžinerijos ir informacinių technologijų vaidmuo Lietuvos teisėkūros procese [in Lithuanian] (The role of system engineering and information technologies in legal drafting in Lithuania). In: Šeinauskas R (ed) Proceedings of the conference IT'2002. Kaunas University of Technology, Kaunas, pp 367–376

Costake N (2007) General requirements for digital government. In: Anttiroiko A, Mälkiä M (eds) Encyclopedia of digital government, vol 2. Idea Group, Hershey, pp 859–868. https://doi.org/10.4018/978-1-59140-789-8.ch130

Čyras V (2007) On formalisation of the goal concept in law. Eng Appl Artif Intell 20(5):601–608. https://doi.org/10.1016/j.engappai.2006.11.010

Čyras V (2009) The concept of "goals" in legal informatics. In: Jakob R, Philipps L, Schweighofer E, Varga C (eds) Auf dem Weg zur Idee der Gerechtigkeit: Gedenkschrift für Ilmar Tammelo. LIT Verlag, Vienna, pp 187–196

Čyras V, Lachmayer F (2008) Transparent complexity by goals. In: Wimmer MA, Scholl HJ, Ferro E (eds) Electronic government. EGOV 2008, Lecture notes in computer science, vol 5184. Springer, Heidelberg, pp 255–266. https://doi.org/10.1007/978-3-540-85204-9_22

Dennett D (1989) The intentional stance. MIT, Cambridge

Dennett D (1996) Kinds of minds: toward an understanding of consciousness. Basic Books, New York

Dworkin R (1986) Law's empire. Harvard University Press

Grönlund Å (2007) Electronic government. In: Anttiroiko A, Mälkiä M (eds) Encyclopedia of digital government, vol 2. Idea Group, Hershey, pp 634–642. https://doi.org/10.4018/978-1-59140-789-8.ch097

Hafner C, Berman D (2002) The role of context in case-based legal reasoning: teleological, temporal, and procedural. Artif Intell Law 10(1–3):19–64. https://doi.org/10.1023/A:1019516031847

Hage J (2005) Studies in legal logic. Springer, Dordrecht

Jhering R (1877) Zweck im Recht. Breitkopf & Härtel, Leipzig. English edition: Jhering R (1913) Law as a means to an end (trans: Husik I). Boston Book Company, Boston

Jhering R (1924) Geist des römischen Rechts auf den verschiedenen Stufen seiner Entwicklung. Breitkopf & Härtel, Leipzig (1st edn 1852-1865). Scientia Verlag, Aalen (1993)

Kaufmann A, Hassemer W, Neumann U (2004) Einführung in Rechtsphilosophie und Rechtstheorie der Gegenwart, 7. Auflage. C.F. Müller, Heidelberg

Larenz K, Canaris C (1995) Methodenlehre der Rechtswissenschaft, 3. Auflage. Springer, Heidelberg

Oskamp A, Lauritsen M (2002) AI in law practice? So far, not much. Artif Intell Law 10(4): 227–236. https://doi.org/10.1023/A:1025402013007

Sartor G (2006) Fundamental legal concepts: a formal and teleological characterisation. Artif Intell Law 14(1–2):101–142. https://doi.org/10.1007/s10506-006-9009-x

Sergot M (2001) A computational theory of normative positions. ACM Trans Comput Log 2(4): 581–622

Summers R (2006) Form and function in a legal system: a general study. Cambridge University Press, New York

Traunmüller R, Wimmer M (2004) E-government: the challenges ahead. In: Traunmüller R (ed) Electronic government. EGOV 2004, Lecture notes in computer science, vol 3183. Springer, Heidelberg, pp 1–6. https://doi.org/10.1007/978-3-540-30078-6_1

Valente A (1995) Legal knowledge engineering. IOS Press, Amsterdam

Van Hoecke M (2002) Law as communication. Hart, Oxford

van Lamsweerde A (2009) Requirements engineering: from system goals to UML models to software specifications. Wiley

Westerman P (2007) Governing by goals: governance as a legal style. Legisprudence 1(1):51–72. https://doi.org/10.1080/17521467.2007.11424659

Wimmer M (2006) Implementing a knowledge portal for egovernment based on semantic modeling: the e-government intelligent portal (eip.at). In: Proceedings of the 39th annual Hawaii international conference on system sciences (HICSS'06), vol 4, p 82b. IEEE Computer Society. https://doi.org/10.1109/HICSS.2006.215

Wintgens LJ (2006) Legisprudence as a new theory of legislation. Ratio Juris 19(1):1–25. https://doi.org/10.1111/j.1467-9337.2006.00315.x

Chapter 30
Standard Cases, Hard Cases, Emergency Cases and Scurrile Cases in Jurisprudence

30.1 Why Solving Cases by Machines?

This chapter explores the characterisation of four types of cases. The context is solving cases by computers. Standard cases correspond to the German Normfall, which was introduced by Fritjof Haft. Standard cases (also clear cases) are important in automated form proceedings and are cases that can be made subject to legal machines. A hard case needs a court decision and cannot be solved by computers. Emergency cases have recently been actively discussed. They appear in unexpected and exceptional situations in which there cannot be a differentiated ex post assessment by the authorities, but there must be a rapid decision by the actors themselves in a time-critical situation. Scurrile cases (German skurrile Fälle, Latin adj. scurrilis, noun scurra—clown, buffoon; he can also cure) mean bizarre ones and no connotation of rude or indecent. Scurrile cases can be used for learning purposes. Scurrile cases, which are examples of hypothetical cases, can be used in legal argumentation according to the doctrine of precedent.

Suppose that cases are to be solved by intelligent electronic form proceedings (e-forms). Examples are e-government applications. Consider the question 'Can machines solve cases?' At first sight, the answer is 'no'. Regina Ogorek's (2011) condensed analysis concerns how judges solve disputes, and explains the problem. The development of the theory of the judiciary in the nineteenth century has to be taken into account.[1] In a machine culture, there may be an aim to solve standard cases by machines.

Thanks to Meinrad Handstanger and Erich Schweighofer.

---

[1] Ogorek (2011, p. 35) writes: "The judge, whose task it was previously to carry out with dutiful obedience that command of the law (thus as medium of interpretation), who had exclusively to take into account the legislator's intent, was now recognized as a productive creator of law [...] A somewhat all too naive belief in the capabilities of legislative activity is ascribed to the apologists of

© The Author(s), under exclusive license to Springer Nature Switzerland AG 2023
V. Cyras, F. Lachmayer, *Essays on the Visualisation of Legal Informatics*, Law, Governance and Technology Series 54,
https://doi.org/10.1007/978-3-031-27957-7_30

30.2   What Is a Case?

The whole procedure in connection with a case—before or outside the judicial proceedings—aims at a settlement, which solves the case. In this respect the quintessence of a case is a decision concerning conflicting interests or positions. Generally, a legal decision covers three different tiers:

- Legal questions, which generally appear as the problem of how to interpret the relevant legal provisions (or leading cases) concerning the relevant facts.
- Factual questions, which allow the development of the facts of the case; the outcome of the giving of evidence should be a consistent picture of the factual situation that is subject to legal evaluation.
- Interrogatory questions, which concern the handling of evidence and the consideration of evidence. These also solve factual questions in a procedural, but intellectually easier, way.

During the discussions the three dimensions are interconnected. Clarifications for one tier generally involve clarifications for the other dimensions of the decision. The aim of the procedure is the reduction of possible solutions so that a final decision can be reached.

30.3   Standard Cases

Standard cases correspond to the German 'Normfall' (see Haft 2010)—to stress that these cases are the opposite of boundary cases. A process for a normal case allows a set of alternative variants, v_1, v_2,... and can be solved with e-proceedings. This is shown in Fig. 30.1 with a spectrum of parallel positions.

For example, suppose there are two rules:

$$R_1 : if\ C \quad then\ A_1$$
$$R_2 : if\neg C \quad then\ A_2$$

These two rules allow two variations of actions: $v_1 = A_1$ and $v_2 = A_2$. The two rules R_1 and R_2 above can be represented as the conditional process *if C then A_1 else A_2*.

Processes in Computer Science The term 'process' is treated differently in computer science from how it is treated in law and there are different formalisations. For

---

the binding force of statute at the beginning of the last century. The former nurtured false hopes in the all-encompassing completeness of the statutory law; the latter had been responsible for misunderstanding the nature of the judicial process as an automatic, formal process of subsumption: the role of value-based and purposive judgments in the interpretation of the law had been underestimated."

Fig. 30.1 Standard case

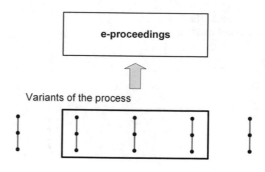

Fig. 30.2 Four variants of the process correspond to four traces in the block-diagram. The traces are $v_1 = \{A_1,B_1\}$, $v_2 = \{A_1,B_2\}$, $v_3 = \{A_2,B_1\}$, $v_4 = \{A_2,B_2\}$

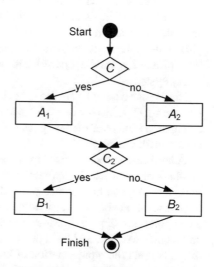

example, the sequence of two conditionals *if C then A_1 else A_2; if C_2 then B_1 else B_2* allows four variations of action sequences: $v_1 = \{A_1,B_1\}$, $v_2 = \{A_1,B_2\}$, $v_3 = \{A_2, B_1\}$, $v_4 = \{A_2,B_2\}$ (see Fig. 30.2). A standard case with a well-defined process flow such as the conditionals above can be implemented with e-proceedings. This is the idea of normal cases in the sense of Haft.

30.4 Hard Cases

Ronald Dworkin in *Taking Rights Seriously* (1977) focuses on legal principles (judicial 'recourse to principle') in his vision of hard cases. However, there are arguments against Dworkin's vision, and the univocal conception of a 'hard case' is rejected: see Waldron (2009) and Kellogg (2013).

Fig. 30.3 Hard cases need a
tribunal decision

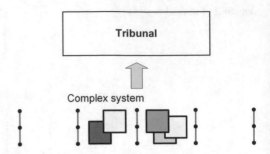

One of the arguments is that the "background elements" of the legal system—"the principles and policies that lie behind the rules and text that positivists emphasize" are split. The assumption is that the background is plainly incoherent. Kellogg (2013) defends a "restrained and participatory, or *socialized*, epistemology for legal principles, leaving space when appropriate for input from outside the adjudicatory system".[2]

Hard cases cannot be solved by a computer and need a tribunal (see, for example, Dworkin 1977). Hard cases arise when the law is not sufficiently settled: when, for example, a fight over the law goes on. Argumentation allows several solutions or is constrained; see below.

A hard case is characterised by a complex combination of different issues, such as conflicts of interests, the appreciation of values, the procedure of taking evidence, interpretation, and the balance of legal principles and legal rules. It is impossible to formalise all this knowledge in advance and to represent it in the knowledge base of a computer (see Fig. 30.3). Moreover the sources of law extend beyond statutory law and include case law and legal doctrine. Wisdom is required to solve a hard case, and this is beyond the representation of knowledge in computers.

Hard cases demonstrate that even judges may have separate opinions. Hard cases provide practice in solving standard cases. In algorithmic regulation, a more experienced team of engineers and jurists can foresee more situations in which the software does not solve the case.

We propose to distinguish between different types of hard cases. Let us call them, first, 'hard cases with more than one plausible solution', and, second, 'hard cases

---

[2]Kellogg (2013, pp. 4–5) writes: "When a dispute stands in relation to a broader and continuing controversy, the time for principled decision may not be ripe [...] This highlights a distinct form of uncertainty that has, nevertheless, been commonly perceived as legal indeterminacy. The perception of indeterminacy in this category of cases derives from the appearance of equal balance among competing interpretations, characteristic of unsettled classification of an emergent form or class of dispute. When the judicial role in such a case is viewed in relation to an emergent or unsettled problem, the perception of intractable difficulty can and should be seen not as a radical indeterminacy, but as representing a stage of inquiry into developing perceptions of underlying conditions [...] This vantage point recognizes a danger implicit in any generalized approval of judicial 'recourse to principle': the influence of ideology and subjectivity in the judicial application of moral principles. Premature recourse to principle (and indeed of constitutional principle) may foreclose fact-based inquiry in unsettled controversies."

with restrictions on the latitude allowed in decision-making'. After this we discuss cases with an unexpected solution, and classify them as hard cases, too.

30.4.1 Hard Cases with Several Plausible Solutions

A case involving complex issues often gives room for more than one plausible solution. The complex pattern may be due to legal complexity (because of the openness of legal texts), to factual complexity (for example, difficulties concerning the establishment of facts because of contradictory expert opinions), or to procedural complexity (based, for example, on a huge number of parties in a case concerning infrastructure or environmental issues). The decision in such—hard—cases follows the line of argument that is the most convincing.

30.4.2 Hard Cases with Restrictions on the Latitude Allowed in Decision-Making

The second type of hard case is characterised by distinctive restrictions on the way in which a decision is made. Therefore it is as difficult to reach a decision in these cases as it is in cases containing complex issues.

Those restrictions concern the period of time during which the decision must be made (e.g., only a very short period is available for a decision with serious consequences), local constraints (e.g., an appropriate visual inspection is not possible) or other comparable circumstances that handicap the making of the decision (such as administrative chaos).

The legal control over such decisions is, above all, constituted by efforts to come to a fair balance between such principles and human rights (which are likewise structured as principles, see Alexy 2012).

Hard Cases Embrace Emergency Cases From the point of view set out above, emergency cases can be understood to be covered within the concept of hard cases. A distinct type of cases described as emergency cases seems to be superfluous.

Even though emergency cases show specific characteristics, when considering the challenges concerning the decision-making process they can be defined as hard cases. Moreover, in general legal orders include provisions concerning such emergency situations (including decision-making in hospitals), for which reason it is advisable to treat such situations as not (completely) unexpected. This is the case under international law, EU law, national law and even regional law, such as that in India.

30.4.3 Cases with an Unexpected Solution

On the other hand, everyday legal life brings up a number of cases showing the following specific pattern:

1. On the basis of the provisions of ordinary laws, the solution of the case seems to be easy; even if it falls under the definition of a hard case, the repertoire of legal skills leads, in general, to a speedy decision.
2. But when it comes to the application of paramount law in the case—particularly domestic constitutional law or European Union law—the multilevel legal system allows solutions that one would not expect from the perspective of the level of ordinary laws.
3. The legal complexity of the multilevel legal system notably (as regards the way in which it is interpreted) allows the parts of ordinary legal provisions to be overridden and replaced by elements of constitutional provisions or provisions of European Union law.
4. The outcome is an artificial legal text (quite often elaborated by constitutional or European courts), a combination, which does not exist as such in the legal texts of the different legal levels.

Such cases can certainly easily be classified as hard cases (cases characterised by legal complexity). Nevertheless the said specific pattern, which is of great importance for legal everyday life, suggests that we should mention this group separately (especially when emergency cases are taken as a specific type of case).

30.5 Emergency Cases

Real life is characterised by restricted resources. Time is one of these restricted resources, particularly in our fast moving network society. Emergency cases appear in unexpected situations that are concerned not with the differentiated ex post assessment by authorities, but with a rapid decision by the actors themselves in a time-critical situation. Extreme time pressure is a feature (see Fig. 30.4). Examples

Fig. 30.4 Emergency situation

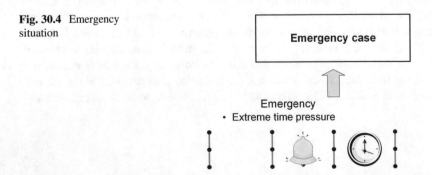

Emergency case

Emergency
• Extreme time pressure

can be provided from decision-making in a hospital. Decision makers are typically ordinary people, for example physicians, who are not legally trained or qualified.

Emergency situations can be classified into three types:

1. Fast-track procedures
2. Break-glass policy situations
3. Life-threatening situations

30.5.1 Fast-Track Procedures

Because of the interests of stakeholders in achieving fast decisions, the legal rules that are applied are reduced to more basic principles, either by law or by practice. Further, the taking of legal evidence is constrained by time pressures, allowing evidence to be given easily, and the resulting decision may easily be appealed against in further proceedings. The following are examples of such fast-track procedures:

- Injunctions (a well-known example, which is to be found in many jurisdictions; there are strict rules requiring proof of an emergency).
- Online dispute resolution, taking the form of either a mediation or an administrative dispute settlement procedure (e.g., the Uniform Domain-Name Dispute-Resolution Policy (UDRP)[3] established by the internet Corporation for Assigned Names and Numbers (ICANN)).
- Consumer arbitration procedures (e.g., SquareTrade,[4] which is used by the eBay electronic marketplace).

30.5.2 Break-Glass Policy Situations

The notions of 'break-glass' and 'emergency access' are distinguished and can be defined in terms of the healthcare requirements for emergency access (see, for example, Davis 2009).[5] The mechanisms for authorising, implementing and revoking break-glass and emergency access are distinguished. "The term 'break-glass' is a metaphor referring to the act of breaking the glass to pull a fire alarm" (Schefer-

---

[3] https://www.icann.org/resources/pages/help/dndr/udrp-en.

[4] https://www.squaretrade.com/.

[5] Davis writes: "In the case of break glass no additional user permissions are required (similar to a fire alarm in a hallway, all users have access to the alarm); however, access may involve alerts to system managers and increased auditing. Examples of break glass include access to one's own records, to records belonging to a spouse, family member or to a VIP. In contrast to emergency access, break glass does not require evaluation of patient consent directives, nor is eminent [sic] threat to patient safety a concern." (Davis 2009, p. 5), emphasis added.

Wenzl and Strembeck 2012, p. 25). A break-glass situation allows the healthcare staff:

> [A]ccess to information without the need to extend existing permissions. Access is provided to information needed but normally not accessible as part of day-to-day need-to-know. The system should document (audit) any actual access for later review. Break the glass may or may not involve harm or risk to life (Davis 2009, p. 5).

Life-Threatening Situations   In healthcare, an 'emergency access' situation allows caregivers access to information that is normally not authorised.[6]

30.5.3   Break-Glass Policies

Break-glass policies are relevant to emergency situations. Below, we follow Schefer-Wenzl and Strembeck (2012), who provide modelling support for break-glass policies in the context of process-related role-based access control (RBAC) models. They formulate a problem from the viewpoint of information systems engineering: "[M]ost process diagrams and corresponding access control models only visualize standard task sequences and do not consider exceptional situations, such as emergency scenarios."[7] Process-related break-glass policies define override rules for subjects to allow the execution of certain tasks in exceptional cases. A typical visualisation of a simple medical examination process modelled as a business activity (BA) that includes task-based entailment constraints is shown in Schefer-Wenzl and Strembeck (2012, p. 27).[8] The use of UML in graphical representations is also demonstrated.

---

[6]Davis (2009, p. 5) writes: "[A]ccess to information specifically extending existing permissions to protected health information when timely access is needed to prevent harm or risk to life. Declaration of an 'emergency' allows specific pre-authorized individuals to gain access to records locally, across the enterprise and potentially extra-enterprise (across policy domains). Emergency access includes situations for which a caregiver would not normally have need-to-know access to a record, or parts of a record or system functions covered by 'least privilege' restrictions. Persons declaring an emergency must be properly authenticated. Anonymous access to protected health information is not allowed."

[7]Schefer-Wenzl and Strembeck (2012, p. 25) write: "In emergency situations, certain subjects sometimes have to perform important tasks although they are usually not authorized to perform these tasks. Break-glass policies have been introduced as a sophisticated exception handling mechanism to resolve such situations. They enable selected subjects to break or override the standard access control policies of an information system in a controlled manner [...] For example, a junior physician shall be able to perform certain tasks of a senior physician in case of emergency."

[8]Schefer-Wenzl and Strembeck (2012, pp. 26–27) write: "The process starts when a patient arrives at the hospital. Subsequently, the "Medical examination" task (t_1) is conducted to reach a medical diagnosis. Next, the "Determine treatment options" task (t_2) is executed to devise an appropriate treatment plan. This treatment plan has to be confirmed by a second physician (t_3). In case the treatment plan includes errors or is incomplete, it must be revised before it is resubmitted for confirmation. Finally, the "Medical treatment" task (t_4) is performed [...] [M]embers of the Junior Physician role are permitted to perform the tasks t_1, t_2, and t_4. Task t_3 ("Confirm treatment") can

Fig. 30.5 Scurrile case

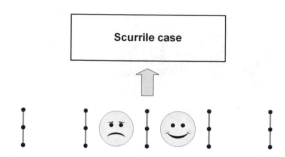

Emergency situations are the concern of software engineers who develop legal machines to assist decision making. We can see that there is a risk of ultra vires actions and the misuse of power.

30.6   Scurrile Cases

Scurrile cases happen in absurd, bizarre, odd, strange, unusual or grotesque situations. Scurrile situations can be used for learning purposes. Examples can be found in textbooks and also in detective stories. Narrative quality is obtained with role-playing actors, who typically have exaggerated comical masks, and juridical problems (see Fig. 30.5).

It is important that scurrile cases demonstrate legal subsumption. Hence legal meanings are revealed. To explain the law, clear graphical descriptions are employed.

Lothar Philipps (2012) writes about so-called trolley cases, and gives references to earlier works, the doctrine of double effect, and the trolley problem,[9] which in the modern form was first introduced by Philippa Foot in 1967. Scurrile cases introduce serious problems and need not be as comical as the role-playing characters in the visuals (see Fig. 30.6).

---

only be performed by subjects assigned to the Senior Physician role. Furthermore, the Junior Physician role is defined as junior-role of the Senior Physician role via a role-to-role assignment ("rrAssign")."

[9] See, for example, Wikipedia, https://en.wikipedia.org/wiki/Trolley_problem: "There is a runaway trolley barrelling down the railway tracks. Ahead, on the tracks, there are five people tied up and unable to move. The trolley is headed straight for them. You are standing some distance off in the train yard, next to a lever. If you pull this lever, the trolley will switch to a different set of tracks. However, you notice that there is one person on the side track. You have two options: (1) Do nothing and allow the trolley to kill the five people on the main track. (2) Pull the lever, diverting the trolley onto the side track where it will kill one person. Which is the more ethical option?"

Fig. 30.6 The trolley problem: should you pull the lever to divert the runaway trolley onto the side track? See Wikipedia, https://en.wikipedia.org/wiki/Trolley_problem

Berman (1983) presents a bizarre example, a scurrile situation, to shed light on the paradoxes of a legal tradition that has lost contact with its theological sources.[10]

We should place scurrile cases in a subset of the hypothetical cases, settled or unsettled. The reason is that scurrile cases serve to raise a problem, in philosophy, ethics or law. However, one might speak about actual scurrile cases, which we would assign to the standard cases or hard cases groups, most probably with an unexpected solution.

Hypothetical cases, again, whether settled or unsettled, are thought experiments. Some hypothetical cases, such as those that serve for legal education, can be assigned to the set of standard cases. Some hypothetical cases, especially those that raise a problem, can be assigned to the set of hard cases.

It should be possible for hypothetical cases that are assigned to the set of normal cases to be solved by machines. We can imagine scurrile cases that serve to test software. Exceptional situations have to be taken into account when designing software tests.

30.7   Settled Actual Cases and Settled Hypothetical Cases

The concepts of settled cases and hypothetical cases and also settled actual cases and settled hypothetical cases are employed in Susan Hurley's analysis (1990). She discusses coherence in practical reasoning. Here the subject matter is "deliberation about what to do when the reasons that apply to the alternatives conflict" (Hurley

---

[10]Berman (1983, p. 165) writes: "If a sane man is convicted of murder and sentenced to death, and thereafter, before the sentence is carried out, he becomes insane, his execution will be postponed until he recovers his sanity. Generally speaking, this is the law in Western countries and in many non-Western countries as well. Why? The historical answer, in the West, is that if a man is executed while he is insane he will not have had the opportunity freely to confess his sins and to take the sacrament of holy communion. He must be allowed to recover his sanity before he dies so that his soul will not be condemned to eternal hellfire but will instead have the opportunity to expiate his sins in purgatory and ultimately, at the Last Judgment, to enter the kingdom of heaven. But where none of this is believed, why keep the insane man alive until he recovers, and then kill him?"

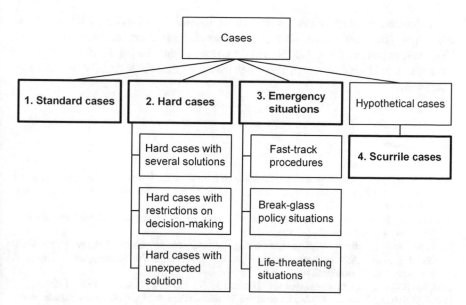

Fig. 30.7 The classification of cases in this chapter

1990, p. 222). Settled cases "may have actually been decided, or may be posed as hypothetical issues, the resolution of which can be taken as evident" (ibid., p. 223). By a 'settled' case she means "a case which, if actual, is such that its resolution is clear to the relevant decision-maker or decision-makers, and which, if hypothetical, is such that its resolution would be clear to the relevant decision-maker or decision-makers were the case to be considered". Hurley further notes: "That a resolution of a particular case is or would be clear does not mean that it cannot be mistaken; the settledness in particular cases is a matter of what is or would be believed to be correct, not necessarily of what is correct". She concludes that "at least as a conceptual matter, not all actually decided cases are settled" (some are problematic) and "some settled cases are hypothetical, not actual" (ibid., p. 223). The doctrine of precedent in law commonly gives settled actual cases more weight than settled hypothetical cases. Hurley also illustrates the point that "status as actual and status as settled do not in fact coincide [. . .] Some actual cases, even some that are settled, may be mistaken" (ibid., p. 245).

30.8   Conclusion: Classifying Cases

An attempt at classifying the concepts discussed is shown in Fig. 30.7. This is not an ultimate classification. Others can be devised that depend on other characteristics of cases.

A Cartesian product of a two-adjective set {*actual, hypothetical*} by a set of four adjectives {*standard, hard, emergency, scurrile*} produces eight combinations. However, we do not think that these eight combinations, which are obtained purely formally, would give an exhaustive explanation of the whole variety of cases and situations.

References

Alexy R (2012) Law, morality, and the existence of human rights. Ratio Juris, 25(1):2–14. https://doi.org/10.1111/j.1467-9337.2011.00499.x. https://ssrn.com/abstract=2009741. Accessed 15 Dec 2022

Berman HJ (1983) Law and revolution: the formation of the Western legal tradition. Harvard University Press, Cambridge

Davis M (2009) Healthcare requirements for emergency access. Health Level Seven International, US. http://www.hl7.org/documentcenter/public/wg/secure/HL7%20Emergency%20Access. doc. Accessed 15 Dec 2022

Dworkin R (1977) Taking rights seriously (1st edn 1977). Harvard University Press, 1999

Haft F (2010) Das Normfall-Buch: IT-gestütztes Strukturdenken und Informationsmanagement, 4th edn. Normfall-GmbH, München

Hurley SL (1990) Coherence, hypothetical cases, and precedent. Oxf J Leg Stud 10(2):221–251. https://doi.org/10.1093/ojls/10.2.221

Kellogg FR (2013) What precisely is a 'hard' case? Waldron, Dworkin, critical legal studies, and judicial recourse to principle. https://doi.org/10.2139/ssrn.222083. https://ssrn.com/abstract=2220839. Accessed 15 Dec 2022

Ogorek R (2011) Inconsistencies and consistencies in 19th century legal theory. German Law J 12(1):34–57. https://doi.org/10.1017/S2071832200016722

Philipps L (2012) Moralische Doppelwirkungen – die Wiederkehr einer Naturrechtlichen Denkfigur aus dem Internet. In: Endliche Rechtsbegriffe mit unendlichen Grenzen: Anthologia. Editions Weblaw, Bern, pp 191–205

Schefer-Wenzl S, Strembeck M (2012) A UML extension for modeling break-glass policies. In: Rinderle-Ma S, Weske M (eds) Der Mensch im Zentrum der Modellierung. EMISA 2012, Lecture notes in informatics, vol 206. Gesellschaft für Informatik, Bonn, pp 25–38. http://subs.emis.de/LNI/Proceedings/Proceedings206/article6772.html. Accessed 15 Dec 2022

Waldron J (2009) Did Dworkin ever answer the crits? In: Hershovitz S (ed) Exploring law's empire: the jurisprudence of Ronald Dworkin. Oxford Scholarship Online, pp 155–182. https://doi.org/10.1093/acprof:oso/9780199546145.003.0008

Printed in the United States
by Baker & Taylor Publisher Services